EXETER MEDIEVAL TEXTS AND STUDIES

General Editors: Marion Glasscoe, M.J. Swanton and Vincent Gillespie

THE VOYAGE OF SAINT BRENDAN

The story of the voyage of the sixth-century Irish saint, Brendan the Navigator, is one of the greatest legends of the Middle Ages. To the nations of medieval Europe the ocean voyage became a metaphor for the perilous journey of the Christian soul in search of the Promised Land, and no spiritual odyssey attracted wider interest.

But Brendan's reach goes far beyond his medieval and monastic context. He is frequently cited as a discoverer of the New World – the search for the mythical St Brendan's Isle was an important motif behind the voyages of Columbus. Brendan's story also has much in common with the Irish seafaring tales we know as *immrama*, and his voyage contributes to our understanding of the history of quest and travel literature, containing as it does echoes of the *Odyssey* and the *Aeneid, Sinbad the Sailor* and the quest for the Holy Grail.

This volume collects the most important versions of the voyage from a variety of cultures and presents them in modern English translations together with contextual introduction, explanatory commentaries and bibliography. The indexes in this new paperback edition allow easy comparison between the different versions.

W.R.J. Barron† was Senior Research Fellow in the School of English, University of Exeter, series editor of *Arthurian Literature in the Middle Ages*, and co-editor with S.C. Weinberg of *Layamon's Arthur: The Arthurian Section of Layamon's* Brut.

Glyn S. Burgess is Emeritus Professor of French at the University of Liverpool. His many books include, as co-author, *The Legend of St Brendan: A Critical Bibliography* (2000) and *The History of the Norman People: Wace's Roman de Rou* (2004).

THE VOYAGE OF SAINT BRENDAN

Representative Versions of the Legend in English Translation with Indexes of Themes and Motifs from the Stories

under the general editorship of

W.R.J. BARRON AND GLYN S. BURGESS

UNIVERSITY
of
EXETER
PRESS

First published in 2002
by University of Exeter Press
Reed Hall, Streatham Drive
Exeter EX4 4QR, UK
www.exeterpress.co.uk

First paperback edition, with indexes, 2005

British Library Cataloguing in Publication Data
A catalogue record of this book is available
from the British Library.

ISBN 0 85989 755 9

Cover illustration by Helen Maclean.
Typeset in Caslon.
Printed in Great Britain by Antony Rowe Ltd, Chippenham.

CONTENTS

PREFACE

Come, my friends,
'Tis not too late to seek a newer world.
Push off, and sitting well in order smite
The sounding furrows.
It may be that the gulfs will wash us down,
It may be we shall touch the Happy Isles . . .
One equal temper of heroic hearts,
Made weak by time and fate, but strong in will
To strive, to seek, to find, and not to yield.

Tennyson's Ulysses, the archetypal voyager, typifies the ambivalence which the ocean inspires in all mankind: challenge and threat, lure and trap, highway and trackless wilderness, path to fortune or to fate. But for the hermit monks of Dark Age Ireland it held a deeper ambivalence as a means of escape from a wicked world, a penitential pilgrimage to seek closer communion with God in distant solitudes. In the spirit of the Desert Fathers they sailed among the wave-washed skerries to high-cliffed half-acres where foam flew among pinnacles of rock. And ever farther and farther until they found their Promised Land – or death.

The process by which Brendan became the archetype of all such sailor pilgrims is not apparent. But its components are evident in what little we know of his life: the remoteness of his era, the great length of his career, wide-ranging over the Christian West, founding abbeys, building churches, the voyages it involved, the sanctity it brought. As always with such charismatic spirits, the life drew elements of myth and legend from many cultures: the odyssey of Ulysses, the voyages of Sinbad the Sailor and Columba the Missioner, fragments of Indo-European folklore, echoes of

Sumerian epics. Its cosmopolitan appeal, carried abroad by Irish missionary enterprise, inspired not only a saint's life (the *Vita Brendani*) but also 'the Voyage of Saint Brendan' (the *Navigatio sancti Brendani*) both written in the international language, Latin. But the power of the *Navigatio* penetrated the *Vita*, producing hybrid versions and itself multiplying so that over 120 manuscripts still survive. All over Europe vernacular versions appeared throughout the later Middle Ages, each finding its own variation on the voyage into the unknown.

With the modern age came new perspectives, new maps recording a new geography, voyages undertaken by laymen in search of new worlds, new markets, adventurers in pursuit of adventure itself. On the expanding horizons ahead of them they glimpsed Brendan's sails, leading them on from island to island. From Columbus to Tim Severin they were drawn to follow in his wake, often in search of self as much as foreign shores. What matter if Brendan never went where they followed him, so long as he lured them on from land to new-found land. As he had passed from island to island, so the legend passed from age to age, bringing to each the meaning of which it was capable, literal or metaphorical. His faith has faded, the New World has grown familiar, Ultima Thule lies still beyond the horizon, men still raise their eyes to the guiding stars. What follows here records something of what they sought, found or failed to find, when the spirit of Brendan was young, the voyage newly begun.

* * * * * * *

The present volume contains an English translation of the *Navigatio sancti Brendani* and of the eight most significant vernacular versions of the legend, translated from the Anglo-Norman, Dutch, German, Italian, Occitan, Catalan, Norse and Middle English. Of particular interest is the presence here of the neglected, indeed almost unknown Catalan version. Also included is William Caxton's version, printed in his *Jacobus de Voragine, The Golden Legend*, one of the earliest books in English. In the case of the Occitan, Catalan, Norse and Middle English versions, new editions have been provided in this volume, as an edition of the original could prove hard to locate. Most versions are translated into English for the first time.

In each version the reader encounters the same structure: a quest for the Promised Land or for Paradise. But each vernacular author has adapted the themes, motifs and personages of the original story to meet the needs of his own audience and culture. Part saint's life, part romance, the *Voyage* conveys to us the exploits, both nautical and spiritual, of one of Europe's greatest legendary figures.

W.R.J. Barron, Exeter
Glyn S. Burgess, Liverpool
October 2001

* * * * * * *

Preface to the paperback edition

The volume as published in 2002 has been revised and expanded by the addition of two indexes, one covering the material found in the introductions to the various versions of the legend, the other being an index to the versions themselves.

In view of the untimely death of Dr Barron in April 2004, I am grateful for the invaluable help provided by Jude Mackley, who has compiled the indexes and assisted in the preparation of camera-ready copy, and for the advice and encouragement of Simon Baker and Anna Henderson of the University of Exeter Press.

Glyn S. Burgess, Liverpool
December 2004

CONTRIBUTORS

W.R.J. Barron† was a Senior Research Fellow in the School of English, University of Exeter.

Glyn S. Burgess is Emeritus Professor of French at the University of Liverpool.

Margaret Burrell is Senior Lecturer in French at the University of Canterbury, Christchurch, New Zealand.

Mark Davie is Senior Lecturer in Italian at the University of Exeter.

Willem P. Gerritsen is a retired Professor of Medieval Literature at the University of Utrecht.

Andrew Hamer is lecturer in English Language at the University of Liverpool.

Peter K. King is a retired Professor of Dutch at the University of Hull.

Jude Mackley is a PhD student at the University of York.

John J. O'Meara is a retired Professor of Classics at Trinity College, Dublin.

Clara Strijbosch is a researcher affiliated to the University of Utrecht.

Jonathan M. Wooding is Senior Lecturer in the Department of Theology and Religious Studies at the University of Wales, Lampeter.

INTRODUCTION
The Life and Legend of Saint Brendan
Glyn S. Burgess

Brendan (Irish Brénainn, Latin Brendanus / Brandanus) is one of
the most famous of all Irish saints. His voyages, whether real or
imaginary, have created one of the most remarkable and enduring
of European legends. So famous did his travels become that he has
long been known as Brendan the Navigator and his name is still
placed high on the list of possible discoverers of the New World.
There is, however, very little secure information concerning his
life, although at least the approximate dates of his birth and death,
and accounts of some events in his life, are found in the Irish annals
and genealogies.[1] The principal works devoted to the saint and his
legend are a 'Life of Brendan' in several Latin and Irish versions
(*Vita Brendani / Betha Brénainn*) and the better known 'Voyage of
Saint Brendan the abbot' (*Navigatio sancti Brendani abbatis*).[2]
Unfortunately, the Lives and the Voyage provide little reliable
evidence of the real St Brendan as they are largely fictional
accounts of his life and travels; they do, however, attest to the
development of his cult in the centuries after his death. An
additional problem is that the precise relationship between the
Vita and the *Navigatio* traditions is uncertain. The form in which
the seven surviving versions of the *Vita* of St Brendan have come
down to us is somewhat confusing, since with two exceptions they
have been conflated with the more popular *Navigatio*; although
they all relate to a common early tradition, these versions differ in
length and content and also on points of detail.[3]

---

1. The dates given there are often slightly at variance with the Christian
calendar, differing by a year or two in some cases.
2. Another text with links to the Irish *Vita* tradition is *Dá apstol décc na hÉrenn*
('The Twelve Apostles of Ireland').
3. Of the Latin Lives only one, known as the Second Salmanticensis Life (or *Vita*

Just when the *Vita* tradition began is uncertain. The surviving copies are not earlier than the end of the twelfth century, but they strongly suggest that a version of the Life was composed before the year 1000. The *Navigatio* was probably written earlier than the *Vita*, perhaps in the second half of the eighth century. It relates Brendan's seven-year voyage in search of the Promised Land of the Saints; thus, unlike the *Vita*, it concentrates on one episode in his life. Around 125 manuscripts of the *Navigatio* have survived; its account of Brendan's travels proved so attractive that during the Middle Ages numerous vernacular translations and reworkings were produced, in a variety of countries and languages. This popularity has inspired the present volume, which brings together, along with a translation of the *Navigatio* itself, the most interesting and significant of these vernacular versions. Readers can thus determine how the various episodes of the *Navigatio* have been reworked and for what purpose, and also assess the extent to which the reworked versions constitute appealing and innovative works of literature.

Any attempt to reconstruct the details of the life of the real Brendan or to understand the nature of the Brendan legend has to be based principally on the Irish annals and genealogies and on the various versions of the *Vita Brendani*. In one set of annals (Inisfallen) we learn that Brendan was born in 486, and all annals agree that he died in 575.[4] The *Navigatio* lists his family as being of the Alltraige, a Munster kingroup, and it brings him into the territory of Corca Dhuibhne. The *Vitae* state that he was born in the parish of Tralee in County Kerry, in the civil division of Annagh, but whether this is based on anything other than speculation derived from later dedications, on misreadings of the *Navigatio* or even on later political developments, cannot be established. Some versions of the *Vita* tell us that Brendan died whilst visiting his sister Brig at the Convent of Annaghdown in County Galway and

---

altera), is unconflated; unfortunately, it is also heavily abbreviated (see Heist 1965, 324-31). Only one short Irish life, known as the First Irish Life and found in the *Book of Lismore*, is unconflated (see Stokes 1890, 99-116, 247-61).

4. If the date of Brendan's birth remains somewhat uncertain, the date of his death, in spite of slight variations in the annals, can be regarded as accurate; it falls into the period for which the annals provide a contemporary record. For references to Brendan in the Irish annals, genealogies and martyrologies see Burgess and Strijbosch 2000, chapter VI.

was buried at Clonfert. According to the annals, Clonfert was founded by Brendan himself in 558; he is in fact often known as Brendan of Clonfert, in part to distinguish him from Brendan of Birr.[5] The precise day on which he died is variously reported in the martyrologies, but 16 May is the most common date and is St Brendan's Day, though pilgrimages to Brandon Mountain are held on two alternative days during the summer.

The Brendan of the *Vita* Tradition Both the *Vita* and the *Navigatio* traditions state that Brendan's father was Findlug (Fynlogus, Findluagh, Findlogh, etc.). His mother's name is found in the *Vita* as Cara or Broinngheal. Brendan's parents were free and well-born and, as indicated above, the family was related to the Alltraige Caille, a clan associated in its turn with the Ciarraige Luachra, a people from north Kerry (a region to which, in fact, the Ciarraige gave their name). Readers of the *Navigatio* or its vernacular descendants are given no information about Brendan's early life. The *Vita* tradition, however, provides an account of his early years. It also preserves what were no doubt originally oral tales of marvels which became associated with him and served to enhance his status as a legendary figure. For example, we are told that before his birth Brendan's mother had a vision that her bosom was filled with pure gold and her breasts were shining like snow (the name Broinngheal means 'bright breast'). When she gave birth to Brendan, Bishop Erc told her that her son would be of mighty birth and filled with the grace of the Holy Spirit.[6] He was baptized at Tobar na Molt in Ardfert by Bishop Erc, who may have been a relative of the family. At first, he was given the name Mobhí (or Mobí), but suddenly a white mist (*broen finn*) descended and he became known as Broen-finn.

The *Vita* tradition also gives the following account of Brendan's early life and the miracles associated with him. After his birth, he

---

5. In addition to founding Clonfert, which became one of Ireland's great ecclesiastical centres, Brendan is reputed to have founded monasteries at Annaghdown (Co. Galway), Ardfert (Co. Kerry) and Inishadroum (Co. Clare).

6. The Lismore Life tells us that a prophet, Bec Mac Dé, told a farmer called Airdre that a worthy king would be born that night. The same night thirty of Airdre's cows produced thirty calves. Next day he found his way to Brendan's house and presented him with the thirty cows and the thirty calves, Brendan's first alms (p. 248).

remained with his parents for a year and was then fostered in Kileedy by St Ita of Cluain Credhail (south-west Limerick), since it was an old Irish custom to allow a monk or nun to provide a child with a religious education. Brendan spent five years with Ita, during which time signs of his special status became apparent. The *Vita* tells us that angels were often seen in attendance on him, ascending and descending above him; Brendan himself considered these angels to be virgins who were fostering him. From Ita, Brendan learnt to believe in God; she taught him the importance of the simple life and of generous charity, impressing on him that he should avoid hating others, embracing evil or trusting in riches.

Brendan spent the early years of his life with Ita. When he returned to his parents, he was taught to read and write by Bishop Erc, at which time it again became obvious that he possessed special virtues. Even at this young age, he performed a number of miracles. His foster father Erc had no milch cow, and when Brendan asked him one day for some milk, he replied: 'God is able to do that, my son.' From that time onwards, there came every day from Slieve League a hind with her fawn, and once Erc had milked her she would return to the mountains.

Bishop Erc finally decided that Brendan should be provided with a religious vocation and again he took him away from his home and fostered him. A story is told of this period. Erc, accompanied by Brendan, was preaching away from home; Brendan, aged about ten, had been left alone in Erc's carriage when a young princess, catching sight of his handsome face, jumped on to the vehicle in playful fashion. Brendan's response was to shout at her, strike her with the reins and drive her away, bruised and weeping. When Erc returned, Brendan was rebuked for his behaviour; as he offered to do penance, he was told to remain alone in a cave until morning. Whilst in this cave, Brendan sang psalms and hymns and his voice could be heard a mile away. Erc himself, entranced, stopped to listen to the singing, and around the cave he could see troops of angels moving upwards towards Heaven and downwards towards the earth. From then on, only a man named Finan Cam, who was filled with the Holy Spirit, could look on the radiance of Brendan's face.[7]

---

7. Another tale is told of a young man who was troubled by enemies. Brendan told him to stretch himself out on the shadow of a pillar, and he then prayed that the boy be saved in the form of a pillar. The enemies came to the pillar and cut

Brendan spent five years with Bishop Erc, during which time he learnt the canon of the Old Law and the New Testament. Then, having reached the age when he could learn 'the rules of the saints of Ireland',[8] he was ready to embark in earnest on religious training. He first returned to his foster-mother St Ita, who told him that he should not learn the rules from female saints in case he was reviled for so doing; she instructed him to set out on a journey and told him that on the road he would be met by a famous warrior of noble race. Brendan set out on a journey to the district of Connaught in Galway, and the warrior he met was a certain Colmán Mac Lenín, whom Brendan urged to repent; he did so immediately and set about building a church.[9] Brendan wished to be trained as a monk by a man named Jarlath, with whose reputation he was acquainted and in whose community he was able to learn all the rules of the Irish saints; he would also have learned there the psalms and the rudiments of Latin.

Jarlath himself benefited from this association with Brendan. He commented that Brendan's divine graces were so manifest that, rather than be his master, he should learn from him. Brendan responded by telling him he should seek his salvation elsewhere; he should build a chariot and take up residence in the place where its two hind-shafts broke. Jarlath set out, accompanied by Brendan; the place where the shafts broke became known as Tuaim dá Ghualann ('Mound of Two Shoulders'). Continuing his journey, Brendan met an angel who instructed him to write down the words of devotion he would dictate to him; in this way, Brendan wrote down the entire sacred rule of the Holy Church.[10]

---

off its head and wounded it in the side. They left the stone beheaded and carried with them the head, in the shape of their enemy. Bishop Erc told them to repent and they did so under his rule (Stokes, *Book of Lismore*, pp. 250-51).

8. For a text of the surviving rule of St Ailbe see Ó Néill 1907.

9. During his journey to Connaught Brendan also encountered a distinguished poet from the courts of the kings of Munster, at Cashel. After a debate at the roadside, he was converted by Brendan. This legend does not appear in the Lismore Life.

10. The Lismore Life tells us that, as Brendan and the angel were crossing the plain, they caught sight of a dead man on a bier, surrounded by wailing friends. Brendan told them to trust in the Lord and their friend would live; he then prayed and the dead man arose. Brendan was taken to the king, who offered him land wherever he liked. But, not wanting to dwell on the plain, Brendan refused (p. 252).

Subsequently, Brendan returned to Bishop Erc to be ordained. Then, fired with ambition to found his own monastery, he took a group of monks and established a community at Ardfert, just a few miles from where he was born. This monastery soon became famous,[11] but Brendan wanted to go farther afield. He may have had a long-standing love of the sea and was certainly aware of the well-established Irish tradition, inspired by Scripture, that a servant of God should abandon home and family and seek a place of solitude.[12] A penitential voyage or pilgrimage of this sort, in which monks by way of exile often settled on one of the islands off the west or north coast of Ireland, was known as *peregrinatio* (Charles-Edwards 1976). As it turned out, the legendary Brendan, and no doubt the historical Brendan as well, was somewhat more ambitious than most of his contemporaries. The fifteenth-century *Book of Lismore* states that his love of God had increased so much by this time that he asked the Lord to 'give him a land secret, hidden, secure, delightful, separated from men'. That night he heard the voice of an angel telling him God had given him what he sought, 'even the Land of Promise' (p. 252).

Brendan responded to this by making his way alone to Sliabh Daidche, where he saw 'the mighty, intolerable ocean on every side and then beheld the beautiful noble island, with trains of angels rising from it' (*Book of Lismore*, ibid.). He stayed there for three days; when he fell asleep, an angel came to him, saying he would teach him how to find the beautiful island he had seen and wished to reach. Brendan wept at what he heard and was filled with joy. He then made the difficult journey to Skellig Michael, eight miles off the coast of Kerry across a very rough sea, where, on a few square yards at the top of a desolate piece of rock, monks had

---

11. On the strength of his foundations Brendan was later placed among the 'twelve apostles of Ireland' and in the course of his travels he met other apostles, for example, Brigid, now ageing, and Finnian of Clonard, whom he met in Leinster. Sometimes known as the tutor to the saints of Ireland, Finnian is the author of a penitential and a letter to Gildas. He is recognized as a monastic founder.

12. Especially Genesis 12: 1 ('Now the Lord had said unto Abram, get thee out of thy country, and from thy kindred, and from thy father's house, unto a land that I will shew thee') and Luke 18: 29-30 ('And he said unto them, "Verily I say unto you, there is no man that hath left house, or parents, or brethren, or wife, or children, for the kingdom of God's sake, who shall not receive manifold more in this present time, and in the world to come life everlasting"').

established an isolated community. It may have been this first experience of hermit-style life which inspired Brendan even more to search for his own earthly solitude; his next step was to go to what is now Brandon Mountain on the Dingle Peninsula and build an oratory there. This provided him with an opportunity not only to concentrate on spiritual matters, but also to make preparations for a sea journey, which, tradition has it, began beneath Brandon Mountain, at what is now Brandon Creek.

The *Vita Brendani* tells us that Brendan and his monks set out in three skin-covered coracles, with three rows of oars for each ship and thirty men in each. After sailing for several years, during which he and his companions had a number of adventures, Brendan returned home, having failed to find the island he was seeking. On his return, he spoke to Bishop Erc and then went to see his foster-mother St Ita, who told him he should have consulted her before setting off on his voyage; to find this sacred place, she said, he must sail in a wooden boat, not as a passenger in the hides of dead animals. Hearing this, Brendan went to Connaught where he built a huge wooden boat. For his second voyage he set sail with sixty companions, and eventually, after two more years and a number of further adventures, they reached the sought-after location, a paradise-like island, beautiful and radiant, a place of peace, rest and permanent good health.[13] The voyages in the *Vita* differ somewhat from the account in the *Navigatio*, where there is a single voyage lasting for seven years and where the monks visit a

---

13. The Lismore Life contains a lengthy description of this island. On the island is an old man who says to them: 'See the plains of Paradise and the delightful fields of the land radiant, famous, lovable, profitable, lofty, noble, beautiful, delightful. A land odorous, flower-smooth, blessed. A place where you will find health without sickness, delight without quarreling, union without wrangling, princedom without dissolution, rest without idleness, freedom without labour, luminous unity of angels, delights of Paradise, service of angels, feasting without extinction, avoidance of pain, faces of the righteous, partaking of the Great Easter. A life blessed, just, protected, great, loveable, noble, restful, radiant, without gloom, without darkness, without sin, without weakness, in shining, incorruptible bodies, in stations of angels, on plains of the Land of Promise. Vast is the light and the fruitfulness of that island, its rest, its lovableness, its dearness, its stability, its security, its preciousness, its smoothness, its radiance, its purity, its lovesomeness, its whiteness, its melodiousness, its holiness, its bright purity, its nobleness, its restfulness, its beauty, its gentleness, its height, its brightness, its venerableness, its full peace, its full unity' (pp. 259-60).

number of islands, four of which (the Isle of Sheep, the whale Jasconius, the Paradise of Birds and the Isle of Ailbe) are visited on seven occasions before they reach their final destination.

Brendan's Voyages: Did Brendan Discover America?   There is no precise evidence that the historical Brendan made a voyage or voyages of the type narrated in the *Vita* or the *Navigatio*. In the *Vita* tradition the account of the voyages is relatively short and lacking in geographical precision. But in the *Navigatio* some of the island visits are described in detail and a good deal of energy and ingenuity has gone into attempting to identify them. The island of St Kilda in the Hebrides, the Faeroe Islands, Iceland, Greenland, Jan Mayen, Madeira and the Azores all feature in such attempts (Ashe 1962). Yet, however convincing these identifications sometimes are, it is impossible to know how they correspond to voyages made by an historical Brendan. If the real Brendan travelled as far as the Faeroe Islands or even Iceland, which is by no means impossible, he would have covered a substantial part of what is now known as the 'stepping-stone' route to North America (the Hebrides, Faroes, Iceland, Greenland), the route taken by Severin in his reconstruction of Brendan's voyage in 1976 and 1977 (Severin 1978).

Brendan reportedly travelled widely in Ireland and visited Scotland; his travels are, however, sometimes difficult to distinguish from those of his namesake Brendan of Birr (see Carville 1997). Both Brendans are mentioned by Adomnán in his seventh-century *Life of St Columba*, the text which provides us with our earliest reference to Brendan of Clonfert (here called *Brendenus mocu Alti* – Alti indicates that he was one of the Alltraige), who met Columba on the island of Hinba.[14] This visit must have taken place after 563, the year in which Columba left Ireland. Hinba used to be identified as the small island of Eileach an Naoimh, one of the four Garvellachs ('Isles of the Sea') in the Firth of Lorn, but this is now doubted and various possibilities have been suggested.[15] A number of churches in Scotland are dedicated to St Brendan and several places are named after him; whether this is on the basis of Brendan's real travels or because of the spread of his cult is unclear

14. See sections 29b and 118b (ed. by A. and M. Anderson).
15. For a recent discussion see Marsden 1995, 117, who suggests that Hinba was the larger island of Jura.

(Forbes 1872, 284-87; Simpson 1935, 75-76). Brendan is also said to have visited St Gildas in Wales and to have performed miracles in connection with this visit.[16] St Gildas is said to have directed the monastery and school at Llancarfan for a year, and legend has it that Brendan himself became abbot of this monastery.[17] It is also probable that Brendan visited Brittany, where place names, personal names and church dedications indicate that he was venerated there at some stage.

Brendan may also have sailed in warmer waters to the south of Ireland. In his book *Legendary Islands of the Atlantic*, William Babcock states: 'It appears likely that St Brendan in the sixth century wandered widely over the seas in quest of some warm island, concerning which wonderful accounts had been brought to him, and found several such isles' (1922, 48-49). If this is true, Brendan could have visited an island or islands in the South Atlantic with the sort of warm climate and paradise-like conditions found in the Promised Land of the Saints. Therefore, however vague our knowledge of the travels of Brendan the Navigator, the possibilities prompt us to ask the question: did Brendan, either by a northerly or a southerly route, reach the New World? Did he sail, like Severin, to Newfoundland or Labrador, or rather disembark either on the coast of what is now the USA or on an island in the Caribbean? Works dealing with the early history of America frequently cite the name of St Brendan. For example, in *Who Discovered America?* Eugene R. Fingerhut writes: 'One of the earliest medieval contenders for the title of discoverer of the New World is St Brendan', and Samuel Morison, in *The European*

16. See the Second Irish Life in Plummer 1922, I, 80-81, and the chapter 'The Latin Life of St. Brendan', in O'Donoghue 1893, 197-214. In the Second Irish Life Brendan is said, after visiting Gildas, to have made two more visits to Britain and built a church in the Isle of Ailec and one named Bleit in the district of Letha.

17. St Machutus (St Malo) is said to have been a pupil of Brendan at this monastery (see Selmer, edition, pp. xviii-xix). The relationship between the Life of St Malo and the Brendan legend remains unclear, but Malo is said in some versions of the *Vita* to have been one of the crew members on board Brendan's boat. See the section entitled 'Les diverses rédactions de la vie de saint Malo' in Ferdinand Lot, *Mélanges d'histoire bretonne (VI-XI)* (Paris: Champion, 1907), pp. 97-206. In the Second Irish Life of Brendan Malo is said to be one of Brendan's fourteen chosen companions. In one of the Lives of St Malo Brendan is said to have made a voyage to Orkney.

Discovery of America, has a lengthy section entitled 'St. Brendan and the Irish, AD 400-600' (Fingerhut 1984, 31; Morison 1971, 13-31).

St Brendan's Isle Whether or not the real St Brendan actually discovered America or visited remote Atlantic islands, he nevertheless retains, through his influence on later voyagers, an important place in the history of exploration. By at least the later thirteenth century, navigators and cartographers were clearly of the view that Brendan had indeed discovered an island or islands in the Atlantic. This belief seems to represent a fusion between the age- old, pagan notion of the Isles of the Blessed, mentioned by Strabo around 50 BC, that of the Fortunate Islands, a concept found in many cultures, and that of the fast-expanding legend of St Brendan the Navigator, which was becoming known through vernacular translations. The earliest allusion to St Brendan's Isles associates them with the Fortunate Isles and it is found on the Hereford *mappamundi* (dating from around 1275): 'Fortunate Insulae sex sunt Insulae Sct Brandani' ('The six Fortunate Islands are the islands of St Brendan'). On this map, these islands are located on roughly the site of the Canary group (in which there are in fact seven islands not six).[18] For several centuries, cartographers routinely included St Brendan's Isle or Isles on their maps, thus inspiring navigators to set out on voyages of discovery. As late as 1721, an organized expedition was launched for this purpose by Don Juan de Mur, Governor of the Canaries; like all the other expeditions, it was unsuccessful. The supposed existence of St Brendan's Isle(s) even exerted a degree of influence over the voyages of Christopher Columbus. In the fifteenth century there were claims by inhabitants of the Azores, Madeira and the Canaries that on occasion an island became visible to them. John B. Thacher, in *Christopher Columbus, his Life, his Work, his Remains*, relates these claims to Columbus's eventual discovery of the New World: 'It was common report for many years before Columbus ever saw the Canaries that the people of Gomera and Ferro reported seeing to the distant west a strange land, and that

18. The Canary Islands had been known from classical antiquity as the Fortunate Islands. See the chapter 'The Fortunate Islands' in Baring-Gould 1868, 524-60, and Manfredi 1996. On the Hereford map see Benedict 1892. It has in fact been alleged that St Brendan himself composed a work on the Fortunate Islands (see Manfredi, p. 229).

frequent excursions were made in that direction in ever fruitless search. Some said this land was the Isle of Antilia. Others said it was the Isle of St. Brandon that they saw' (I, p. 279).[19] We cannot know for certain whether Columbus believed such reports, but Thacher adds that 'they nevertheless produced some effect on his mind'. Columbus's westerly course from the Canaries was partly determined by the 'possibility of his finding the island so long dreamed of by the people of Gomera and Ferro' (ibid.).[20] At first, St Brendan's Isle or Isles were usually situated near the Canaries, Madeira or the Azores. But by the sixteenth century it was commonly thought that there was just one St Brendan's Isle and it was often located in more northerly waters. Babcock reports that the 1544 map purporting to be by Sebastian Cabot places the island of 'San Brandan' close to the scene of his father's explorations, around the latitude of the Strait of Belle Isle, which separates Newfoundland from Labrador. Babcock concludes that the shift of St Brendan's Isle to more western and northerly waters may be partly responsible for the hypotheses that Brendan crossed the Atlantic and reached North America (p. 48).

Why Read the *Navigatio*? One of the charms of the *Navigatio sancti Brendani* and of the resulting vernacular versions is that they can be read in a number of different ways, as thinly disguised accounts of Irish travels and discoveries in the Atlantic Ocean, as seafaring stories in the fashion of the Irish *immrama*,[21] or as allegorical tales

---

19. Gomera is the smallest of the Canary Islands. Babcock reports (p. 47) that apparent confusion between Antil(l)ia and St Brendan's Isle occurs on Behaim's globe of 1492 and on an earlier Catalan map.

20. Flint states that the story of Brendan had 'a most profound effect on Columbus's explorations, and especially on his claim to have found the Terrestrial Paradise' (1992, 91). She adds that the *Navigatio* 'may well occupy an especially crucial place in Columbus's medieval cosmology' (97) and that Columbus's naming of the Golfo de la Ballena brings to mind the Brendan story (159 n. 17). Along with the stories of Sindbad, the *Navigatio* would have 'offered spectacular reinforcement to the sense of moral worth and Christian wonder' which were attached to the adventures of Columbus (210). See also chapter 5 of Flint's book ('The Terrestrial Paradise', 49-181) and also Lecoq 1992.

21. *Immrama* ('rowings about') are stories such as *Máel Dúin*, in which islands visited reflect the search for the Other World. These works are largely the fruit of fertile imaginations.

charting Man's journey through life as he searches for happiness. There are also close links between the *Navigatio* and the monastic culture of its day,[22] and one cannot but be reminded of the great classical texts such as the *Odyssey* and the *Aeneid*, or of the tales of Sindbad the Sailor (whether the latter influenced the Brendan legend or vice versa remains uncertain). Many readers will surely wish to see the various accounts of Brendan's voyage as a combination of all these elements and to read them above all as literary works. The quest for the Promised Land, like the quest for the Holy Grail, is a theme which haunts many ages, and Brendan's voyage continues to inspire novels, poetry, drama and music.[23] In recasting the original Brendan material, the writers of the medieval vernacular versions, and those who continue to make use of Brendan's legend, have grasped the opportunity this material affords for an exploration of the culture and spiritual needs of their own age.

---

22. For Dorothy Bray (1995) the *Navigatio* presents an important ecclesiastical message with regard to monasticism and the religious life. See also Bourgeault 1983.

23. For example, George Mackay Brown (1984, 81-150) has written a play on the subject of St Brendan and John and Elizabeth Paynter (1979, 1984) have produced a musical composition. There is also a poetry cycle in Afrikaans devoted to Brendan by D.J. Opperman (1950). Earlier, the Brendan legend was an important source for Dante's *Divine Comedy* and it also seems to have been used by the writers of Icelandic sagas.

1

The Latin Version

John J. O'Meara and Jonathan M. Wooding[1]

Manuscripts, Editions and Translations The *Navigatio sancti Brendani abbatis* ('Voyage of Saint Brendan the abbot') was one of the most widely read and imitated texts in the Middle Ages, and the consequent range of variant and subsidiary versions has served to make the task of editors a particularly complex one. In addition to the surviving recensions of the canonical text (Burgess and Strijbosch 2000), there also exists a number of translations into vernacular languages, as well as a variety of abridgements and conflations with the more conventional Latin and Irish lives (*vitae / bethada*) of Brendan (Selmer 1959, 103-4; Sharpe 1991, 390-91). The *Navigatio* also spawned a number of imitations, both in Ireland, where the *immram* genre is mostly derived from the *Navigatio*, and in Europe, where evident counterparts to St Brendan occur in a number of voyage tales. From an early date the *Navigatio* was an international tale and this is reflected in its complex textual history. One hundred and twenty-five surviving copies of the *Navigatio*, located across most of the nation-states of modern Europe, indicate, by medieval standards, a very wide readership.

The oldest manuscripts of the *Navigatio* date from the tenth century. The earliest manuscript tradition of the *Navigatio* is entirely continental, and exemplars of the *Navigatio* in Irish manuscripts derive from French and German families of the text (Dumville 1988, 88 n. 9). The *Navigatio* made an early appearance in print, an English version being printed by Caxton in 1483; Latin and vernacular versions were reprinted intermittently throughout the early modern period.

The popularity of the work was doubtless more as a tale of wonders than as a saint's life. The interest of the *Navigatio* was very

---

1. The introduction to this chapter has been written by Jonathan M. Wooding; the translation, by John J. O'Meara, is published by permission of Colin Smythe.

often seen as being more historical and geographical than theological. Columbus undoubtedly read the *Navigatio*, and St Brendan's Isle appeared on maps as late as the modern period. The Bollandists, by contrast, were notably unimpressed by the *Navigatio* and refused to print it or the *Vita* (by then most likely only available in conflation with the *Navigatio*) in the *Acta sanctorum* (Esposito 1938, 344).

The first modern editions of the *Navigatio* were those which eschewed the continuous tradition of the text in favour of an attempt to reconstruct the primary text from manuscripts. The rich body of material presented problems of scale and nineteenth-century editions were typically diplomatic texts, or they were based on a few recensions with limited reference to the range of variant readings. The earliest edition, by Achille Jubinal (1836), was taken from two Paris manuscripts and it included a useful introduction and a discussion of the Old French versions. This edition had only a limited print-run. In 1871 Carl Schröder published a new edition based on MS Leipzig, Pauliner Bibliothek 844 and collated with Jubinal's edition and one other manuscript. Cardinal Moran (1872), in his *Acta sancti Brendani*, printed the text from a Dublin manuscript (Archbishop Marsh's Library, Z.3.1.5, the Codex Kilkenniensis or Codex Ardmachanus), along with other documents relating to the saint's cult.

These texts, particularly those published by Moran, formed the basis of most discussions of the *Navigatio* prior to 1959, the year in which Carl Selmer published an edition from a *codex optimus* (MS Ghent, Universiteitbibliotheek 401), with variants from seventeen further manuscripts, selected from among an identified total of 120. Although in technical terms this was an adequate edition, several weaknesses can be identified. James Carney (1963, 37-39) demonstrated that the editor's reconstruction of the opening sentences of the text, which are concerned with the identity and genealogy of the saint, was poor. Selmer's unlikely theory concerning the date and place of authorship also led him to questionable conclusions regarding the composition and form of the early text (1959, xxviii-xxix). Esposito (1961) was also critical of the editor's apparent belief that the text preserved some record of the discovery of America.

Though it has a copious textual tradition, the *Navigatio* is – the later recensions aside – a relatively homogeneous text, and the readings of the manuscripts bear witness to an original common version. Most variants are relatively minor and in many cases the readings of the original text can be established with confidence. A new edition would be useful, especially to shed light on its complex textual history. Giovanni Orlandi has undertaken a critical edition of the text based on the collation of a larger range of manuscripts; so far only the introductory volume and a preliminary version of the text have appeared (1968). An edition by Michaela Zelzer (Vienna) is in progress. Orlandi's edition has identified a number of variants from Selmer's edition, of greater and lesser importance. The most notable is his identification that the last portion of Selmer's text, §XXIX, which provides an account of St Brendan's death, is not present in the earliest versions, demonstrating that so far as genre is concerned the original *Navigatio* was almost completely distinct from a saint's *vita*.[2]

Setting aside the Middle English version in the *South English Legendary* and Caxton's printed version, the first English translation of the *Navigatio* was O'Donoghue's translation of Moran's edition (1893). In 1965 J.F. Webb made the first full translation of Selmer's text. However, the translation by John J. O'Meara (1976), printed in the present volume, is in general more satisfactory; it takes account of the *corrigenda* published in reviews of Selmer's edition, especially those of Carney.

Authorship The *Navigatio* is anonymous, which is not unusual for a text dating from the early medieval period. The text itself does not record explicitly where or when it was written. It is written in a clear, mostly culturally neutral Latin idiom and, although it may draw on earlier tales and traditions, this does not obscure the fact that, as we have it, it is clearly the work of a single, immensely gifted and original author who would appear to have been a monk. That he was an Irishman is evident from his use of genealogical and topographical details, as well as from some words and names – for example the great fish Iasconius, whose name is from Old Irish *íasc* 'fish'[3] – and the occasional instance where we suspect that the Latin syntax represents a calque on Old Irish sentence structure.[4]

The author had available to him traditions concerning the deeds of St Brendan, who had lived some two hundred years before the text was written. Stories of the voyages of St Brendan were doubtless already in circulation, as can be seen by references in works which

---

2. We cannot rule out the possibility, however, that an early text in the stemma simply lost its final folio.
3. John Carey has kindly drawn my attention to the Hisperic Latin word *(s)calta* (§XVII), translated by O'Meara as 'fruit' (though it is more commonly translated as 'flower'). This is likely to reflect Irish origin (see Herren, *Hisperica Famina*, 166, Harvey and Power, 'Hiberno-Latin *scaltae*', 277-79).
4. For example the opening line *'filius . . . nepotis'*, which is a calque upon either Irish *'macc . . . moccu'* or (later) *'macc . . . ua'*('son of . . . of the sept of').

cannot have been influenced by the *Navigatio*, such as the *Vita Columbae* ('Life of Columba') and the *Vita Machutis* ('Life of St Malo').[5] The author also had access to stories of voyages made by St Ailbe and his brethren as well as accounts of the journeys of more recent marine pilgrims (*peregrini*), who, probably in the early 700s, had voyaged from the western coasts of Ireland and Scotland in search of a 'hermitage in the ocean' (*herimum in ociano*). This activity, in imitation of the Desert Fathers' retreat into the wilderness, was inspired by texts such the *Vita Antonii* ('Life of St Antony') of Athanasius, the *Historia monachorum* ('History of the Monks') of Rufinus and the *Vita Pauli primi eremitae* ('Life of Paul the First Hermit') of St Jerome. These texts, or works which cited them, were also used by the author of the *Navigatio*. Whether or not the author had available to him an early version of the *Vita Brendani* is unclear. That the *Vita* is of early medieval date appears likely in view of the citation of its details in the *Litany of the Pilgrim Saints* (*c*.800-900). While the *Navigatio* and the *Vita* have certain themes in common (see below), there is no definite evidence of the influence of one upon the other in their primary detail, though the two texts were later to be conflated.

In terms of style, the author has an eye for narrative consistency and a very delicate touch when representing detail, which has frequently inspired his audience to see a degree of verisimilitude in descriptions of details which are clearly of metaphysical character (e.g. Ashe 1962; Severin 1978). Details of the monastic life are lavishly described. More fanciful details are sometimes subtly understated.[6]

At the very beginning of the text, St Brendan is introduced by the words *Sanctus Brendanus, filius Finlocha, nepotis Alti de genere Eogeni, Stagni Len Mumenensium ortus fuit*: 'Saint Brendan, son of Finlocha, of the sept of the Alltraige of the Eóganacht of Loch Léin, was born in Munster.' This bears witness to the author's detailed knowledge of Munster genealogy, though, as it stands, the genealogy itself is defective. The Alltraige cannot be described as located in the territory of the Eóganacht of Loch Léin (Ó Corráin 1969, 27-37; 1970, 19-22). Some attempts to date the text have treated this as reflecting a particular

---

5. See Adomnán, *Vita Columbae* III.17, ed. Anderson and Anderson, 206-7; for the *Vita Machutis* see Mac Mathúna 1994b.
6. A very striking example of this is in the respective descriptions of what lies beneath the transparent sea in the *Navigatio* (§XXI) and *Immram Máele Dúin* (§XXIII). In the *Navigatio* there are schools of fish 'lying in herds like pastures . . . so numerous that they looked like a city of circles'. In *Immram Máele Dúin* (inspired in this case by the *Navigatio*) there are actual 'roofed strongholds and a beautiful country . . . and a drove of herds' (ed. Stokes 1889, 55).

historical claim. Donnchadh Ó Corráin, however, in a personal communication, suggests that in all probability the text is corrupt at this point. If this is so, the defect must have occurred very early in the textual tradition, as it is common to all exemplars.

The detail in the *Navigatio* concerning sites in Corca Dhuibhne (west of Dingle, Co. Kerry) is clearly based on local knowledge of their orientation. The mountain on which Brendan pitches his tent (cf. Daniel 11: 45) in the 'distant part of his native region where his parents were living' (§IV)[7] is described as 'extending long into the ocean', which is an adequate description of the elevation of the north side of Brandon Mountain, and though the description of Brandon Creek, Feohanagh, as 'having entry for only one boat' (*ubi erat introitus unius nauis*) would appear to understate its size very slightly there can be little doubt that this is the location that the author had in his mind's eye.

These elements point to the author having been an Irishman. The author need not necessarily have been resident in Ireland at the time of writing. An Irish *peregrinus* on the continent could just as easily have composed the text. Dicuil, writing in Aachen in 825, includes in his *De mensura orbis terrae* ('Of the Measurement of the Earth' (ed. Tierney 1967)) details of the voyages of Irish *peregrini* which he had probably acquired from earlier residence in Iona (Wooding 2000b). These voyages include accounts of the Faroe Islands and Iceland, and the same voyages appear to have been known to the author of the *Navigatio* – for example, the fantastic description of the islands inhabited by sheep and birds appears to have been based on an account similar to the one used by Dicuil in his description of the Faroe Islands. This does not mean, of course, that Dicuil himself was the author. The author we are looking for would perhaps have been a slightly earlier figure, albeit one whose knowledge of the experience of ocean voyaging by the *peregrini* was similar to Dicuil's.

Selmer's candidate for author of the *Navigatio* was such an Irish exile. On the basis of the distribution of the earliest manuscripts, he attempted to locate him in tenth-century Lotharingia (Selmer 1950); he even went as far as to ascribe authorship to a specific person, Israel Episcopus. However, Selmer's views have not found acceptance (Lapidge 1993). The mid-tenth-century date of the earliest recension of the text and the overall textual tradition indicate a date of

---

7. I suspect that this passage is intended to highlight the tension between the ties of kin and the monastic vocation (cf. Matthew 10: 37).

composition considerably earlier than the *floruit* of Israel. Moreover, the gap, probably two centuries or greater, between the original composition and the Lotharingian exemplars does not argue for an early date for these manuscripts within the stemma. The fact that the earliest textual tradition is continental does not prove continental authorship – even for texts of known Irish authorship the earliest copies are often exclusively in continental manuscripts. Claims based on manuscript tradition are of limited value for determining the provenance of the tale.

Date and Context If we seek evidence which will assist us in dating the text itself, as opposed to the earliest manuscripts, we can identify a number of details which can be dated with some degree of precision. In a brief discussion of the relationship between the *Vita Albei* ('Life of St Ailbe') and Munster historiography, Herbert (1999) has suggested that the reference in the *Navigatio* to St Ailbe's voyage may be part of a tit-for-tat comparison between the voyaging traditions of the two saints. Herbert dates the *Vita Albei* to the period between 721 and 742, and the *Navigatio* can plausibly be dated to the same century. Dumville (1988) has placed the text before *c.*786 on the basis that Brendan's Alltraige / Eóganacht genealogy relates to a period in which there were close connections between these two peoples.

As the *Navigatio* incorporates details seemingly derived from datable monastic sea voyages between the late 500s and the early 800s, these may also be used to suggest a *terminus post quem* by which certain sources were available to the author of the *Navigatio*. Perhaps the most plausible contribution to the *Navigatio* by genuine voyaging is a description of the Faroe Islands (§IX). Dicuil (ed. Tierney, 76-77) states that Irish anchorites lived on these islands from *c.*730 onwards, and if the details in Dicuil and the *Navigatio* derive from the same source this would seem to rule out a date much before the mid 700s. We may yet hope for other evidence of cited sources. The wealth of liturgical detail in the *Navigatio*, such as the antiphons chanted in the Office (§XII and §XVII), would seem to offer possibilities for dating.[8]

An upper limit for the composition of the text is harder to set (see Orlandi 1968, 72); the textual tradition would suggest a date no later than the ninth century. But the overall context seems to be a pattern

---

8. See Stevenson 1998, 314. My colleague Tom O'Loughlin, who kindly read this introduction in typescript, informs me that the antiphons are of an undoubtedly early type. The close resemblance of these to the antiphons in the Antiphonary of Bangor has been noted by Curran 1984, 169-77.

of voyaging and its commemoration in literature centred on the period c.730-830.

Content and Structure The text is structured around a series of episodes connected by a symmetrical narrative, based on the feasts of the monastic year (Bourgeault 1983; Bray 1995; O'Loughlin 2000, Ch. 9). For convenience, these are outlined here by reference to the chapters as numbered in the accompanying translation, though it should be noted that these chapters derive only from late manuscripts and that in all probability the text originally contained no divisions. The structure of the text can be broken down into the following divisions:

(1) Barrind's account of the journey to *Insula deliciosa* and thence to the *Terra repromissionis sanctorum* (§I)

(2) Brendan obtains permission for his voyage from the elders and departs (§§II-V)

(3) The journey to the Isle of Sheep / Paradise of Birds archipelago. The start of the symmetrical cycle (§§VI-IX)

(4) Adventures on the ocean. The circuit of voyages with occasional northward diversions into the perilous zone. Final return to the Isle of Sheep / Paradise of Birds archipelago (§§X-XXVII)

(5) The eastward voyage to the *Terra repromissionis sanctorum*. Thence to *Insula deliciarum*. The return to Ireland (§XXVIII)

(6) The death of Brendan (§XXIX)

The narrative begins with the genealogy of the saint (§I). A vision of the Promised Land of the Saints (*Terra repromissionis sanctorum*), which will be Brendan's destination, is revealed to him through the visit of Barrind,[9] who tells him of a visit he had made to this place with Abbot Mernoc.[10] The two men had set off across the sea from Mernoc's monastery on *Insula deliciosa* ('Isle of Delights'), itself located off the coast of Slieve League in Donegal.[11]

What was for Barrind simply a place to visit and for Mernoc a place of regular retreat became for Brendan what is termed in other Latin saints' lives 'a higher place of pilgrimage' (*potioris peregrinationis locus*), i.e. the personal destination which would be the ultimate goal of his *peregrinatio*

---

9. The name Barrind is a 'pet name' or hypocorism *Barr-find* 'little / dear Finn / Finnian'.

10. Mernoc is a hypocoristic name for St Ernán (*Mo-Ern-óc* 'my little/dear Ernán').

11. Slieve League is rendered *Mons lapidum*. See Carney 1963, 39, who identifies *Insula deliciosa* with *Inis Caín*, a monastery of St Ernán (though the discussion of its location is inaccurate).

(see Charles-Edwards 1976). Brendan then shuts himself up for forty days with fourteen chosen companions (§II). This is followed by a visit to St Enda (in Aran), then by retreat to Brandon Mountain (§IV). After this (§V), the monks build a boat; they are joined by three supernumerary companions, who have left without permission of their abbot (for which reason Brendan predicts that they will not return). They set out in the direction of the solstice.

Events henceforth are episodic. After forty days they come to the rocky island (§VI); a brother is tempted and dies, but his soul is saved (§VII); a youth gives them food (§VIII); they come to the Isle of Sheep, where they stay until Holy Saturday (§IX); the first encounter with Jasconius, the giant fish, takes place (§X); they land in the Paradise of Birds, where birds chant the canonical hours (§XI); they visit the monastery of the surviving followers of St Ailbe (§XII); they drink of the soporific well (§XIII); they sail north and encounter the Coagulated Sea (§XIV); they spend Easter again on the Isle of Sheep, Jasconius and the Paradise of Birds (§XV); they sail for forty days and encounter a sea monster (§XVI); they sail north and come to the Isle of the Three Choirs or Anchorites (§XVII); a bird brings them grapes and they land on the island from which they came (§XVIII); they encounter the gryphon (§XIX); they spend Christmas in St Ailbe's community and Easter on the Isle of Sheep, Jasconius and the Paradise of Birds (§XX); they come across the clear sea (§XXI), the Crystal Column (§XXII), the Isle of Smiths (§XXIII) and the fiery mountain (§XXIV); they meet Judas Iscariot (§XXV) and Paul the Hermit (§XXVI); they again spend Easter on the same sites (§XXVII); they visit the Promised Land of the Saints and return to Ireland (§XXVIII); Brendan dies (§XXIX).

This brief analysis of the structure of the *Navigatio* reveals a number of features. Criticism of the text's geography has been distracted by the tension existing between, on the one hand, those who would reconstruct the sequence of episodes in terms of a half-recalled voyage via a stepping stone route to America and, on the other hand, the sceptics of such readings. In amongst this debate, it is not often noted that the author had both a vision of the geography of his ocean and a conception of its chronological relations to the lives of other saints.[12] Brendan was a sixth-century saint and tradition had it that

---

12. There is a continuous tradition of criticism of the *Navigatio* which views it as representing a voyage to America or Canada (see, Introduction, pp. 9-11). Suggestions that Brendan discovered North America, however, depend on a reading of the text as a single westward voyage by the saint (see esp. Little 1945; Chapman 1973; Severin 1978; Wooding 2000b).

Ailbe was a contemporary of the fifth-century Patrick; therefore, in reality Ailbe should be dead by Brendan's time. When the latter visits Ailbe's community (XII), the author is careful to note the length of time (eighty years) which has elapsed since Ailbe's time.

The voyage takes place in the Atlantic, to the west and north-west of Ireland. Most critics of 'rationalizing' readings of the text have pointed out that the voyage to the Promised Land of the Saints is reached after a voyage in an *easterly* direction and for this reason cast doubt on those who would read the *Navigatio* as a voyage to the western Atlantic. A far westward voyage it certainly is not, but not because the Promised Land lies in the east. Initially, Brendan leaves Ireland and sets sail on the ocean. He reaches the Isle of Sheep / Paradise of Birds and then voyages for seven years in a cycle. To get to the Promised Land of the Saints, he eventually goes *east* from the Paradise of Birds. After that, he returns via *Insula deliciarum* (§XVIII). The latter is clearly the same place as *Insula deliciosa* in chapter I (Bieler 1976; O'Meara 1976, xviii-xix and *pace* Carney 1963).[13] Barrind and Mernoc went west from *Insula deliciosa* to the Promised Land of the Saints. The Promised Land of the Saints is therefore west of *Insula deliciosa / deliciarum*, but east of the Paradise of Birds. The Promised Land of the Saints is to the *west* of Ireland, able to be reached from a liminal space in the ocean between Ireland and other islands. It is not the uttermost west, nor east. The Isle of Smiths (§XXIII) and the coagulated sea (§XIV) are both reached after a voyage northward from the Paradise of Birds. The north constitutes a zone of peril (see Borsje 1996, 164).

Sources The *Navigatio* clearly uses earlier sources, which fall into several categories. It has a close relationship with other voyage tales, the priority of which has not yet been clearly established with respect to the *Navigatio* (Dumville 1976; Mac Mathúna 1994a). The *Navigatio* makes reference to the tradition of the voyage of the brethren of St Ailbe. This is mentioned in the ninth-century *Litany of Pilgrim Saints* (Hughes 1959; Sanderlin 1975) and in the *Vita Albei* (§XXIX, ed. Heist 1965, 129). Of non-Irish sources, texts relating to desert monasticism are clearly known to the author. The episode in which one of the brethren is possessed by a devil in the form of an Ethiopian boy (§VII) is in all probability based on an episode in Athanasius (*Vita Antonii*, §VI). The description of the monks

---

13. At least to the author of the *Navigatio*, who may have been conflating separate locations in Irish tradition.

swarming from their cells on *Insula deliciosa* derives from Rufinus's *Historia monachorum*.[14] Paul the Hermit is clearly the 'first hermit' of Egypt commemorated by St Jerome in *Vita Pauli primi eremitae*, which the author of the *Navigatio* appears to have used.

The story is an eschatology, and typically the events of the Bible, as well as possible reference to apocrypha, are close at hand. Selmer has documented the direct quotations from Psalms; the many indirect citations of Scripture remain largely uncatalogued. Discussion of the sea monsters, following the example of Borsje (1996), is also a *desideratum*. O'Loughlin (1999) has argued that the description of the river and distances in the *Terra repromissionis* derives from the Book of Revelation. Esposito (1960) and Dumville (1988) have suggested that the presence of Enoch and Elijah in the *Tír Tairngire* ('promised land') in the *Immram Snédgusa ocus Maic Riagla* ('The Voyage of Snédgus and Mac Riagla') indicates strongly that the author of the *Navigatio* had in mind the very same place, where Enoch and Elijah await the end of the earth (McNamara 1975, 25-27). Esposito (1960) maintained that the Irish had access to a specific tradition, available in Brittany, which located Enoch and Elijah's land in the ocean. The evidence for the latter is persuasive, but not compelling.

Zimmer (1889) argued strongly that the *Navigatio* was dependent on Virgil's *Aeneid*, an argument which was convincingly dismissed by Thrall (1917); some influence, however, perhaps indirect, remains more than likely.

Genre The *Navigatio* is first and foremost a monastic tale of a monk who is drawn from the timeless task of 'fighting the good fight' (cf. 1 Timothy 6: 12, 2 Timothy 4: 7) in the wilderness to set forth on a search for a revealed higher place of exile. In many ways, the tale is unique in structure, although many of its motifs are paralleled in Old and Middle Irish *echtrai* ('adventures') and *immrama* ('voyages'), as well as in Middle Irish and Latin hagiography and 'visions' (Old Irish *físi* / Latin *visiones*).

In Irish tales such as *Echtrae Condle* ('The Adventure of Condle'), *Baile in Scáil* ('Phantom's Prophecy') and *Immram Brain* ('The Voyage of Bran') tokens are brought to draw the recipient to an immanent otherworld (Carey 1982-83; McCone 2000). In the *Vita Brendani* the saint is vouchsafed a vision from a mountain top of a *Terra secreta* ('secret place') in the ocean, while in *Dá Ápstol décc na hÉrenn* ('The Twelve Apostles of Ireland') a flowering branch is carried on the

---

14. I owe this identification to my research student Dan Tipp.

breeze to an assembly of clergy (Plummer 1922, 96). In the *Navigatio* Brendan's vision is more mundane, being acquired from Barrind by word of mouth, although, like St Ailbe and the monks Snédgus and Mac Riagla (§XVII, ed. Stokes 1888, 21), he does pick up a flowering branch while on his voyage (§XVIII).

When setting off on his voyage, Brendan takes with him three monks who have left without permission. This motif is also seen in the episode concerning the attempt by Cormac Ua Liatháin to voyage north from Iona in the *Vita Columbae*, where his voyage fails because he has taken along with him a brother who has departed without his abbot's permission. In the *immrama* such supernumerary figures also fulfil the function of extras who are marked for a different fate, though there they are not monks.

Various locations are shared between the *Navigatio*, the *immrama* and *vitae*, especially the two longer *immrama* of Máel Dúin and the Uí Corra. Examples are too numerous to be listed here in full, but they include the Crystal Column, the Coagulated Sea, the Isle of Sheep, various islands where processions are held and islands where the occupants throw objects at the boat, in the manner of the Isle of Smiths. These parallels were traditionally taken as evidence that the *Navigatio* was a Latin text derived from an established genre of *immrama*. But, as Carney (1963), Mac Mathúna (1994b) and others have shown, it is more likely that the *Navigatio* is the source for *Immram Máele Dúin*, which was itself used by the author of *Immram Ua Corra*. Carney has also speculated that *Immram Brain* may be modelled on an older version of the *Navigatio*, but this remains to be demonstrated convincingly. Such a work would have been completely different to the *Navigatio* which we now have.[15]

In terms of genre, then, we may conclude that the evidence points to the *Navigatio* as having developed originally from the type of voyage episode (perhaps inspired by native *echtrai*) found in the *vitae* of several early Irish saints, for example Saints Columba, Patrick and Ailbe.[16] These can reasonably be seen as a sub-genre of Latin *navigationes*, of which St Brendan's is the only one to be developed as the *leitmotiv* of an entire tale.[17] At the moment we should regard the

---

15. David Dumville informs me that he hopes to publish Carney's surviving correspondence on this theory.
16. For example, the various voyages of Cormac Ua Liatháin in Adomnán, *Vita Columbae* II.42, 168-69), also I.20, 46) and the voyage of Macc Cuill in Muirchú, *Vita Patricii*, 104, see Bieler 1979).
17. Likewise, Brendan is the only saint to be the subject of voyage narratives in Irish such as *Dá apstol décc na hÉrenn* and the poem 'Mochen Mochen a Brénaind'. Other

immram genre as a direct translation of the concept – as well, perhaps, as the term – into vernacular literature.[18]

The Author's Purpose At the centre of the *Navigatio*'s structure lies the monastic life; in terms of narrative structure the text is an allegory of monastic progression. The monks are not on a pilgrimage or a mission; the three latecomers aside, they are following their monastic vocation with permission and guidance and alternately fast, pray and row. Every year, they celebrate the festivals of the calendar in the same places; they exist in a life of monastic *stabilitas* and *stasis*, until they are called to a higher place. Such a structure almost defies any attempt at narrative progression. Later, vernacular versions of the *Navigatio* insert into the story an element of progressive education and purification which are lacking here. The only reason given for the length of time taken to reach the Promised Land of the Saints, which Mernoc and Barrind reached in only a few hours, is the steward's statement: 'You could not find it immediately because God wished to show you his varied secrets in the great ocean' (§XXVIII).

There may be retarding factors. The three latecomers are not destined to find the Promised Land of the Saints (§XII) and the last of these must be jettisoned before this Promised Land can be found (§XXIV). In the *Vita Brendani* an additional retarding factor occurs; here the *Terra secreta* is a sacred place, which the saint's hide boat cannot enter because it is made of dead flesh. In the *Navigatio* this motif is absent, as the hide boat seems to present no obstacle (but the saint himself, it is observed, abstains from eating the flesh of animals and has done so since his ordination, §XVI). From the beginning, Brendan himself is doubtless worthy of entry to the Promised Land of the Saints, though this distinction may hint at the need for his companions to become worthy through their experiences. If anything, however, the experiences described by the steward as 'trials' (§XV) seem only likely to cause regress rather then progress. Brendan is concerned that, contrary to the requirements of his vocation as famously set out by Augustine in *On the Work of Monks*, he is living on food provided by God, rather than by dint of his own labours (§XXVI). The example of Paul the Hermit shows that this is a higher calling, and Paul's life without any food at all may be a satire on the extreme asceticism of the *Céli Dé* in the ninth century. The *Vita*

---

tales of clerical voyages, such as *Immram Snédgusa ocus Maic Riagla*, are not about saints.
18. On the *immram* genre see Dumville 1976 and Mac Cana 1980, 43; 76-7. *Immram* (literally 'rowing about') seems likely to be a translation into Irish of *navigatio*.

Pauli presents a conflict between the vocation of the monk and that of the hermit, which is echoed in the *Navigatio* and may echo the concerns leading to the ban on *peregrinatio* in the ninth century (Hughes 1960).[19]

To attempt to tie the *Navigatio* to contemporary events, however, may be to miss the point of the story. Orlandi has identified the *christianorum persecucio* ('persecution of the Christians') in chapter XXVIII with the Viking raids (see Dumville 1988). The *Navigatio*'s eschatology is, however, more generally millenarian in character (cf. Revelation 20). It is not an urgent narrative; its cyclical nature reflects the circular path of the monastic year and the religious life. The text arose from social circumstances very like those which produced the romances of the twelfth century, in a mentality which R.W. Southern famously defined as characterized by the journey motif (1953, 212-18). In the hierarchical society of Ireland, exile was a common phenomenon. In monasticism, ascetic exile was its reflex, and allegorical tales of quests in the 'desert' were perhaps a logical development. In the *Navigatio* this quest is given a specific and especially holy destination, and as in the Old French *Queste del Saint Graal* tension is created between the normal moral development of the allegorical tale and the requirement of purity in the person who will attain the sacred place which is the object of the quest. As in the story of the Grail, the resolution is uniquely achieved, in this case by making the tale an allegory of the monks' quest to sustain the 'good fight' (§I) and maintain their purity, not simply to *attain* it. To sustain the tension of this tale, the author packed it with lavish detail of the voyages being made by his contemporaries on the ocean and of the monastic life which they lived in it. In this way, the *Navigatio* appeals to the monastic reader and the armchair traveller alike. There is certainly a need for future criticism to treat of the religious content of the work in greater depth. The voyage on the sea has been seen as evidence of 'le naturalisme celtique', in the words of Ernest Renan, and with respect to this reading details such as the monastic structure and the motifs of monsters, symmetrical pillars and the miraculous feeding of the monks have tended to be explained away (Wooding 2003). Monasticism, however, is the subject of the story and such detail is crucial to the interpretation of this unique religious allegory.

---

19. The motif of the brethren who depart without permission (cf. *Anglo-Saxon Chronicle*, s.a. 891) is probably another exploration of this theme of the tension between the eremitic and communal life.

I Saint Brendan, son of Findlug, descendant of Alte, was born among the Eoganacht of Loch Léin in the land of the men of Munster. He was a man of great abstinence, famous for his mighty works and father of nearly three thousand monks.

When he was fighting the good fight, in a place called Clonfert of Brendan, there arrived one evening one of the fathers whose name was Barrind, a descendant of Niall. When this Barrind was plied with many questions by the holy father, he wept, prostrated himself on the ground and stayed a long time praying. But Saint Brendan lifted him up from the ground and embraced him, saying:

'Father, why should we be sad during your visit? Did you not come to encourage us? Rather should you give joy to the brothers. Show us the word of God and nourish our souls with the varied wonders that you saw in the ocean.'

When Saint Brendan had finished his remarks, Saint Barrind began to describe a certain island, saying:

'My son Mernoc, steward of Christ's poor, left me and sought to live the life of a solitary. He found an island near Slieve League, called the Delightful Island. Then, a long time afterwards I heard that he had many monks with him, and that God had shown many wonders through him. So, I set out to visit my son. At the end of a three-day journey, as I was approaching, he hurried with his brothers to meet me. For the Lord revealed to him that I was coming. As we were crossing in a boat to the island the brothers came, like bees swarming, from their various cells to meet us. Their housing was indeed scattered but they lived together as one in faith, hope and charity. They ate together and they all joined together for the divine office. They are given nothing to eat but fruit, nuts, roots and other greens. But after compline each remained in his own cell until the cocks crowed or the bell was struck. Having stayed overnight and walked round the whole island, I was brought by my son to the sea shore facing west, where there was a boat. He said to me: "Father, embark in the boat and let us sail westwards to the island which is called the Promised Land of the Saints which God will give to those who come after us at the end of time."

'We embarked and sailed, but a fog so thick covered us that we could scarcely see the poop or the prow of the boat. But when we had spent about an hour like this a great light shone all around us, and there appeared to us a land wide, and full of grass and fruit. When the boat landed we disembarked and began to go and walk round that island. This we did for fifteen days – yet we could not find the end of it. We saw no plants that had not flowers, nor trees that had not fruit. The stones of that land are precious stones. Then on the fifteenth day we found a river flowing from east to west. As we pondered on all these things we were in doubt what we should do.

'We decided to cross the river, but we awaited advice from God. In the course of a discussion on these things, a man suddenly appeared in a great light before us, who immediately called us by our own names and saluted us, saying: "Well done, good brothers. For the Lord has revealed to you the land, which he will give to his saints. The river there marks the middle of the island. You may not go beyond this point. So return to the place from which you departed." When he said this, I immediately questioned him where he came from and what was his name. He said: "Why do you ask me where I come from or how I am called? Why do you not ask me about the island? As you see it now, so it has been from the beginning of the world. Do you feel the need of any food or drink or clothing? Yet for the equivalent of one year you have been on this island and have not tasted food or drink! You have never been overcome by sleep nor has night enveloped you! For here it is always day, without blinding darkness. Our Lord Jesus Christ is the light of this island."

'Straightaway we started on our journey, the man coming with us to the shore where our boat was. As we embarked in it he was taken from our eyes and we passed through the same darkness to the Delightful Island. When the brothers saw us they rejoiced with great joy at our arrival and complained of our absence for such a long time, saying: "Why, fathers, have you left your sheep wandering in the wood without a shepherd? We knew of our abbot going away from us frequently somewhere or other – but we do not know where – and staying there sometimes for a month, sometimes for a fortnight or a week or more or less." When I heard this, I began to console them, saying to them: "Think, brothers, only of good. You are living undoubtedly at the gate of Paradise. Near here is an island which is called the Promised Land of the Saints where night does not fall nor day end. Your abbot Mernoc goes there. An angel of the Lord guards it. Do you not perceive from the fragrance of our clothing that we have been in God's Paradise?" The brothers then replied: "Abbot, we knew that you were in God's Paradise in the wide sea; but where that Paradise is, we do not know. We have indeed often noticed the fragrance exuding from our abbot's clothes when he returns from there after the space of forty days." I stayed on with my son for two successive weeks without food or drink. Yet our bodies were so satisfied that to others we seemed full of new wine. And after forty days I received the blessing of the brothers and the abbot and set off with my companions on the return journey to my cell. I shall go there tomorrow.'

When they heard these things, Saint Brendan and all his community prostrated themselves on the ground, glorifying God and saying:

'The Lord is just in all his ways and holy in all his works. For he has revealed to his servants such great wonders. He is blessed in his gifts, for he has nourished us today with such a spiritual foretaste.'
When they had said this, Saint Brendan spoke:

'Let us go to repair our bodies and to the washing of feet in accordance with the new commandment.'
When that night was over, Saint Barrind, having received the blessing of the brothers in the morning, set out for his own cell.

II   Saint Brendan, therefore, when fourteen brothers out of his whole community had been chosen, shut himself up in one oratory with them and spoke to them, saying:

'From you who are dear to me and share the good fight with me I look for advice and help, for my heart and all my thoughts are fixed on one determination. I have resolved in my heart if it is God's will – and only if it is – to go in search of the Promised Land of the Saints of which father Barrind spoke. How does this seem to you? What advice would you give?'
They, however, having learned of the holy father's will, say, as it were with one mouth:

'Abbot, your will is ours. Have we not left our parents behind? Have we not spurned our inheritance and given our bodies into your hands? So we are prepared to go along with you to death or life. Only one thing let us ask for, the will of God.'

III Saint Brendan and his companions, therefore, decided to fast for forty days – but for no more than three days at a time – and then to set out. When the forty days were over he said good-bye to the brothers, commended all to the man put in charge of his monastery, who was afterwards his successor there, and set out westwards with fourteen brothers to the island of a holy father, named Enda. There he stayed three days and three nights.

IV Having received the blessing of the holy father and of all the monks that were with him, he set out for a distant part of his native region where his parents were living. But he did not wish to see them. He pitched his tent at the edge of a mountain stretching far out into the ocean, in a place called Brendan's Seat, at a point where there was entry for one boat. Saint Brendan and those with him got iron tools and constructed a light boat ribbed with wood and with a wooden frame, as is usual in those parts. They covered it with ox-hides tanned with the bark of oak and smeared all the joints of the hides on the outside with fat. They carried into the boat hides for the makings of two other boats, supplies for forty days, fat for preparing hides to cover the boat and other things needed for human life. They also placed a mast in the middle of the boat and a sail and the other requirements for steering a boat. Then Saint Brendan ordered his brothers in the name of the Father, Son and Holy Spirit to enter the boat.

V While Saint Brendan remained alone on the shore and blessed the landing-place, three brothers from his own monastery came up, following after him. They fell immediately at the feet of the holy father, saying:

'Father, leave us free to go with you wherever you are going; otherwise we shall die on this spot from hunger and thirst. For we have decided to be pilgrims for the days of our life that remain.'

When the man of God saw their trouble, he ordered them to enter the boat, saying:

'Your will be done, my sons.'

And he added:

'I know why you have come. One of you has done something meritorious, for God has prepared a suitable place for him. But for you others he will prepare a hideous judgement.'

VI   Saint Brendan then embarked, the sail was spread and they began to steer westwards into the summer solstice. They had a favourable wind and, apart from holding the sail, had no need to navigate. After fifteen days the wind dropped. They set themselves to the oars until their strength failed. Saint Brendan quickly began to comfort and advise them, saying:

'Brothers, do not fear. God is our helper, sailor and helmsman, and he guides us. Ship all the oars and the rudder. Just leave the sail spread and God will do as he wishes with his servants and their ship.'

They always had their food, however, at evening time. When they got a wind, they did not know from what direction it came or in what direction the boat was going.

When forty days were up and all the victuals had been consumed, an island appeared to them towards the north, rocky and high. When they came near its shore they saw a high cliff like a wall and various streams flowing down from the top of the island into the sea. Nevertheless they failed totally to find a landing place where they could put in the boat. The brothers were greatly harassed by the lack of food and drink. So each took up a vessel to try to catch some of the fresh water. When Saint Brendan saw this, he said:

'Do not do that. What you are doing is foolish. God does not yet wish to show us a place to land, and do you want to be guilty of plundering? The Lord Jesus Christ after three days will show his servants a landing-place and a place to stay, so that our harassed bodies will be restored.'

When, then, they had circled the island for three days, on the third day about three o'clock they found an opening where one boat might enter. Saint Brendan stood up immediately and blessed the entry. It was a cutting with rock of remarkable height on either side, straight up like a wall. When they had all disembarked and stood outside on land, Saint Brendan forbade them to take any equipment out of the boat. As they were walking along the cliffs of

the sea, a dog ran across them on a path and came to the feet of
Saint Brendan as dogs usually come to heel to their masters. Saint
Brendan said to his brothers:

'Has not God sent us a good messenger? Follow him.'

Saint Brendan and his brothers followed the dog to a town. On
entering the town they caught sight of a great hall, furnished with
beds and chairs, and water for washing their feet. When they had
sat down Saint Brendan gave an order to his companions, saying:

'Beware, brothers, lest Satan lead you into temptation. For I can
see him persuading one of the three brothers, who came from our
monastery to follow after me, to commit a bad theft. Pray for his
soul. For his body has been given into the power of Satan.'

The house where they were staying had hanging vessels of different
kinds of metal fixed around its walls along with bridles and horns
encased in silver.

Then Saint Brendan spoke to the one who usually placed bread
before the brothers:

'Bring the meal that God has sent us.'

This man stood up immediately, found a table made ready and
linen and a loaf for each of marvellous whiteness and fish. When all
were brought before him, Saint Brendan blessed the meal and said
to his brothers:

'Give praise to the God of Heaven who gives food to all flesh.'

The brothers sat back, therefore, and glorified God. In the same
way they found as much drink as they wanted. When supper was
over and the office of compline said, he spoke:

'Rest now. There is a well-dressed bed for each of you. You need
to rest, for your limbs are tired from too much toil.'

When the brothers had fallen asleep, Saint Brendan saw the devil at
work, namely an Ethiopian child holding a bridle in his hand and
making fun with the brother already mentioned to his face. Saint
Brendan got up immediately and began to pray, thus spending the
whole night until day. In the morning when the brothers had
hurried to the divine office and later had gone to the boat, they saw
a table laid out just like the day before. And so for three days and
three nights God prepared a meal for his servants.

VII After that Saint Brendan with his companions set out again, saying
to the brothers:

'Make sure that none of you takes anything belonging to this island with him.'

But they all replied:

'God forbid, father, that our journey should be desecrated by any theft.'

Then Saint Brendan said:

'Look, our brother whom I referred to a few days ago has a silver bridle in his bosom given to him last night by the devil.'

When the brother in question heard this, he threw the bridle out of his bosom and fell before the feet of the man of God, saying:

'I have sinned, father. Forgive me. Pray for my soul, that it may not perish.'

Immediately all prostrated themselves on the ground, praying the Lord for the brother's soul. As they rose from the ground and the holy father raised up the brother, they saw a small Ethiopian jump out of his bosom, wailing with a loud voice and saying:

'Why, man of God, do you expel me from my dwelling, where I have lived now for seven years, and make me depart from my inheritance?'

Saint Brendan replied to this voice:

'I order you in the name of the Lord Jesus Christ not to injure any man to the day of judgement.'

Turning again to the brother, the man of God said:

'Receive the body and blood of the Lord, for your soul will now leave your body. Here you will be buried. But your brother here, who came from our monastery with you, has his burial place in Hell.'

And so when the Eucharist had been received, the soul of the brother left his body, and before the eyes of the brothers was received by the angels of light. His body, however, was buried on the spot by the holy father.

VIII   The brothers then went with Saint Brendan to the shore of the island where their boat was. As they were embarking a youth came up carrying a basket full of bread and a jar of water. He said to them:

'Receive a blessing from the hand of your servant. A long journey lies ahead of you until you find consolation. Nevertheless neither bread nor water will fail you from now until Easter.'

Having received the blessing they began to sail out into the ocean.
They ate every second day. And so the boat was borne through
various places of the ocean.

IX   One day they saw an island not far from them. When they began to
steer towards it, a favourable wind came to their help, so that they
did not have to exert themselves more than their strength could
manage. When the boat stood to at the harbour, the man of God
bade them all get out of the boat. He got out after them. When
they began to go round the island they saw large streams of water,
full of fish, flowing from various springs. Saint Brendan said to his
brothers:

'Let us carry out the divine service here. Let us sacrifice the
Spotless Victim to God, for today is Maundy Thursday.'

They stayed there until Holy Saturday. Walking round the island
they found various flocks of sheep – all of one colour, white. The
sheep were so numerous that the ground could not be seen at all.
Saint Brendan called his brothers together and said to them:

'Take what you need for the feast from the flock.'
The brothers, hurrying according to the command of the man of
God to the flock, took one sheep from it. When they had tied it by
the horns, it followed the brother who held the rope in his hand as
if it were tame to the place where the man of God was standing.
Again the man of God spoke to one of the brothers:

'Take a spotless lamb from the flock.'
The brother hurried and did as he had been enjoined.

On Good Friday, while they were preparing for the service, a man
appeared to them holding in his hand a basket full of bread, that
had been baked under the ashes, and the other things that were
necessary. When he placed these before the man of God, he fell
prone on his face three times at the feet of the holy father, saying:

'How have I deserved, O pearl of God, that you should eat, on
these holy days, of the labour of my hands?'
Saint Brendan lifted him up from the ground, embraced him and
said:

'Son, our Lord Jesus Christ chooses a place for us where we can
celebrate his holy Resurrection.'
The man replied:

'Father, here you will celebrate Holy Saturday. Tomorrow, however, God has ordained that you celebrate the masses and the vigils of his Resurrection in the island that you see nearby.'
While he said this he prepared to serve the servants of God and do whatever was necessary for Holy Saturday.

When, on Holy Saturday, all was ready and brought to the boat, the man said to Saint Brendan:
'Your boat cannot carry any more. I, therefore, shall bring to you after eight days whatever food and drink you will need until Pentecost.'
Saint Brendan said:
'How do you know where we shall be after eight days?'
He replied:
'Tonight and on Easter Sunday until midday you will be in the island that you see nearby. Afterwards you will sail to another island, which is not far from this one towards the west, and which is called the Paradise of Birds. There you will remain until the octave of Pentecost.'
Saint Brendan also questioned him on how the sheep could be so big there as, one could see, they were. They were indeed bigger than cattle. He replied:
'No one takes milk from the sheep in this island, nor does winter put any strain on them. They stay in the pastures always, day and night. As a consequence they are larger here than in the parts you come from.'
They set out for the boat and began to sail, each party having blessed the other.

X When they approached the other island, the boat began to ground before they could reach its landing-place. Saint Brendan ordered the brothers to disembark from the boat into the sea, which they did. They held the boat on both sides with ropes until they came to the landing-place. The island was stony and without grass. There were a few pieces of driftwood on it, but no sand on its shore. While the brothers spent the night outside in prayers and vigils, the man of God remained sitting inside in the boat. For he knew the kind of island it was, but he did not want to tell them, lest they be terrified.

When morning came he ordered each of the priests to sing his mass, which they did. While Saint Brendan was himself singing his mass in the boat, the brothers began to carry the raw meat out of the boat to preserve it with salt, and also the flesh which they had brought from the other island. When they had done this they put a pot over a fire. When, however, they were plying the fire with wood and the pot began to boil, the island began to be in motion like a wave. The brothers rushed to the boat, crying out for protection to the holy father. He drew each one of them into the boat by his hand. Having left everything they had had on the island behind, they began to sail. Then the island moved out to sea. The lighted fire could be seen over two miles away. Saint Brendan told the brothers what it really was, saying:

'Brothers, are you surprised at what this island has done?'
They said:

'We are very surprised and indeed terror-stricken.'
He said to them:

'My sons, do not be afraid. God revealed to me during the night in a vision the secret of this affair. Where we were was not an island, but a fish – the foremost of all that swim in the ocean. He is always trying to bring his tail to meet his head, but he cannot because of his length. His name is Jasconius.'

XI When they were sailing near the island where they had spent the three days, and came to the western edge of it, they saw another island almost joining it, separated only by a small channel. There was plenty of grass on it; it had groves of trees and was full of flowers. They started circling it, looking for a landing-place. As they were sailing on its southern side they found a stream flowing into the sea and there they put the boat in to land. As they disembarked, Saint Brendan ordered them to draw the boat with ropes up along the river-bed with all their might. The width of the river was about the width of the boat. The father sat in the boat. So they carried on for about a mile until they came to the source of the stream. Saint Brendan spoke:

'Our Lord Jesus Christ has given us a place in which to stay during his holy Resurrection.'
And he added:

'If we had no other supplies but this spring, it would, I believe, alone be enough for food and drink.'

Over the spring there was a tree of extraordinary girth and no less height covered with white birds. They covered it so much that one could scarcely see its leaves or branches. When the man of God saw this, he began to think and ponder within himself what it meant or what was the reason that such a great multitude of birds could be all collected together. He was so tormented about this that the tears poured out and flowed down upon his cheeks, and he implored God, saying:

'God, who knows the unknown and reveals all that is secret, you know the distress of my heart. I implore your majesty to have pity and reveal to me, a sinner, through your great mercy your secret that I now look upon with my eyes. I rely not on what I deserve or my worth, but rather on your boundless pity.'

When he said this within himself and had taken his seat again, one of the birds flew from the tree, making a noise with her wings like a hand-bell, and took up position on the side of the boat where the man of God was sitting. She sat on the edge of the prow and stretched her wings, as it were as a sign of joy, and looked with a peaceful mien at the holy father. The man of God immediately concluded that God had listened to his plea, and spoke to the bird:

'If you are God's messenger, tell me where these birds come from or for what reason they are congregated here.'
She replied immediately:

'We survive from the great destruction of the ancient enemy, but we were not associated with them through any sin of ours. When we were created, Lucifer's fall and that of his followers brought about our destruction also. But our God is just and true. In his great judgement he sent us here. We endure no sufferings. Here we can see God's presence. But God has separated us from sharing the lot of the others who were faithful. We wander through various regions of the air and the firmament and the earth, just like the other spirits that travel on their missions. But on holy days and Sundays we are given bodies such as you now see so that we may stay here and praise our Creator. You and your brothers have now spent one year on your journey. Six still remain. Where you celebrated Easter today, there you will celebrate it every year. Afterwards you will find what you cherish in your heart, that is, the Promised Land of the Saints.'

When she said this, she lifted herself off the prow and flew to the other birds.

When the hour of vespers had come all the birds in the tree chanted, as it were with one voice, beating their wings on their sides: 'A hymn is due to thee, O God, in Zion, and a vow shall be paid to you in Jerusalem.' They kept repeating this versicle for about the space of an hour. To the man of God and his companions the chant and the sound of their wings seemed in its sweetness like a rhythmical song.

Then Saint Brendan said to his brothers:

'Repair your bodies, for today our souls are filled with divine food.'

When supper was over they performed the divine service. When all was finished, the man of God and his companions gave repose to their bodies until midnight. Waking, the man of God aroused his brothers for the vigil of the holy night, beginning with the versicle: 'Lord, open my lips.' When the holy man had finished, all the birds responded with wing and mouth, saying: 'Praise the Lord, all his angels; praise him, all his powers.' So it was as for vespers – they chanted all the time for the space of an hour. When dawn rose they chanted: 'May the radiance of the Lord, our God, be upon us!' – with the same tune and for the same length of time as at matins and lauds. Likewise at terce they chanted the versicle: 'Sing praises to our God, sing praises! Sing praises to our king. Sing praises in wisdom.' At sext they chanted: 'Shine your countenance, Lord, upon us, and have mercy on us.' At nones they chanted: 'How good and pleasant it is that brothers live together as one!' In this way, day and night, the birds gave praise to the Lord. And so Saint Brendan refreshed his brothers with the feast of Easter until the octave day.

When the days of the octave were over he said:

'Let us take supplies from the spring. Until now we had no need of water except to wash our hands and feet.'

When he said this, the man, with whom they had previously spent the three days before Easter and who had given them food for the feast of Easter, came to them in his boat which was full of food and drink. He took all of this out of the boat, stood before the holy father and said:

'Men, brothers, here you have enough until the holy day of Pentecost. Do not drink from the spring here. It is strong to drink. I shall tell you what kind it is: if a man drinks it, sleep will overpower him and he will not awaken for twenty-four hours. It is only when it is outside of the spring that it has the taste and quality of water.'
When he had received the holy father's blessing, he returned to his own place.

Saint Brendan remained where he was until the beginning of the octave of Pentecost. For the chanting of the birds revived their spirits. On Pentecost, however, when the man of God had sung mass with his brothers, their steward came, bringing with him whatever was necessary for the celebration of the feast day. When they had sat down together for the meal, the steward spoke to them, saying:
'You have a long journey ahead of you. Take the full of your vessels from the spring here and dry bread which you can keep until next year. I shall give you as much as your boat can carry.'
When all this had been finished, he received the holy father's blessing and returned to his own place.

After eight days Saint Brendan had the boat loaded with all the things the steward had brought to him, and had all the vessels filled from the spring. When all was assembled at the shore, the same bird with speedy flight came and sat on the prow of the boat. The man of God understood that she wanted to tell him something. Then in a human voice she said:
'Next year you will celebrate with us the holy day of Easter and the time you have just spent with us. And where you were this year on Maundy Thursday, there you will be next year on that day. Similarly you will celebrate the vigil of Easter Sunday where you formerly celebrated it, on the back of Jasconius. After eight months you will also find an island which is called the Island of the Community of Ailbe and there you will celebrate Christmas Day.'
When she had said this, she returned to her own place. The brothers stretched the sail and steered out into the ocean, while the birds chanted, as it were with one voice: 'Hear us, God, our Saviour, our hope throughout all the boundaries of the earth and in the distant sea.'

XII   Then the holy father, with his group, was driven here and there for three months over the space of the ocean. They could see nothing but sky and sea. They ate always every second or third day. One day there appeared to them an island not far away. When they were approaching the shore, the wind drew them away from landing. They, therefore, had to circle the island for forty days, and still they could not find a landing-place. The brothers in the boat implored God with tears to give them help. Their strength had almost failed because of their utter exhaustion. When they had persevered for three days in frequent prayer and abstinence, a narrow landing-place appeared to them, just wide enough to take one boat only; and there appeared before them there also two wells, one muddy and the other clear. The brothers then rushed with their vessels to drink the water. The man of God, watching them, said:

'My sons, do not do a forbidden thing, that is, something without permission of the elders who live in this island. They will freely give you the water that you now want to drink in stealth.'

When they disembarked and were wondering in which direction they should go, an elder of great gravity met them. His hair was snow-white and his face was shining. He prostrated himself three times on the ground before embracing the man of God. But Saint Brendan and those with him raised him from the ground. As they embraced one another, the elder held the hand of the holy father and went along with him the distance of about two hundred yards to a monastery. Saint Brendan stood with his brothers before the gate of the monastery and asked the elder:

'Whose monastery is this? Who is in charge of it? Where do the inhabitants come from?'

The holy father kept questioning the elder in various ways, but he could not get one answer out of him: he only indicated with his hand, with incredible meekness, that they should be silent. As soon as the holy father realized that this was a rule of the place, he spoke to his brothers, saying:

'Keep your mouths from speaking lest these brothers be defiled by your garrulousness.'

At this remonstrance eleven brothers came to meet them with reliquaries, crosses and hymns, chanting the versicle: 'Rise, saints of God, from your dwellings and go to meet truth. Sanctify the place, bless the people, and graciously keep us your servants in peace.'

When the versicle was finished the father of the monastery embraced Saint Brendan and his companions in order. In the same way his community embraced the companions of the holy man.

When they had exchanged the kiss of peace, they led them to the monastery as the custom is in western parts to conduct brothers in this way with prayers. Afterwards the abbot of the monastery with his monks washed the feet of the guests and chanted the antiphon: 'A new commandment.' When this was done the abbot led them in great silence to the refectory. A signal was sounded, hands were washed, and then the abbot made them sit down. When a second signal sounded, one of the brothers of the father of the monastery got up and served the table with loaves of extraordinary whiteness and some roots of incredible sweetness. The brothers sat mixed with their guests in order. There was a full loaf between every two brothers. The same server, on the sounding of the signal, gave the brothers drink.

The abbot for his part was urging on the brothers, saying with great glee:

'In joy and fear of the Lord, drink in love now water from the well from which you wanted to drink in stealth today! The feet of the brothers are washed every day from the other, muddy, well that you saw, because it is always warm. We have no idea where the loaves that you see are baked or who carries them to our larder. What we do know is that they are given to his servants from the great charity of God by means of some dependant creature. There are twenty-four of us brothers here. Every day we have twelve loaves for our food, a loaf between every two. On feast-days and Sundays God increases the supply to one full loaf for each brother, so that they can have supper from what is left over. Just now on your coming we have a double supply. Thus Christ feeds us from the time of Saint Patrick and Saint Ailbe, our father, for eighty years until now. Yet neither sign of old age nor weakness spreads in our limbs. On this island we need nothing to eat that is prepared by fire. Neither cold nor heat ever overcomes us. And when the time comes for masses or vigils, we light in our church the lights that we brought with us from our homeland under divine predestination. They burn till day and still none of them is reduced in any way.'

After they had drunk three times, the abbot sounded a signal in the usual way. The brothers rose all together in great silence and gravity from the table, and preceded the holy fathers to the church. Behind them walked Saint Brendan and the father of the monastery. As they entered the church twelve other brothers, genuflecting quickly, met them on their way out. When Saint Brendan saw them he said:

'Abbot, why did these not eat along with us?'

The father replied:

'Because of you our table could not hold us all together at one sitting. They will now eat and will miss nothing. Let us now, however, go into the church and sing vespers so that our brothers, who are eating now, will be able to sing vespers after us in good time.'

When they had finished the office of vespers Saint Brendan examined how the church was built. It was square, of the same length as breadth. and had seven lights – three before the altar, which was in the middle, and two each before the other two altars. The altars were made of crystal cut in a square, and likewise all the vessels were of crystal, namely patens, chalices and cruets and other vessels required for the divine cult. There were twenty-four seats in a circle in the church. The abbot, however, sat between the two choirs. One group began from him and ended with him, and it was likewise with the other. No one on either side presumed to intone a verse but the abbot. No one in the monastery spoke or made any sound. If a brother needed anything he went before the abbot, knelt facing him, and requested within his heart what he needed. Thereupon the holy father taking a tablet and stylus wrote as God revealed to him and gave it to the brother who asked his advice.

While Saint Brendan was reflecting upon all these matters within himself, the abbot spoke to him:

'Father, it is now time to return to the refectory so that all that we have to do will be done while there is light.'

This they did in the same way as before. When they had completed the day's course in order, they all hurried with great eagerness to compline. When the abbot had intoned the versicle: 'God, come to my aid', and they had together given honour to the Trinity, they began to chant the versicle: 'We have acted wrongly, we have done iniquity! You, Lord, who are our faithful father, spare us. I shall sleep in peace therefore, and shall take my rest; for you, Lord, have placed me, singularly, in hope.'

After that they chanted the office of the hour. When the order of psalms had been completed, all went out of the church, the brothers bringing their guests, each to his cell, with them. But the abbot and Saint Brendan remained seated in the church to wait for the coming of the light. Saint Brendan questioned the holy father on their silence and their community life:

'How could human flesh endure such a life?'

The father replied with great reverence and humility:

'Abbot, I confess before my Christ. It is eighty years since we came to this island. We have heard no human voice except when singing praise to God. Among the twenty-four of us no voice is raised except by way of a signal given by a finger or the eyes, and that only by the elders. None of us has suffered ill in the flesh or from the spirits that infest the human race, since we came here.'

Saint Brendan said:

'May we stay here now – or not?'

He replied:

'You may not, because it is not the will of God. Why do you ask me, father? Has not God revealed to you, before you came here to us, what you must do? You must return to your own place with fourteen of your brothers. There God has prepared your burial-place. Of the two remaining brothers, one will stay abroad in the Island of the Anchorites, and the other will be condemned by a shameful death to Hell.'

While they were thus conversing a fiery arrow sped through a window before their very eyes and lit all the lamps that were placed before the altars. Then the arrow immediately sped out again. But a bright light was left in the lamps. Saint Brendan again asked:

'Who will quench the lights in the morning?

The holy father replied:

'Come and see the secret of it. You can see the tapers burning in the centre of the bowls. Nothing of them actually burns away so that they might get smaller or reduced in size, nor is there any deposit left in the morning. The light is spiritual.'

Saint Brendan asked:

'How can an incorporeal light burn corporeally in a corporeal creature?'

The elder replied:

'Have you not read of the bush burning at Mount Sinai? Yet that bush was unaffected by the fire.'

They kept vigil the whole night until morning, Then Saint Brendan asked leave to set out on his journey. The elder said to him:

'No, father. You must celebrate Christmas with us until the octave of the Epiphany.'

The holy father, therefore, with his company stayed that time with the twenty-four fathers in the Island of the Community of Ailbe.

XIII When the feast-days were over the blessed Brendan and his followers brought provisions into the boat and received the blessing of the holy men. He then sailed out to the ocean as fast as he could. Whether by rowing or sailing, the boat was carried to many different places until the beginning of Lent. One day they saw an island not far in front of them. When the brothers saw it they began to row eagerly, because they were then very distressed from hunger and thirst. Their food and drink had failed three days before. When the holy father had blessed the landing-place and all had disembarked from the boat, they found a clear well, a variety of plants and roots in a circle around the well, and various kinds of fish swimming along the river-bed into the sea. Saint Brendan said to his brothers:

'God has given us here a comfort after our toil. Gather the plants and roots which the Lord has prepared for his servants.'

So they did. When they poured out the water to drink it, however, the man of God said to them:

'Brothers, take care that you do not use too much of these waters, lest they lie heavily upon your bodies.'

The brothers interpreted the prescription of the man of God in different ways. Some of them drank one cup, others two, and the rest three. The last were overcome by a sleep of three days and three nights; others by a sleep of two days and two nights; the remainder by a sleep of a day and a night. But the holy father prayed unceasingly to God for his brothers, because through their ignorance such a danger had come upon them. When the three days' sleeping were up, the holy father spoke to his companions:

'Brothers, let us flee from this threat to our lives lest something worse happen to us. The Lord gave us sustenance, but you did yourself damage with it. Leave this island, then, taking provisions from the fish, and prepare what you need for a meal every third day up to Maundy Thursday. Likewise for the water – a single cup for each brother each day and equally for the roots.'

When they had loaded the boat with all that the man of God had ordered, they set sail and made out to sea in a northerly direction.

XIV After three days and three nights the wind dropped and the sea coagulated, as it were – it was so smooth. The holy father said:

'Ship the oars and loosen the sail. Wherever God wants to direct the boat, let him direct it!'

The boat, therefore, was carried around for twenty days. Afterwards God raised a wind favourable to them again, from west to east. They then set sail out to sea and sped on. They ate always every third day.

XV One day an island that looked like a cloud appeared to them a long distance away. Saint Brendan said:

'My sons, do you recognize that island?'

They said:

'No, not at all.'

He said:

'I recognize it. That is the island where we were last year on Maundy Thursday. That is where our good steward lives.'

The brothers began to row for joy as fast as their strength could support. When the man of God saw this, he said:

'Children, do not tire your limbs foolishly. Is not the all-powerful God the pilot and sailor of our boat? Leave it to him. He himself guides our journey just as he wills.'

When they came near that island, the same steward came to meet them in a boat, and led them to the landing-place where they had disembarked the previous year. He praised God and embraced the feet of every one of them, beginning from the holy father right down to the last, saying:

'God is wonderful in his saints. The God of Israel will himself give valour and strength to his people. Blessed be God.'

When the versicle was over and everything had been taken from the boat, the steward pitched a tent and made ready a bath – for it was Maundy Thursday – and clothed all the brothers with new garments and served them for three days. The brothers for their part celebrated the Passion of the Lord with great attention until Holy Saturday.

When the services for Holy Saturday were completed, spiritual victims sacrificed and supper taken, the steward said to Saint Brendan and those that were with him:

'Go and embark in the boat so that you may celebrate the vigil of the holy Sunday of the Resurrection where you celebrated it last year. And celebrate the Sunday itself until midday in the same way. Afterwards, steer for the island which is called the Paradise of Birds, where you were last year from Easter until the octave of Pentecost, and bring with you all the food and drink that are necessary. I shall come to see you on the Sunday after Easter.'

So they did. The steward loaded the boat with loaves and drink and flesh and other good things, as much as it could take. Saint Brendan gave a blessing and embarked. They set sail immediately for the other island.

When they came near the spot where they should disembark from the boat, they saw the pot which they had left behind the year before. Then Saint Brendan disembarking from the boat with his brothers chanted the hymn of the Three Children right to the end. When the hymn was finished, the man of God warned his brothers, saying:

'My sons, watch and pray, that you do not enter into temptation. Reflect on how God has subjected the savage beast under us without any inconvenience to us.'

The brothers, therefore, spent the vigil scattered over the island until matins. From then until about nine o'clock each of the priests offered mass. Then the blessed Brendan sacrificed the Spotless Lamb to God and said to his brothers:

'Last year I celebrated the Resurrection of the Lord here. I wish to do the same this year.'

They then set out for the island of the birds.

As they came near the landing-place they had chosen on that island, all the birds chanted, as if with one voice, saying: 'Salvation belongs to our God who sits upon the throne, and to the Lamb!' And again: 'The Lord God has given us light. Appoint a holy day, with festal branches up to the horn of the altar.'

Thus they chanted and beat their wings for a long time – for about half an hour – until the holy father and his holy companions and the contents of the boat were landed and the holy father had taken his place in his tent.

When he had celebrated there with his community the feasts of Easter, the steward came to them, as he had told them beforehand, on Sunday the octave of Easter, bringing with him all the food needed for human life. When they sat down to table, the same bird again sat on the prow of the boat, stretching her wings and making a noise like the sound of a great organ. The man of God then realized that she wished to convey a message to him. The bird said:

'God has ordained for you four points of call for four periods of the year until the seven years of your pilgrimage are over, namely, on Maundy Thursday with your steward who is present every year; Easter you will celebrate on the back of the whale; the Easter feasts until the octave of Pentecost with us; Christmas you will celebrate with the Community of Ailbe. Then after seven years and great and varied trials you will find the Promised Land of the Saints that you seek. There you will live for forty days, and afterwards God will bring you back to the land of your birth.'

When the holy father heard this, he prostrated himself on the ground with his brothers, giving thanks and praise to his Creator. When the venerable elder had finished this, the bird returned to her own place.

When they had finished eating, the steward said:

'With God's help I shall return to you with your provisions on the feast of the coming of the Holy Spirit upon the apostles.'

Having received the blessing of the holy father and all that were with him, he returned to his own place. The venerable father remained there the number of days indicated. When the feast days were over, Saint Brendan ordered his brothers to prepare to sail and fill the vessels from the well. They brought the boat to the sea, while the steward came with his own boat laden with food for the brothers. When he had placed all in the boat of the holy man, he embraced all of them and then returned where he had come from.

XVI The venerable father and his companions sailed out into the ocean and their boat was carried along for forty days. One day there appeared to them a beast of immense size following them at a distance. He spouted foam from his nostrils and ploughed through the waves at a great speed, as if he were about to devour them. When the brothers saw this they called upon the Lord, saying:

'Deliver us, Lord, so that that beast does not devour us.'

Saint Brendan comforted them, saying:

'Do not be afraid. You have little faith. God, who always defends us, will deliver us from the mouth of this beast and from other dangers.'

As the beast came near them he caused waves of extraordinary height to go before him right up to the boat, so that the brothers were more and more afraid. The venerable elder also raised his hands to Heaven and said:

'Lord, deliver your servants, as you delivered David from the hand of Goliath, the giant. Lord, deliver us, as you delivered Jonas from the belly of the whale.'

After these three pleas asking for deliverance, a mighty monster passed near them from the west going to encounter the beast. He immediately attacked him, emitting fire from his mouth. The elder spoke to his brothers:

'Look, my sons, at the great deeds of our Saviour! See how the beasts obey their Creator. Wait presently for the outcome of this affair. This battle will do us no damage. It will redound to the glory of God.'

When he had said this the wretched beast that pursued the servants of Christ was cut into three pieces before their eyes. The other returned after his victory to where he had come from.

Another day they saw at a distance a very large island full of trees. While they were drawing near its shore and disembarking from the boat, they saw the end portion of the beast that had been slain. Saint Brendan said:

'See what wished to devour you! You now shall devour it! You will stay a long while in this island. Take your boat, therefore, out

of the water high up on the land and look for a place in the wood
where your tent can stand.'
The holy father himself determined the spot where they were to
stay.

When they had carried out the order of the man of God and had put
all the utensils in the tent, Saint Brendan said to his brothers:
    'Take your provisions from that beast, enough for three months.
For tonight its flesh will be devoured by beasts.'
They were engaged until vespers in carrying up as much flesh from
the shore as they required, in accordance with the instruction of
the holy father. When the brothers had done all this, they said:
    'Abbot, how can we live here without water?'
He answered them:
    'Is it more difficult for God to give you water than food? But go
to the southern part of the island and you will find a clear well and
many plants and roots. Bring me the proper amount of supplies
from there.'
They found everything as the man of God had foretold. Saint
Brendan, therefore, remained three months, because there was a
storm at sea and a strong wind and variable weather with rain and
hail.

The brothers went to see what the man of God had said about the
beast. When they came to the place where the body was before,
they found nothing but bones. They hurried back to the man of
God and said:
    'Abbot, it is as you said.'
He replied to them:
    'I know, my sons, that you wanted to test me, to see if I spoke
the truth or not. I shall tell you another sign: a portion of a fish will
come there tonight, and tomorrow you will eat of it.'
On the following day, indeed, the brothers went out to the place
and they found as the man of God had said. They brought back as
much as they could carry. The venerable father said to them:
    'Keep it and preserve it carefully with salt. You will have need of
it. For God will make the weather fine today, tomorrow and after
tomorrow. The swell of the sea and the waves will fall. Then you
will leave this place.'

When these days were over Saint Brendan ordered his brothers to load the boat, to fill the containers and other vessels and collect plants and roots for his own use. For the father from the time of his ordination to the priesthood tasted nothing in which the spirit of life drew support from flesh. When all was loaded into the boat, they raised the sail and set off in a northerly direction.

XVII One day they saw an island a long distance away from them. Saint Brendan said:

'Do you see that island?'

They replied:

'We do.'

He said to them:

'Three choirs of people are in that island: one of boys, another of youths, a third of elders. And one of your brothers will remain on pilgrimage there.'

The brothers asked him which of them it was. As they were preoccupied with the thought and he saw that they were sad, he said:

'There is the brother who will remain here!'

The brother indicated was one of the three who had followed after Saint Brendan from his monastery. When they were embarking in the boat in their fatherland, he had spoken of their future.

They approached the island until the boat put in at the shore. The island was extraordinarily flat, so much so that it seemed to them to be level with the sea. It had no trees or anything that would move with the wind. It was very spacious and covered with white and purple fruit. There they saw the three choirs, as the man of God had foretold. The space between one choir and another was about the throw of a stone from a sling. They moved continuously here and there, one choir, however, at a time standing in one place and chanting: 'The saints will go from strength to strength and they will see the God of gods in Zion.' While one choir finished this versicle, another choir stood and began to chant the same song, and this they did without any intermission. The first choir was made up of boys in white garments, the second choir was clothed in blue garments, and the third in purple dalmatics.

It was ten o'clock when they put in at the landing-place on the island. When midday came all the choirs began to chant together, singing: 'May God be merciful to us . . .' to the end of the psalm, and 'Be pleased, O God, to deliver me . . .' and likewise the third of the psalms for sext: 'I kept my faith . . .' and the prayer for mercy as above. Likewise at three o'clock they chanted another three psalms: 'Out of the depths' and 'Behold how good', and 'Praise the Lord, O Jerusalem.' At vespers they chanted: 'A hymn is due to thee, O God, in Zion', and 'Bless the Lord, O my soul, O Lord my God', and the third of the psalms for vespers: 'Praise the Lord, children.' They then chanted, while seated, the gradual psalms.

When they had finished this chant, a cloud of extraordinary brightness covered the island, but now they could no longer see what they had seen, because of the denseness of the cloud. Nevertheless they continued to hear the voices of those singing their ordinary chant without interruption until matins. Then the choirs began to chant, singing: 'Praise the Lord from the heavens', then 'Sing to the Lord', and the third of the psalms of matins: ' Praise the Lord in his saints.' After that they chanted twelve psalms in the order of the Psalter. When day dawned the island was cloudless, and immediately they chanted the three psalms: 'Have mercy on me, O God', 'God, my God, from the dawn I keep watch for thee', and 'Lord, my refuge.' At terce they chanted another three psalms, that is: 'All peoples', and 'God, in your name', and the third: 'I have loved, because . . .' with the Alleluia. They then offered up the Spotless Lamb and all came to communion, saying:

'Take this holy body of the Lord and blood of the Saviour for everlasting life.'

When the sacrifice was over, two members of the choir of youths carried a basket full of purple fruit and placed it in the boat, saying:

'Accept fruit from the Island of Strong Men, give us our brother, and set forth in peace.'

Then Saint Brendan called the brother to him and said:

'Embrace your brothers and go with those who summon you. It was a good hour that your mother conceived you, seeing that you have deserved to live with such a community.'

When he had embraced all, including the holy father, Saint Brendan said to him:

'Son, remember the great favours God conferred on you in this life. Go, and pray for us.'
He immediately followed the two youths to their school.

The venerable father and his companions set sail. When it was three o'clock, he ordered his brothers to refresh their bodies with the fruit of the Island of Strong Men. As he said this the man of God took one of them. When he saw its size and that it was full of juice, he expressed wonder and said:
'I have never seen or gathered fruit of such size.'
They were all of equal size and like a large ball. The man of God then asked that a vessel be brought to him. He squeezed one of the fruits and got a pound of juice from it, which he divided into twelve ounces. The holy father gave an ounce of the juice to each of the brothers. One fruit, therefore, fed one brother for twelve days so that he always had in his mouth the taste of honey.

VIII After some days the holy father prescribed a fast for three days. Then when the three days were over a great bird was seen flying near the boat, carrying a branch of an unknown tree. At the tip of the branch was a cluster of grapes of extraordinary redness. The bird dropped this cluster from its beak into the saint's lap. Then Saint Brendan called the attention of his brothers and said:
'Look at the meal that God has sent you. Take it.'
The grapes of this cluster were as big as apples. The man of God divided them, one each among his brothers, and so they had food until the twelfth day. Again the man of God renewed with his brothers the same fast for three days.

Now on the third day they saw an island not far from them, covered completely with densely planted trees bearing the same crop of grapes of such incredible fertility that all the trees were bent down to the ground, with the same fruit of the same colour. No tree was barren, nor was there a tree of any other kind in that island. The brothers then put into harbour. The man of God disembarked and began to walk round the island. It had a perfume like that of a house filled with pomegranates. Meanwhile the brothers were waiting in the boat until the man of God should return to them. All the while the breeze bore in on them a sweet perfume, so that they were tempted to be heedless of their fasts. The venerable father found six copious wells full of flourishing plants and roots of many kinds. He then returned to his brothers, carrying with him some of the first fruits of the island and said to them:

'Disembark, pitch your tent and refresh yourselves with the good fruits of this land that the Lord has shown us.'

And so for forty days they fed on the grapes and on the plants and roots of the wells. But at the end of that time they embarked, bringing with them as much of the fruits as their boat could carry.

XIX   When they had gone on board, the boat's sail was hoisted to steer where the wind directed. After they had sailed, the bird called the Gryphon appeared to them, flying from far away towards them. When his brothers saw it they started saying to the holy father:

'That beast has come to devour us.'

The man of God said to them:

'Do not be afraid. God is our helper. He will defend us on this occasion too.'

The bird stretched her talons to seize the servants of God. Just then, suddenly, the bird which on the earlier occasion brought them the branch with the fruits, flew swiftly up to the Gryphon, which immediately made to devour her. But that bird defended herself until she overcame and tore out the eyes of the Gryphon. The Gryphon then flew high up into the sky so that the brothers could scarcely see her. But her killer pursued her until she killed her. For the Gryphon's body fell into the sea near the boat before the eyes of the brothers. The other bird returned to her own place.

XX   Not many days afterwards, Saint Brendan and his sailors caught sight of the Island of the Community of Ailbe. There he celebrated Christmas with his brothers. When the feast-days were over, the venerable father received the blessing of the abbot and his community and then sailed round the ocean for a long time – except for the feasts mentioned, that is Easter and Christmas. For during them he rested in the places mentioned.

XXI   It happened on one occasion that as Brendan was celebrating the feast of Saint Peter the Apostle in his boat, they found the sea so clear that they could see whatever was underneath them. When they looked into the deep they saw the different kinds of fish lying on the sand below. It even seemed to them that they could touch

them with their hands, so clear was that sea. They were like herds
lying in pastures. They were so numerous that they looked like a
city of circles as they lay, their heads touching their tails. His
brothers asked the venerable father to celebrate his mass in silence,
lest the fish would hear and come up to pursue them. The holy
father smiled and said to them:

'I am surprised at your foolishness. Why are you afraid of those
fish when you were not afraid of the devourer and master of all the
fish of the sea, sitting and singing psalms, as you often did, on his
back? Indeed you cut wood and lit a fire and cooked meat there!
Why then are you afraid of those? Is not our Lord Jesus Christ God
of all fish, and can he not reduce all living things?'

When he said these things he began to intone as loudly as he could.
Others of the brothers kept their eyes on the fish all the time.
When the fish heard him singing, they came up from the bottom
and began to swim in a circle round the boat – in such a way that
the brothers could not see beyond the fish anywhere, so great was
the multitude of the different fishes swimming. Still they did not
come near the boat, but kept swimming at a distance in a wide arc.
And so they kept swimming here and there until the man of God
finished mass. After this, as if they were taking flight, they all swam
by different paths of the ocean away from the sight of the servants
of God. It took eight days for Saint Brendan, even with a favouring
wind and all his canvas stretched to the full, to cross the clear sea.

XII   One day when they had celebrated their masses, a pillar in the sea
appeared to them that seemed to be not far distant. Still it took
them three days to come up to it. When the man of God
approached it he tried to see the top of it – but he could not, it was
so high. It was higher than the sky. Moreover a wide-meshed net
was wrapped around it. The mesh was so wide that the boat could
pass through its openings. They could not decide of what substance
the net was made. It had the colour of silver, but they thought that
it seemed harder than marble. The pillar was of bright crystal.
Brendan spoke to his brothers:

'Ship the oars and take down the mast and sail. Let some of you
at the same time take hold of the meshes of the net.'
There was a large space, roughly about a mile, at all points between
the net and the pillar, and likewise the net went down a similar

distance into the sea. When they had done what they had been ordered, the man of God said to them:

'Let the boat in through one of the meshes, so that we can have a close look at the wonders of our Creator.'

When they had gone in and looked around here and there, the sea was as clear to them as glass, so that they could see everything that was underneath. They could examine the foundations of the pillar and also the edge of the net lying on the sea bed. The light of the sun was as bright below as above the water.

Then Saint Brendan measured the four sides of the opening of the net: it was about six to seven feet on every side. They then sailed throughout the whole day near one side of the pillar and in its shadow they could still feel the heat of the sun. They stayed there until three o'clock. The man of God kept measuring the one side. The measurement of each of the four sides of that pillar was the same, namely about seven hundred yards. The venerable father was engaged for four days in this way around the four angles of the pillar. On the fourth day, however, they found a chalice, of the same substance as the net, and a paten, of the same colour as the pillar, lying in a window in the side of the pillar facing the south. Saint Brendan took hold of these vessels immediately, saying:

'Our Lord Jesus Christ has shown us this wonder, and given me these two gifts, so that the wonder be manifested to many in order that they may believe.'

Then the man of God ordered his brothers to perform the divine office and then refresh their bodies, for they had had no slack time in which to take food or drink since they had seen the pillar. When the night was over the brothers began to row towards the north. When they had passed through an opening in the net they raised the mast and sail, while some of the brothers still held the meshes of the net until all was made ready on the boat. When the sail had been spread, a favouring wind began to blow behind them so that they did not need to row but only to hold the ropes and rudder. So their boat was borne along for eight days towards the north.

XXIII   After eight days they caught sight of an island not far away, very rough, rocky and full of slag, without trees or grass, full of smiths' forges. The venerable father said to his brothers:

'I am troubled about this island. I do not want to go on it or even come near it. But the wind is bringing us directly there.'

As they were sailing for a moment beside it, a stone's throw away, they heard the sound of bellows blowing, as if it were thunder, and the blows of hammers on iron and anvils. When he heard this the venerable father armed himself, making the sign of the Lord in all four directions, saying:

'Lord, Jesus Christ, deliver us from this island.'

When the man of God had finished speaking, one of the inhabitants of the island was seen to come out of doors apparently to do something or other. He was very shaggy and full at once of fire and darkness. When he saw the servants of Christ pass near the island, he went back into his forge. The man of God blessed himself again and said to his brothers:

'My sons, raise the sail higher still and row as fast as you can and let us flee from this island.'

Even before he had finished speaking, the same savage came to the shore near where they were, carrying a tongs in his hands that held a lump of burning slag of immense size and heat. He immediately threw the lump on top of the servants of Christ, but it did no hurt to them. It passed more than two hundred yards above them. Then the sea, where it fell, began to boil, as if a volcano were erupting there. The smoke rose from the sea as from a fiery furnace.

But when the man of God had got about a mile away from the spot where the lump fell, all the islanders came to the shore, each of them carrying a lump of his own. Some of them began to throw the lumps after the servants of Christ into the sea, the one throwing his lump over the other, all the while going back to the forges and setting the lumps on fire. It looked as if the whole island was ablaze, like one big furnace, and the sea boiled, just as a cooking pot full of meat boils when it is well plied with fire. All day long they could hear a great howling from the island. Even when they could no longer see it, the howling of its denizens still reached their ears, and the stench of the fire assailed their nostrils. The holy father comforted his monks, saying:

'Soldiers of Christ, be strengthened in faith unfeigned and in spiritual weapons, for we are in the confines of Hell. So, be on the watch and be brave.'

XXIV   On another day there appeared to them, as it were through the clouds, a high mountain in the ocean, not far away towards the north. It was very smoky on top. Immediately the wind drew them very fast to the shore of that island until the boat stopped a little distance from the land. The cliff was so high that they could scarcely see the top of it. It was also the colour of coal and unusually perpendicular, just like a wall. The one remaining of the three brothers, who followed after Saint Brendan from his monastery, jumped out of the boat and began to walk up to the base of the cliff. Then he cried out:

'Alas for me, father, I am being snatched from you and am powerless to come back to you.'

The brothers straightaway began to turn the boat from the land and call on the Lord, saying:

'Have mercy on us, Lord, have mercy on us.'

The venerable father and his companions saw how the unhappy man was carried off by a multitude of demons to be tormented and was set on fire among them. He said:

'Alas for you, my son, that you have received such fate as you have deserved while living.'

Again a favouring wind brought them towards the south. When they looked back for a distance at the island, they saw that the mountain was no longer covered with smoke, but was spouting flames from itself up to the ether and then breathing back, as it were, the same flames again upon itself. The whole mountain from the summit right down to the sea looked like one big pyre.

XXV   When Saint Brendan had sailed towards the south for seven days, there appeared to them in the sea the outline as it were of a man sitting on a rock with a cloth suspended between two small iron fork-shaped supports about a cloak's length in front of him. The object was being tossed about by the waves just like a little boat in a whirlwind. Some of the brothers said that it was a bird, others a boat. When the man of God heard them discussing the matter among themselves, he said:

'Cease arguing. Steer the boat to the spot.'

When the man of God drew near, the waves, glued as it were in a circle, kept them at a distance. They found a man, shaggy and unsightly, sitting on a rock. As the waves flowed towards him from every side, they struck him even to the top of his head. When they receded, the bare rock where the unhappy man was sitting was exposed. The wind also sometimes drove the cloth hanging in front of him away from him, and sometimes blew it against his eyes and forehead.

Blessed Brendan questioned him as to who he was, or for what fault he was sent here, or what he deserved to justify the imposition of such penance? The man replied:

'I am unhappy Judas, the most evil trader ever. I am not here in accordance with my deserts but because of the ineffable mercy of Jesus Christ. This place is not reckoned as punishment but as an indulgence of the Saviour in honour of the Lord's Resurrection.'

That day was in fact the Lord's day.

'When I am sitting here I feel as if I were in a Paradise of delights in contrast with my fear of the torments that lie before me this evening. For I burn, like a lump of molten lead in a pot, day and night, in the centre of the mountain that you have seen. Leviathan and his attendants are there. I was there when he swallowed your brother. Hell was so joyful that it sent forth mighty flames – as it always does when it devours the souls of the impious. But here I have a place of refreshment every Sunday from evening to evening, at Christmas until the Epiphany, at Easter until Pentecost, and on the feasts of the Purification and Assumption of the Mother of God. After and before these feasts I am tortured in the depth of Hell with Herod and Pilate and Annas and Caiphas. And so I beseech you through the Saviour of the world to be good enough to intercede with the Lord Jesus Christ that I be allowed to remain here until sunrise tomorrow, so that the demons may not torture me on your coming and bring me to the fate I have purchased with such an evil bargain.'

Saint Brendan said to him:

'May the Lord's will be done! Tonight until the morning you will not be eaten by the demons.'

The man of God questioned him again, saying:

'What is the meaning of this cloth?'

The other replied:

'I gave this cloth to a leper when I was procurator for the Lord. But it was not mine to give. It belonged to the Lord and the brothers. And so it gives me no relief but rather does me hurt.

Likewise the iron forks, on which it hangs, I gave to the priests of the temple to hold up cooking-pots. With the rock on which I sit I filled a trench in the public road to support the feet of those passing by, before I was a disciple of the Lord.'

When the evening hour had darkened the sea, an innumerable number of demons covered its surface in a circle, shouting and saying:

'Go away, man of God, from us. We cannot come near our companion until you go away from him. Neither have we dared to look on the face of our chief until we return his friend to him. You have taken our mouthful away from us. Do not protect him this night.'

The man of God said to them:

'I do not protect him, but the Lord Jesus Christ allowed him to remain here this night until morning.'

The demons retorted:

'How can you invoke the Lord's name over him, when he is himself the betrayer of the Lord?'

The man of God said to them:

'I order you in the name of our Lord Jesus Christ that you do him no evil until morning.'

When, therefore, that night was passed, and when the man of God had begun to set out on his journey, an infinite number of demons was seen to cover the face of the ocean, emitting dire sounds and saying:

'Man of God, we curse your coming as well as your going, since our chief whipped us last night with terrible scourges because we did not bring to him that accursed prisoner.'

The man of God said to them:

'Your curse does not affect us, but rather yourselves. The man whom you curse is blessed; he whom you bless is cursed.'

The demons answered him:

'Unhappy Judas will suffer double punishment for the next six days because you protected him in the night that has passed.'

The venerable father said to them:

'You have no power over that, nor your chief: God will have the power.'

And he added:

'I order you and your chief in the name of our Lord Jesus Christ not to inflict on him more torments than before.'
They answered him:
'Are you the Lord of all, so that we obey your words?'
The man of God said to them:
'I am his servant, and whatever I order, I order in his name. My service lies in those matters which he has assigned to me.'
The demons followed him until Judas could no longer be seen. They then returned and lifted up the unhappy soul among them with great force and howling.

XVI But Saint Brendan and his comrades sailed towards the south, glorifying God in all. On the third day there appeared to them a small island far away to the south. When his brothers had begun to row faster and they had come near the island, Saint Brendan said to them:
'Men, brothers, do not tire your bodies overmuch. You have enough toil. It is seven years to the coming Easter since we left our fatherland. You will now see Paul the spiritual Hermit, who has lived in this island for sixty years without any bodily food. For the previous thirty years he got food from an animal.'
When they had got to the shore they could not find a landing-place because of the height of the cliff. The island was small and circular – about two hundred yards in circumference. There was no earth on it, but it looked a naked rock like flint. It was as long as it was broad and as it was high. When they had rowed around the island they discovered a landing-place so narrow that it could scarcely take the prow of the boat and disembarkation was very difficult. Saint Brendan then said to his brothers:
'Wait here until I return to you. You may not go on land without permission from the man of God who lives in this spot.'

When the venerable father had come to the top of the island, he saw two caves, the entrance of one facing the entrance of the other, on the side of the island facing east. He also saw a minuscule spring, round like a plate, flowing from the rock before the entrance to the cave where the soldier of Christ lived. When the spring overflowed, the rock immediately absorbed the water. When Saint Brendan had come near the door of one of the caves, the elder came out to meet him from the other, saying:

'How good and joyful it is that brothers live together.'
When he said this he requested Saint Brendan to order all the
brothers to come from the boat. As they embraced him and sat
down he called each of them by his own name. When the brothers
heard this, they greatly wondered not only at his power of divining,
but also at his dress. For he was entirely covered by his hair from
his head and beard and other hair down to his feet, and all the hair
was white as snow on account of his great age. They could see only
his face and eyes. He had no other clothing on him except the hair
that grew from his body.

When Saint Brendan saw this he was discouraged within himself
and said:
    'Alas for me who wear a monk's habit and have many owing
allegiance to me by virtue of being monks: Here I see sitting before
me a man already in the angelic state, untouched by the vices of
the body, although he is still in human flesh.'
The man of God said to him:
    'Venerable father, how great and marvellous are the wonders
that God has shown you that he did not show to any of the holy
fathers! You say in your heart that you are not worthy to carry the
habit of a monk. But you are greater than a monk! A monk uses the
labour of his hands with which to clothe himself. But God from his
own secret supplies feeds and clothes both you and your
companions for seven years. And I, unhappy, sit here like a bird on
this rock, naked but for my hair.'

Saint Brendan then questioned him on his coming and where he
came from and for how long he had endured such a life there. The
other answered him.
    'I was brought up in the monastery of Saint Patrick for fifty years
where I looked after the cemetery of the brothers. One day, when
my director had pointed out to me the place to bury one who had
died, an unknown elder appeared to me and said: "Do not make a
grave there, brother, for it is the burial place of another." I said to
him: "Father, who are you?" He said: "Why do you not recognize
me? Am I not your abbot?" I said to him: "Saint Patrick, my abbot?"
He replied: "I am he. I died yesterday. That is the place of my
burial. Make the grave of our brother here and tell no one what I
have told you. But go tomorrow to the sea shore. There you will

find a boat. Embark in it and it will bring you to the spot where you will await the day of your death."

'In the morning I went, in accordance with the holy father's command, to the shore and found exactly what he had told me I would find. When I had embarked, I sailed for three days and three nights. After that I let the boat go wherever the wind would drive it. Then on the seventh day this rock appeared to me. I got on to it immediately, letting the boat go and kicking it with my foot so that it would go back to there it came from. Straightaway I saw it ploughing waves like furrows through the plains of the sea so as to return to its home. But I stayed here. About three o'clock in the afternoon an otter brought me a meal from the sea, that is, one fish in his mouth. He also brought a small bundle of firewood to make a fire, carrying it between his front paws while walking on his two hind legs. When he had put the fish and kindling in front of me he returned where he came from. I took iron, struck flint, made a fire from the kindling and made a meal for myself on the fish.

'Thus it was for thirty years – always every third day the same servant brought the same food, that is one fish, to do for three days. I ate a third of the fish each day. By God's grace I had no thirst – but on Sunday a trickle of water came forth from the rock, and from this I could drink and fill my little container with water to wash my hands. Then after thirty years I found these two caves and this well. On it I live. For sixty years since, I have lived on this well without nourishment of any other food. I have been ninety years on this island, living on fish for thirty years and on the food afforded by the well for sixty. I lived for fifty years in my native land. The sum of the years of my life until now is one hundred and forty. Here I have but to await in the flesh, as I have been assured, the day of my judgement. Go then to your native land, and bring with you vessels filled with water from this well. You must do this since you have a journey before you of forty days, which will take you till Holy Saturday. You will celebrate Holy Saturday and Easter Sunday and the holy days of Easter where you have celebrated them for the last six years. You will then, having received the blessing of your steward, set out for the Promised Land of the Saints. There you will stay for forty days and then the God of your fathers will bring you safe and sound to the land of your birth.'

XXVII   Saint Brendan, therefore, and his brothers, having received the blessing of the man of God, began to sail towards the south for the whole of Lent. Their boat was carried hither and thither, and their only food was the water which they had got on the island of the man of God. This they took every third day and, remaining untouched by hunger or thirst, all were joyful. Then, as the man of God had foretold, they came to the island of the steward on Holy Saturday. As they arrived at the landing-place he came to meet them with great joy, and helped each of them out of the boat on his arm. When they had finished the divine office for the holy day, he spread supper before them. When evening came they embarked in their boat, and the steward came with them.

When they had set sail they found the fish immediately in his usual place. There they sang praise to God all night and masses in the morning. When mass was over, however, Jasconius began to go his own way, and all the brothers who were with Saint Brendan began to call on the Lord, saying:

'Hear us, God, our Saviour, our hope, throughout all the boundaries of the earth and in the distant sea.'

Saint Brendan comforted his brothers, saying:

'Do not be afraid. You will suffer no evil. Help for the journey is upon us.'

The fish went in a straight course to the shore of the island of the birds. There they stayed until the octave of Pentecost. When the season of feast-days was over, the steward, who was with them, said to Saint Brendan:

'Embark in your boat and fill your water vessels from this well. This time I shall be the companion and guide of your journey. Without me you will not be able to find the Promised Land of the Saints.'

As they embarked in the boat, all the birds that were on the island began to say as it were with one voice:

'May God, the salvation of all of us, prosper your journey.'

XXVIII   Saint Brendan and those who were with him sailed to the island of the steward, who was with them, and there they took on board provision for forty days. Their voyage was for forty days towards the east. The steward went to the front of the boat and showed them the way. When the forty days were up, as the evening drew on, a great fog enveloped them, so that one of them could hardly see another. The steward, however, said to Saint Brendan:

'Do you know what fog that is?'

Saint Brendan replied:

'What?'

Then the other said:

'That fog encircles the island for which you have been searching for seven years.'

After the space of an hour a mighty light shone all around them again and the boat rested on the shore.

On disembarking from the boat they saw a wide land full of trees bearing fruit as in autumn time. When they had gone in a circle around that land, night had still not come on them. They took what fruit they wanted and drank from the wells and so for the space of forty days they reconnoitred the whole land and could not find the end of it. But one day they came upon a great river flowing through the middle of the island. Then Saint Brendan said to his brothers:

'We cannot cross this river and we do not know the size of this land.'

They had been considering these thoughts within themselves when a youth met them and embraced them with great joy and, calling each by his name, said:

'Happy are they that live in your house. They shall praise you from generation to generation.'

When he said this, he spoke to Saint Brendan:

'There before you lies the land which you have sought for a long time. You could not find it immediately because God wanted to show you his varied secrets in the great ocean. Return, then, to the land of your birth, bringing with you some of the fruit of this land and as many of the precious stones as your boat can carry. The final day of your pilgrimage draws near so that you may sleep with your fathers. After the passage of many times this land will become known to your successors, when persecution of the Christians shall have come. The river that you see divides the island. Just as this land appears to you ripe with fruit, so shall it remain always without any shadow of night. For its light is Christ.'

Saint Brendan with his brothers, having taken samples of the fruits of the land and of all its varieties of precious stones, took his leave of the blessed steward and the youth. He then embarked in his boat and began to sail through the middle of the fog. When they had passed through it, they came to the island called the Island of Delights. They availed themselves of three days' hospitality there and then, receiving a blessing, Saint Brendan returned home directly.

XXIX The brothers received him with thanksgiving, glorifying God who was unwilling that they should be deprived of seeing so loveable a father by whose absence they were for so long orphaned. Then the blessed man, commending them for their love, told them everything that he remembered happening on his journey and the great and marvellous wonders God deigned to show him. Finally he mentioned also the speed of his approaching death – emphasizing its certainty – according to the prophecy of the youth in the Promised Land of the Saints. The outcome proved this to be correct. For when he had made all arrangements for after his death, and a short time had intervened, fortified by the divine sacraments, he migrated from among the hands of his disciples in glory to the Lord, to whom is honour and glory from generation to generation.

Amen.

2

The Anglo-Norman Version

Glyn S. Burgess

Manuscripts, Editions and Translations Benedeit's Anglo-Norman version of the *Voyage of Saint Brendan* is preserved in six manuscripts, two of which are fragments. Editions are normally based on MS A, London, British Library, Cotton Vespasian B X (I), which dates from the first half of the fourteenth century. It presents a text of 1,834 lines written in double columns containing forty-four lines each; a diplomatic transcription was published by H. Suchier in 1875. The text was first edited by F. Michel in 1878, then subsequently by E.G.R. Waters (1928) and by I. Short and B. Merrilees (1979). A number of translations have appeared, in English (Margaret M. Sherwood 1918), French (J. Marchand 1940; Short and Merrilees 1984), German (E. Ruhe *et al.* 1977), Spanish (M. Lemarchand 1986) and Italian (R. Bartoli and F. Cigni 1994).

Authorship In the Prologue the author gives his name as 'danz Benedeiz' ('Li apostoiles danz Benedeiz', l. 8). The term *danz* (Latin *dominus*) is a title of address equivalent to the modern 'Dom', and the name *Benedeiz* (oblique case *Benedeit*) is the English Benedict or the French Benoît. It is probable that the author was a Benedictine monk, although neither the title *danz*, also applied at the time to the nobility, nor the name Benedeit, provides absolute proof of this. In l. 8 Benedeit also refers to himself as 'li apostoiles'. At the time, the term *apostoiles* normally designated the pope, but it could also refer specifically to St Peter, the first pope, as in l. 1034 of the text ('A saint Perrunt li apostorie'). In his edition, Waters proposes, but largely rejects, the meaning 'bishop', which, he says, would preserve an archaic sense of the Latin *apostolicus* (p. xxvii). He also suggests that *apostoiles* could be taken as an adjective meaning 'belonging to the monastery' (*ibid*). E. Walberg had earlier suggested that the word was a nickname applied to a monk named Benedeit (an interpretation which would probably require the whose text the present translation is based, propose 'missionary, envoy'. If Benedeit means that he is charged with a divine mission of education and that this mission will be accomplished through his telling of the story of St Brendan, one could perhaps translate as 'missioner'.

The author remains unidentified. Waters mentions two Benedicts: (i) a chaplain to William the Conqueror, who later became archdeacon of Rouen, and (ii) Benedict of Gloucester, who wrote a Latin life of St Dubricius and was a Benedictine monk in the abbey of St Peter of Gloucester (pp. xxvii-xxix). In Waters's opinion, however, neither of these Benedicts can be identified convincingly as the author of our poem. Another identification, made by M. Dominica Legge (1967, 45-48), concerns a monk by the name of Benedict from the abbey of Bec in Normandy. This Benedict came over to England with the abbot of Westminster, Gilbert Crispin; the latter was a former resident of Bec, where his name is recorded immediately before that of Benedict. If this is the Benedict who composed the *Voyage of Saint Brendan*, it is possible, as Legge suggests, that Anselm, Archbishop of Canterbury and a life-long friend of Gilbert, introduced him to Queen Matilda, the wife of Henry I.

Patron and Date The suggestion of a link between Benedeit and Queen Matilda, and therefore between the Anglo-Norman poem and the court of Henry I, raises the question of the identity of the patron mentioned by Benedeit in the first line of his Prologue. This Prologue is preserved in four manuscripts (ABCD), in three of which (ABD) the opening line is addressed to 'Donna Aaliz la reïne' (with minor variants). Benedeit's patron would thus be Adeliza of Louvain, the second wife of Henry I, whom he married in 1121 after the death of his only son William in the White Ship disaster of 1120. However, in the remaining manuscript (C) the name *Mahalt* 'Matilda / Maud' is found in place of *Aaliz*. This would be a reference to Henry's first wife, Matilda (formerly Edith), the daughter of Malcolm III of Scotland, who spent her early years in a convent and married Henry in 1100. Matilda was a lady of considerable learning, who corresponded with archbishops Lanfranc and Anselm and with Bishop Hildebert of Le Mans; she died in 1118.

Both Matilda and Adeliza were generous patrons of scholars and poets, but Matilda might have been more interested than Adeliza in the activities of a Celtic saint. Matilda was a Scot and Brendan is known to have visited Scotland and founded monasteries there in the sixth century. In ll. 4-6 of his poem Benedeit expresses the hope that his patron will use her influence to bring a great war to a conclusion, and the war referred to is more likely to have been the hostilities between Henry and his brother Robert, which came to an end at the battle of Tinchebrai in 1106, than any conflict taking place during the comparatively peaceful early 1120s. Matilda is certainly known to have possessed a significant amount of power and influence: during her husband's absence she sat in the king's court (*curia regis*) and she is described by the chronicler Robert of Gloucester as having had 'a most beneficial influence on the condition of England under Henry I'. Adeliza, on the other hand, in the words of the *Dictionary of National Biography*, 'took no part in politics, but devoted herself to soothing and pacifying the disappointed and sullen king'. Moreover, after what had happened to his son, a tale involving a perilous journey by sea might not have been appropriate for Henry's court in the early 1120s! But although Matilda is in many ways a more likely patron for Benedeit's work than Adeliza, the scribe's reference to Matilda in MS C could, as Waters points out, have resulted from a 'misreading or historical error' (p. xxv), or the address to Adeliza could owe more to rhetoric and an author's traditional eulogy of a patron than to reality or genuine expectations of political influence on Adeliza's part. But if Matilda was the original patron and the poem merely re-dedicated to Adeliza, the probable date of composition would be the first few years of the twelfth century, perhaps 1101-1106. If Adeliza was the patron, a date shortly after 1121 is likely.

Content and Structure The poem begins with a Prologue (ll. 1-18), but it contains no formal Epilogue. A possible division of the remaining 1,816 lines of the narrative is:
  (1)   Brendan's vision of Paradise and Hell and preparations for the voyage (ll. 19-208)
  (2)   Departure and the first cycle of island visits (ll. 209-892)
  (3)   Encounters with animals and with infernal islands (ll. 893-1210)
  (4)   Visits to Judas and Paul the Hermit (1211-606)
  (5)   The visit to Paradise and return to Ireland (1607-834)
Section (1) includes Brendan's genealogy and career (ll. 19-38), his desire to see Paradise and Hell (ll. 39-72), the consultation with Barrind and the story of his godson Mernoc (ll. 73-106), the selection of the monks, the construction of the boat and the arrival of three latecomers (ll. 107-208). Section (2) includes the first visit to the four islands to which the monks return on a cyclical basis (the Isle of Sheep, ll. 371-434, the Whale, ll. 435-78, the Isle of Birds, ll. 479-620, the Isle of Ailbe, ll. 621-778) and also three visits which are experienced only once (the Uninhabited Island, ll. 241-370), the Coagulated Sea, ll. 779-92, the Intoxicating Spring, ll. 793-824). Section (3) introduces events of a more dramatic nature: animal combats (ll. 893-952, 1001-30), the Great Pillar

(ll. 1063-96), visits to hellish islands (ll. 1097-1210). Section (4)
prepares in different ways for the visit to Paradise (Judas, ll. 1211-1486,
St Paul the Hermit, ll. 1505-1606). Section (5) includes a description
of Paradise (ll. 1673-1702) and the return of Brendan and the monks to
Ireland (ll. 1801-34).

Source There can be no doubt that the principal source of Benedeit's
version is the *Navigatio sancti Brendani*. The main episodes of Benedeit's
narrative remain more or less identical to those in the *Navigatio*. In both
texts Brendan and his monks set out from Ireland and return there, and
the main purpose of their journey is to visit a paradise-like island. In
both texts they visit a number of islands, return to four of them on a
cyclical basis and experience some testing adventures, including
dramatic encounters with animals. They pass close to Hell, visit Judas
and Paul the Hermit and finally achieve their aim. But Benedeit omits
two complete episodes found in the *Navigatio*: the Island of the Three
Choirs and the Island of Grapes. Several other short sections (the visit
made by Barrind to the Promised Land of the Saints, the visit of
Brendan and his monks to Aende, the measuring of the pillar and the
canopy, and the voyage on the back of Jasconius) are also omitted. The
Navigatio does not contain a passage equivalent to ll. 39-70 of Benedeit's
version, in which Brendan prays to God that he may be shown Paradise
and Hell. Nor is there any sign in the *Navigatio* of the disappearance of
the third latecomer in mysterious circumstances (ll. 1499-1510) or of the
entry through the gates of Paradise (ll. 1709-34).

   In one or two cases Benedeit has made a substantial change to an
episode. In his version, Brendan's visit to Barrind (ll. 73-106) replaces
the visit of Barintus to Brendan. For Benedeit, it is a dragon not a bird
which attacks the griffin (ll. 1007-30). In the *Navigatio* Brendan and his
monks are permitted to wander alone through Paradise, whereas in
Benedeit's version they have an angel as their guide (ll. 1729-810). But
in both texts all the common episodes follow each other in the same
order, except for the Coagulated Sea (ll. 789-93), which in the *Navigatio*
precedes rather than follows the Intoxicating Spring (ll. 794-820). Some
sections are re-arranged by Benedeit, e.g. the Uninhabited Island
episode (where in the Latin text a bridle, not a chalice, is stolen), the
Isle of Ailbe and the feeding of the monks after the first animal combat.

   Benedeit's version is certainly not a literal translation of the *Navigatio*
and it is in the detail of the two texts that the major differences are to be
found. Having compared the two versions, Waters concludes that
Benedeit possessed an 'independent attitude' towards his source and
produced 'a complete re-telling of the story contained in the *Navigatio*'

(pp. ciii-civ). Gone is a good deal of the ecclesiastical material, e.g. the list of canonical hours which are celebrated on the Isle of Birds and the liturgical versicles found frequently in the *Navigatio*. Details of the direction taken by the monks are often omitted by Benedeit, as are many of what Waters calls 'needless repetitions' (p. cii).

A complete catalogue of the changes made by Benedeit and of the material he added is beyond the scope of this Introduction (for a fuller discussion see Waters's edition, pp. lxxx-cv), but amongst his additions are a number of didactic passages aimed at reminding the public of God's ever-present powers (ll. 241-46, 371-76, 472-78, 819-20, 953-58, 1173-82). Short and Merrilees also stress the Anglo-Norman poet's 'gift for visual description' (p. 21). Benedeit seems to revel in the account of the infernal island, clearly in reality an erupting volcano, which gives off putrid smoke and is said to be 'stinking more than rotting flesh' (l. 1106); from it molten rock rains down on the travellers (ll. 1123-30). Judas's extraordinary sufferings are detailed with the brio of a torturer extolling his art (ll. 1353-424). Throughout the narrative, descriptions of persons and objects are enlivened by small, but significant embellishments which are not found in the source: the messenger on the Isle of Sheep has 'white hair and youthful eyes' (l. 407), Paul the Hermit has 'the expression of an angel and a body redolent of Heaven' (ll. 1531-32).

Genre In so far as it tells the story of the hero's life from birth to death, the Anglo-Norman version is a hagiographic text (after l. 1834 MS A reads *Explicit vita sancti Brendani* 'Here ends the Life of Saint Brendan'). Like other saints, Brendan is an imitator of Christ, an independently minded, virtuous individual who shows others the way to eternal happiness. But in many senses Benedeit's poem is more of an adventure story than a saint's life. The emphasis is on action and movement rather than on repentance or martyrdom; it is the attainment of a precise goal which is fundamental, rather than merely the avoidance of sin or the importance of leading a pious life. Benedeit's poem has even been described as a romance. Written in octosyllabic rhyming couplets, which later in the twelfth century will become the norm for the new genre of romance, the poem is dominated by a quest and the material is presented by means of varied episodes, all of which contribute to the attainment of the goal in question. The *merveilleux* element, so common in later romances, is certainly not absent, nor is the feeling that the hero is a quasi-divine or mythical figure (he has been linked with Moses and with the figure of the Irish god Bran). Benedeit is certainly the first writer in French literature to make use of Celtic material, which will soon have such a significant role to play as inspiration for writers of Arthurian romance. Romance is also essentially aristocratic literature, with stories often being composed for a specific patron. This is clearly the case with Benedeit's poem, which was composed in the vernacular at the request of the queen herself. One can therefore assume that Benedeit's poem, even with its strong clerical and didactic purpose, was aimed at the entertainment of court society (which would, of course, have included clerics, as well as knights and ladies).

Romance has always been able to fuse didactic functions with elements of wish-fulfilment, as Benedeit's narrative does, and to explore the recesses of human behaviour, emotions and aspirations. Romance authors also like to exploit the symbolic properties of such things as objects, numbers and actions, the interpretation of which is both challenging to the reader / listener and crucial to the meaning of the work. In Benedeit's narrative, for example, the monks are told to take away precious stones as signs or tokens of Paradise ('Enseignes de paraïs', l. 1802), and this both recalls and explains the occurrence of precious stones earlier in the poem, which act as pointers to the monks' eventual success (ll. 275-76, 676-86, 1067-85, 1681-92). Animals, such as those taking part in the violent combats which occupy the poem's central episodes (ll. 893-952, 1002-30), also have symbolic importance, representing, like other objects in the text, either God and Paradise or the Devil and Hell. Numbers too have significance (see Caulkins 1974), especially 3 (ll. 134, 188, 260, 897, 994, etc.), 7 (the number of years occupied by the voyage and the number of monks, twice 7, initially chosen for the journey, ll. 866, 874, 1596, 1617) and 40 (ll. 133, 183, 631, 1640). The four elements themselves (earth, fire, air, water), fundamental to the medieval view of the world and capable of assuming both a positive and a negative function within a text, are exploited to the full by Benedeit (see Burgess 1995a).

The Author's Purpose Benedeit's poem can be read as an account of a spiritual quest undertaken by servants of God or as an adventure story, an account of exciting and dramatic happenings at sea (e.g. the discovery after a lengthy period at sea of an uninhabited island, an encounter with a speaking bird, the sight of fearsome clashes between monsters from the deep). The action in the poem is stimulated by Brendan's desire to see Paradise and Hell and informed by constant allusions to God's power and presence, which are manifested in many ways (the arrival of helpful messengers, meetings with those who know both the length and the outcome of the journey, prayers swiftly answered, etc.). But the heroic struggle against the unknown, which is always to the fore as the journey progresses, goes beyond the scope of a spiritual quest.

Benedeit keeps the two levels of his narrative under perfect control and maintains constant and profound links between them. There can be no doubt that it was his intention to have his poem fulfil a social function, in that the success of Brendan's mission should act as a stimulus to the desire of all Christians to reside in Paradise after their death. Benedeit concludes his poem by stating that Brendan's example led to more than a thousand people entering the kingdom of God (ll. 1833-34, another addition to his source). But Benedeit also had the task of entertaining the queen and court society. To do this he had to involve the audience's emotions, which he does through the exploitation of the dramatic possibilities of his material and by challenging their intellectual capacities, something he accomplishes by making use of such devices as thematic and linguistic repetition and, as mentioned earlier, the symbolic richness and ambivalence of objects and motifs.

One theme which runs throughout Benedeit's version is that of knowledge, a concept of importance to the understanding of the self, both as Christian and as courtier. The voyage is to a great extent a quest for knowledge. Significantly, Brendan's personal quest and that of his companions differ. Brendan is initially inspired to enter a monastery by his knowledge of what Scripture says (l. 23); the knowledge that he must commit himself to God leads to his desire to see Paradise and Hell. Whilst on his voyage, he never fails to seek information about the islands visited (ll. 413, 502-5, 714-16). He wishes to acquire knowledge of all aspects of the places he has reached and he questions his interlocutors avidly; for example, he asks the abbot of the Isle of Ailbe about the place and its occupants, 'who they were, how they lived, how long they had been there, from whom and by whom they received their supplies' (ll. 714-16). However, Brendan himself, unlike his monks, also possesses divine foreknowledge. He knows where he has to build his boat (ll. 157-58), he knows that one of his monks will commit theft on the uninhabited island (ll. 309-26), he knows the secret of the moving island (ll. 467-78) and he knows that he is permitted to take a chalice from the great pillar (ll. 1091-96).

The monks, on the other hand, know far less than their master. As they sail from island to island, they are learning, or are supposed to be learning. They acquire their knowledge in the painful school of experience; sometimes, when a word of warning would have been appropriate, Brendan lets them learn the hard way (ll. 227-28, 467-78); sometimes he warns them to no avail (ll. 807-12). But they do succeed in making progress in this respect, and at a critical moment in the poem, after the fight between the griffin and the dragon, Benedeit can tell us that, thanks to the Holy Spirit, Brendan and his monks now possess great knowledge ('Par l'espirit Deu mult sunt savant', l. 1030). The knowledge they acquire will ultimately be sufficient to allow them to visit Paradise, but their stay there comes to an end when they are told they lack the knowledge which would allow them to go any farther (ll. 1787-88).

Waters states that Benedeit inserted realistic and poetic touches into his narrative in order to 'bring the whole marvellous story within the comprehension of ordinary mortals' (p. cii). Benedeit clearly wanted the 'ordinary mortals' in his audience to appreciate the subtleties and complexities of a sea voyage. The detail with which he describes the search for a harbour (e.g. ll. 247-64) and his accounts of the panic and despair experienced by sailors in trouble at sea (ll. 229-34, 898-916) betoken a man with knowledge of nautical matters and an interest in day-to-day life. At no time, even in Paradise, are matters such as diet, physical suffering and meteorological conditions forgotten. He knows that the circumstances of daily living are as crucial to the monks who have to survive at sea for seven years as they are for any Christian in his audience.

In the *Navigatio* Brendan's lengthy journey is said to have been an opportunity for God to show him 'his varied secrets in the great ocean' (§XXVIII). But, as Short and Merrilees observe, Benedeit has turned into 'a trial of faith what in his original was a quest for adventure undertaken explicitly out of curiosity' (p. 20). Benedeit's Brendan seems to have a more complex relationship with God than his counterpart in the *Navigatio*. From what the angel tells him, Brendan could see that God wanted him to undertake the voyage (ll. 140-44). When the monks have scrambled off the back of the sea creature on to their boat, Brendan tells them that God wished to bring them to this place because he intended 'to teach them more' (l. 474). God's unceasing supply of miracles (l. 1001) and the constant suffering which the monks undergo are all aimed at increasing what Benedeit calls their *oür* or *bon oür* 'good fortune' – Latin *(bonum) augurium*. This fortune is not luck or chance, but the opportunity for success which God bestows on those who maintain faith, even in adversity (ll. 362, 1176). *(Bon) oür* is something which can, as Brendan tells the monks, easily be lost by negligent behaviour, such as foolish fear or lack of faith (ll. 921-22). But when complete trust in God, no matter how terrifying the circumstances, is allied to the acquisition of knowledge and commitment to prayer and the proper expenditure of effort, God's *vertud* 'power' (ll. 364, 1620, 1814, 1830) will grant admission to his kingdom. But if Benedeit, who has said what he knows and done what he can (l. 15), is concerned primarily with God's law ('lei divine', l. 2), he is never unmindful of man's law ('lei de terre', l. 3), by which humans have to live until they are finally judged (ll. 1248, 1484, 1503, 1559). He also knows that he lives in a cruel world, in which he will receive mockery and censure if his work does not reach the required standard (ll. 14-16). Just as Brendan requires God's *defens* 'protection' (l. 1006), Benedeit will need the queen's protection ('Mais tul defent', l. 13) if he is to cope successfully with the rigours of the task assigned to him.

My lady Adeliza the queen, through whom divine law will prevail and secular law be strengthened, and through whom this great war will be brought to an end, by virtue of the military power of Henry the king and the wise counsel you embody, the missioner Dom Benedeit greets you a thousand times and more. He has undertaken the commission you gave him in accordance with his ability and put into writing in the vulgar tongue, as you commanded, the story of the holy abbot, Saint Brendan.[1] But take care that he is not derided, since he says what he knows and does what he can; one should not find fault with such a servant. It is rather he who is capable, but unwilling, who ought properly to suffer. (18)

This saint of God was of royal birth and of Irish descent; being of royal lineage, it was fitting that he should devote himself to a noble cause.[2] He was well aware of what the Scriptures say: 'He who flees the delights of this world will have so much delight with God in Heaven that he could not ask for more.' Accordingly, this royal heir forsook false honours in favour of true ones. To show humility, and to live in this world yet be exiled from it, he donned monk's clothing, adopting both the habit and the discipline; later, he was elected abbot against his will. As a result of his great gifts many others came to him and adhered fully to the monastic order; under him, in various places, the saintly Brendan had three thousand monks, all taking their example from him because of his abundant virtue.[3] (38)

Abbot Brendan, a man of very great wisdom, solid and sound in judgement and of great righteousness, made up his mind to pray unceasingly to God, on his own behalf and that of his entire lineage, both the living and the dead, since he was a friend to all. But he had one particular desire, concerning which he began to pray to God repeatedly, asking him to show him the Paradise where Adam was lodged in the beginning, that place which is our rightful heritage and of which we have been deprived. Brendan believed that, as Holy Scripture tells us, it was a place of true glory; nevertheless he wanted to see for himself that place where he ought rightfully to dwell. But Adam had sinned; as a result he and we ourselves were expelled from it. Brendan prayed fervently to God that he would show him this place clearly; before he died, he longed to see the future abode of the good, as well as the place where the evil would dwell and the reward they would receive. (64)

He prayed that at the same time he might see Hell and the suffering which would be undergone there by the faithless who, out of pride, take every opportunity to show hostility towards God and his law; such people have in them no love or good faith. Brendan wished to accomplish his desire with God's support, so he decided first of all to make confession to a servant of God, a hermit named Barrind, a man of virtue who led a saintly life. This faithful servant of God lived in the forest together with three hundred monks; wishing to have his support, Brendan would take advice from him. Accompanying his account with inspiring stories and appropriate maxims, Barrind related to him at length what he had seen on land and sea when he went to visit his godson Mernoc, who had formerly been a brother in the place where Barrind was abbot. But Mernoc had been very eager to find a place of solitude elsewhere; with the advice of his abbot and godfather he had set sail on a mission, which turned out well, for he managed to reach the place which none but the pious can enter: this was on an island in the ocean, where no wind blows and where he was nourished by the scents which the flowers of Paradise gave off. For the island of Paradise lies very close to the one to which Mernoc had sailed and where he lived as if in Paradise, within hearing of the singing of the angels. Barrind later went to visit him and saw there the things which he recounted to Brendan. When he heard what Barint had seen there, Brendan was all the more willing to accept his advice and set about his preparations with greater urgency.[4] (106)

He chose fourteen of his monks, those he saw to be the best, and told them what he had in mind; he wanted to know from them whether it would be a wise thing to do. When they had heard what he said, they all responded as one; they were unanimous in their view that he should undertake this mission boldly and begged him to take them with him as sons of his, firm in their faith. Brendan replied:

'I am telling you this because I want to have every confidence in you, rather than take you with me and then regret it.'

They gave him the assurance that they would not hinder him. When he had heard their words, the abbot took those he had chosen into the chapter house, where he addressed them like a man of good sense:

'My lords, we do not know how difficult it will be to accomplish what we have planned. But let us pray to God that he will guide us and conduct us there at his pleasure. In the name of the Holy Spirit, let us fast in order that he may guide us there; let us fast three days each week for a period of forty days.' (134)

They all did without delay what he had commanded them, and the abbot did not cease his prayers day or night, until God sent down to him an angel from Heaven to act as his guide for the whole of the journey he was to make. The angel so inspired him in his heart that he quickly and clearly perceived that God favoured his journey; Brendan then took leave of his brothers, whose most tender father he was, telling them about his mission and how he intended to entrust it to God. He commended them all to his prior, telling him how he should take care of them; Brendan commanded them to obey the prior and serve him loyally as their abbot. Then he kissed them and departed; they all wept most bitterly because their father had refused to take with him more than fourteen of their brothers. (156)

Brendan made his way towards the ocean where he knew from God that he was to embark; he did not turn aside to visit his family, for he had a more worthy destination in view. He went to the coast, but had no intention of remaining there long. He came to the rock which peasants now call Brendan's Leap; it juts out far into the ocean, like a promontory.[5] Beneath this promontory was a harbour, where a very small, narrow stream flows into the sea; it flowed straight down from the cliff-top – no one before Brendan, I believe, had ever descended this escarpment. It was to this very place that Brendan had wood brought for the construction of his boat: on the inside it was all made of pinewood and on the outside it was covered with ox hide. He had it caulked so that it would sail swiftly and speed over the waves; in it he placed such gear as was necessary, as much as the boat could carry. To this he added the provisions they had brought with them; he put in food enough for no more than forty days, saying to the brothers:

'Go aboard and give thanks to God, for the wind is favourable.' (186)

They all went aboard and Brendan followed them. But suddenly three men appeared, running towards them and, with outstretched arms, calling loudly to Brendan, saying:

'We have come from your monastery and followed you here; abbot, let us enter your service and come with you, my lord, on your voyage across the sea.'

Brendan recognized them and welcomed them, fully aware of what would befall them. The abbot did not conceal from them what he had learned from God. Instead, he said to them:

'Satan will carry off two of you, just as he did with Abiram and Dathan.[6] The third will be greatly tempted but will have God's protection.'

Having said this, Abbot Brendan raised both hands and prayed fervently to God that he should protect his faithful from torment; then the saintly priest raised his right hand and made the sign of the cross over them all. (208)

They raised the mast and spread the sail; the faithful servants of God departed forthwith and the wind, coming from the east, drove them westwards. Everything, save sea and cloud, disappeared from their view. Although the wind was favourable, the monks were not idle; they rowed as hard as they could, wanting to make their bodies suffer to ensure that they saw what they had set out to see. They sailed for fifteen days until the wind slackened; all the brothers were dismayed by the lack of wind. But the abbot, whose courage never failed, then rebuked them:

'Put yourselves under God's protection and let none of you be afraid. When the wind is blowing, sail along with it; when there is no wind, then you must row!'

So they took to the oars, calling upon the grace of God. For they did not know which way to head or which ropes to haul, in which direction to steer or set their course. All the brothers voyaged without wind for a full month and made no complaint. As long as their food lasted, they were able to row hard without growing weak. Then their food and their strength failed; this made them greatly afraid. (240)

At a time of great need, God is never far from his faithful followers; so no one should be lacking in faith. Anyone who undertakes a voyage in God's name should do all he is able; God will provide for his needs. They sighted land, vast and mountainous; the wind favoured them once more and blew steadily; having been struggling to row, they were now driven towards it without further hardship. But they were unable to find a landing-place where their boat could be moored, for the land had so many rocks all around it that no one dared put ashore. The lofty mountains soared upwards towards the sky and stretched far out over the sea; from the chasms under water the sea swirled up, causing great peril. They spent three days going up and down in search of a harbour; when they found one, hewn in the grey limestone, they put in, but there was only room for a single ship. The harbour was set in pale rock; once they had tied up, they all disembarked, following the path which led them where they were to go. It took them straight to a castle which was large, splendid, and beautiful; it had the appearance of a truly royal place, an emperor's magnificent estate. They all made their way inside its walls, which were of solid crystal, and saw a palace constructed entirely of marble; none of the buildings was made of wood and the golden gems with which the walls were covered gave off a bright light. But one thing displeased them greatly: there was no one in the city. So they gazed at the lofty palace and entered in the name of peace. (280)

Brendan went into the palace and sat down on a bench. He saw no one other than his own followers and began to speak to them, saying:
    'Go into the kitchens and see if there is anything we need there.'
They did so and found what they most desired, a supply of food and plenty to drink. The dining utensils were of gold and silver, very fine and beautiful; in this place they had entered they found an abundance of everything they required. The abbot said to them:
    'Take some of this for ourselves; but do not take too much, that I forbid you; let each of you pray God that you do not break faith with him.'
The reason the abbot wanted to warn them was that he knew what was going to happen. They took away a good supply of provisions, but did not take too much. They ate as much as they pleased, but only what they needed at the time; not forgetting to praise God, they begged fervently for his mercy. They ventured to take up quarters there and, when it was time, lay down to rest. (308)

When they were all asleep, suddenly Satan came to tempt one of them, putting in his mind the desire to steal some of the gold he saw gathered together there. The abbot was awake and clearly saw how the devil had that monk in his power and how he was holding out a golden chalice to him – no treasury has one more precious. The monk got up, went to take it and at once stowed it away secretly; having committed the theft, he returned to his bed to sleep. From where he lay, the abbot saw everything and observed how this monk roamed about at night; the darkness did not prevent Brendan from seeing. He saw everything without a candle; since God wished to reveal all this to him there was no need for a candle to be lit in addition. They remained there three days in all, departing on the fourth day. Brendan said to them:

'My lords, I beg you, do not take anything away with you from here, not even a scrap of food, nor any water to prevent thirst.'

Weeping profusely, he said to the brothers:

'Look, my lords, this man is a thief.'

The monk saw that the abbot knew about the theft and realized how he had found out about it. Confessing his sin before everyone, he threw himself at the abbot's feet, hoping for pardon. The abbot said:

'Pray for him; you will see him die this very day.' (340)

Before everyone, in full view, the devil emerged from the monk, crying:

'Tell me, Brendan, why do you drive me from my dwelling?'

Brendan said what he had to say to the brother, pardoned him and then absolved him. As soon as he had received communion, death took him in the sight of everyone. His spirit went to Paradise, where God granted him great repose. They buried the body, commending it to the care of God. He was one of the three brothers whom the father superior had taken on board. (354)

Then they went to the harbour on the shore, where suddenly a messenger appeared before them, bringing them bread and water and asking them to accept it with the words:

'Have no fear, no matter what danger you meet with; whatever you see, do not be afraid. God will grant you good fortune; by the grace of Almighty God you will see what you are seeking. Have no concern about lack of provisions; you will not want for anything until you reach the place where you can take on a fresh supply.'

Bowing low, he handed them the provisions and departed without another word. (370)

Now the servants of God perceived that they were journeying under God's direction; the miracles they had witnessed proved this beyond doubt. Seeing clearly that God would feed them, they never ceased praising him and set off at once, sailing before the wind. God's protection was about them and for a good part of the year they sailed over the sea, suffering extreme hardship. Then, as they had hoped, they sighted land, which came into view on the distant horizon; they turned their vessel in that direction and none of them showed any reluctance to row. Then they slackened the ropes and lowered the sail; reaching the shore, they quickly disembarked. They saw great numbers of sheep, all with white fleece and as large as stags in this country. The abbot said to them:

'My lords, we shall not leave here until the third day. Today is Maundy Thursday, which commemorates the agony suffered by the son of God; he is our tender and ever-present friend, who has now sent us what we need in order to celebrate this festival. Make sure the boat is pulled ashore. Take one of these sheep and prepare it for Easter Day. Let us ask God's permission for this, since we can find no one else here.' (402)

They did as he commanded and remained there for three days. On the Saturday a messenger came to them and greeted them in God's name. He had snow-white hair and youthful eyes and had lived a long life without experiencing any misfortune. He brought them bread from his own country, many large, white, unleavened loaves, promising faithfully that, if they lacked for anything, he would provide it for them. The abbot asked him about the nature of the place; I do not know how helpful he was, but he did say a little about it,[7] replying:

'We have everything here our hearts can desire.'
The abbot said:
'There are sheep here, as large as I have ever seen anywhere.'
The other replied:
'This is no marvel. None of the ewes here is ever milked; the winters are not unpleasant and none of the sheep sicken or die. Brendan, board your ship and go to the island you can see over there; tonight you will land on that island and tomorrow you will celebrate your feast-day there. You will leave that island tomorrow before nightfall. Why so soon? You will find out! Then you will return without difficulty, sailing close to this coast. Next you will go to another place where I too am going; I shall follow you and find you there, very close to this place, and bring you a large store of provisions.' (434)

Setting sail without more ado, Brendan made his way to the island which he could clearly see. God provided a favourable wind and he

soon reached it, although he had crossed a very large stretch of sea –
this is how things turn out for those whom God guides. They landed
without difficulty and all the brothers disembarked, save the abbot
who remained on board. That night and the next morning they
celebrated a splendid and most sincere service to God; when they had
finished their celebration, in the boat as if it were in church, they took
out the meat they had placed in the boat and made preparations to
cook it, going in search of firewood with which to make their meal on
the island. When the meal was prepared, the steward said:

'Now be seated.'

But then they all shouted out very loudly:

'Help, lord abbot, wait for us!'

For the whole island was moving and drawing farther away from the
boat. The abbot said:

'Do not be afraid; call fervently upon the Lord God! Bring all our
gear and join me in the ship!'

He threw out to them very long ropes and poles, but all this made
their clothes wet. They all boarded the ship, but their island moved
away very rapidly; at ten leagues distant they could still see the fire
they had made on it. (466)

Brendan said to them:

'Brothers, do you know what frightened you? It is not an island on
which we performed our celebration; rather is it a beast, a sea creature
larger than any other. Do not be amazed at this, my lords! God wished
to bring you here because he intended to give you the clearest
possible lesson; the more you see of his marvels, the more firmly you
will believe in him. The Divine King made this creature before any
other beast in the sea.'[8]

After Abbot Brendan had said this, he sailed a great distance over the
sea; then they sighted land, rising high and clear, just as the brother
had told them. They swiftly drew towards it and landed; they were
not reluctant to disembark and nothing daunted them. They pushed
their boat ashore and made their way up a stream, using ropes to drag
the boat. At the head of the stream was a tree, as white as marble; it
had very broad leaves spotted with red and white. The tree rose
towards the clouds, as far up as the eye could see; from its summit,
right down to the ground, it was a mass of thick branches, extending
over a wide area. Casting shade a good distance around and

completely blocking out the light, the tree was covered all over with white birds – none more beautiful have ever been seen. (500)

Seized with amazement, the abbot besought God, his counsellor, to explain to him what this might be and the meaning of this large assembly of birds; he asked God in his majesty to let him know what this place could be to which he had come. When he had finished his prayer, one of the birds flew down. Its flight sounded as sweet as the striking of a bell and, once it had settled on the ship, Brendan addressed it sweetly and gently:

'If you are a creature of God, pay heed to my words! Tell me who you are, what your duties are in this place, both your own and those of the other birds, for you seem very beautiful to me.'
The bird replied:

'We are angels and once lived in Heaven; we fell from on high to this lowly place, along with that arrogant and wretched creature who through pride rebelled and rose up treacherously against his lord. He was made master over us and it was his duty to feed us with the aid of God; because of his great wisdom, we were forced to accept him as our master. But his pride caused him to become a great traitor; he scorned God's command, yet once he had done so we served and obeyed him as before. For this we have lost our heritage, the kingdom of truth. But since it was not our fault, we enjoy all this thanks to the power of God; we do not share the suffering of those who displayed pride as he did. The only hardship we endure is this: we are deprived of the majesty of God, the presence of glory and the joy of being before God. The name of the place, about which you enquired, is the Paradise of Birds. It is now a year', he said to them, 'that you have been toiling over the sea; there are still six more ahead before you reach Paradise. You will suffer much pain and hardship as you travel back and forth over the ocean; each year you will celebrate Easter on the back of the beast.' (552)

After uttering these words, the bird returned to the tree from which it had flown down. Towards eventide, as the day drew to a close, the birds began to sing hymns. They sang very loudly with sweet voices, and in their hymns they gave thanks to God. In their exile they were acknowledging the comfort the monks were bringing them; never before had the Lord God sent any human beings there. Then the abbot said:

'Did you hear how these angels welcomed us? Praise God and give thanks; he loves you more than you can imagine!'
Leaving the boat in the channel, they ate on the shore and then sang compline with a great many psalms, after which they all lay down upon their beds and commended themselves to Jesus. They slept as those do who are weary and have undergone great hardship. But, nevertheless, at cock-crow they said their pre-dawn matins; the birds in chorus joined in the responses. (578)

In the early morning, when the sun was shining, there suddenly appeared God's faithful messenger, through whose instruction they received their guidance and by whose gift they obtained their provisions. He said to them:
   'I shall provide you with an abundance of food; you will easily have enough for the octaves of Pentecost. After your hardships rest is required, so you will remain in this place for two months.'
Then he took his leave and departed; on the third day he returned and subsequently visited the company twice a week; they did exactly what he told them and placed themselves completely under his guidance. When the time came to depart, they began to make their boat watertight, stitching ox hides over it, for those already on it were completely worn through. They had with them plenty of replacements to ensure that their boat would remain seaworthy; they got themselves a good supply of everything they needed so as not to perish for lack of provisions. The messenger brought them bread and water, as much as they wanted. He reckoned what they needed for a full eight months; the boat could not bear any more weight. When he had kissed each one of them, they took their leave and so departed; with tears in his eyes, the messenger indicated the direction in which they should head. Suddenly the bird appeared on the mast and told Brendan to set sail, informing him that he had a long voyage ahead and many hardships to endure. He would have to wait a full eight months before he could reach land, before they reached the Isle of Ailbe where they would spend Christmas. Once the bird had spoken, Brendan delayed no longer; the boat departed with the wind directly behind it. (620)

They sailed swiftly over the sea, thanking God for such a favourable wind; then the wind increased and they were in constant dread of danger and great suffering. After four months they sighted land, but reaching it proved difficult; at long last, however, in the sixth month, they did finally see an end to it all. They made land, but nevertheless could not find a landing-place; they circled the island for forty days before putting into a harbour, for on shore they were faced with rocks and high mountains. Then, very belatedly, they found a place suitable for their purpose, an opening made by a stream. Those who hauled the boat upstream took a rest, for they were weary; then the abbot said:

'Let us disembark and go in search of what our bodies need.'
So one by one the abbot and all his companions disembarked. They came upon a spring with two outlets, one clear and one cloudy; dying of thirst, they ran towards it, but the abbot said to them:

'Restrain yourselves! I forbid you to partake so soon, until we have spoken to someone. We do not know the nature of the streams we have found.' (650)

The monks were daunted by the abbot's words and kept their great thirst in check. Shortly afterwards a tall, elderly man appeared abruptly. They would have been afraid, had it not been for his habit; for he was a monk. Saying nothing to them, he approached and fell at Brendan's feet. Brendan raised him up with his own hand; with great humility the old man bowed low and began to kiss the abbot and all the others. Then he took Brendan by the right hand to conduct him to the place where he lived, beckoning the others to come and see a most excellent place. As they went, the abbot asked where it was that they had come to, but the other kept silent and made no reply. He welcomed them warmly and with the greatest pleasure, and they proceeded until they came in sight of the place they were making for: a fine and beautiful abbey, none more holy in all the world. (672)

The abbot of the place had his relics and treasures brought out: crosses, reliquaries and gospel books, studded with amethysts and adorned with gold and precious stones, still uncut, and censers of solid gold, set about with gems. Their vestments were covered with gold, none so brightly coloured in all Arabia, and with jacinths and sards, huge and perfect; their clasps were no less brilliant with topaz and jasper. All the monks were robed and they went outside with their abbot; with much joy and great friendliness they formed a procession. Having all kissed each other, they took one another by the hand and led Brendan and his company into their abbey, where they performed a splendid and joyous service to God; they did not wish to make the occasion too solemn. Then they went to eat in the refectory where, except for the readers, everyone remained silent; in front of them they had sweet, white bread, wholesome and full-flavoured. In place of cooked food they had roots, which satisfied them better than delicacies. With it they had a full-flavoured drink: water sweeter than sugared wine. (704)

When they had had their fill, they rose and made their way to the church, singing psalms. All the brothers processed, singing the *miserere*[9] until they reached the choir stalls, except for those who had been serving the meal; they now took their turn in the refectory. Once the canonical service had been sung and the bell rung, the abbot of that place led them out and told them about the place and its occupants, who they were, how they lived, how long they had been there, from whom and by whom they received their supplies.

'There are twenty-four of us living here in this holy place. It is eighty years since Saint Ailbe the pilgrim came to his end; he was a wealthy man with vast estates, but he abandoned everything for this place. When he went in search of seclusion, a messenger from God appeared to him and brought him here, where he found a place already prepared for him: this monastery which still stands here. When in various places we heard that Ailbe the pious lived here, we gathered here together in God's name because of our great love for him. As long as he lived, we served him and obeyed him as our abbot; after he had taught us about his order and established us here securely, God took him to be close to him. He died eighty years ago; since then God has sustained us so well that no hardship has befallen us, no illness has affected our bodies, no suffering or affliction. The food we have comes to us from God; we know of no other source, have no one to serve us and never see anyone bringing it. But each day we find it ready; there is never any need for us to seek it elsewhere. Invariably, each working-day, we have a whole loaf between two of us; on feast-days I have one all to myself for supper and each of us has his own. As for the two springs which you saw and from which you almost took some water, the clear one is cold and we drink from it, the cloudy one is warm and we use it for washing. Also, at the appropriate time, our lamps are lit; even though the flame burns in the lamp none of the wax or oil is used up. The lamp lights up by itself and goes out by itself; we have no brother in charge of it. We live here without concern and without any difficulties in our life. Before we learned of your coming, God wanted us to provide for you, so he gave us more than we normally receive; I know he wanted us to welcome you. Only on the eighth day after Epiphany will you leave here; until then, you will stay here, and then and only then take your departure.'

Then Brendan said:

'There is no place, however pleasant, where I would so willingly remain.'

The abbot replied:

'Go in search of that which made you leave your homeland; then you will return to your country and die where you were born. You will leave here in a week's time, on the octave of Epiphany.' (778)

When the day set by the abbot arrived, Brendan took leave of him. One abbot accompanied the other and all the monks went with him; they set sail and a wind sent by God carried them away from the Isle of Ailbe. They sailed the seas for a very long time with no idea of where land was to be found; the wind dropped, their provisions ran out and keen hunger and burning thirst increased. The sea became so calm that it was difficult to make progress; it grew dense as a morass and there were those in the boat who thought their situation hopeless. But God sent a strong wind to assist them and they sighted land and saw a shoreline. The famished monks realized that God had intended them to reach there, for they discovered a landing-place which seemed destined for them. Finding a clear stream with fish in it, they caught more than a hundred of them; the herbs they found in the bog and marshy ground all around them supplied their needs.[10]

The abbot said:

'Take care not to drink too much.'

But paying no heed to what the abbot had said, they drank what their thirst required and secretly consumed so much at that time that they were considered fools as a consequence; for sleep overtook them and caused them all to lie slumbering. Those who had drunk too much lay prostrate, some for one day, some for two and some for three whole days. Brendan prayed for his monks, whom he saw to be drunk; when they regained consciousness, they all realized how foolish they had been. The abbot said to them:

'Let us leave here quickly lest you become negligent again; it is better to suffer honest hunger than to neglect God and one's prayers to him.' (820)

They sailed away from there and voyaged until Maundy Thursday. Then Father Brendan returned to the island he had visited the previous year. Suddenly their host, the white-haired old man, appeared; he had a tent erected for them at the harbour and had the weary men bathed and provided with fresh clothes. They celebrated the Last Supper and the Washing of Feet, as is decreed in Scripture, and remained there until the third day. On the Saturday they left and sailed towards the fish. The abbot said to them:

'Let us disembark!'

Then they saw the cauldron they had lost the year before; the great fish had kept it and now they had found it once more upon its back. This time they felt more secure in their stay on the fish and celebrated their festival splendidly, continuing without ceasing all night until morning; they celebrated Easter Day, but were not unmindful of the hour for their departure. They tarried no longer than midday, at which time they reloaded their boat; shortly the saint departed and made swift progress towards the birds they had visited before. They caught sight of the white tree and the birds upon the branches. From far out at sea they could hear how the birds were welcoming them; they went on singing until the pilgrims reached the shore. They hauled their boat upstream to where they had moored it the last time. Suddenly their host was there again, pitching a tent. His ship was laden with provisions and he said to them:

'You will be here for a little while and with your permission I shall go back; you will remain here without any difficulties until the octave of Pentecost. Do not be afraid; I shall not fail to return. When you need help, I shall provide it.' (864)

They secured their boat with chains and remained there for seven weeks. When the time came to depart, one of the birds came swooping down; it circled round them and then settled on the yard-arm. Seeing that it wished to speak, Brendan told everyone to keep quiet.

'My lords', said the bird, 'you will return here to this place of repose every year for seven years; each year you will spend Christmas on the Isle of Ailbe. You will celebrate the Last Supper and the Washing of Feet in the place your host has prescribed; each year you will celebrate the festival of Easter on the beast.'

When it had spoken these words, it returned to the tree from which it had flown down. The boat was floating in deep water and each of them kept a look out for their host; he was not long in coming and arrived with a boat laden with provisions. From his ship he loaded theirs with good supplies of great worth, and then called upon the son of the Virgin Mary to care for this company. They fixed a time for their return and shed tears as they departed. (892)

They ran freely before the wind, which drove them towards the west; the sea was calm and dead and sailing over it was difficult. After they had voyaged for forty-five days, a chill ran through their veins; an immense fear gripped them because their ship began to pitch dangerously and the swell was such that the ship nearly turned over on them. Then something else occurred which terrified them more than any other peril they had experienced; a sea-serpent came towards them, pursuing them more swiftly than the wind. The flames coming from it burned as brightly as firewood in a furnace; the blaze was huge and burning hot, causing them to fear for their lives. The body was extraordinarily large and it bellowed louder than fifteen bulls; its teeth alone would have been a great threat to them, even if there had been fifteen hundred of them in the boat.[11] On the surface, the waves which it churned up were like those created by a great storm. As it neared the pilgrims, Brendan the true divine said:

'My lords, do not give way to fear; God will avenge you. Take care that foolish fear does not make you desert God or lose your chance of success. For no one under God's protection should be afraid of a roaring beast.' (924)

Having said this, he prayed to God; what he had prayed for was not long delayed. They saw another beast coming to attack the first one; as the first beast was heading straight for the boat, the second roared with rage at its approach. The first beast, recognizing its opponent, turned away from the boat and drew back; raising their heads very high, the two beasts began to fight, fire spewing forth from their nostrils and rising swiftly up towards the clouds. They gave each other blows with their fins, which they used like shields, and with their claws. With teeth as sharp as spears they cut and wounded each other; blood spurted forth from the violent bites which their teeth made in their huge bodies and the wounds were very deep and the waves stained with blood. The battle was fierce and the sea greatly disturbed. Finally, the second beast won the day, killing the first and tearing it so violently with its teeth that it ripped it into three parts. Having achieved its act of vengeance, it returned to its lair. (952)

No one should ever despair, rather one's faith should grow stronger when one sees that God so readily provides food and clothing, as well as aid in times of grave danger and succour from the jaws of death. The abbot said to them:

'Let us ignore all else, for one should serve such a lord.'

They replied most willingly to this:

'We know how much he cherishes us.'

The next day they sighted land and felt sure they could reach it; they made swift progress and disembarked to rest their weary bodies. They set up their tent on the grass and drew their boat up on to dry land. As they were landing, the strong winds intensified and Brendan knew from the humid air that the weather was about to become very unpleasant; a gale had got up and their provisions were running low. Nevertheless, despite the danger they faced, they were undaunted. (976)

The abbot had spoken so seriously to them, and God had always given so much to them, that they could have no concern about anything whatever on their journey. Then, not long afterwards, the third part of the fish arrived, the waves driving it in such a way that they brought it to their shore; the storm drove it swiftly in order that it might provide them with relief. Then Brendan said:

'See, brothers, what was once your enemy has now become, thanks to God, an aid for our relief; you will have food for a good while. Have no fear, this will be something we can eat, however it may look to us; take as much as you judge necessary to suffice for three months.'

They did his bidding and provided themselves with food for this period of time; they filled up their barrels with sweet water from the springs and gathered firewood. When the wind was right, they set sail.[12] (1000)

God's miracles never cease. Another danger now beset them; had this one been the first, the danger it posed would not have been any the less, in fact it would have been greater. But the confidence they had in God and his protection meant that they were not afraid. A flaming griffin swooped down from the sky and stretched out its claws to seize them; its jaws were afire, its claws very sharp. It could have carried away in its claws any plank in the ship, however strong the timber might be. As a result of its violent approach and the wind which it generated, the ship nearly capsized. But whilst it was pursuing them over the sea in this way, a dragon arrived, flaming in all its brilliance; it flapped its wings, stretched out its neck and directed its course towards the griffin. The battle took place in the air above them and the flames from the two of them lit up the sky; in sight of everyone, they attacked each other with blows, flames, bites and thrusts. The griffin was huge and the dragon slender; the former was the stronger, the latter the fiercer. The griffin was killed and fell into the sea, so those who had dreaded it were avenged; the dragon departed, having won its victory. The monks gave thanks to God in his glory and continued on their way; through the spirit of God they were full of knowledge. (1030)

The festival of Saint Peter, who was killed in the gardens of Nero, came round and the monks gave praise to the glory of the first pope. When the abbot was conducting the service, as the law prescribes, he sang in a voice which was clear and loud, and the brothers all said:

'Fair lord, dear father, sing more quietly; if you do not, you will be the death of us all. For where the sea is deep, each wave is so clear that we can see right to the bottom, where we can see a host of fish; so large and fierce are the fish we can see that we have never heard of any like them. Should the noise arouse them, we would not, you must realize, escape death.'

Considering them most unwise, the abbot smiled and rebuked them:

'My lords, why are you afraid of such a thing? How you abandon your beliefs! You have endured dangers greater than this and God was always there to protect you all; something like this has never befallen you before. Repeat your *mea culpa*', said Brendan to them.

He sang more loudly and very clearly; the fierce sea creatures rose up and swam all round the ship, rejoicing in the day's celebrations. After the monks had sung the hymns appropriate to the day, each fish went its way. (1062)

They sailed on, and in the open sea they clearly sighted a huge pillar made of pure jacinth without an ounce of any other material. The jacinth was sapphire-blue and whoever possessed it would be truly rich; it towered up towards the clouds and reached right down to the sea bed. Surrounding it was a canopy, extending from its summit right down to sea level, finely wrought with precious gold; it could not have been made for all the riches in the entire world. Brendan sailed in that direction, but it seemed to him that it took a long time to reach it. With the sail raised, he passed beneath the canopy with his monks and his boat; just where the pillar went down into the sea he saw an emerald altar. The shrine was made of sardonyx, the pavement of chalcedony; within the pillar a beam of pure gold was fixed as a support and the lamps were made of beryl. The monks feared no danger and remained there until the third day, all of them singing mass turn by turn. Brendan made up his mind that he should not seek to understand God's mysteries and said to his monks:

'Accept my decision; let us leave here and depart!' The abbot took with him a magnificent crystal chalice; he knew he was not turning away from God, since he took it as a means of serving him. (1096)

The pilgrims had travelled a long way, but still they did not know when their journey would end. Nevertheless, they did not become faint-hearted, for the farther they travelled, the more they toiled; yet toil alone would never have caused them to give up until they had seen what they sought. An island appeared before them indistinctly, shrouded in dark fog and mist; putrid smoke arose from it, stinking worse than rotting flesh. It was wrapped in deep darkness and they had no desire to spend any time there; from far out at sea they could hear that they were hardly welcome there. They tried very hard to steer clear of it, but could not avoid heading that way, for the wind drove them there. The abbot explained the situation to them clearly, saying:

'You must realize that you are being driven towards Hell; never have you been in such great need of God's protection as now.'
He made the sign of the cross over them, fully aware that the pit of Hell was close; the closer they got, the more of its evil they witnessed. The valley became darker, and from deep gorges and pits huge, flaming blades came flying. The roaring wind sounded like the blowing of bellows; no thunder could roar so loudly. Along with the blades came sparks, burning rocks and flames, soaring so high into the air that they blotted out the daylight from them. (1130)

As they approached a mountain, they saw a man who terrified them. This devilish fellow was huge and he emerged from Hell, all ablaze; in his hand he carried an iron hammer, big enough to have made a pillar.

When he became aware of their presence, his eyes flaming like a burning fire, he could not wait to prepare his instruments of torment; with flames spewing from his throat, he bounded into his forge and rushed out again with his blade as red as flame. The tongs in which he held it would have made a load for ten oxen. He raised it up to the heavens and flung it straight at them; a whirlwind does not travel faster when the wind sucks it up into the air, nor does the bolt from a crossbow or the shot from a sling. The higher it went the more it glowed; as it travelled, it took on new force. It began to split up, then became solid again, but instead of falling on them, it passed them by. At the spot where it fell into the sea, it continued to burn like heather in a clearing; for a very long time the blade went on burning in the sea with huge flames. The wind so drove the ship that they managed to make their escape from there. (1162)

Running with the wind, they sailed on; looking back repeatedly, they saw the island aflame and covered in smoke. They could see many thousands of demons and hear the laments and weeping of the damned; from the smoke which spread high into the air a dreadful stench reached them. They bore all this as best they could and avoided it as well as they were able. When a pious man suffers many hardships, hunger, thirst, cold and heat, anxiety, sadness and great fear, the good fortune he enjoys from God becomes all the greater. So it was with them, once they had seen where the damned are lodged; their belief in God intensified and they were not inclined to lose faith. They went forward fearlessly, for they knew that what they were doing was right. As early as the next morning they saw an island close to them, a mountain shrouded in mist; a strong wind drove them in that direction and they soon reached the shore. But the mountain rose up to such a great height that they were quite unable to see just how high the summit was; it did not descend towards the shore as much as it extended up above the mist. The earth was completely black and they had never met anything like it in the whole of their voyage. For a reason they did not understand, one of their number jumped out of the boat and was lost to them. They all heard what he said to them, but only the abbot actually saw him with his own eyes:

'My lord, believe me, I am now being snatched away from you because of my sins.'

The abbot saw him dragged away by a hundred demons, who made him howl with pain. The monks left there and went elsewhere, looking all around them fearfully; the smoke on the mountain lifted and they saw the open jaws of Hell. Hell spewed forth fire and flames, burning rods and blades, pitch and sulphur; then it sucked them in again, for they belonged there. (1210)

Then, arming them with the sign of the cross, Brendan guided them across the sea. On the sea they sighted something jutting up, just as if it were a rock; it was indeed a rock, but they could not credit it with any certainty. Then the abbot said:

'Let us not tarry! Let us find out what it is and hasten towards it.'
Making their way towards it, they discovered something they scarcely expected; they found a naked man sitting on the rock which they had reached. In great distress, he was battered, lacerated and torn to shreds; his face was draped in a cloth and he was clinging to a pillar. He clung tenaciously to the stone so that the waves would not drag him under, but the sea battered him violently and his death knew no end. One wave struck him so hard that he almost lost his grip; the next one hurled him upwards. He had danger in front of him and danger above him, danger behind him and danger below him; torment to the right and torment no less terrible to the left. When the waves made their assaults on him, he bemoaned his fate with these words of woe:

'O Jesus, King of Glory, will my death never come, winter or summer? Jesus, you who move the entire firmament, your mercy is so good. Jesus, you who are so full of pity, shall I never be released at any time? Jesus, son of Mary, I do not know if I ought to beg for mercy. I cannot, I dare not, for my crime was so great that judgement has already been passed on me.' (1248)

When Brendan heard him lamenting in this way, he felt more grief than he had ever known. Raising his hand, he made the sign of the cross over them all and then made a great effort to approach him; as he was approaching, the sea remained calm and no wind or gale disturbed it. Brendan said to him:

'Tell me, poor wretch, why do you suffer this torment? In the name of Jesus, on whose name you call, I command you to tell me; tell me truly who you are and about the crime for which you are here.'
Brendan was prevented by his tears from saying more, so he fell silent, and the other replied in a low voice; he was very hoarse and greatly exhausted:

'I am Judas who once served Jesus whom I betrayed. I sold my lord and hanged myself out of grief. I feigned affection in order to kiss him and created discord when I ought to have created peace. I am the one who had the keeping of his money and squandered it by stealth; for he ordered that all the gifts given to him should be handed over to the poor. I concealed the money in my purse and that is why suffering has come upon me; I thought that it could be concealed from him who created the starry heavens. I denied succour to God's poor; now they are rich and I am a beggar. I am the traitor who hated God, who handed the innocent lamb over to the wolves. When I saw him in Pilate's hands, I became very downcast. When I saw him in the hands of the Jews, the holy one handed over to those cruel men, and when I saw that their worship of him was merely taunts and their crown was one of thorns, and again when I saw him treated so vilely, you must know that I was overcome by grief. (1290)

'Then I saw him led to his death; from his tender side I saw blood oozing. When I saw him hanging on the cross, having been sold to his death by me, I immediately offered to give back the thirty pence; but they would not accept repayment. I did not repent prudently; in my madness I killed myself, and since I had not confessed I am condemned eternally. You see nothing of the suffering I endure in Hell. This is a period of respite from my pains, which I have on a Saturday evening; I have such respite all day Sunday until evening and for the fifteen days of Christmas I am here, relieved of my great suffering, and also at the feasts of the Virgin Mary I have none of my terrible suffering. At Easter and Pentecost I have no more suffering than that which you can see. On Sunday evening I go from here to endure torment.' (1316)

Then Brendan said to him:
    'Tell me now, since you have such respite here, in what place do you live your life of torment and suffering? Where do your acts of expiation take place? When you depart from here, where do you go?'
Judas replied:
    'The devils' domain is near by; it is only a short distance away. I am just far enough away not to be able to hear them. There are two Hells close by and it is a great torment to endure them; very close to here are two Hells, whose activity never ceases, summer or winter. The lesser of the two is terrible and very grievous for those who are there.

Those who suffer in that place think that, compared to them, the others suffer no hardship. Apart from myself, not a single one of us knows which of the two is the more agonizing; no one else has to undergo more than one, but I in my misery have endured both. One is on a mountain, the other in a valley; they are separated by the salt sea. The sea divides the two Hells, but it is astonishing that it is not all ablaze. The one on the mountain is the more grievous, the one in the valley the more terrible; the one close to the sky is warm and clammy, the one near the sea cold and stinking. I spend one day and night up there, and then remain for the same period down below. One day I go up and the next day I come down; so there is no end to my torment. I do not alternate Hells in order to get any relief, but so that my suffering will increase. (1358)

'On a Monday, both day and night, I am whirled round on the wheel. Wretch that I am, I am impaled upon it and whirl about as swiftly as the wind; the wind propels it through the air, and all day long I go round and round. Then the next day I am hurled about in a state of complete numbness; I fly across the sea into the valley, to the other Hell where there is so much suffering. There I am immediately thrown into chains and reviled by the devils; I am laid on a bed of spits and on top of me they pile lead and rocks. My body, as you see, is all pierced through by being spitted there; I am, as you see, full of holes. On Wednesdays I am hurled up above, to the place where my plight is altered; for much of the day I boil in tar, which makes me black as you see me now. Then I am taken out and put to roast there, bound to a post between two fires; the iron post is set up there for me and me alone. It is as red as if it had lain ten years in a fire with the bellows blowing; because of the tar, the fire takes hold to increase my torment. Again I am thrown into tar and smeared with it so that I burn more fiercely. No marble could be so hard that it would not be melted if placed upon it, but I am so inured to this torment that my body cannot perish. This pain, however agonizing, lasts a whole day and night. (1388)

'Then on a Thursday I am brought down to the valley to suffer the opposite form of torment. I am put in a cold place, which is very dark and gloomy and I am so cold there that I long to be back in the fire which burns so fiercely; it seems to me that there is no torment in which I could feel worse than I do in the cold. Thus each torture does not seem so severe when I am first placed in it. On Fridays I come back up to where so many forms of death await me; then they flay my whole body so that there is no skin on the outside. With a burning stake they thrust me down into soot mixed with salt; then as a result of this torment a completely new skin is soon formed. They flay me thoroughly ten times a day and force me down into the salt. Then they make me drink the molten lead and copper, scalding hot. On a Saturday they cast me down where other devils vary my torments. I am put in prison; in the whole of Hell there is nothing so terrible, in the whole of Hell no place so foul. I go down into it without a rope and lie there without light, in darkness and stench; the stench is so great that I constantly fear my heart will burst. But I cannot vomit because of the copper which they make me drink there. Then I swell up greatly and my skin stretches; I am in agony and ready to burst. Such heat, such cold, such stench does Judas suffer, and such pain. As yesterday was Saturday, I came here in the early afternoon and today I remain at rest in this place. Shortly, I shall have a painful evening. Soon a thousand devils will arrive; when they get hold of me, I shall have no respite. But if you are a man of such wisdom, ensure that I get some rest tonight! If you are of sufficient merit, set me free tonight! I know full well that you are a pious and holy man, since you have come to such a place without any concern.' (1438)

Brendan wept profusely at Judas' great suffering; he asked him to tell him the meaning of the sheet which was wrapped round him and whence came the rock to which he clung and from whom. Judas replied:

'In my life I did a little good and a great deal of folly. I now perceive the good and the bad and know which of them was dearer to me in my heart. With the alms of which I was the keeper I bought a sheet for a poor naked man; thanks to this I have the sheet I wrap round my mouth to prevent me from drowning. When the wave strikes me full in the face, I get some protection from it. But in Hell it is of no use to me, as it was not my own money which bought it. At a stream, where many men used to perish, I constructed a small mound and then laid a strong footbridge over it. As a result many were saved at that place; this is why I enjoy some alleviation of my extreme suffering.' (1462)

When evening approached, Brendan saw he was telling the truth; he saw a thousand devils coming with their instruments of pain and torture and heading straight for that unhappy creature. One of them darted forward and grabbed him with a hook, but Brendan said to them:

'Let him remain here until Monday morning.'

They replied defiantly that they would not be prevented from taking him. Then Brendan said:

'This is my command to you and I invoke Jesus as my protector.'

The devils were compelled to leave Judas; in the end they achieved nothing. Brendan remained there all night, greatly angering all the devils. There were some nearby; they were very anxious for dawn to break. Aggressively and with raucous voice they said that he would have twice his normal suffering. The abbot replied:

'He shall have no more punishment than has been decreed.'

Now that it was bright daylight, the devils departed with Judas. (1486)

Brendan continued on his way; he was well aware that God was his true protector, and the monks all knew they were safe under the guidance of God. They gave thanks to God for their journey and all their provisions. When all the companions were counted, one of their number was missing; they did not know what had become of him nor in what place he had been seized. They knew how the other two had fared, but were concerned for this one. The abbot, who knew all about him, said to them:

'God has done what he pleased with him. Do not worry about this; continue on your way. You must realize that judgement has been passed on him, either for repose or for torment.' (1504)

As soon as they set out, they saw, standing alone in the sea, a lofty mountain; they soon reached it, but the shore was steep and forbidding. The abbot said to them:

'I shall go ashore; let no one move apart from myself!'

He climbed the mountain and walked a good distance before discovering anything. He made his way through a rocky area and suddenly came upon a boulder; all at once there emerged from this place a man with a devout and religious air. He called to Brendan to approach, for, thanks to God, his name was known to him; then he kissed him and told him to bring his companions along, leaving no one behind. Brendan went and fetched them and they secured the boat to the rock. The other man named them all individually:

'Come here and kiss me!' They did so and he led them to his dwelling, showing them the way; there, as he urged, they rested. They marvelled at him and his clothing. He was clad in nothing other than his hair, which covered him like a veil, and had the expression of an angel and a body redolent of Heaven. No snow could be whiter or clearer than this brother's hair. Brendan said to him:

'Dear, good father, tell me who you are.'

He replied:

'Willingly. My name is Paul the Hermit. Here I am free from all suffering and have been here for a very long time, having arrived at this place through the guidance of God. In my earlier life, I was a hermit living in the woods. That was the life I had chosen and I served God as best I could, in accordance with what little understanding I had. In his goodness he accepted this and rewarded me more abundantly than I merited. He commanded me to come to this place where I could await my heavenly reward. How did I get here? I went aboard a boat which I found all ready for me. God guided me swiftly and gently; when I arrived here the boat went back.[13] (1552)

'I have been here for ninety years; the climate is good and it is always summer. Here I await the Day of Judgement, as I have been commanded by God. I am here in flesh and bones; free from hardship, I have constant repose. Only at the Last Judgement will the spirit leave my body; I shall be reborn with the just because of the life I have led. For all of thirty years I had a servant who cared for me constantly, an otter which regularly, three days each week, brought me fish and fed me with it; never did a week go by when it did not bring me three fishes, each of which provided me with a complete meal. Round its neck hung a satchel packed full of dry seaweed, with which I could cook my fish. He who provided all this was a true Lord! For the first thirty years of my stay here, I was fed in that way; I was so well nourished by the fish that I had no need to drink anything. Our Lord did not trouble himself at all to supply such provisions, or anything else in addition. After thirty years, the otter did not return; this was not out of reluctance or because it despised me, but because God did not want my body alone to have any further provisions from elsewhere. He created for me here the spring which supplies everything I require; it seems to anyone who takes a drink from it that he has been fully satisfied. I have lived on water for sixty years and on fish for thirty; that makes ninety. I had already been on earth for fifty years and now my age is one hundred and forty. Brother Brendan, I have now told you how pleasant my life is. But you are on your way to Paradise; you have been searching for it for nearly seven years. You will first go back to the land of the good host, with whom you spent some time. He will lead you, and you will follow him to Paradise, the home of the pious; take with you some of this water and use it to ward off hunger and thirst. Get aboard your boat and do not delay! No one should fail to profit from a favourable wind.'

Then he gave them leave to go; thanking him for his kindness, Brendan accepted it. (1606)

Then the monks set off towards their host. The clouds were very dark and they sailed for a long time before getting there, even though they took a direct route. With great difficulty they arrived on the Thursday of the Last Supper; as before, they stayed there until they had to leave. On the Saturday they came upon the fish; as in past years they prepared a feast upon it, fully aware that the fish had now been their servant for seven years. They praised God for this; because of God's most certain power, they had sustained no loss there. The next day they set off again, sailing with such wind as they found and heading straight towards the Island of Birds, where they would stay for two months. They remained there with great joy, awaiting the guidance of the good host, who would accompany them on the voyage which was so fine and good. The host made all the necessary preparations, for he knew what a long journey it would be; he knew precisely what they would need and for this reason he equipped them as best he could. Then they set sail, the host along with them, and were never to return there. They set their course for the east, never once losing their way; having someone on board to act as their guide, they sailed with joy and pleasure. For forty days without interruption they maintained their course over the high seas and sailed along, seeing nothing other than the sea and the sky above them. But then, by the grace of the Divine King, they approached the fog which surrounded the Paradise over which Adam had held sway. (1646)

Huge clouds created such darkness that the sons of Adam were helpless; the thick fog blinded every person who approached, with the result that he completely lost his sight unless God gave him the vision required to penetrate the cloud. Then the host said:

'Do not delay; fill the sail with wind!'

As they approached, the cloud opened up the width of a street; they entered the fog and at its heart found a broad path. They put their trust in their host because of the cloud which surrounded them; amassed on both sides, it was vast and thick. For three days they travelled straight along this path, which opened up before them; on the fourth day they emerged from the fog and the pilgrims were full of joy. They came out of the fog and caught sight of Paradise. First of all, a wall appeared, rising up towards the clouds; there was no parapet or passage-way, battlement or tower. None of them knew for sure what material it was made from, but it was whiter than any snow and its maker was the Sovereign Lord. All of a piece and with no carvings on it, it had been constructed without the slightest effort. But the gems, with which the wall was covered, shone brightly. There were many exquisite chrysolites containing drops of gold; the wall was ablaze, burning brightly with topaz, chrysoprase, jacinth, chalcedony, emerald and sardonyx. Jasper together with amethysts shone brightly along the borders; the jacinth there was clear, with crystal and beryl. The light reflected from one to the other; he who had set them possessed great skill. They gave off a great light from their colours, which were so bright.[14] (1694)

The mountains, made of solid marble, were high where the sea beat against them, far from the wall. Above the mountain of marble was another mountain of pure gold; on top of that was the wall enclosing the flowers of Paradise. Such is that wall, set high above us, where our home ought to have been. They made their way straight towards the entrance, but it was very difficult to enter. Dragons, burning like fire, were there to guard it and right at the entrance hung a sword; anyone who did not fear it was not wise. Its point was turned down, its hilt upwards, so I am not surprised they were afraid. It dangled down and whirled around, making them dizzy just to watch it; no iron, rock or diamond was proof against its cutting edge. Then they saw a very handsome young man coming towards them, God's messenger, who told them to come ashore; this they did and he greeted them, naming them all by their rightful names and kissing them gently. He quietened the dragons, making them lie on the ground, very humbly and peaceably; he summoned an angel to hold the sword in check, so the entrance was clear and they entered into certain glory. (1728)

The young man moved forward, accompanying them through Paradise. They saw a very fertile land of beautiful woods and meadows; the meadows form a garden which is permanently in full bloom. The flowers there smell very sweet, as befits the home of the pious; it is a place of delightful flowers and trees, of superb fruit and aromas. There are no clumps of brambles, thistles or nettles, and no trees or herbs which do not exude sweetness. The flowers and trees bear fruit all year round, with no seasonal changes to delay them; there is permanently pleasant summer there with fruit on the trees and flowers always in bloom. The woods are always full of game and there is good fish in all the rivers; the rivers there run with milk, and such plenty is to be found everywhere. The reed beds exude honey through the dew which comes from Heaven, and there is a mountain there, made of gold; no treasure-house has a stone so massive.[15] There the sun shines brightly and unceasingly; there is no wind or gale to stir a single hair and no clouds coming from the sky to obscure the sun. Those who live there will experience no hardship, and harsh winds will be unknown, as will heat and cold, affliction and hunger, thirst and privation. There will be a plentiful supply of whatever one desires and everyone will be certain they will not lose what they want most; it will be there at all times and always ready. (1766)

Brendan saw all this joy and the time he had spent in contemplation of it seemed very short; he would like to have remained there a long time. The youth led him onwards a good distance, instructing him in many matters and explaining carefully and indicating to him what delights awaited each of them; with Brendan following him, the host advanced towards a mountain which was as high as a cypress tree. From there they could see visions for which they knew no explanation; they saw angels and heard how they rejoiced in their coming. They heard their great melody, but they could not endure this for long, since their nature could not take in or comprehend such great glory. The host said to them:

'Let us go back! I shall not take you any further; you cannot be permitted to go on, as you have insufficient knowledge. Brendan, you can see this Paradise, for which you frequently besought God; farther on, there is a hundred thousand times more glory than you have seen.

For the present, you will learn no more until you return. Where you have now come in the flesh, you will return in spirit. Now go; you will return and await the Day of Judgement here. Take some of these stones, as tokens of hope.' (1800)

Once the host had spoken these words, Brendan departed, bearing tokens of Paradise. Brendan took his leave of God; the beloved saints of Paradise and the young host guided them until they all went on board their boat. He made the sign of the cross over them and they quickly raised their sail. Their saintly host remained behind, for Paradise was his rightful realm. The monks went on their way joyfully with no wind to hold them back; in three months they were back in Ireland, thanks to God's great power. The news spread throughout the country that Brendan had returned from Paradise. It was not only the families which rejoiced; the joy was shared by all. Brendan's dear brethren in particular were delighted to have their good father back. He often told them of his journeying, where things went well and where there were difficulties; he told them how, whenever he had needed to ask God for something, it had been provided, and he related the whole story of how he had found what he had been looking for. Many of them embarked on a saintly life because of the power they saw in him. As long as he lived in this world, Brendan was of great assistance to many people, thanks to God's power; when his end finally came, he went back to the place destined for him by God. Through his efforts, more than a thousand people followed him to the kingdom of God. (1834)

3

The Dutch Version

Willem P. Gerritsen and Peter K. King[1]

Manuscripts, Editions and Translations The anonymous Middle Dutch poem *De reis van Sint BranDaan* ('Saint Brendan's Voyage') is known from two manuscripts, both dating from *c*.1400. The famous Van Hulthem manuscript, now in the Royal Library in Brussels, presumably originated in (or near) that city; it contains a variety of Middle Dutch texts, almost all of which are written in verse. *De reis van Sint Brandaan* is the first text in the manuscript; due to the loss of a leaf, the first 323 lines of the poem are missing. The other codex, the so-called Comburg manuscript, was probably written at Ghent; in the sixteenth century it was acquired by a German humanist, Erasmus Neustetter (1522-94), a former student at the University of Louvain, and taken by him to the Comburg, a foundation of secular canons near Schwäbisch Hall in south-western Germany. The manuscript remained there until after the Napoleonic era, when it was placed in what is now the Württembergische Landesbiblothek in Stuttgart.

The 'Comburg' and the 'Hulthem' texts of the poem (C and H) differ in many places. However, the variants seldom concern matters of content, as most of them represent the discarding of obsolete or uncommon words and expressions (the 'Comburg' text seems less affected by this modernising tendency). Both texts derive from a common Middle Dutch ancestor, which probably dated from the early thirteenth century and is supposed to have been for the most part a faithful translation of a German original, now lost. This German poem (O) is thought to have originated around 1150 in the Rhine region (Middle-Franconia); its contents, however, and to some extent its wording, can be reconstructed hypothetically from three versions deriving from it, independently of each other. The stemma contains

---

1. The Introduction and Notes to the Dutch version have been written by Willem P. Gerritsen. The translation is the work of Willem P. Gerritsen and Peter K. King.

three branches: (i) a hypothetical poem (C/H), represented by C and H, (ii) a hypothetical Middle High German poem (M/N), represented by a Middle High German poem (M) and a Middle Low German poem (N), (iii) a Middle High German prose version (P), preserved in four manuscripts and no less than twenty-two early editions, all printed between 1476 and 1521.

Versions C and H have been edited synoptically by E. Bonebakker (1894). More recently, H. Brinkman and J. Schenkel have published a diplomatic transcription of the Comburg manuscript (1997). A critical edition, based on C and H and also on the German versions, was published by M. Draak (1949), who attempted to reconstruct the original Middle Dutch text (C/H). Draak's edition also contains a Modern Dutch verse translation by the poet Bertus Aafjes. A recent critical edition by W.P. Gerritsen and S. Oppenhuis de Jong, based on C, includes a synoptic translation by the poet Willem Wilmink (1994).

The *Reis* Branch The Middle Dutch poem represented by C and H belongs to a corpus of German and Dutch texts usually referred to as the *Reis* ('Voyage') branch of the Brendan legend. This differs in many respects from the well-known *Navigatio sancti Brendani* and its derivatives. The principal difference involves the motivation of Brendan's voyage: in the *Reis* the saint's voyage is undertaken as a penance for his burning of a book containing descriptions of the marvels of God's Creation, to some of which he refused to give credence. An angel orders Brendan to build a boat and put to sea in order to discover for himself what is true and what false. His wanderings, which last no less than nine years, involve a series of fantastic adventures. He encounters sea monsters, meets monks and hermits living in great isolation, observes several infernal and heavenly places and visits the Earthly Paradise and the beautiful land of the Walserands (who turn out to be former angels punished by God for standing aloof from Lucifer's revolt). He also perceives the sounds of a human world below the surface of the sea. A dwarfish creature floating on a leaf and measuring the sea with a stylus and a cup teaches him that God's marvels are limitless. Belying his unbelief, many of Brendan's adventures demonstrate that everywhere in the world God's grace is manifest.

Content and Structure In the manuscripts the text of the poem is not divided into chapters or paragraphs. The following breakdown of episodes aims to guide the reader through the text. To facilitate comparison with other versions the order of episodes is based on O as reconstructed by Strijbosch (2000). Asterisks after the number indicate a scene which is lacking in C/H but present in P. Line numbers between square brackets indicate episodes which have been moved from their original position in the story.

(1) Prologue (1-20)
(2) The burning of the book and its consequences (21-78)
(3) The building of the ship (79-136).
(4) Brendan finds a giant's skull washed ashore (137-260)
(5) A sea-dragon is overcome by a flying stag (261-92)
(6) Landfall on the back of a fish (293-342)
(7) The ship is threatened by a horrible mermaid (343-67)
(8) Encounter with the ghosts of dishonest servants (368-420)
(9) The Liver Sea and the submerged magnet (421-45)
(10) Visit to a monastery situated on a rock (446-518)
(11) Meeting with a recluse, once King of Pamphilia and Cappadocia (519-624)
(12) Burning souls in the mouth of a volcano (625-99)
(13) The first Paradise castle; a monk steals a precious bridle (700-802)
(14) Visit to the second castle: the Earthly Paradise (803-62)
(15) The thieving monk is abducted by devils and returned (863-1008)
(16) ...
(17) The crew is put to sleep by a siren (1009-31)
(18) The devils' island (1032-1114)
(19) ...
(20) Brendan's vision of Heaven (1115-50)
(21) The ship is surrounded by shoals of fish (1151-2202)
(22) Encounter with a hermit floating on a clod of earth (1203-1304)
(23) Encounter with Judas (1305-1556)
(24) The burning birds (1557-96)
(25ᵃ) *Multum bona terra* (1597-1814)
(25ᵇ) Discussion with the Walserands (1815-2068)
(26) The ship is surrounded by a sea serpent [2111-2160]
(27) Contact with a human world below the sea surface [2161-2202]
(28ᵃ) ...
(28ᵇ) ...
(29) Encounter with a dwarf man floating on a leaf (2069-2110)
(30) ...
(31ᵃ) The book is full [2203-18]
(31ᵇ) The lost anchor [2179-2202]
(32) ...
(33) Homeward journey and Brendan's death (2219-62)
(34) Epilogue (2263-84)

Sources A thorough investigation of the sources of the *Reis* by Clara Strijbosch (1995, English version 2000) has provided new insights into the complicated genesis of the text. She argues that the lost German Brendan poem (O), which originated in the Rhine region around 1150, must have been a fairly drastic reworking of the *Navigatio*. Only a few episodes in the latter text are found in the Dutch and German texts representing O, and they have all been radically altered; some are almost unrecognisable. A greater number of episodes can be shown to be related to twelfth-century texts concerning the marvels of the East and the natural and supernatural aspects of Creation. On the other hand, Irish narrative materials – among them earlier versions of the *immrama* of *Máel Dúin* and *Ua Corra*, as well as of the *Vita Brendani* – have played a part in the genesis of the 'Voyage'. The twelfth-century poet of O must have been familiar with a collection of stories of Irish origin, which he used (and transformed) when adapting and modernising the traditional *Navigatio* story. The thirteenth-century Middle Dutch version, C/H, was in its turn an adaptation of O. The episode of the heathen giant (episode 4 in the above list), not found in the German texts, is probably an interpolation by the poet of C/H. On the other hand, some episodes whose presence in O is attested by the German versions must have been absent from C/H, either because of the hazards of textual transmission or by a process of deliberate adaptation. The account of Brendan's return journey in C/H suggests a reworking of the more elaborate narrative in O.

Author's Purpose Whereas in the *Navigatio* the narrative is continuously focused on Brendan's attempt to reach a Promised Land across the Ocean, the 'Voyage' story concentrates on amazing natural and supernatural phenomena and on various manifestations of the afterlife. The Brendan of the 'Voyage' is a saint, but a saint lacking in faith, a doubting Thomas. His lack of faith causes him to burn the book, as a result of which he is ordered to replace it by relating all the marvels he has witnessed during his voyage. This new motivation for the voyage enabled the poet to include a series of exciting adventures. The focus of the work has been altered: what is important in this version is the central lesson that God's omnipotence and his grace are beyond human comprehension.

Let me tell you the story of a man in Ireland who, many years ago, saw manifold signs from God. If you are willing to believe this, you will hear of some real marvels, my lords. May the Holy Spirit be my guide, who put words into the mouth of Balaam's she-ass (Balaam was a heathen) when it saw an angel barring its way with a flaming sword; it shied and warned its master.[1] May this same Spirit that gave the ass the power of speech also open my mouth now.[2] (20)

This man was certainly a saint, and his name was Brendan. He was abbot of an Irish monastery with some three thousand monks, and he served God faithfully. During his study of old books, he came across various signs of God's handiwork: that there were two paradises above the earth, that there were many marvels in the world and huge islands in the sea. He also read that there was another world under this one, where it is night during our daytime. He read that there were three heavens, and that fish existed with forests growing on their backs. This he dismissed as quite incredible. He also read that God took pity on Judas by granting him his mercy on the eve of every Sunday. That was just too much for Brendan, who would not believe it unless he saw it with his own eyes. He cursed the writer and threw the book angrily into the fire.[3] He was to pay dearly for this, for as he stood watching the book being consumed by the flames, one of God's angels came to him, saying:

'O Brendan, my friend, this is an evil thing you have done. All because of your anger the truth is being lost. All right, let the book burn; you will soon learn whether it was true or false. Jesus Christ commands you to sail the seas for nine years; then you will discover what is true and what is not.'

So Brendan was to do full penance for burning the book and to suffer great hardships for cursing it as he journeyed where God commanded him. (78)

Greatly troubled by God's message, Brendan, the holy man, prayed to Christ, for his Mother's sake, to protect his soul in whatever should transpire. Then he went straight to the coast and had a sturdy and trustworthy ship built. The mast was made of pinewood; the sail was carefully cut out and sewn to the leeches. The hull was firmly riveted, like the ark which Noah built in fear of the approaching flood. The anchor was made of steel, to ensure a good anchor-hold if he needed it. He had supplies taken on board for a crew of eighty, enough for nine years, and included a small chapel with its own bells and relics. He also took along from Ireland a hand-mill and a kneading trough, and even blacksmith's tools. Everything was then ready for departure. Brendan was to survive the journey without mishap, but one of the two chaplains he took with him got into serious trouble. He stole a valuable bridle; when the Devil discovered this, he dragged him off and the chaplain had the very hell to pay until Brendan's prayers succeeded in gaining his release. (136)

While they were in the process of embarking, Brendan found an enormous skull which had been washed up onto the beach by the tide.[4] The cranium, the like of which he had never seen, was all of five feet across. Brendan ordered it in God's name to tell him about its former life, and the head then spoke to him:

'Though it is not easy for me, I will tell you how my life once was. I was a pagan. I was tall, at least a hundred foot, and strong. And for my living I used to wade out into the sea and plunder ships sailing along this coast. One day a storm blew up, and although the water normally only came up to my chest I would have needed to be twice the height to avoid losing my footing. So I met my end by drowning – so indeed all things must come to an end, except in Hell where sinners are tormented for ever, and in Paradise where the blessed live in perpetual bliss.'

At this point Brendan interrupted him:

'If I could prevail upon God to restore your life, would you then be baptized and strive to do God's will? I could then absolve you of your sins and you could still go to Paradise.'

'Would I then have to die again?' the pagan asked.

'Yes indeed,' Brendan replied. 'You cannot avoid that.'

'But supposing I were baptized and yet still unable to resist the Devil's temptations – after all he is lying in wait day and night, ready to ensnare people – and I fell to stealing again, or if I should do things strictly forbidden by our Creator, I would end up in Hell once more. Then I should be punished much more severely than now. I know that the Bible says that those who sin after receiving baptism are tormented far worse in Hell than we who have not known God's laws.[5] It must be worse for those who abandon God's laws, when they ought to know better, than for me when I am not even baptized. What is more, I would have to go through the pain of dying all over again, when you feel all your movements failing and when you can no longer eat or drink, and when you lose your memory and your voice. When my arteries burst, my soul would go back again to Hell. No, even if the whole world were yours and made of solid gold, and even if you gave it all to me with two thousand years to enjoy it, I would still refuse, such is my fear of death. So I prefer to go back to my tortures in the darkness.'

'Go then, wherever God wills,' said Brendan.

So the pagan returned to the place where God had sent him, and Brendan returned to the ship as God had commanded him. (260)

They took their leave of friends and relatives, and after commending them to God's mercy they set sail. With their oars out and the sail set to the wind, they soon got under way. Oh, how beautifully the ship took to the water! But before long they ran into serious trouble, for a strange beast, like a sea serpent, threatened to swallow up the ship. But just as it opened its jaws (which were several fathoms wide), the clouds above opened and out came a remarkable beast like a winged stag. In no time it drove the serpent away, right out of sight, and then disappeared again into the clouds. When Brendan saw this, he thanked God for his deliverance. (292)

They sailed on for a time over a calm sea until Saint Brendan sighted a fair shore, which he reckoned to be six miles long or more. The island rested on the back of a fish. It is said in the book that this is where a river flows into the sea, and that the fish had fed for a long time on the food in that fresh water. The island was covered with wood and the brave crew of godly men brought their ship into a harbour and went ashore to inspect the beautiful island. They also went in search of wood to cook food, for they were very hungry. They hung up the cooking kettle and soon found a dry tree. But when they put the axe to it, the whole island plunged under water so that the holy man and his crew could scarcely regain their ship. They scrambled aboard, and sang God's praise that in his mercy he had rescued them from that peril. The island meanwhile had vanished completely. This was the third miracle they witnessed. Still alarmed and confused, they sailed away in a stiff breeze. The holy abbot said:

'It must have been a fish which submerged this island. It must have been very old indeed to have all that wood on its back.'

Praying God constantly that in his mercy he would soon bring them to dry land, they sailed on, only to encounter more wonders. (342)

This time it was a fearful monster, coming towards the ship as if to capsize it.

'There is no need to be afraid,' said Brendan; 'we have done nothing to harm it. Let our ship sail on in God's hands and he will protect us.'

The monster was half fish and half woman[6] with a hirsute body, and it kept circling the ship. Saint Brendan and his monks fell to their knees and prayed for deliverance, until God heard their prayer and the fearful monster dived down next to the ship; and all day long they heard it gurgling on the sea bed. (367)

After sailing on for many days, they came to an island where Brendan observed a strange kind of torment. There were souls in human guise walking on the sea,[7] suffering from heat and cold.

'Whatever kind of creatures are you,' Brendan called out, 'that can walk on the sea like that?'

'We are poor souls,' they answered, 'who have to do everlasting penance. If only we, in God's name, had given clean water to the poor, our lot would have been a better one. In our lives we were stewards and butlers, and our masters gave us food and drink to distribute to the poor. But we kept it for ourselves, and now God shows us no mercy. We suffer greatly from the cold and the heat and are tortured by thirst. Though the sea is always at hand, we can assure you truly that not in a hundred years can we drink one drop of it. Help us, Brendan; please help us.'

Then Brendan prayed for them without ceasing, so that in the end God granted them one drink of water and allowed them to moisten their heads. Then they all bowed down to Brendan, who turned away with tears in his eyes and wrote down a record of God's action. After that Saint Brendan ordered his good ship to sail away from there. The poor souls, who went on walking in torment upon the sea, wailed in lamentation. (420)

For a while they sailed on in calm waters, but suddenly they heard a blustery wind and a storm struck them, so that their ship was driven northwards towards the Liver Sea.[8] If they ended up there, none of them would come out alive. They came so close that

Brendan could see the wrecks of many ships and masts sticking up
out of the water, like a forest swaying to and fro. Once again God
rewarded Brendan's virtue. A voice from Heaven called to him:

'Set your course eastwards! Ahead of you there are rocks in the sea
which cause ships great distress. Whenever a ship with iron rivets
comes near to them, they attract it and hold it fast.' (445)

A wind rose, carrying them to the east, towards a cliff on which was
a magnificent monastery. In it were monks who had served God
diligently for many years. They anchored there that night under the
cliff, and Brendan climbed to the top where he found the
brotherhood at their sacred duties. He could not imagine how they
had got there, unless it were by God's power. Their life was pure
and simple, unlike the monks in our country! They all greeted him
on arrival:

'Welcome, Lord Brendan!'

There were seven of them and they received their daily food from
the Earthly Paradise. At noon a dove and a raven brought to their
table three and a half loaves and a fish, already cooked. They warmly
invited Brendan to join them at their meal, but he wisely said:

'God, the Lord of Paradise, would in his wisdom have provided
me with food if he had considered me worthy of it. I gladly accept
his will. He clearly did not mean me, wretch that I am, to share the
fourth loaf with you, since he broke it in half, so leaving me out.
Now you must all go and eat together in his name; believe me, I do
not mind going without. Every day God provides you with food on this
barren rock. To me he gives fish, fruit and bread; I have all I need from
him in my ship. Pray to God that my poor soul may come into his
kingdom.'

No sooner had he said this than the heavenly messenger brought
him his share. When they had eaten together (so the book tells us),
Brendan took his leave and returned to the ship. (518)

A south-westerly wind got up, driving them back in a north-easterly
direction upon a rough sea, which was very unpleasant. They came
to a rock, rising so high out of the sea that they could not see the
top of it. A man, as hairy as a bear, was sitting on top. He was quite
alone; a recluse with only the sky and the sea around him. Brendan
asked him how he had got there.

'I am subject to those monks you visited this week,' he said. 'I have been sitting alone on this rock for ninety-nine years, and all that time God has sent me my food every day. He is my only consolation, for since coming here I have had no change of diet, nor, until you came, have I seen another living soul.'

Then Brendan asked him what sort of life he had led before coming there, and the recluse replied:

'Truly, I was once a powerful king, and Pamphilia and Cappadocea were my kingdoms. There I married a beautiful woman, and it is for this reason I am now suffering grievously – for she was my sister. She bore me two sons who brought me great misery. The older one was a mere lad when I killed him in a fit of anger. The other was standing near a ship when he was struck down by lightning. On top of all, that I killed my wife. With all those sins heaped upon me, I was afraid of God's wrath and shortly afterwards left my lands, my friends and relatives, and took ship to go to the pope and confess my sins. But a fearful storm arose and my ship foundered; all my companions were drowned and I alone managed to escape to this high rock, where I lament for my sins to him who is my maker, hoping for mercy for my great misdeeds. And, indeed, every day I hear a heavenly chorus.'

Brendan then asked him:

'Tell me, good sir, how can you survive here without clothes when the winter comes? I have read about hermits who served God by denying themselves every comfort and eating nothing but herbs. Yet they sought the protection of woods or caves, or even of shrubs and reeds, to escape the cold.'

'If I can preserve my soul,' the recluse said, 'my bodily needs are quite unimportant while I am here. If the cold is too much for me, I crawl into a crack in the rock[9] and wait for the wind to drop. I believe it is God's will that the very bones of my body must wait for doomsday on this high rock. God be with you; I will say no more. May God, our good Lord, grant us all his heavenly kingdom hereafter.' (624)

Saint Brendan sailed on with his godly crew. The wind and the waves into which they had to sail soon exhausted them. And so they were driven by the wind to a distant, fearful land where, so the book tells us, they saw one of the mouths of Hell. Inside, countless poor souls were screaming with agony as they twisted and turned in the burning mountain. In the everlasting flames nothing could be heard but the tormented cries of 'woe is me' and the gnashing of teeth by the damned, hurled high into the clouds amidst the flames. Brendan called out to the officer in charge of this Hell:

'What is the meaning of that great clamour I hear inside?'

One of the executioners answered:

'Here are corrupt and unjust leaders and rulers, wayward women, dishonest stewards and false magistrates; false witnesses too, and traitors. They are all here, assembled in this great abyss. The foul mouths of all these people are punished here for the evil things they said; and this is their just reward, because it was their scheming that caused their masters to extort meagre gains from poor folk. That is why they have to burn here in this furnace. And there are other souls here who fell into sin, into pride and greed and all kinds of evil, or who harmed their fellow Christians. They are now held for ever in this place, because they persisted in their evil ways and would not do penance.'

'Brendan, good sir,' the poor souls cried, 'we are consumed by this fire. Pray for us, Brendan!'

The Devil ordered Brendan to go away.

'I tell you,' he said to the captives, 'he can do nothing for you. Your cries are quite futile. You had neither the desire nor the heart to do God's will. So there is no way you will ever receive mercy.' (699)

A vile stench enveloped them, so Brendan turned away and soon came to an island where they were again in trouble. They were plunged into pitch darkness and could see nothing, though light came from the sea-bed, which seemed to be made of gold. In the darkness of the depths God had set precious stones all around, including huge carbuncles. For three days and nights they lay there in trepidation, seeing no sun, moon, or stars, only everlasting darkness. Then Brendan ordered them to launch the dinghy; they clambered boldly into it and rowed to the island. (724)

After they had landed, Saint Brendan, we are told, left the boat; in high spirits they set foot on the beach. With Brendan they followed a river until they came to a castle, more beautiful than anything ever seen by Christian mortal. The walls were of pure gold, the

pillars of carbuncle shone more brightly than the sun. In front of
the castle there issued from a spring four gushing streams of
exquisite delicacies: balsam, syrup, olive oil and honey. It all
seemed quite amazing to them. Round the spring stood a ring of
beautiful trees: cedars, plane trees, pines and vines and many
others, with so many of the finest plants growing under them that
it would take me a year to describe all the glorious array in front of
the castle. Oh, how difficult it was for the monks to tear
themselves away from that place! They saw the roof of the castle
gleaming as if it were made of peacock feathers, and the whole
building was decked out as if an emperor were going to hold a
banquet there. (776)

The monks could not resist the temptation to go and see what was
inside. It was then that one of them stole a costly bridle, for which
he was severely punished. As he was looking at it, a devilish voice
told him to take it, but he did not realize why he was hearing that
voice. The Devil reminded him what an impression he would make
at home, riding with such a bridle. He touched it and saw how it
shone and glittered as it moved; he could not take his eyes off it.
He quickly took the bridle and hid it under his habit. For this he
would later pay dearly, when the Devil carried him off to Hell. (802)

After the monks had looked round, they all left the castle. Not far
from there, Brendan saw another castle, even more beautiful than
the one where the monk had stolen the bridle. The country for
miles around was bathed in light from the castle. There was no
night there, no frost or snow, nor were there cold winds or rain. A
venerable old man with long hair and a grey beard was sitting in
front of the heavy gates.[10] Young men were streaming in and out of
the gateway – according to the book from which my story comes,
they were angels. In the gateway itself a young man stood swinging
a flaming sword in a wide arc. That must be the angel called
Cherubin, who allows no one to pass who does not belong to the
throng of angels. Then Saint Michael appeared – may he eventually
lead us all to Heaven! Surrounded by other angels, he seized one of
the monks and dragged him through the gateway by his habit, his
arms and his hair. The angel with the flaming sword barred the way
to the other monks.
    'Come,' said Brendan, 'we must not wait here too long. We have

already experienced more harm than good here. God in his wisdom has reduced our numbers and, whether for good or ill, we must leave our brother here. These walls tower above us as far as the eye can see. I want to return to the ship before we lose anyone else.'
This was, according to my book, the Earthly Paradise. (862)

They went aboard again, wishing to sail away from that dark region, when one of the monks noticed that the sea-bed was all of gold. With great joy they jumped overboard and brought up handfuls of gold with which, when they returned home again, they endowed a great many churches. Suddenly they heard the noise of a raging gale, and a storm crashed round them with lightning flashes, as if the sky itself was falling upon them. Then a horde of devils came to claim the man who stole the bridle and carry him off to the abyss, where he would be tormented with his fellow sufferers. One of them grabbed the monk, tied him up with the bridle and announced the sentence for such theft. He dragged him away like a dog over rough ground into his master's presence. A great howl went up when the devils saw him in their midst – those who are guilty of the same crime may think that it will not be the same for them, but they are wrong. Unless they repent and do penance for their sins, they too will be tormented by the devils in Hell. (902)

Saint Brendan was sick at heart that he had lost one of his monks because of his sin. Choking back his tears, he said:
'If I had not had so little faith, God would not have added this disaster to all my other hardships. If he allows this to happen, my voyage will last a very long time. I will not go any further, O Lord, if you do not return my monk to me. I will stay here on my knees, praying to God, until he makes the Devil release my monk from his awful torment.'
As they called upon God, weeping bitterly, to hear their prayer for the sake of his mother, a bright light, shining from two blazing horns, appeared in the heavens, and a voice came from it:
'What are you now blaming me for, Brendan? I have done nothing; the Devil took him because he was a thief. Why are you angry with me? I have done you no wrong. You know that Adam was committed to Hell for five thousand years for stealing an apple – and such is the fate of your monk; he was sentenced as a thief and delivered into Hell.'

'Spare him his life, O Lord,' Saint Brendan prayed again. I will be his advocate and mediate for him.'
They threw themselves down with outstretched arms, beseeching God their Creator so insistently and with such weeping and wailing that Almighty God at last commanded the Devil to do Brendan's will and return the monk to his ship at sea. (957)

Without delay, the fiend of fiery Hell, furious that he had to carry the monk back to the ship, slung him roughly on his shoulder and gave him a rough ride for forgetting God when he stole the bridle from the castle. When he got to the ship, he bellowed angrily:

'Damn you, Brendan! This is all your doing! You do not let me keep what is rightly ours; that was a really dreadful trick you played on us.'
He had found the monk a heavy load as he staggered along on what seemed a very long journey, while the monk kept on singing the litany, all the time pressing down on his neck. At last he landed on the ship and dumped him roughly in the hull. He was so changed that they scarcely recognized him; his body and his beard were covered in pitch, his skin was scorched black and shrivelled up, and he was covered in wounds and bruises. The Devil screamed horribly and fled away from the good mariners. Brendan wept for joy, but he said to the bridle thief:

'If only you had left the bridle alone and been willing to ride with a normal halter, you would not now have such a burnt head, all covered in pitch. What is more, you have caused a serious delay in our voyage.'

'If only that bridle had never been made!' the blackened chaplain cried.
Then Brendan burst out laughing. (1008)

Having rescued his chaplain from Hell, Brendan continued his journey, sailing on mile after mile. Then one day Brendan heard the singing of a siren – a creature which puts to sleep anyone who hears it singing, and its joyful song means that rough weather is approaching. Then Brendan fell to his knees and prayed to God that he might escape the creature as quickly as possible. The helmsman fell asleep, followed by all the others, all of them quite unconscious. Meanwhile, the ship drifted aimlessly towards a burning mountain. (1031)

A tall, black man emerged from it and shouted to them as loudly as he could from his huge mouth, making them wake up with a start. He called to them to come closer so that he could give the helmsman further directions. So Brendan gave the order to sail nearer the mountain. But, as soon as they got within earshot, they realized that it was just a fiendish trick, for the Devil's messenger called out:

'If I had the chance, master Brendan – but God will not give it to me – I would make sure you had a rough ride ahead with that ship of yours. You would soon pay for having done us ill, I can tell you. But since God will not deny you anything, I cannot get the mastery of you. Your prayers are so effective that you get everything you want. If only you would desist from enjoying my suffering so much. You deprived me of the bridle thief who is sitting there behind you sweating with fear and dreadful memories.'

'True; that is his penance,' Brendan answered. 'He must be washed clean. I have a good mind to throw him overboard – then he will get really clean.'

The monk curled up with shame and, terrified, hid under one of the thwarts, dreading what was to come. The Devil chuckled aloud to see him so afraid. When he had stopped laughing, he asked Brendan to give him back the chaplain, saying he would give him a good scrubbing because he stank to high heaven. But the kind and gentle Brendan replied:

'You cannot have the chaplain, and you are wasting your time with your fine words. I am tired of listening to you.' (1087)

He then ordered the helmsman to head out to sea. But a host of fiends rose up out of the mountain, following him with huge burning torches and with arrows, ready for battle. They began furiously hurling them down at the crew. But God, the good Lord, intervened and shielded them from harm. Thicker than any hailstorm, the brands and arrows rained down all round the ship. The monks strained at the oars to escape the horde, and as they got away the devils continued their vain attack, until the monks realized that with God's help they were out of all danger. (1114)

They now sailed confidently on, and God granted Brendan the sight of hosts of angels carrying countless souls on high above the ship. The air was filled with their hymns praising God. Brendan was granted this because God wanted him to know where these spirits were destined for. He saw a heavenly temple with ten beautiful choirs. No man could ever destroy this, only God; no mortal could describe its glory. Sitting in his ship, Brendan descried the two beautiful paradises and then felt he had finally overcome all the perils of the deep; he could now start the journey home. So he prayed earnestly to the good Lord, who had so often saved him, that he would quickly bring him back to his own country. (1150)

Suddenly a storm blew up, carrying him and his crew far out to sea. The howling wind and lashing waves terrified them. What is more, they ran into a mass of fish near the surface. Deeper down, they saw fishes of all kinds, resembling cows and wild bulls.

'This must be the Liver Sea, about which I have read so many marvels,' said Brendan. 'But it is amazing to me how the sea bed here can provide enough food for them all. Yet God our Lord is powerful enough to provide even them with their daily food.'

He told one of his chaplains to fetch parchment and write down at once all these things as they truly were, and he ordered the helmsman to heave to, so that a faithful record could be made of the scene of the fish swimming there. The monks were very much afraid that the fish might sink the ship. But Brendan gave them all possible reassurance:

'Dear brothers, trust in God! For his sake we set sail. He will protect us; he has everything in his power, for he is almighty. And blessed Mary too – may she protect us from evil if this be her son's will. And may all the hosts of Heaven save us from this sea. Now say "Amen" all of you, and pray to our heavenly Father.' (1202)

The wind died down to a breeze and they saw ahead of them a human being. He was in great hardship, floating upon the sea on nothing more than a piece of turf. How could he survive the raging of the sea if God did not protect him? He tried to get away from the ship, but Brendan called out to him that he wanted to speak to him in God's name. As if in response, the patch of earth came to rest. When Brendan came up with him, he said to the man:

'Are you suffering like this for the sake of God, or are you facing the perils of the sea because of your own sin? If so, there is hope for you, for I am an ordained abbot vested with the stole granted by God, so that at all times I can absolve sinners and ease their burden. If you have done any such thing, I will receive you into God's grace.'

'In me,' the recluse answered, 'you would have a poor replacement for the chaplain you lost outside Paradise, Brendan. For ninety-nine years in this sea God has granted me food and all my sustenance. I want to live by his mercy and according to his commandments. There are others like me; God our Father is so bountiful that in his mercy he feeds us with bread from Heaven. He answered our prayers when your monk was returned to you, after being carried off by the Devil outside the magnificent hall where he stole the bridle. The men who are spending the rest of their lives on the cliff top, as well as the hairy man on the rock, also came to your aid, praying to God so that you got your chaplain back.'

'Then in God's name,' Brendan said, 'tell me more about these people – how they live and how they came to be there. They live such holy lives that they deserve to go to Heaven.' (1264)

The recluse answered very humbly:

'We were born in a town called Vaserijn,[11] in a country where God was unknown. Because of the grievous sins of the people, the town and all the country surrounding it was swallowed up in an abyss, and all the wicked people met a dreadful fate. But God saved some of our brothers on that high cliff. It is God's power that sustains them, just as it is God's power that brought me here. There are others like me, floating adrift on sods in the sea. It was because of my sins that I was parted from them and have to be alone now. When the country was flooded and many strongholds were drowned, as were the great cities of Sodom and Gomorrah, pieces of grassy turf were torn away. I will cling to this piece to my dying day. May God bring us all safely to Heaven. Now you must head northwards; you will see great marvels there.'

A sudden gust of wind parted them before they could take leave of the hermit; each of them went where God would lead them. (1304)

In a short time the ship covered a great distance. For days on end it was swept on and on by a hurricane. And all the while Brendan understood that in this way he was paying dearly for burning the book. He had to watch helplessly as the ship was carried along by the tempest for more than a thousand miles. If God had not guided them on their journey, they would not have survived it. (1319)

One day Brendan caught sight of a hirsute, naked man, sitting alone on a burning rock. He was in agony, for while one of his sides was frozen to the bone, the other was scorching by the rock; he was receiving the just reward for his deeds. He had a cloth flapping in front of him which kept off some of the heat. He suffered agonies from heat and cold at the same time. This was how he fared every Sunday – but he himself enjoyed it; it seemed a real holiday to him. Every Monday at first light, the Devil and his henchmen came to carry him back to Hell. When Brendan and his men were close enough to see how he was suffering, they were moved to pity. Brendan asked the poor man where he came from:

'I am poor Judas,' the sinner answered, 'paying now for my treachery. For selling to no good purpose him who created me and gave me life, I now have to endure this fearful punishment. Just when I might have shown remorse for this ghastly sin, the evil fiend came and cast me into despair and counselled me to hang myself, so denying myself penance. Such was my death, and so I must suffer this torment. If I had repented and prayed for mercy, I would have been saved, for so faithful is God; he would have received me just as he forgave the Jew who pierced him with a spear as he hung on the cross. He even forgave the murderer hanging next to him, because he repented. So, too, he would have forgiven me, if I had repented. But now there's no hope for me. (1377)

'At the moment all is well with me because of the grace allowed me in honour of Sunday, and if it were like this every day I should have no complaints, though it is not all that pleasant. But the day after tomorrow all this will be taken from me. Then I shall be in bottomless Hell, where I burn in endless torment, with the devils howling round me. O, sir, if only I were dead, if only I could die, then I would not go on suffering this endless torture. The heat and cold I must bear here I do not call suffering. But there is no light in Hell. There it is everlasting darkness and eternal pain; woe is the day that the man was born who must suffer there! The heat that is there – it would melt a whole mountain of steel thrown into it before you could blink. If only I could stay here, I would think I had been saved. I am much more afraid of the torments in the days ahead than of what I suffer now.' (1417)

Then Brendan asked:

'If anyone prayed for you, would God have pity on you?'

'Oh, no, it would be to no avail,' poor Judas answered. 'I can expect no mercy from God. I have lost all hope of help, except for this cloth hanging in front of me, which is a great help and comfort. It would help me even more if I had not stolen it from our Lord when I was with him – and yet it gives me protection from this fire. But I was so ashamed of what I had done that I gave it away to one of his poor followers; ever since then he has prayed to God for me. And although it does protect me from the fierce flames, it is still not the same as if it had been rightly mine. Yet because I gave it willingly, it helps me more now than any of the world's goods which might be given me. This shows how much good comes of what is done and given freely during one's lifetime. For prayers and penitential acts often come too late, and a person who, during his lifetime, does not give in God's name, cannot really be helped by what is done after his death. (1458)

As he finished speaking, Judas began to cry out. At daybreak on Monday, he felt the fearful torment approaching and screamed so loudly that the blood rushed from his eyes:

'Woe upon me,' he cried, 'wretched creature; would that I had never been born! There will never be any reprieve in the way I must go, for this is my just desert.'

Then Brendan ordered the relics to be brought up and placed on the gunwale, to warn off the devils which Judas's loud cries had led him to expect. And there they came, a great host of them, so that the air and sea seemed to be all fire and flame.

'We ought to be gone from here', the scorched chaplain cried in great anguish.

They flew over the ship, belching foul pitch and flames from their mouths, and sulphurous fire, seething and raging as it fell into the water, burning it up like straw. They intended to drag Judas off to Hell and torture him there. (1496)

But Brendan ordered the fiends to desist and to leave Judas alone. Meanwhile, he prayed God that Judas might be spared the hellish torment for one night longer. He prayed so long and fervently that God granted his desire. The devils set up a chorus of bellowing and braying since they had to return without him. But, as their mighty

ranks returned to Hell, they screamed threats that they would
torment him the more fiercely for not being able to take him away
at that time. Brendan, on his ship, was greatly distressed by these
threats. (1515)

The following morning, very early, the devils returned, bringing
sharp, red-hot hooks, which they promptly thrust into Judas. They
dragged him roughly away by his legs, stone and all. When they had
carried him off a little way, they shouted back, jeering at Brendan,
    'For this we will torture him much more than he has ever been
tortured before'.
    'On the contrary,' Saint Brendan shouted back at them, 'he will
not be tormented any more severely for spending the night here
with me; no matter how you rant at me. By God Almighty, I care
nothing for your threats.'
And with these words he commanded the rebels to do no more to
Judas than they had previously done. So they carried him off,
yelling loudly in his agony. Brendan ordered the crew to follow the
poor soul, but the devils were too swift for the ship. Then, in the
distance, they saw a huge column of smoke, which was where the
punishment was being carried out. (1556)

Saint Brendan continued his voyage, with God's blessing, to the
farthest end of the world, as far as a rocky coast. There they saw
what looked liked burning birds flying out of a fiery mountain,
uttering all kinds of pitiful cries. An unfathomable sea, thundering
against the west coast, could be heard miles away. Shortly after
this, they saw spurt from the mountain a flame so huge that the
sparks were as big as ovens and the coals like ships' masts. This was
clearly a place of torment and suffering. On one side of the
mountain flowed a stream of black, boiling water; on the other side
was a stream of wind and water colder than anything in existence.
This made progress very difficult; on one side was merciless heat,
and on the other such cold that the bark was splitting from the
trees. So Brendan ordered the whole crew, monks and seamen
alike, to man the oars, which they did at once; they did not dally
there. But it took them almost two years to travel back as far as
they had travelled in one day in the other direction. (1596)

When the ship with its weary crew finally got away from that inferno, they came upon one of the most beautiful places in existence. They could scarcely believe their eyes. In its fields, corn, vines and every fruit imaginable were growing – without any cultivation. There was every sign of prosperity: fish in plenty in its waters, the meat of every animal, wild and tame, that the heart could wish. There were no harmful animals there. This ever-verdant land is Multum Bona Terra and it lies far beyond human ken. If the waves had not carried the ship there at that time, we should never have known about it. As soon as Saint Brendan and his crew landed amidst so much sweetness, they felt their fatigue and suffering falling from them. As they started exploring this beautiful country, they saw a vast mountain rising up out of sight. Clouds hung over it; no living creature could reach it, except by flying; the sea came up to its foot. This mountain, the finest they had ever seen, was called Mount Sion. In some trepidation they started climbing a steep path, and as they climbed they caught sight of an unbelievably magnificent castle rising from the slope. The gates were guarded by fearful dragons and snakes, continuously pouring out fire from their gaping mouths. But in the name of God Saint Brendan commanded them to allow him and his company to enter immediately. (1654)

The book says that the walls were of crystal, set with brilliant stones,[12] and with a great circle of various animals skilfully cast in copper and bronze, some running, others crawling. Anyone seeing these for the first time might well take to his heels, since they were all moving as if they were alive. Every conceivable beast was represented there: lions, panthers, unicorns, leopards, elephants, stags and hinds, as well as all kinds of horrible snakes. In the middle of the castle ran a fast-flowing river whose powerful waters drove the beasts round unceasingly in a circular motion. The visitors clearly saw the figures jumping up, calling out and chanting from time to time, as if they wanted to leave the wall and escape. Among them were a number of curious monsters, partly hairy and partly smooth, such as had never before been seen. Every creature which had ever existed was portrayed there, from the mighty lion to the fish in the river. Here there were stags and does being chased by greyhounds, wild boars being hunted in woods and cornfields by huntsmen blowing their horns. And there were many more amazing things, too many to recount. In the walls horses with magnificent saddle-cloths cantered round, while others were held by knights. Flags fluttered, while a large crowd of women looked on, and watchmen blew their horns. If you did not know better, you would think they were alive. (1721)

I can truly tell you of many more wonders in this splendid castle. The pinnacles, outside and in, glittered like the rising morning star. There were six thousand towers along the walls, and they and all the rooms, both large and small, glittered like firelight. Nothing was lacking there, save whatever smacked of discomfort and poverty. There were costly couches with silk fly-nets draped above them. The floor was of snow-white glass, with gold inlaid figures gleaming in it. (1743)

So much for the richness of the hall. The courtyard stood in the shade of magnificent cedars and numerous other trees which kept off the rain. There was a lawn under the trees which was always green and lush. There were golden bowls hanging everywhere, finer than the most priceless treasures in normal dwellings. The perpetual singing of the birds in the trees could be heard throughout the castle. There was an even more beautiful palace, decorated with gold and precious stones set in ivory, with a floor of saphire and glass. I do not believe there ever was or will be anything more beautiful in the whole world. The whole building was cast in bronze; never was anything more beautifully built and stronger than the castle which Brendan saw that day. The monks feasted their eyes on all there was to see; there were beautiful fountains there, and mills singing as if they had tongues, so that the mountains and valleys afar off echoed with their sounds. The book also tells us of fish darting in the streams and all kinds of other delights for the enjoyment of the occupants. This has been recorded for us by Saint Brendan. (1792)

'We ought to get away from here,' said the scorched chaplain, 'before we have trouble. If you ask me, there must be a master of all these marvels you see here. And if they should see us, we shall not be able to escape. Maybe they will treat us so harshly that we shall regret the day we ever came here, even the day we were born. All this is the work of strange creatures that are not concerned with God. They have such strange customs that they might do us all

sorts of harm, as those others did when they caused us such troubles at the burning mountain.'
The helmsman too appealed to Brendan and the monks to return to the ship. (1814)

When they had embarked and set off again, they were pursued by a host of strange creatures – in the book they are called Walserands.[13] They were furious that Brendan's party had escaped them. They were quite extraordinary: they had boars' heads and teeth like wolves, human hands but dogs' legs, human bodies, but long necks like cranes. They wore silk clothing above their shaggy legs. They were all screaming at once and holding in their hands drawn bows with sharp arrows in them. They had long beards and growled like bears. They were clearly furious that Brendan had managed to leave their castle. (1838)

Then Brendan gave the order:
   'Let the ship slow down, but remain in the current so that these fearful monsters cannot shoot us. I wish to find out what they want and whether they believe in God.'
He went and stood in the prow and adjured them by God in his might, and by all that he had created or brought into life in Heaven and in earth, that they should let him approach in peace; he wanted to speak to them. Quietly they laid down their bows and all fell silent. Saint Brendan addressed them, saying:
   'Do you know who God is? Answer please!'
Then one of them said:
   'Brendan, you have seen many marvels on your journeys to many lands. Now God, whom you have just said you love more than we do, sent you here. But, however well you may know him, note that we know him better than you do. We all saw him sitting on his throne even before Lucifer's fall.' (1870)

'I must contradict you there,' Brendan interrupted, 'though I should not. A wise man has written that even the angels do not dare claim that they have seen God face to face. You are trying to fool me. I tell you straight, you cannot deceive me with such tales. What you say is quite untrue; it is all lies. What on earth are you dreaming of? No eyes have ever seen him, so marvellously bright is he. You are completely deceived. How could those piggy eyes of yours ever come where they could see God on high, whom the angels themselves cannot see face to face? Where exactly did you see him then? When he was the Son here on earth; he was also crowned in Heaven. Here he was Son and there Father. But there he was Father, Son and Holy Spirit, all three, and the one supreme Lord. You seem to me remarkably stupid. God's power is everywhere, in Heaven and in the depths. Yes, even in Hell if one should seek him there – and you mean to say that you have seen God?' (1908)

The strange creature spoke again:
'Brendan, you will not believe what you do not understand, but you shall regret that and suffer for it. You stupidly burned the book containing the truth. How much suffering that has caused you! Now you have seen with your own eyes things you refused to believe before. Happy are they, and wise, who believe God's word, and yet have not seen him. And does not Saint John record how Thomas, that saintly man, lost his faith? Although God had foretold it, when the news of Christ's resurrection came, he would not believe it, unless he saw with his own eyes that Christ had risen. He had to touch him with his own hands and feel his wounds. Then Christ appeared to him and said: "Thomas, I will manifest it to you; see here my wounds. Will you now acknowledge that I am arisen, since you have seen me and touched my wounds?" Then doubting Thomas said: "Now, Lord, I believe that you have risen." "You are more blessed, now that you believe", said Christ. "Those who believe shall be richly rewarded. But more blessed are they who have not seen and yet believe." Just think, Brendan, how Christ loves those who believe.' (1948)

The swine's mouth continued speaking:
'Brendan, let me explain. We were angels, consisting of such radiant light that we could look upon God; I assure you that this is true. Then it happened that Lucifer was planning to gain by force a higher place in Heaven than he had, but we took no notice. Yet, when Lucifer fell, we all had to fall too. Then God spoke to us Walserands, saying that we had behaved like swine. For swine with their evil nature do not strive after good, lying as they do in the mire or other muck, and feeling as much at home there as in a clean place. Because, in fact, we made swines of ourselves, God has sentenced us Walserands to take on the appearance of swine.' (1974)

He continued:

'Half of us is shaggy, like a dog; we could hardly be more extraordinary. We deserved that because in Heaven we behaved like dogs. A dog, after all, never attacks someone it knows, who calls the animal by its name. However fond it is of its master, it will not attack anyone threatening him, but will stand quietly by. And because we did him no harm and took no part in the rebellion, God gave us this country as a reward. That is why we are so fortunate; we are spared Hell and will not be tormented by Lucifer's evil fellows, who torture souls. Our hope is in God in Heaven.' (1996)

Then Brendan said:

'We have been into your castle. The splendour and riches we saw there made a huge impression on us. Whoever assembled all that magnificence must have remarkable talent. Under God's guidance we left the castle without taking anything from it. As far as I know, we have done nothing to be ashamed of, or for which we should be punished. If anything has been taken, I should be very sorry. But God knows that we have not taken anything. After all, if God had not brought us here under his protection and bound the dragons, they would certainly have devoured us as we entered the gates. But now I would like to know where you were while we were in the castle.' (2020)

'We were abroad', the Walserand answered. 'We went off with sixty legions through the forest to invade the country of the dragons. We ran into real difficulties there and were very nearly taken prisoner. They had in the past often pestered us by stealing our corn, and that is why we went over there to take the battle into their own territory. We had a mighty army, but they put as many in the field against us and sealed off all the escape routes. Never since the time God ordained that they should for ever belong to the Devil and face endless despair had they been so enraged and vicious. But we will say no more about that, unless you would like to come back with us to the palace where we will receive you honourably?'

'No, I think not', said the holy Brendan. 'We must be on our way. May God go with us, and protect you too.'

When Brendan wanted to depart – according to the book this happened on the eleventh day – he got into difficulties. The strange creatures shouted out to him in their own language, offering him treasures and food, but he refused everything.

'We do not need your food and we should not take anything from you.'
He then set full sail, heading out to sea and leaving the Walserand coast behind him. (2068)

The book tells us about a little man whom Brendan saw, scarcely an inch tall and floating on a leaf. He had a cup in his left hand and a small stylus in his right; he had the sad task of dipping the stylus into the sea and letting the water drip off it into the cup. When the cup was full, he emptied it into the sea and started filling it again. When Brendan asked him why he was doing that, he answered:

'I am measuring the sea. It is my destiny to go on doing this, to see if I can finish measuring the sea before doomsday.'

'But that is impossible!' Brendan cried.

'Just as it is impossible for me to finish measuring the sea before doomsday,' the little man on the leaf answered, 'so it is impossible for you to be able to see all the wonders of God's creation in the sea and on the land, much of which is still unknown to you. Your spiritual children, the monks you left at home in your monastery, need your encouragement. They are praying to God, who has so often saved you, that he may protect you. God's angel may guard you. I must not dally any longer.' (2110)

One morning, eleven days later, they ran into fearful difficulties; never had they known such fear. An enormous sea monster came swimming towards them with its jaws, fathoms wide, open as if it was going to swallow their ship. To their horror it swam for three whole days ahead of the ship. Then, if the book is to be believed, it curled round in a huge circle and swallowed as much as it could of its own tail; it completely encircled the ship. For fourteen days they were carried along in this ring, and whenever the monster moved, the ship was thrust high up into the clouds or cast down into a bottomless abyss. This went on hour after hour, and in the end they took to the dinghy, intending to try to row to land. But the monster was so terrifying that the helmsman broke down in tears. To comfort him Brendan said:

'Men, do not lose heart. You know that God has already delivered us in wonderful ways. This monster will go away and then the sea will calm down and all will be well.'

Suddenly the weather became beautiful; they were completely becalmed, and without any wind the ship did not move at all. For four hours the ship lay there, scorched by the blazing sun. At last a sudden gust of wind thrust the ship on its way. The fish dissappeared into the depths. Once more God had delivered them. (2160)

After a short time they came to a place where the water seemed to be of such a thin substance that they could clearly hear sounds coming up from the depths. They heard bells ringing, priests singing, horses neighing, birds singing and dogs barking. There was the sound of trumpets and the cheerful noise of men and women singing and dancing. What struck the crew most was that the noise seemed to come from close by, and yet they could see nothing. By common consent they decided to measure the depth by dropping a rope weighted with a stone. The heavy stones soon reached the bottom and then they dropped anchor. They soon regretted this, though, for the anchor was immediately trapped and held on the sea-bed. For hours they were held fast, wondering who could be holding the anchor down there.

'I do not know what we should do now', said the helmsman. 'If I cut the rope, we will have no means of anchoring. Help us, O Lord, and deliver us, for your mother's sake. In this way we will never bring our voyage to an end.'

So they lowered the sail. (2202)

After some time Brendan asked Noah, one of his chaplains, whether they had seen any wonders which he had not recorded in the book.

'Father abbot,' replied Noah, 'I stopped doing that long ago. Thank God; the book is full.'

'Then it is my wish,' said Brendan, 'that we offer the book as quickly as possible to the Virgin Mary. So now we will set sail for home. With God's consent, our pilgrimage will soon be ended.' (2218)

At these words, they hoisted the sail to the mast top and hauled on the sheets. They confidently cut the anchor rope and headed for their own country, arriving there quickly and safely. Saint Brendan took the book and carried it in solemn procession with all the

monks to the beautiful monastery. The monks, clerics and lay
brothers according to God's disposition, came to meet them and
prepared a great homecoming for the returning brethren. Brendan
devoutly laid the book containing all the wonders on the altar.
(2238)

Then an angel appeared, bearing a message from God.

'Welcome, Brendan,' said the angel. 'Your journey is accomplished. Remain here on earth as long as you will. When you no longer
wish to stay here, then come to Heaven where your throne stands
ready.'

Gladly Brendan then prepared himself for death. Once more he
sang mass, and when he had finished singing it was time for him to
take leave of life. God did him the great honour of sending Saint
Michael the angel himself to fetch his soul. Brendan's body was laid
to rest with great solemnity, and over his grave a church was built
with nine magnificent altars. These represent the nine years
mentioned in the book, which he had spent wandering abroad
wherever God had sent him. (2262)

Now I pray and advise everybody not to despise Brendan's
adventures, which often caused him to suffer severely. Nobody
should believe that they were nothing but lies. For the record of his
vicissitudes, described in Latin, can be consulted in many
monasteries and in other religious places, where it is kept in high
esteem, because God showed Brendan many of his hidden marvels.
The *Spiegel Historiael* testifies to this, too.[14] Pray now to Saint
Brendan, God's faithful servant. Ask him to pray for us all now and
in the future. This he will not fail to do, for he is in the Heavenly
Paradise where Christ our Lord will hear him for his dear mother's
sake. Amen. Amen. (2284)

4

The German Version

Willem P. Gerritsen and Clara Strijbosch

Manuscripts, Editions and Translations Like the Middle Dutch poem, the Middle High German prose version ultimately derives from the lost Brendan poem (O), which is assumed to have originated in the Rhine region around the middle of the twelfth century (see the Introduction to the Dutch version). This anonymous prose version (P), which probably dates from the late fourteenth or early fifteenth century, is known from four fifteenth-century manuscripts, written in upper German (Swabian) dialects, as well as from a long series of early printed books, beginning *c.*1476 (Augsburg: Anton Sorg) and ending in 1521 (Augsburg: Hans Froschauer). Three of the four manuscipts have been known for a long time; the fourth has only recently attracted attention. The Brendan text in the Gotha manuscript (g), dating from the first half of the fifteenth century, is assumed to constitute a reliable version of the original prose text; the Munich and Heidelberg manuscripts (m and h), dating from the third quarter of the fifteenth century and *c.*1460 respectively, represent a somewhat later stage in the textual tradition; both are illustrated with pen drawings. The recently discovered Berlin manuscript (b), copied by Casper Rembolt at the end of the fifteenth century or the beginning of the sixteenth century, is closely related to the version in MS h.

Although the author/editor of P seems to have modernized his original in many ways, this late medieval German prose version provides invaluable evidence of the contents of the twelfth-century poem (O). A critical edition of the German prose text, based on a number of early printed books, was published by C. Schröder in 1871. The Brendan text in the Heidelberg manuscript (h) was edited and translated into Modern German by G.E. Sollbach in 1987, and a microfiche edition in colour was published in 1993 by U. Bodemann and K.A. Zaenker. The Brendan text in the Gotha manuscript (g) was edited by M.-L. Rotsaert (1996). The

Berlin manuscript (b) was recently edited by R. Hahn (1998), but there has as yet been no edition of the Munich manuscript (m).

The present translation is based on the Gotha manuscript (Gotha, Forschungs- und Landesbibliothek, Chart. A 13), edited by Rotsaert (1996). Problematic passages have been checked against photographs of the manuscript. Words or passages in italic, missing or incomprehensible in MS g, have been supplied from MS h. Episode numbers referring to episodes listed below are given in the margin at the beginning of each episode. Readings of other manuscripts, in so far as they assist the interpretation of the text, are given in the Notes.

Content and Structure   In manuscript g the text of the poem is not divided into chapters or paragraphs. The following breakdown of episodes may guide the reader through the text. To facilitate comparison with the Dutch and other versions, the order of the episodes is based on that of O as reconstructed by Strijbosch (2000). Asterisks after the number indicate a scene which is lacking in P (manuscript g) but is present in the Middle Dutch C/H.

(1)   * * *
(2)   The burning of the book and its consequences
(3)   The building of the ship. Departure
(4)   * * *
(5)   A sea dragon is defeated by a flying stag
(6)   Landing on the back of a fish
(7)   The ship is threatened by a horrible mermaid
(8)   Encounter with the ghosts of dishonest servants
(9)   The Liver Sea and the submerged magnet
(10)   Visit to a monastery situated on a rock
(11)   Encounter with a recluse, a former king
(12)   * * *
(13)   The first Paradise castle; a monk steals a precious bridle
(14)   Visit to the second castle: the Earthly Paradise
(15)   The thievish monk abducted and returned
(16)   The Liver Sea again
(17)   The crew is put to sleep by a siren
(18)   The devils' island
(19)   Brendan loses his cowl and retrieves it
(20)   * * *
(21)   * * *
(22)   Encounter with a hermit floating on a small clod of earth
(23)   Encounter with Judas
(24)   The burning birds

(25^a)   *Multum bona terra*
(25^b)   Discussion with the Walserands
 (26)   The ship is surrounded by a sea serpent
 (27)   Contact with a human world below the surface of the sea
(28^a)   The dwarf Bettewart and the hermit
(28^b)   * * *
 (29)   * * *
 (30)   Heilteran (in MS g after 31a/b)
(31^a)   Brendan records the marvels he has seen
(31^b)   The anchor is cut away. Bettewart tows the ship
 (32)   * * *
 (33)   Homeward journey and Brendan's death
 (34)   Epilogue

Sources and Author's Purpose For information on the sources of O and the purpose of the work, see the Introduction to the Dutch version above.

1   Long ago, there was a most holy abbot named Saint Brendan.[1] He
was a native of Ireland and abbot of a famous monastery. Once upon a
time he came across a book in which he found descriptions of great
marvels which God had created in Heaven, on earth and at sea. He
also read therein that there were three heavens, two paradises, nine
purgatories and many uncultivated lands; and that there was a world
beneath us, under the earth, and whenever it was night with us, it was
daytime for them. He also read that there were great marvels in the
sea, and in particular that there were fishes there grown so old and so
large that great woods and tall trees had sprung up on their backs. He
also read that, by God's compassion, Judas enjoyed some relief from
his hellish pain every Saturday.[2]

2   Unable to believe these things, he burned the book in which they
were written. As he was standing beside the fire in which the book
was burning, an angel came down from Heaven and said:
    'My lord Brendan, why have you burned the truth? Do you not
believe God able to work greater marvels than those you have read
about in this book? I therefore order you on behalf of the living God to
prepare yourself to put to sea, in order to experience for yourself the
marvels you read about, and others as well. You must remain at sea for
five[3] whole years, sailing from marvel to marvel. This is God's will, in
order that you may acknowledge that you have burned the truth.'
Saint Brendan was shocked, for he feared our Lord's wrath; yet he had
to be obedient. The angel ascended to Heaven and Saint Brendan
prayed our Lord to be taken under his protection; then he would
gladly carry out his commandment.

3   He ordered a large ship to be built and had it strengthened with broad
iron strips. It was built in the fashion of *Noah's ark*. He gave order for
sufficient food and clothing to be carried aboard, as well as everything
that would be needed in the way of provisions, and whatever he and
twelve of his brethren and all their crew would need for nine years at
sea. He had a chapel constructed in the ship, consecrated it and
provided it with many relics. He selected twelve of the holiest monks
he could find in Ireland, who willingly accompanied him and happily
obeyed him. All of them finally came home with him, except for one
who was dragged off to Paradise. The devil also took one from them,
whom they regained by prayer, as you will hear later.

Now you will hear what great marvels they witnessed. When the ship had been fully fitted out, they took leave of their friends and went aboard in God's name. In great anxiety, they put out to sea, hoisted the sail and sailed for well over six-and-a-half months without discovering any great marvel.

5 One morning, shortly afterwards, they saw a serpent coming towards them. It emerged from a mountain in the sea, opened its jaws and threatened to devour them. Startled, they urgently invoked our Lord, and God came to their aid. The clouds above opened and out of them came a beautiful animal, shaped like a stag and flaming like fire. It swooped down and dragged the serpent, screaming horribly, up into the air. Thus God rescued them from the first peril.

6 After that, the ship approached a forest, which was green and pleasant; there they moored their ship, walked into the forest and gathered dry sticks for a fire. One *of them* came upon a dry tree and wanted to cut it down. As soon as he cut into the wood,[4] the forest filled with water and they sank swiftly. Just in time, they got into the ship, after which the forest submerged completely.

'This was one of the fishes I read about in the book I burned', said Saint Brendan. 'They are so old and so large that forests grow on their skins; I have now discovered the truth about this.'

When the *forest* submerged and the fish thus went under water, the waves of the sea would have drowned them if God had not protected them.

'Ah!' said Saint Brendan, 'how many years old this fish *must be* for this large forest to have grown on its back.' Then they prayed our Lord that he might help them reach land.

7 When they had left this marvel behind them, they immediately got into difficulty once more. They saw a horrible sea monster coming towards them through the waves; its forepart was like that of a man, its back like that of a fish. It threatened to seize hold of the ship and overturn it.

'Keep going!' urged Saint Brendan, 'Do not give way to fear; God will protect us. Let it go ahead; it cannot harm us.'

The animal had a hairy body and a horrible face. It circled the ship for a long time, clearly wanting to drag them down. Saint Brendan fell to his knees and prayed God to protect them. Then the sea monster left them and submerged near the ship. All day long they heard it *roaring*[5] and raging at the bottom of the sea. Saint Brendan realized that here was one of the nine purgatories.

8   Then the waves of the boiling sea cast them ashore *on another island*. They came to a place where they saw a lake, around which souls in human shape were walking. Saint Brendan asked them what they were doing there.

'Alas, Brendan', one of the souls replied, 'we find ourselves in great pain. In this way we shall suffer terrible heat until Doomsday, since we have shown so little mercy to the poor. We are suffering the utmost pain from *thirst* and heat. However close the lake is to us, we are not allowed to enjoy refreshing ourselves. Oh, dear Lord Brendan, pray God that he may save us from this bitter torture for the sake of his holy martyrs.'

Saint Brendan prayed our Lord to allow the poor souls to refresh themselves a little. God granted them this and allowed every one of the souls to have a good drink from the lake and to splash some water on his head with his hand. The souls bowed down gratefully to Saint Brendan and thanked him with all their heart for having obtained God's mercy for them and the chance to drink. Thereupon Saint Brendan left, and when he sailed away the poor souls screamed so miserably and loudly that he felt such pity that his eyes overflowed with tears.

9   When Saint Brendan had left the souls, a terrible thunderstorm with high winds struck them and drove them far into the Liver Sea, so that they would have remained stuck in it if God had not helped them.[6] They saw in the Liver Sea many ships which were stuck there, their masts rising high above the surface; there were so many of them that it looked like a forest of tree trunks. Saint Brendan prayed to our Lord to indicate what was the best thing to do. Thereupon, a voice speaking to him on God's behalf was heard, saying:

'Brendan, sail on without fear; God is with you. Go to your right *because if you go left, you will be lost, for there is a stone which attracts all the iron which comes close to it, which has destroyed many a ship with people and goods.*'[7]

10   Then Saint Brendan turned with his ship to his right and *sailed* towards a cliff, on which stood a beautiful monastery. Having given the order to moor the ship, he climbed the mountain alone until he

reached the monastery. Seven very holy monks lived there, worshipping God constantly day and night. When Saint Brendan came to them and saw their holy Christian life, he was filled with joy and stayed with them overnight. At noon, God sent them their food by means of a raven which brought them three and a half loaves of bread and a fried fish. God did this every day and they lived on no other food than that which came to them from Heaven. They invited Saint Brendan to eat with them, but he said:

'If God wanted me to eat this food, or if I was worthy of it, he would have sent me my share as well, because he knows I am here. If I had deserved in God's eyes to eat his food, he would not have sent you only half a loaf, but would have left it whole; that would have been my share. Because he did not send more than a half loaf for every one of you, you must eat your food alone. Praise God for the grace he shows you. God well knows that I have enough food in my ship.'

But God did not want to let him down, and he sent food from Paradise for him as well. When they had eaten, Brendan commended himself to their prayers; having taken his leave, he left them and returned to the ship.

11   When Brendan had returned to the ship and they had pushed off from the shore, a westerly wind drove them to a coast in the east. Then Saint Brendan saw a white rock, floating far away in the sea. Alone on top of it sat a holy man, as hairy as a bear. Saint Brendan asked him how he had got there, and the good man said:

'I belong to the brethren whom you visited last night, and I have been sitting on this stone for ninety-nine years. God made my hair grow to serve as clothing. And since the day I first sat here I have never seen any human being except you and never partaken of any solid food.'

'How do you protect yourself against the weather?' asked Saint Brendan.

'I do not care much about the state of my body', the holy brother replied, 'as long as I can save my soul. But there is a hole in this rock; when the weather turns bad, I crawl into it until it is over.'

'Since you belong to the brethren whom I visited last night', said Saint Brendan, 'why are you not with them? They live a holy life, since God feeds them with bread from Heaven.'

The good man replied:

'My penance here still seems to me to be too easy. I will die on this rock and here my bones will wait for Doomsday.'

And then the good man said to Saint Brendan:

'May God take care of you. I will not be saying anything more to you.'

13   Saint Brendan sailed on with his brethren until they reached an island, where it was so dark that they could see neither sky nor anything else. The sea bottom was made of pure gold and the shingle of nothing but precious stones: carbuncles, sapphires, diamonds and many other gems. The stones were dark from the spume the sea had swept there. There they remained for fifteen days without light and in great unease. Unable to escape from there, they *left* the ship. They did not know where to go until they came to a reed-bordered stream and followed its course until they reached the most beautiful hall any human being had ever set eyes on. The walls were of gold, the columns of gold and carbuncle and the roof consisted of nothing but peacock feathers. The hall was permanently illuminated: within it carbuncles and gold shone like the sun. In front of the hall rose a spring which divided into four streams. One stream contained wine, another milk, the third oil and the fourth honey. The sight of it filled the brethren with joy. From this spring all *herbs* and roots had received their power. Moreover, there were *five hundred* chairs[8] in the hall, which were beautifully covered with precious cloth and silk. Whatever one could wish for was there in that hall. Now among them was a monk who, out of sheer madness which possessed him, took a precious horse-bridle from the hall. His delight in the hall made him act without knowing what he did – he came to regret it, as you will hear.[9]

14   Going further, they saw a fair castle, which was even more beautiful than the hall they had entered before. The castle wall shone so splendidly with gold and precious stones that it would have illuminated a whole country. In the castle neither rain nor snow fell, nor were there any thunderstorms; it was always bright and beautiful. In front of one of the gates of the palace sat an old white-haired man called Enoch. And at the second gate sat another old man called Elia. But in front of the third gate stood a beautiful young man, wearing a red hood and holding a flaming sword in his hand. This young man leapt among Saint Brendan's monks and grabbed one of them who

was a very holy monk. He dragged him inside through the gate and closed it. When Saint Brendan *and the other monks* saw this, they were all shocked. They left, grief-stricken that their companion had been taken from them. The walls of the castle were so high that they would not have been able to see the pinnacles, and it was so bright that no one could describe it fully. Then Saint Brendan understood that it was a Paradise. Leaving this Paradise, they arrived once more at the dark place where they had left the ship. Then one of the monks noticed that the sea bed consisted of pure gold and the shingle of pure gems. They were delighted and gathered so much of the gold and the precious stones that they could build many a beautiful church and monastery with them. When they had gathered both carbuncles and other precious stones from the sea wrack, the silt and the mud, they shone so brightly that they could see very clearly in the dark.

15   When they had carried enough of them to their ship, they sailed far away. Having reached the high sea, they heard a horrible raging and howling which made them think that Heaven and earth were going to collapse. Terrible thunder and lightning brought all the brethren to despair. Amidst the noise and thunder the Devil arrived with a great host, screaming and raging so that the skies resounded. Coming close to the ship, he screamed horribly:

'Brendan, you must now deliver the thief to me.'
And with these words he took hold of the monk who had stolen the bridle in the hall near the Paradise. He tied him up with the bridle and took him away, dragging him over bushes and sticks and hurting him so much that he bitterly regretted the theft.

And when the Devil dragged the monk to Hell, Saint Brendan and all his brethren prayed our Lord earnestly, with tears in their eyes, on behalf of their companion.

'Oh Lord', Saint Brendan prayed, 'what do you blame us for? Why do you let this misery come upon us and allow the Devil to disgrace us in this way? We will never leave here, unless we get our brother back.'
They all fell on their knees and prayed until he heard them. Thereupon, they saw a light hovering above them which shone like a fiery horn; from it a voice called, saying:

'Oh Brendan, why are you angry with me? I did not do you any wrong. The Devil has taken one brother from you; he had the right to do so, because the monk had stolen a bridle. You well know that Adam had to go to Hell because of a small piece of fruit and with him five ages of the world.[10] Now your brother has been caught in the act of theft and been carried off to Hell.'

'Dear Lord', implored Saint Brendan, 'do not let the Devil have power over your little band. Don't let our name as Christians be defiled by him. Whatever my monk did to you, I will help to recompense and atone for.'

They all prayed to God until he showed mercy. God commanded the Devil to carry the monk into the ship on his back. Then the Devil called the monk, struck him and injured him so much that God forgave him for ever having seen the bridle, for the Devil was furious that he had to carry him to the ship. When he came near the ship, the Devil screamed horribly at Saint Brendan and shouted:

'Woe to you, Brendan, and all your company, for because of you we cannot keep anybody in our Hell.'

He threw the monk violently into the ship; the monk had become so black with the pitch which had dried on him that they did not recognize him at first. His hair and beard had hardened because of the pitch and resin and he had been scratched and bruised miserably by the reeds and sticks, when the Devil had dragged him through them. They all crossed themselves; thereupon, the Devil quickly fled, and they praised our Lord for giving them back their comrade.

16   Then the sea carried them to a place where they saw many large ships floating; they contained so many goods that, if distributed, they would be sufficient for the whole world. From one of the ships came the loudest, most miserable screaming ever heard; for the ships were stuck in the Liver Sea and the people died there in great numbers. Innumerable griffins dived down on them and, carrying the dead upwards with them, devoured them. In the ship just mentioned eighty-four people died.[11] Brendan saw their souls sitting on the masts, waiting for God's judgement as to their destination. He saw a host of devils, lying in wait for the souls; the Devils took eighty-one souls which fell to them and Saint Michael did not get more than three. Saint Brendan secretly lamented that the Devil obtained so many souls and Saint Michael only a few belonging to God. Saint Brendan clearly saw Saint Michael chasing away the Devil from the ship and letting him go ahead with his souls. The devils made an incredible noise; they raged and threw the souls up and down, hurting them so much that they cried out miserably when they were carried

off to Hell with great violence. Then the devils left, and holy angels descended from Heaven with lovely singing, came down to Saint Michael in the ship and led the three souls upwards to the kingdom of Heaven with great joy and songs of praise.

17 When all this was over at last, they resumed their journey and once more got into great difficulties, because they saw a beast coming towards them with a human body and face, but from the waist downwards it was a fish. It is called a siren, a very lovely creature with a beautiful human shape; it sings so well and its voice is so sweet *that* whoever hears it cannot resist sleep and does not know what he is doing. When this sea monster *approached them*, the shipmen fell asleep and let the ship drift: the monks too forgot themselves completely because of its voice and did not know where they were.

18 Then the ship drifted towards a mountain made entirely of fire. Out of the mountain appeared a black man, shouting loudly at them with a terrible voice. They were frightened; and he yelled:
'Come over here! I will show you where to sail.'
Saint Brendan ordered the ship to be turned towards him. *When they were near him*, the Devil said to Saint Brendan:
'If I had the courage to provoke God, you, Brendan, you old monk, and all your comrades would die by my hand and I would throw you into the fire. You should pay me for all the souls we have lost here *as a result of* your prayer. Because of you we are unable to retain any soul, since God does not refuse your prayer. You are causing us great damage: you robbed us of the bridle thief *who is sitting aft there with you and who stole the bridle before the Paradise.*'[12]

When the monk understood that the Devil recognized him, he was terrified. Sweating with fear, he felt terribly ashamed because of the theft. Then Saint Brendan said:
'He has been punished sufficiently, having had trouble in cleaning off the resin and pitch with which you made him look so frightful.'
'The suffering we made him undergo was only very little', the Devil replied. 'If you had left him to us, this pain would have been only the beginning.'
When the Devil saw the monk's terror, he mocked him and, taking a piece of burning slag, so large that he could barely carry it, threw it at him in the ship. The monks in the ship were close to despair, but

Saint Brendan comforted them. Then the Devil demanded that the helmsman hand over the monk who stole the bridle, so that he might torment him a little; he pressed him hard in the ship. Saint Brendan said:

'If God wishes it, our man will not be yours. We will stay out of your reach, for as far as I am concerned it is not pleasant to remain with you.'

They turned the ship away from him towards the sea, and saw how many devils came running towards them on the shore, carrying glowing, burning arrows with them, which they threw and shot in the direction of the holy men. At last God came to their aid, so that no harm was done to them. Burning arrows fell into the ship like rain from Heaven. The monks fled as best they could.

19   After that, Saint Brendan lost a cowl;[13] he did not know where it had gone. Because he did not want to allow the devils the honour of having his cowl, he ordered his men to turn back, so that he could retrieve it. The monks grumbled and said that, even if it were of gold, they would not return; they preferred to withdraw without resisting. Then the monk who had been scorched earlier said:

'Dear lord Saint Brendan, I have many cowls; take them all to replace your cowl, so that we need not go back. For, if you had come as close to them as I did, you would avoid them forever. Nobody will be able to find it, anyway.'

'I want to get back the cowl because, if it remains in their possession, they will poke fun at it', answered Saint Brendan. 'They should never be fortunate enough to gain this much from us. They should yield to us, those wicked hounds of Hell.'

The sailors obeyed him and turned back. Then the devils came towards them so furiously that they nearly despaired and were shocked and frightened. But Saint Brendan recited the psalm *Deus misereatur nostri*.[14] When the Devil hears psalms being recited, it is not in his power to stay; Saint Brendan relied on this. They defeated the devils and put them to flight, as Saint Brendan had known all along they would. Then he retrieved his cowl; it was lying near the shore. That night Saint Brendan remained in the neighbourhood of the burning mountain until dawn.

22   Now there came a favourable wind which drove them far out to sea, where they discovered a very holy man floating on the sea on a piece

of turf; he had nothing to keep himself alive but the turf and God's power. Without this, he could not have held out for so long amidst the raging waves.[15] When the good man saw the ship coming towards him, he tried to get away from it. Saint Brendan begged him for God's sake to turn back and talk to him. Thereupon, the turf stayed still until Saint Brendan had reached it. He asked the good man how he had come to find himself on the turf and whether he was sitting there for God's sake or had been put there because of a crime. Saint Brendan said he would help him, if he wished, adding that he was a priest; did he not require spiritual things of him? Then the good man on the turf said:

'You must know that the chaplain you lost in front of Paradise was taken into Paradise instead of me. I have been on this turf for nineteen years, during which time God has fed me with his bread from Heaven. *I will wait here forever for his mercy and follow his divine commandments and be obedient. You should also know that I have other brethren, whom God feeds with his heavenly bread.* It was because of their intervention that your chaplain, who stole the bridle, was given back to you contrary to God's will; some of them are in the monastery where you spent the night. You have seen another one sitting on the rock in the sea. He has often assisted us in praying to God to grant you things you asked of him. God often fulfills the prayers my brother said for you.'

'Oh holy man,' Saint Brendan answered, 'tell me more about your brothers who, as I saw, strive greatly for God's mercy and live a good Christian life.'

'I will tell you how we came here', said the good man on the turf. 'We had a monastery in a town called Mararin.[16] Now this country and city were so full of sin that it was submerged with its people and property. My brothers remained on the rock where you visited them. God kept me alive on the white rock, as well as my brother whom you also visited; because of our sins we were separated from each other when the land went under. When this turf you see here emerged, God helped me to get on to it. I have to atone for my sins here and will never have shelter until the time when I reach eternal rest. Now may God protect you', said the good man to Saint Brendan. 'You will proceed onward now and there you will see great marvels.'

After the good man had given them directions, a wind got up which soon carried them a good three hundred and fifty miles away from the turf. The sea began to swell[17] and rage, and it drove the ship forward into a dark fog. At this place the sea rushes into the abyss of Hell. But God pulled the ship back, so that they would not be carried off into it. Although they were terrified, their ship was in God's hands. God wanted Saint Brendan to be under his protection, so that he experienced all the marvels himself and discovered the truth he had read about in the book.

23 Sailing a little further, Saint Brendan saw a naked man sitting on a stone. Sitting alone he was suffering great pain. His body was half frozen, so that the flesh was peeling off his bones. His other side was burning so badly that *great holes opened in his body, from where the flames burst out higher than his head.* Before his eyes a small cloth was *hanging,* which drove the heat away behind his back. From above hail fell down, which fortified him a little. To this bare rock he came every Saturday night and sat there until Sunday noon; then the devils came and dragged him back from there into the abyss of Hell. When Saint Brendan saw him in this pain, he asked him who he was.

'I am the poor sinner Judas, who betrayed God', the man said. 'I hanged myself in desperation. If I had not killed myself *but had felt real remorse,* God would have shown mercy to me. So I have to suffer infernal pain eternally; I am forever beyond help. But because God shows me a little mercy I am enjoying a short respite until noon tomorrow. Then the devils will come from Hell to carry me back to great torment.'

Saint Brendan asked: 'Do you suffer even greater pain than I see being inflicted upon you here?'

'Ah, Brendan, if it was only this pain I had to suffer, I would not complain at all', poor Judas answered. 'However great this pain is, my anxiety about tomorrow hurts me as much as the pain you see me enduring here. Tomorrow, when I am back in Hell, they will throw me once more into boiling sulphur and pitch, in which I stew and writhe forever. This frost and heat here have been given me by God's compassion, so that I enjoy respite from the devils' torment every Saturday night until noon on Sunday. But then I have to go into the terrible heat, which is so bad that even a mountain of steel would melt in it. Oh, how hot it is! That will be my welcome. Oh, would to God that this night may last a long time!'

'Tell me', said Saint Brendan, 'would a prayer be of some help to you? If so, I am willing to pray earnestly to God, together with all my brethren.'

'All prayers for me are in vain', Judas replied, 'for God will no longer have mercy on me. Look at this cloth hanging here before my eyes; it protects me a little against the heat. I stole it from God when I was with him and felt such a bitter regret that I gave it to a poor man – that is why it helps me here; but I also suffer because I stole it.'

That night Saint Brendan stayed with him, and on Sunday at noon Judas uttered the loudest lament ever heard. He cried out miserably:

'Woe is me, woe is me forever, now I have to go into unimaginable pain.'

When Saint Brendan heard this, he ordered all his relics to be brought on deck and fell to his knees in prayer, for on hearing Judas lamenting and screaming he realized that the devils were about to fetch him. When the devils arrived, the sea seemed to be pure fire. The monk who stole the bridle cried:

'We should have left here earlier.'

The devils flew around the ship, and from their jaws they belched smoke, pitch, sulphur and fire into the ship, so that all the men on board almost perished from the stench. As they flew over the sea, they dropped large pieces of sulphur and pitch and blazing logs, and the sea burned as if it had been set on fire. When they seized hold of Judas, Saint Brendan ordered them to leave him for a little while; he prayed God, for Brendan's sake, to give him respite that night. God granted him that. When the devils had to leave him there for the time being, they screamed, viciously threatening to treat him worse.

When morning came, they returned with great clamour and with burning hooks which they thrust into Judas; they dragged him with them and inflicted severe pain on him, cursing Saint Brendan and yelling:

'He will have to suffer more than he did before!'

'He will not!' said Saint Brendan. 'I command you by the living God not to treat him worse than before.'

Then they had to obey him and with great violence they dragged Judas into the eternal torment. Saint Brendan sailed after him to see what they did to him. But, from where they were, they could not see him and behind the devils a bluish smoke arose.

24　When Saint Brendan sailed towards it, he saw a mountain which consisted of pure fire at one side, and *from the mountain he saw a stream flowing down*, which, fiercely hot, boiled and burned. From the other side of the mountain came a cold wind and a stream of water – nothing was ever colder; and a loud screaming arose from it. Saint Brendan realized that it was a place of torment.

They saw a bird[18] flying up the face of a cliff, and also heard all kinds of voices crying in the mountain; the air was filled with laments. At the western side of the mountain flowed an unfathomable lake which struck the mountain so violently that they heard the blows at a distance of nine miles. On the other side of the mountain flew blazing firebrands as if a whole wood there was aflame. On the north side of the mountain it was so cold that the solid stones cracked and the bark peeled away from the trees. Then Saint Brendan ordered the ship to turn away from the water and the boiling lake. In three years they could hardly get back to where they had earlier sailed *in one day*.

25[a]　Having sailed for eight years, they arrived in the ninth year in a land where they found the greatest bliss and beauty which can be found anywhere on earth. The land was so bountiful that everything one wanted was found there, corn and wine and all the fruit needed, all without labour. There was meat to be had with no need to breed animals, and the birds were tame and the fish came spontaneously to men. No wolf or snake or any harmful creature ever entered that land, and it is always green there. This land is called *Bona Terra* and it lies far from the inhabited world. If God had not wanted the sea to carry them there, they would never have got there. When they arrived in the land, it smelt as sweet there as in Paradise; and the scent took away from them all fatigue and hardship.

Saint Brendan went ashore with eleven of his brethren; they saw a beautiful castle floating high in the air so that no living creature could reach it unless it could fly very high. They found a bridge which they crossed. When they climbed the mountain on which the castle had been erected, they saw curious animals, dragons and serpents, lying on the mountainside. Saint Brendan ordered them to lie still, and they let him pass into the castle. Then they saw that the castle wall was made of pure crystal, encrusted with many precious stones, and that all the marvels on earth were sculpted on the wall, in copper, bronze and brass. There were animals, such as lions, bears, boars, leopards and elephants; every kind of animal ever created was sculpted on the wall as figures in relief. At first sight one fancied them alive; they had been sculpted thereon in masterly fashion. They looked as if they were walking in the wood: one was lying, another sitting; here a bear was fighting with a boar, there dogs were running after hares and stags, there one could see animals disporting themselves in every way imaginable. All this was sculpted *on one side of* the wall. The other side was sculpted with all kinds of birds which seemed to be flying and floating in the air: the eagle, the vulture, the sparrow-hawk and all sorts of other birds, wild and tame, large and small, just as if they were alive. On the third side one saw all kinds of fish, large and small, as if they were swimming in the water. On the fourth side were all kinds of human pastimes: here jousting, there fighting, yonder falconry, there hunting, here dancing, yonder caroling, there riding, here men and women talking to each other; there big fights were being fought, yonder kings and lords seated under pavilions. One could see there all kinds of blazons, on shields, helmets and banners; also all kinds of crafts and all the trades people plied at that time. One could also see all kinds of stringed instruments being played and entertainment of all sorts – everything was sculpted on the crystal walls.

The pinnacles on the walls were beautiful and bright; they shone inside and out, like the morning star. In the castle were seven hundred towers and as many magnificent rooms. Everywhere in the castle gold shone like tinder in a fire, and in the rooms were very comfortable beds, covered with multi-coloured silk cushions and surrounded with precious tapestries. In the castle was a building with a floor as clear as glass, blue and hard as steel; it contained mosaics of gold interspersed with precious stones. In the courtyard and in the keep there was always light and radiance, beauteous as the sun. There no one ever gets wet.

Now they saw a cedar tree standing in the garden; at its foot was a lovely meadow, green and beautiful. On the cedar tree hung many golden drinking-bowls and jugs, and under it stood beautiful tables, set with the finest dishes one could imagine. In the cedar tree birds were continuously singing cheerful songs. There were also the loveliest springs, sparkling high, clear and cool; in the streams flowing from the springs many large, beautiful and lively fishes were swimming. In the building the greatest bliss in all the world was constantly to be found. They attentively observed these marvels and the bliss in the castle, and Saint Brendan described everything in detail. When they had carefully examined the mountain, the building and the walls, inside and out, Saint Brendan said:

'Here is great joy, and gold and precious stones. All of you, my companions, will have to take great care that nobody removes anything, so that things will not turn out for us as they did when our brother stole the bridle. Now we should go quickly to our ship, so that the Devil will not lay snares and deceive us.'

25^b They immediately left the castle, and when they had reached the ship, they saw coming towards them odd-looking beings, with heads like swine, hands like humans and necks like cranes. Below the waist they were hairy, and they wore silk clothes; each carried a quiver with arrows and had a bow in his hand. They growled furiously, like swine and with outstretched tails angrily approached the shore, heading straight for the ship. The monks counted themselves lucky to be in the ship *and* not to have encountered them on their way. Since they were such horrible, frightening beings, Saint Brendan ordered:

'Get the ship away from here quickly, so that they cannot shoot at us. I wonder whether they have knowledge of God; I want to speak to them about God.'
Standing on the afterdeck,[19] Saint Brendan hailed them. He mentioned God to them and ordered them in the name of the living God to keep peace with him until he had talked to them.

As soon as they heard the name of God, they laid down their bows of horn and all were silent, save for one among them who spoke, saying:

'Brendan, you have experienced great marvels and seen many a strange land. Now God, of whom you spoke just now, has sent you here. You should know that we knew God at one time better *than you do*: when he was enthroned in his majesty, we saw him and knew him. Before Lucifer fell, we were in his sight. Now I say to you, Brendan, you do not want to believe what you have not seen. That has brought you great trouble, for you burned a book which told the whole truth. Therefore they are wiser who believe that God has worked much greater marvels without number, as you know from what God said to Saint Thomas when he let him feel his wounds. Jesus then said to him: "Thomas, when you *feel* me, you believe and you are blessed, but

more blessed are those who believe without touching or seeing."[20]
Thereby you shall know, Brendan, that God has shown great love to
those Christians who believe.'

'Who has told you about God in so much detail?' asked Saint
Brendan.
He answered:
'We were close to him in Heaven and lost our beautiful appearance
because we were Lucifer's followers when he was thrown out of
Heaven. When he rose against God, we did not have enough
judgement to be able to love or fear God. We also lacked discernment
of what was good or bad for us to do. When Lucifer fell, God saw our
lack of judgement and cast us out, together with Lucifer and the
other angels who fell with him, who did have the power of judgement.
But he did not want to let us keep our angelic beauty and appearance
and changed us to look like this: the swine's head is because, like
swine, we lacked judgement. The swine does not know what to love
or fear, nor even its own nature; often it prefers to be in dung than in
clear water. We also had to have bodies like dogs, because once we
had the habits of a dog; for a dog does not bark at someone he knows,
however much that person steals from his master. We did the same in
Heaven: we left Lucifer unreported when he rose against God, and
did not stop him. Because we did not suggest it, God in his mercy
excluded us from Lucifer's company and did not cast us into Hell.
God gave us the land and we have hope that in the future he will
show us some mercy.'

Then Saint Brendan said:
'We set foot on your mountain, which at the front is made of gold
and precious stones, with pleasant dwellings like Paradise. We left
just as we came, without harming you or taking any of your
possessions. We went in ignorance and regret at having entered your
domain. If God had not been with us, the serpents would have
devoured us. I wonder where you came from.'
Then one of them said:
'We had gone off to a foreign land; there six hundred hellish
legions had stationed themselves along the roads. We had to fight
them and had marched out against them. They did great damage to
our lands, for they cannot bear us not to endure their suffering; they
cause us every kind of harm they can. We had to defend ourselves

against them. Then a thousand wood goblins[21] and as many demons came to their aid in obstructing the roads, the paths and the streets.'

'What are those wood goblins and demons?' asked Saint Brendan.

'These are reeds and trees with which they had barred the paths and roads', one of them answered. 'We have never got into any greater trouble since we were cast from Heaven. Now this beautiful land is ours, and we have no other punishment than the loss of the loving vision of God. Now I will not talk to you any more, except to ask you to come with us to our home, where we want to welcome you and your men.'

Then Saint Brendan said: 'No, we had better not. We want to return to Ireland; may God give us favourable winds.'

In this way they left there and bade farewell to that strange company. They would have liked to give them treasures, but Saint Brendan did not want them to do so.

26   When Saint Brendan and his brethren set off on the journey back to Ireland, they sailed in comfort until early on the morning of the eleventh day. Then a gigantic fish came swimming towards them, behaving as if it was going to swallow the whole ship, so widely did it open its jaws. It was so big that they sailed alongside it, as fast as they could, *for four whole weeks*, before they reached the end of the fish. When they thought they were ahead of it, it caused a very dangerous situation for them, for it curled its tail round into its mouth; for fourteen days they had to remain in the ring, unable to get out. Whenever the fish moved, the upsurge of the water was so high that it raised the ship as if intending to carry it up into the air; then the ship crashed down as if falling into the abyss. On the skin of this fish wood and grass were growing. They were in great distress.

At last the fish let them sail out of the surge; *as it swam away, the waves rose in such a flood* that the noise of it could be heard over a great distance. Building up, the waves rose high above the ship so that the brethren became terribly frightened. They would have despaired, had not Saint Brendan comforted them, saying:

'Keep up your spirits. God has saved us from many a dangerous situation; he will do so again. When this fish gets ahead of us, the sea will calm down.'

27 With its turbulence the sea swept them many thousands of miles away. Then the winds died down and the weather became so hot that they nearly perished. The ship lay still; neither oars nor sail were of any use. In this way they had to lie still in the heat for four weeks.

At last there came a great gust of wind which drove them onward to a place where the sea was very clear and in many parts completely dry. They heard an astonishingly loud noise of people and cattle roaring. They also heard bells ringing, mass being sung, the noise of cattle being driven, of dancing, parading, singing, crying, lamenting and laughing, trumpeting, cows bellowing, horses neighing – they heard noise of every kind.[22] Saint Brendan was very puzzled, for they could see nothing but water and sky, yet they heard the noise. Then Saint Brendan said:

'I wonder where this noise comes from; it sounds so near and yet we cannot see anybody. What do you suggest? Shall we take the ship forwards or backwards? For I have to find out what may be here.'

They did not know what to do for the best. Then they cast their sounding line into the water and soon sounded the bottom. Thereupon, they dropped their anchors after it, which were immediately held so fast that they could not recover them; they did not know what to do. They urgently invoked the Lord and lowered their sail; they were in great trouble.

28ª Now their screaming and shouting was heard by a dwarf. He emerged from a wood, where the water had risen above the sky and the trees; the water could not damage either the sky or the wood. He saw the way in which the ship was held by a contrary wind, and he immediately ran into the wood. There a hermit had his dwelling and he told him how the ship was held where the water reached its end and its point of return, saying that those on board were urgently invoking God and the Virgin Mary – he supposed they were Christians – and that they were asking whether they could come and help them.[23] He answered 'Yes' – he was happy to learn that they were Christians. Together they left the wood and went to the sea, where they *had* a small boat, and both went aboard; the dwarf made the boat move quite fast, for they were both happy to come to their aid.

Then Saint Brendan called out:

'There in a mist I can see a small boat with one sail coming towards us. I trust that God is sending us his help.'

The boat moved towards them, and in it they saw a hermit and a dwarf. The man was old and his clothes were made of the hair of wild animals, intertwined and woven. In his hand he had an abbot's staff which had once been given to him by Saint Brendan. The dwarf sat aft and steered the boat; the dwarf was called Bettewart and was hideous to behold; he had a long beard and beautiful, long hair and was fully clothed and equipped. He sang with fervour, but they did not understand his singing well. He had a wide mouth and his voice resounded like a bronze horn. All the clothes he wore were made of precious cloth and silk; and he was very strong, for he moved the boat with great power. His beard reached down to his knees.

When they reached the ship, the hermit said to them:

'Turn back at once with your ship, for I hear four winds coming; if they take hold of you, they will cause you severe damage and you will get into great distress and difficulty.'

Then Saint Brendan suspected that he was a devilish apparition and said:

'Unless it upsets you, I would like you to join us in this ship, for we carry many relics with us. We would like, with God's help, to sing a mass here.'

The hermit understood very well that Saint Brendan was afraid he was an illusion and a devilish apparition, and he moved towards them rapidly. They helped him aboard; then he fell down, arms spread in a cross, before the reliquary, for he was a chosen vessel of God. They thereupon received *him with great dignity and together they sang a beautiful mass and all of them received* the Blessed Sacrament.

Then the dwarf told them that the world had reached an end and that the noise they heard came from another world beneath the earth. Then Saint Brendan was well aware that he had burned the truth.

31[a-b]   While at sea, Saint Brendan wrote down in a book all the marvels he had experienced at sea. Thereafter, they cast off their anchor ropes and hoisted their sail. The dwarf towed the ship in such a way that it moved quite fast, for he was very strong and powerful. When they reached the sea, they looked out over the Liver Sea and saw many ships that had been stuck there for a long time.

30 Soon afterwards they reached the coast, where Saint Brendan saw an old grey-haired monk[24] riding. He wore rich clothes, his beard had been threaded with pure gold and he wore a sable cloak, which had been studded with pure carbuncles which enable one to see at night. A beautiful eagle, looking as if it was going to take flight, had been worked upon it with gold and precious stones. This lord was virtuous and brave and he ruled over the whole country. He rode a small mule with one black ear. The value of the clothes he wore was as much as a thousand marks. The name of this lord was Heilteran.[25] When Saint Brendan saw him he knew him well and felt joy in his heart, for he realized that they had come close to their homeland.

'Now, keep up your spirits,' he said to his brethren, 'and praise God, for we are now home in our own country and have, if God so wills it, overcome all our troubles.'

33 With these words they reached the shore and disembarked. Then the holy man and the dwarf, who had come to them, said farewell and sailed away in their boat. When Saint Brendan and his men set foot ashore and landed in Ireland, and came to the town and entered it, all the people there came towards them and welcomed them with great honour. Now Saint Brendan, when at sea, had recorded all the marvels in a book. He took the book and carried it into his monastery. All his brethren followed him and Saint Brendan placed the book on the altar of our Lady. Thereupon, a voice was heard from God, welcoming him kindly and saying to him:

'Brendan, if you wish, come to me.'

Then Saint Brendan prepared himself for a sung mass, which he celebrated with great devotion. When the mass was ended, Saint Brendan died and his soul went to God.

34 Therefore, we will pray Saint Brendan that, for our sake, he will pray God that our lives may be brought to a happy end. Amen

5

The Venetian Version

Mark Davie

Manuscripts and Editions The hundred years between *c.*1250 and 1350 were a period of intense literary activity in the cities of northern and central Italy, in which texts representing the whole range of medieval Latin culture were translated into the various emerging vernaculars. This activity included four distinct versions of the Brendan legend. Two of these are reasonably close to the Latin *Navigatio*: (i) the earliest (turn of the fourteenth century) and the most faithful from western Tuscany, probably Lucca; (ii) more eclectic in its use of the *Navigatio* (which the author tries to abbreviate, often rather clumsily and introducing illogicalities into the narrative), from the university city of Bologna. Much the longest and most original version comes from Venice and represents a development of the Brendan tradition quite distinct from the other, somewhat pedestrian versions. Its influence is attested by the fact that it is the only one of the Italian versions to survive in more than one MS (two from the fifteenth century, one of which is incomplete, plus a fourteenth-century fragment) and by the fact that it is the source of the fourth Italian version, another Tuscan text which closely follows the Venetian text for most of its length (although it abbreviates some of its more prolix descriptions, particularly towards the end) and which retains linguistic traces of its Venetian model. Indeed, the extent to which Brendan was associated with Venice in the Italian mind is indicated by the fact that the Lucchese version states that he was born there.

The Venetian version was therefore the natural choice, among the Italian versions, for inclusion in this volume. There have been two editions of this text based on the only complete MS (Milan, Biblioteca Ambrosiana D 158 inf., beginning of the fifteenth century), by Francesco Novati (1892) and by Maria Antonietta Grignani (1975, 3rd edn 1997). Novati's edition provided a glossary and linguistic analysis, and Grignani published a separate glossary (1980), but there is no modern Italian or any other translation, and several passages remain obscure. The text is discussed in Renata Bartoli's survey of all the Romance versions of the *Navigatio* (1993a), and it was the subject of an unpublished dissertation at the University of Trento by C. Boscolo (1997).

Authorship The text gives no clue to the identity of the Venetian author, but two indications in the first few pages give the work a specifically Venetian character. The first is the direction in which the pilgrims travel. It is not a casual slip when, at the end of the text, they set out on their return journey sailing west; already in §I Mernoc urges Barrind: 'My father, go aboard the boat and let us sail towards the east, that we may go to the island which is called the Promised Land of the Saints.' In the *Navigatio*, needless to say, the monks set off sailing towards the west, true to the text's Irish origin; but for a Venetian it would be much more natural to suggest sailing towards the Levant, always the focus of the maritime republic's expansion and exploration. There is a further trace of Venetian nautical experience in §IV, where the *Navigatio* describes the construction of Brendan's ship – 'a light boat ribbed with wood and with a wooden frame, as is usual in those parts'. The Venetian text goes further and gives it a name: 'and he called it a cog (*coca*).' The similarity of the name to the Irish *curagh* is almost certainly fortuitous, but the *coca* or *cocha* was a type of merchant ship which became common in the Venetian fleet from the thirteenth century onwards (Lane 1966, 233-34).[1]

Date and Context Venice and its hinterland played a major part in the diffusion in Italy of much of the literature of northern Europe, both Latin and vernacular. The progress of this Brendan text, with a Venetian version followed by a Tuscan one, is therefore not untypical for a work originating north of the Alps; what is unusual is the survival of the Venetian text alongside its Tuscan derivative. There is no other text in Venetian on a comparable scale from this period; indeed, such was the prestige of French as a literary language, and the corresponding lack of widely read local vernacular, that the most substantial original works in the region were written, if not in Latin, either in French (if in prose, Marco Polo's *Divisament dou monde* being the best-known example) or in the curious linguistic hybrid known as Franco-Venetian (if in verse, the elaborations of the Roland legend, *L'Entrée d'Espagne* and *La prise de Pampelune*). In these circumstances it is difficult to date

---

1. I am grateful to Claudia Boscolo for this reference.

the Venetian *Brendan* with any certainty. Novati assigned it to the end of the thirteenth century; Bartoli places it within a broad time-span ranging from 1270 to 1350, but inclines to a date relatively early in this range. Grignani, however, does not hesitate to place it squarely in the fourteenth century, and this seems the safest assumption given the lack of any comparable text written in Venetian before 1300. As regards its place of origin, there is a general consensus on both linguistic and cultural grounds that it comes from Venice itself, rather than any of the cities of the hinterland; the author's evident familiarity with maritime matters clearly suggests this.

Source Direct verbal correspondences as well as the overall structure of the narrative make it clear that the Venetian text is, in essence, a translation of the Latin *Navigatio*. We do not know the exact text which the Venetian writer used, or whether, indeed, there were one or more intermediate versions between the *Navigatio*, as we now have it, and its Venetian derivative. Novati inclined to the view that the changes of substance in the Venetian version belong to an earlier Latin version, now lost; but in the absence of any direct evidence of such a version this can be no more than speculation. In the analysis which follows, therefore, the Venetian version is compared directly with the *Navigatio* as it is represented by Selmer's edition and by the translation in this volume.

Content and Structure [2] For the first two-thirds of the text the Venetian version follows the *Navigatio* closely, making only small-scale changes, usually to add some practical or realistic detail: when the abbot Ailbe refers to the burning bush seen by Moses on Mount Sinai (§XII), the Venetian adapter adds 'which is in Armenia'; when the voyagers are given a basket of enormous grapes from the Island of Strong Men (§XVII), not only does Brendan squeeze the juice into a basin but he weighs the fruit, finding that each grape weighs a pound and has skin 'as thick as an oxhide'; where the *Navigatio* assumes that its readers know what 'the bird called the Gryphon' is (§XIX), the Venetian heightens its monstrous nature, describing it as 'part bird and part beast and part fish' with a curved beak and claws and with wings as sharp as razors.

---

2. Here and in the translation, chapter numbers are those of the Latin *Navigatio*, which usually but not always coincide with the unnumbered divisions of the Venetian text. The Venetian text has chapter headings, mainly written in Latin, which have been omitted in the translation.

The most consistent additions to the first part of the *Navigatio* are in the liturgical texts. Not only does the Venetian adapter faithfully reproduce the details of the psalms and canticles which the brothers sing at the various feasts punctuating their journey, he frequently spells out the reference which is given in an abbreviated form in the *Navigatio*, as if to identify the texts for an audience unfamiliar with the daily office. Thus, when the *Navigatio* states in §XV that the voyagers on reaching the Paradise of Birds for the second time 'chanted the hymn of the Three Children right to the end', the Venetian version helpfully adds, '[They] began to sing the song of the three young men, Ananias, Azarias and Misael, that is the psalm which begins: "O all ye works of the Lord . . ." '. Sometimes the liturgical material is expanded, as in Brendan's prayer in §XVI for protection against the sea monster, where in addition to the *Navigatio*'s references to the divine protection given to David and Jonah, the Venetian text also adds references to Daniel, Joseph and Moses. Again in the account of the texts sung by the three choirs on the Island of Strong Men (§XVII), the Venetian writer goes one better than the *Navigatio*, giving the psalms for sext and nones as well as those for midday, terce and vespers.

In the last third of the *Navigatio*, however, the Venetian adapter shows a progressively freer attitude to his original. The change is first apparent in §XXI, where the *Navigatio*'s enigmatic description of the submarine creatures which the brothers could see under their ship ('they were like herds lying in pastures . . . so numerous that they looked like a city of circles as they lay, their heads touching their tails') prompts a truly exotic catalogue of animals in the Venetian text: 'It was like a great city with houses and towers [. . .]; and they looked like sheep and goats, pigs, dogs, wolves, oxen, donkeys, lions, griffins, bears, mules, buffaloes, camels, dragons, elephants and deer.' Later in the same chapter, the text adds the curious detail of an island where the trees grow out of the ground at sunrise and sink beneath the surface when the sun sets. The chapters which follow contain substantial additions as the Venetian text dwells at length on the lurid details of the pains of Hell (§§XXIII and XXIV), and gives a much more circumstantial account of the life of Judas (§XXV).

The turning point in the relationship between the two texts comes almost at the end of the *Navigatio*, in the meeting with Paul the Hermit (§XXVI). Here the Venetian author introduces the first of the descriptive passages which will be such a distinctive feature of the text's final episodes, the Paradise of Delights and the Promised Land of the Saints. Outside Paul the Hermit's cave is what the *Navigatio* described as 'a minuscule spring, round like a plate, flowing from the rock before the entrance to the cave'. In the Venetian version the water from the spring flows into an elaborately decorated basin, inset with precious stones and with carved figures corresponding to the signs of the zodiac which 'were in constant motion around the water, making a very sweet sound as they moved'. No explanation is given for this addition, but it anticipates the similar astrological carvings on the arch leading to the castle of Bel Veder, which are described a few pages later in the Venetian text.

There are two other notable changes in the Paul the Hermit episode. In the *Navigatio*, Brendan, on hearing of the unparalleled austerity of the hermit's life and the extent to which he had eliminated his dependence on material needs, laments the inadequacy of his own version of the religious life. The hermit consoles him by reminding him of the special signs of God's favour which he has received: '[. . .] You are greater than a monk! A monk uses the labour of his hands with which to clothe himself. But God from his own secret supplies feeds and clothes both you and your companions for seven years'. Sanctity, in other words, is manifested in not depending on normal human means of survival. The Venetian text, however, draws exactly the opposite conclusion; here the hermit says to Brendan: 'You are a true and good monk – and more than a monk, for the majority of monks do not work, but you work hard, labouring all day with your hands on the boat, and praying with your heart and tongue.' The true religious, for the Venetian author, is one who does an honest day's work, not using his vocation as an excuse to be exempted from the practical obligations of daily life.

The final change is in Paul's account of how he was miraculously fed for thirty years by an otter bringing him a fish every three days, together with the means of making a fire on which to cook it. The *Navigatio* here follows a hagiographical tradition going back, ultimately, to the biblical story of Elijah fed by ravens in the desert. The Venetian author, either unaware or forgetful of this tradition, seeks to heighten the miraculous element by making a fish emerge from the sea every three days of its own accord, carrying the wood for the fire in its hind paws [*sic*] and expiring at the hermit's feet ready to be cooked – an innovation whose effect is bathetic rather than impressive. In all these respects the Venetian version of the Paul the Hermit episode – with its mixture of the exotic, the would-be symbolic, the down-to-earth and the bizarre – anticipates the qualities which will characterize the lengthy, and quite independent, account of the two paradisal islands which then follows.

Paul the Hermit is the last substantial episode in the *Navigatio* (§XXVI). After this, §XXVII repeats the pattern of the previous six years with the observance of Easter on Jasconius and the meeting with the Steward, who then accompanies the pilgrims on the final stage of their journey to the Promised Land of the Saints. This, the final goal of their voyage, receives only the briefest description before the travellers' return journey and Brendan's death are recounted in the space of a few lines. The Venetian author seems to have found this abrupt ending unsatisfactory, and pausing for only half a sentence to note the repetition of the liturgical pattern ('When the feasts of Easter and Pentecost were past . . .'), he embarks on the most original part of his narrative. The Steward proposes to guide the travellers, not to the Promised Land of the Saints which has been their goal from the outset, but to somewhere quite new: 'The Paradise of Delights, that place which God ordained upon earth, in the middle of the world, as a garden for his friends from the beginning of the world.' Only after this has been described at length do they then set sail again and, passing through the fog described in the *Navigatio* (§XXVIII), come to the Promised Land of the Saints, which in turn is described in even greater detail.

The description of the Paradise of Delights begins with the statement that it contained 'so many things quite unlike those which are found elsewhere that they can hardly be written down', and ends on the same note: '. . . And many other things in great numbers, such that anyone who tried to describe them would seem merely foolish.' In between, the passage could indeed be infinitely extended, as one exotic detail follows another with little overall coherence. The centrepiece of the episode is a mysterious castle, richly furnished and showing every sign of being inhabited, but with no visible trace of its occupants; it is fortified with towers and battlements and is approached by a bridge over a wide river. This castle appears to derive from the same strand of Celtic mythology as the 'great hall' set with a sumptuous dinner which the travellers encountered early in the *Navigatio* (§VI), but to have come to the Venetian text from an independent source which, to judge from the name of the castle, Bel Veder, seems likely to have been a French courtly romance. But any narrative function which the castle might have is ignored as the Venetian author minutely describes every aspect of its surroundings, sometimes simply giving an impression of abundance (trees bearing every kind of fruit in every degree of ripeness, including date palms, sugar cane and cinnamon), at others suggesting an enigmatic and unspecified symbolic meaning (a river with streams of clear water,

milk, wine and oil, each bearing different precious stones and metals).
Precious stones, indeed, are a recurring feature, whether described
generically or identified in lists borrowed from the book of Revelation.
A passage describing carved reliefs on an arch leading to the castle
appears to have a didactic function, with panels depicting the signs of
the zodiac, scenes of biblical history from the Old and New
Testaments, the existing world order ruled by the pope and the
emperor, and the last judgement; but this gives way once more to
passages of mere enumeration (the table vessels inside the castle, again
made of a range of precious stones, and fabulously large and colourful
birds) until the Steward abruptly announces that the allotted forty
days for their visit are up and they must move on.

The transitional narrative of the voyage through the fog coincides
with the introduction of a first-person narrator ('the Steward led me to
the boat and told us all to embark . . .'), who remains intermittently
present throughout the visit to the Promised Land. Much of what is
described there is in a similar vein to the previous episode, and is if
anything even more exotic: there is a catalogue of prodigiously large
fruit ('pomegranates with seeds as big as walnuts, bean pods a yard
long [. . .], cherries as big as peaches'), and another of 'strange
creatures of all shapes and sizes' with a variety of skin coverings and
any number ('up to twelve') of limbs, heads and eyes. But there is
more to the Promised Land of the Saints than this. As the travellers
approach their goal, the Steward tells them that their journey has been
an allegory of the soul's journey to salvation: 'You have experienced in a
small way how it is through many trials and tribulations that we can see
Paradise, which is called the kingdom of God. There is no other way to
get there, except through many tribulations of the body and the soul;
that was the way which was taken by all God's saints, and by him who
took our nature and became a man like other men.' As they emerge
from the fog into the dazzling light of a sun which never sets (briefly
mentioned as 'a mighty light' in the *Navigatio*, §XXVIII), he explains
that this sun 'is not like the sun which appears among the signs of the
zodiac', but 'is the glorious God, who reveals here something of his
power to his saints'. Later an angel appears and sings a love song, 'such
as a young maiden might sing to her lover', which is 'the song of the
soul of the just, which seeks for its bridegroom the Son of God, who is
a fair youth, noble, wise, virtuous and bold, courteous, sagacious, rich
and full of joy'. These elements represent a new level of religious
sophistication which has hitherto been absent in the text and which, in
its mixture of the language of courtly love with traditional Christian
imagery, is quite unlike the spirituality of the *Navigatio*. For all the

differences in scale and profundity, we are in recognizably the same spiritual climate in which Dante wrote the *Divine Comedy*; and it is matched by a new response of mystical rapture in the pilgrims: 'The brethren were so filled with joy and comfort at all these things that they were oblivious of anything else, but just stood there, looking and listening to these precious things, their souls almost abandoning their bodies in an ecstasy of love.' This aspiration to a level of being which rises above the senses is a counterbalance to the text's sometimes prosaic concern with material well-being, in particular to the absence of hunger, most graphically illustrated in the comment at the end of the text that when the travellers finally returned home they were 'fair, plump and [. . .] younger than they were when they set out'.

The angel appears to signal the end of the episode when, having concluded his song, he turns to the pilgrims and says: 'Today is the last of the forty days which God has granted you to see and smell and touch everything here. So now prepare yourselves to return to your home.' But by now the author's descriptive invention is almost unstoppable, and the expected ending is repeatedly delayed. The next paragraph begins: 'When we had seen these things and were preparing to depart to . . .', but this leads to a whole new sequence of seven springs, rivers, horses, churches (each of a different precious stone) and altars; there is another column carved with biblical scenes, a set of bells chiming with the harmony of the heavens, and finally a bridge which stops short of crossing to the far shore. Again the travellers accept that this is as far as they can go, and turn back; but again they set off exploring in another direction until they come to the bank of a river which they cannot cross. Again they are met by 'a handsome young man, finely dressed and very pleasing to behold' who repeats with almost comical insistence that they are to take home as many precious stones as they can carry. But equally indefatigable is the author's didacticism, and almost on the very last page the young man embarks on a retelling of the story of Adam and Eve. When he finally bids the travellers farewell, Brendan gives his companions one last chance to acquire souvenirs of their journey ('So Saint Brendan told his brethren that they could confidently gather every kind of fruit of the island, and every kind of gem, and could take whatever they wanted') before embarking on their ship and setting sail – towards the west, implying that the Promised Land was in the east, the traditional location of the Garden of Eden. The Venetian text thus maintains its dual character – its fascination with fabulous wealth on one hand, and its religious didacticism on the other – right to the end.

The Author's Purpose The author clearly shares the fascination of the Venetian merchant class with exotic places and material abundance, and it is reasonable to assume that, whether or not he himself belonged to this class, they were the audience for whom he was writing. Reading the text one is repeatedly reminded of the most famous of all Venetian travellers' tales, Marco Polo's *Divisament dou monde*, written at the very end of the thirteenth century; both texts have the same sharp eye for detail and the same astute appraisal of the material value of what they describe. But at the same time the Venetian *Brendan* retains, and in some respects expands, its devotional character, with the careful attention given to the liturgical material, the explicit allegorization of the journey, and the mystical language of the last few pages. These elements suggest an author who was a cleric, albeit one who was not immune to the materialism of the secular world – a member of the parochial clergy, perhaps, or of one of the mendicant orders. This would be in keeping with the anti-monastic gloss added to the Paul the Hermit episode, for the parish clergy and the friars shared the laity's resentment of the privileges enjoyed by the enclosed monastic orders. But this is no more than speculation. What is clear is that the Venetian text is further testimony to the power of suggestion of this remarkably adaptable narrative, which is able to reflect the concerns of a late-medieval urban society of merchant adventurers, just as its source had expressed the very different spiritual and imaginative life of an earlier age at the other extremity of Europe.

I Saint Brendan was born in Munster, the son of Findlug, nephew of Alte, of the family of the Eogenacht, from a place called Stagnile.[1] He was a man of great contrition and abstinence and of many virtues, and he was the abbot of some three thousand monks.

Once when he was in his place of penance in a monastery called Brendan's Leap of Virtue, it happened that at the hour of vespers there came to him a holy father and monk whose name was Barrind, who was his nephew. Saint Brendan asked him about many things, wanting to learn from him news of where he had been and whether he had seen or heard any strange thing. And as they were earnestly talking, Barrind began to weep and threw himself on the ground, and remained so for some time devoutly in prayer. As he was thus rapt, Saint Brendan took him and raised him up and kissed him, saying to him:

'Father, why are you so sorrowful and lost in thought? Do you think that we are grieved at your coming? You must surely know that we have great joy at your coming, and so you should bring joy to all of us and show us consolation, and greet the brothers in this place. May it please you to speak to us some good word of God for the nourishing of our souls, telling of the many miracles which you have seen in those parts of the ocean where you have been.'

At these words, Abbot Barrind began to speak about an island, saying:

'My son Mernoc is the Steward of Christ's poor; he left me, not wishing to remain with me, but choosing rather to live in solitude. And as he journeyed he came upon an island near a mountain called Lapisilis,[2] which is very sweet and delightful, and there he remained for a long time. Later I was told that he had many monks under him, and that God had shown through him many miracles and wonders. I went to see him, and when I was near where he was he came three days' journey to meet me with his brothers; and by this I know that God revealed my coming to him. Our journey was by boat, and as we neared that island many monks came from different parts to meet us, all dressed in different ways, and crowding more densely than swarms of bees; although they were from different places and dressed in different ways, they were all good and wise and united in faith, hope and charity. They had a church where they gathered for the divine office; and they ate nothing but bread and nuts and the roots of various plants. When the brothers had devoutly sung compline in the church they went to their cells; each had his own cell, and remained there in prayer until the first bell, and when the cocks crowed they went to rest. We travelled over the whole island until my son took me to the western seashore, where his boat was, and he said to me: "My father, go aboard the boat and let us sail towards the east, that we may go to the island which is called the Promised Land of the Saints, which God will give to those who will come after us." [3]

'When we had embarked and set sail, a cloud came up and covered us on all sides, so densely that those in the stern could hardly see the prow; and this darkness lasted for the space of an hour. And when this fog lifted, there arose a great light, and there appeared to our sight a spacious land, full of precious plants and flowers and many fruit trees, such as fair apple trees laden with apples, and many other kinds of fruit. The boat sailed to the shore and there it came to rest, whereupon we disembarked and began to explore up and down the length of the island for the space of fifteen days, never coming to the end of it. And there was no plant without flowers or tree without fruit; and on the ground were many kinds of precious stones of delightful colours. At the end of the fifteen days we came upon a great river; and there appeared to be no way to cross it, for it seemed to run from the rising of the sun to its setting.

'So we stood looking at all these things, not knowing what to do; for we wanted to cross over this river. And as we stood there waiting for guidance from God, and discussing among ourselves, there appeared before us a very handsome man, radiant with light, who greeted us and called us all by name, and then said to us: "O men and brothers, servants of God, you are welcome; rejoice, be comforted, and fear not. For in truth the Lord God has brought you here, and in his great grace has shown you this land, which is the land that you have been seeking and which he will give to his saints. And know that half the land is on this side where you are, and the other half is beyond this great river which you seek to cross; but God does not wish you to go any further, so contain yourselves in patience and return whence you have come." When he had spoken thus, one of the brothers asked him where he was from and what he was called. "Why do you ask me where I am from and what I am called?" he replied. "Ask me rather about this island; and if you want to know about it, take a good look all around you. As you see it now, so it has been from the beginning of the world. Now tell me, do you need anything to eat or drink, or clothes to wear? I will tell you the truth: you are neither hungry nor thirsty, nor do you need any clothing or sleep. Today it is a year since you came to this island with your companions, and you have neither eaten nor drunk, nor have you been weighed down by sleep or seen night fall, for it has been always day. Learn now that in this place night never falls, but it is always light; it never rains, nor does any cloud appear to disturb the air. No one ever knows hunger or thirst or sleep or infirmity; it is never wearisome to stay here, and there is no grief over anything; nor can anyone ever grow old or die. And the great light that is here is not from the sun or the moon or any stars, but it is the light of the precious Lord our God, from whom all good things come, all grace and all light. He has been very gracious to you, for few are those who are worthy to experience what you have seen and heard." And having spoken thus, he immediately made as if to depart, saying: "Now leave this place, and I will come with you to the shore where your boat is." When we reached the shore, we boarded the boat, and the man was seen no more.

'We set sail, and in a short time there came again the same fog and darkness as before, and it lasted for the space of an hour; we passed through it and came to the island so rich in flowers and trees. We sailed on, as God guided us, until we found our brothers, who had been waiting for us with great desire to see us; and they were overjoyed at our coming. Our long absence had cost them many tears and much anxiety, and they had spoken much about us, having waited for us with great sorrow for a year and eighteen days. Then they said to us: "Our lords and fathers, you have been away so long; why did you leave us without a guide in this dark wood, like men who are lost? We know that our lord abbot often goes away to a place by himself, and we do not know where, or how far away it is; sometimes he stays away for a month at a time, sometimes two weeks, and sometimes just one week or less, and then he returns safe and sound. But you have been away too long, and it is no wonder that we have been sad and anxious." When I heard the brothers' words I began to comfort them, saying: "My dearest brothers, think only good of this matter; for you are in a good place, and you are speaking not far from the gate of the Paradise which God planted in this world. The precious island which is called the Promised Land of the Saints is near at hand; and on this island it is never night and the day never ends; it is always light and the air is clear, and the birds never cease to sing sweetly of spring. Every kind of plant is in flower, and the trees are all laden with flowers and fruit. There is no hunger or thirst or headache there, nor sadness or anxiety of any kind, so great is the joy and delight, and one never wearies of being there. Abbot Mernoc, my companion and my son in Christ, goes often to this island, and it was he who found the way to this precious place. And you should know that an angel of God, wondrous to behold, guards this place, and no one can go there without his permission." And I added, "Can you not tell from the fragrance of our clothes that we have been in Paradise?"[4]

'Then the brothers answered: "O Abbot, we did indeed know by that fragrance, and by other things, that you have been in a good place. We would gladly learn from you where this Paradise is, for we do not know. And we tell you that the fragrance of your clothes has lasted forty days since you returned from that place." I told them that I had been in that precious place for the space of two weeks with my son Mernoc, and that we had not eaten or drunk or slept; and we were so filled with joy and delight at what we saw, that we were fully satisfied, as if we had eaten to our hearts' content. Then, when the forty days had passed and we had received the blessing of the brothers and the Abbot Mernoc, I came back with my brothers to return to my cell, to which I had to go on the morrow.'

When he heard these things, Saint Brendan threw himself on the ground with all his company, praising the Lord God and saying:
'Praised be the Lord God in all his ways; for he is holy in all his works, and he has revealed to his servants all these things and such great marvels. May he be blessed for his gifts, by which he has fed us with such spiritual food and drink.'
Then Saint Brendan said to his brothers:
'Let us go and eat bodily food, according to our custom.'
So it was done; and, when the night was past and he had received the blessing of the brothers, in the morning Saint Brendan went to his cell, and let his nephew Barrind depart.

II   Then Saint Brendan chose from his whole congregation seven good
      brothers, and he shut himself up with them in the refectory, and
      spoke thus to them:

      'You, my companions in penance – for so we have been – I pray
      you to advise me, for my heart and my thoughts are all united in a
      single purpose. I am resolved, provided it is the will of God, to
      journey to that land of which Abbot Barrind spoke, the Promised
      Land of the Saints, and not to rest until I am there. Now, what do
      you think, and what advice will you give me?'

      And they, recognizing the purpose of this holy father, almost at
      once and with a single voice said to him:

      'O Abbot, this purpose which is yours is ours also. Do you not
      know that we have left our families and our worldly inheritance to
      serve God? We are ready to come with you to death or life, provided
      it is the will of God.'

      So they ended their discussion and went away; and Saint Brendan
      ordered that they should all keep a fast for forty days, and then set
      out on their voyage.

III   When the forty days' fast was completed and he had taken leave of
      his brothers, he embarked on his boat and began to make his way
      towards the west; and he came to a certain island, the island of a
      holy father called Enda.

IV   He sought his blessing and that of all the monks who were with
      him, and journeyed to the farthest point of that country. His family
      lived there, but he did not wish to see anyone; instead he climbed a
      very high mountain to see the extent of the ocean. And he saw a
      place nearby called Saint Brendan's Seat, which was the place from
      which he set out; he went down the mountain and made a haven
      there, for there was entry for one boat. Saint Brendan and all those
      who were with him brought tools, and there they built a boat, very
      strong and light, to sail the open sea. They made it very strong and
      all of wood, according to the way in which they built boats in that
      country; and he called it a cog.[5] When the cog was finished and
      properly ballasted, he covered it on the outside with ox leather, and
      painted it red, and sealed all the joints in the wood; then he greased
      the boat and the leather all over with butter, and in the boat he put
      two oxhides and enough butter to grease the boat when it was
      necessary. Then he put in it sufficient food and drink for forty days,

and various things to cook and to make what they needed. He set up a mast in the middle of the boat, and furnished the boat with everything else that it needed. Then Saint Brendan commanded his brothers in the name of God the Father and the Son and the Holy Spirit to embark on board the boat, and he remained alone on the shore.

V   When he had blessed the haven and his brothers, there came to him three brothers from his monastery. When they came to him, they threw themselves on the ground at his feet and said:

'O Father, Father, let us come with you to the place where you are going; if you do not let us come, we shall die of hunger and thirst on this very spot. Know that we have resolved among ourselves to be pilgrims all the days of our life.'

When the saint saw their distress, he commanded them to enter into the boat, saying:

'Be it as you will, my dear sons.'

Then he said:

'I know how you come to be here: this brother has done good works, and in truth God has prepared a good place for him; but for you others a dark and evil place.'

VI   Then Saint Brendan embarked in the boat and, spreading the sail, he began to sail towards the south; there was a good wind, and all he had to do was keep the sail in place. So he voyaged for forty days; and at the end of forty days the wind dropped, and they had to row. They rowed so far that they were weary and could labour no longer. Then Saint Brendan began to encourage and comfort them, saying:

'My brothers, have no fear, for God is our guide and helmsman, and so he will provide for us what we need. So ship all the oars and put the other fittings of the boat in their place, and leave the sail unfurled; and let God do as he wills with his servants and with this boat.'

They ate always at the hour of vespers; and the boat sailed on, wherever the winds carried it.

When the forty days were ended, they had eaten all their food; and towards the north they came upon an island which was very steep and rocky. As they approached the shore they saw a very high cliff, as sheer as a wall. There were many streams flowing down from the mountain into the sea, but they could not find any harbour where they might bring the boat to rest. The brothers, suffering from hunger and thirst, all took the vessels and filled them with water to drink, and they brought this water on to the boat; but when Saint Brendan saw what they were doing, he said:

'Do not do that, for what you are doing is madness. Since God does not wish to show us a harbour, why do you seek to seize what is his by force? I am not pleased that you have taken this water' – and he threw it away.

After three days Jesus Christ allowed them to enter the harbour; and they moored the boat, went ashore, and explored the island looking for something to eat. They had sailed around the island for three days before they found this haven; and at the hour of nones they came into a very narrow harbour, so narrow that the boat could barely enter it. Before they entered Saint Brendan made the sign of the cross and blessed the harbour. There was a great rock, very high, sheer like a wall, and cleft down the middle. And they all disembarked and came ashore. Then Saint Brendan ordered them all not to take anything from the boat. As they went up from the seashore, a dog came to meet them, and greeted Saint Brendan, fawning at his feet as if welcoming its master. Saint Brendan said to his brothers:

'Does it not seem that God has sent us a good messenger? So follow him without fear, wherever he leads you.'

So Saint Brendan and his brothers followed the dog until they came to a castle; and going inside they found a large hall, where there were many beds to lie on and chairs to sit upon and water in vessels for washing their feet. As they sat down, the saint addressed his brothers thus:

'Brothers, be on your guard lest Satan should deceive you or should lead you into temptation. I see him deceiving one of the three brothers who came after us from our monastery; and he is about to commit a wicked theft, to the loss of his soul, for his soul is already given into the devil's hands.'

The house where they were was full of vessels hanging on the walls, of different kinds of metals, and also of bridles and horns decorated with silver.

Then Saint Brendan said to his steward, who was accustomed to give the brothers their bread:

'Serve the dinner which God has sent us.'

So he immediately got up to serve the meal; and as he went through the lodgings, he found the table ready laid with cloths and white bread and cooked fish, and pure white sheets on all the beds. When they were at table and Saint Brendan saw everything so well prepared, he pronounced the blessing along with his brothers, speaking this verse:

'Give thanks unto the God of Heaven, who giveth food to all flesh.'[6]

They sat down to table and began to eat, devoutly praising God; and they had as much as they wanted to drink. And when they had finished eating, they gave thanks to God, and the saint said to his brothers:

'Go, and worship God until evening, and then let everyone go and sleep in his bed and rest, for your limbs are weary and worn out with all the rowing you have done.'

When the brothers were asleep Saint Brendan saw the devil at work tempting one of his brothers. He saw a black boy who had a bridle in his hand, and was playing with it at the feet of one of the brothers. Immediately Saint Brendan got up and began to pray, and he remained in prayer until it was day. At the appointed time he ordered the brothers to say the office. When they had finished saying the office, they were about to go back to the boat. But they saw the table full of things to eat, so they stayed there eating and drinking as much as they wanted. And the food lasted them for three days; so they stayed three days in that place, and God sent them what they needed.

VII When the three days had passed, they boarded the boat to continue their journey. The holy father said to the brothers:

'Take care, all of you, that no one has taken anything from this place.'

They replied:

'God forbid that any of us should have stolen anything, to bring dishonour on our journey.'

Then the holy father said:

'You see this brother of ours, of whom I spoke to you yesterday? He has taken a silver bridle and has hidden it in the devil's bosom;

the devil has given it to him, and he has taken it without my permission. Now let him know what he must do, for we could all perish because of this sin.'

As soon as the brother heard this, he took the bridle from under his clothing and threw it at the abbot's feet, saying:

'Holy father, forgive me, for I know I have sinned; pray to God for my soul, that it may not perish because of this theft.'

All the brothers were dismayed, and devoutly threw themselves on the ground and began to pray to God for his soul. When the brethren arose from their prayer, the brother who had committed the theft got to his feet and stood in great shame and misery before the abbot. And they all saw a black boy come out from under the clothes of the brother who had the bridle, crying out with a loud voice:

'Holy father, why do you drive me out from my place by your prayers? Know that these past seven years I have been constantly with this brother, trying to tempt him into some mortal sin, but I have never been able to tempt him until this past night. You do me wrong, Abbot, for because of you I have to change my dwelling place and leave my inheritance!'

To this Saint Brendan replied:

'I command you in the name of the Father and of the Son and of the Holy Spirit, who is our Lord Jesus Christ, that you depart and do no harm to any man until the Day of Judgement.'

So as they all watched, the devil departed; and, turning to the brother, he said:

'Make your confession straightaway to a priest, for then you will die and your soul will leave your body. Your body will remain in this place and will be buried here; and the soul of your brother who came with you from the monastery is in Hell.'

The brother immediately made his confession and devoutly received the body of our Lord Jesus Christ. The abbot and the brothers began to dig his grave; and as soon as he had received the blessed sacrament, he died, and his soul was taken by the angels and borne up to Heaven. When the brothers saw this, they buried his body in that place and said the office for him in the proper way.

VIII   Then the brothers went down to the shore with the abbot, and they all embarked in the boat. But before they left the shore there came a young man bringing them a basket full of bread and a large jar full of water, and he said to them:

'Receive this blessing from the hand of a servant of God. Know that you are to make a long journey; you will succeed, and you will find consolation in the place where you are going; and this bread and water will last you until Easter day.'

When they had received these things and given thanks, they set sail towards the west. And they ate every third day, and sang the office at all the fixed hours.

IX One day, as the boat was sailing hither and thither, they sighted an island not far off, so they sailed towards it; there arose a favourable wind, so the boat soon reached the harbour without their having to row. When they were in the harbour, the abbot commanded them all to leave the boat, while he remained behind. As they explored the island, they discovered many rivers of clear water and many springs, full of different kinds of fish; and when they reassembled in one place, the abbot commanded that they should observe the office there, and sing mass and give communion to the whole company, for it was Maundy Thursday. So it was done, and they had supper there, and remained there until Holy Saturday.

As they were exploring the island, they found a great flock of sheep, as white as cotton and as big as oxen, covering the whole land. Saint Brendan called his brothers and told them that they should confidently take these beasts for food and for their other needs; so they took just one sheep and cut off its head, and also a lamb for the blessing, and did with it what was required, as seemed best to them. When everything was ready for the feast of Easter, which was the next day, there appeared to them a man carrying a large sack of bread which had been baked in the embers, and other things to eat. He put it down on the ground in front of Saint Brendan, and then devoutly prostrated himself at his feet three times, saying fervently:

'O pearl of God, how has this happened to me, who am not worthy that such a person should appear at this holy time to eat my bread, which I have made by my own labour and with my own hands?'

Saint Brendan took him by the hand and raised him from the ground and, giving him his blessing, said:

'My son, you are welcome. Know that our Lord Jesus Christ has provided for us, in these holy days, this place to celebrate the feast of Easter, which is the feast of his holy Resurrection.'
The man answered:

'Father, you will stay here to do what you have to do on Holy Saturday, which is today; but early tomorrow you will be on that island which you see over there, and there you will make your resting place and will sing mass and say the other hours. For it pleases God that you should do so on that island and not on this one.'

So the abbot had everything loaded into the boat ready to go to that place early the next morning. When the boat was fully laden, the man said:

'Sir, the boat is so full that it cannot hold any more; but do not worry about the things that you lack. Set off whenever you like, and after eight days I will send you all you need to eat and drink, and it will be enough to last you until the feast of Pentecost.'
To this Saint Brendan replied:

'How do you know where we will be in eight days' time?'
The man said:

'In the early hours of tonight you will be on that island which you see close by, and you will stay there tomorrow until the hour of sext; then you will sail to another island to the west of that one, not far from it, which is called the Paradise of Birds, and you will stay there until the octave of Pentecost.'

Then the abbot questioned him about the sheep, why they were so big and so white and why there were so many of them, and he replied:

'You should know that on this island there is good grass and dew which falls full of manna, and the air is very temperate and wholesome, so it is a very good place for them; and no one milks them when they have finished suckling their lambs, there is no winter to cause them to die of cold or infirmity, and no one to kill them or butcher them. So they live as they please, wandering or remaining still day and night at will; that is why they are so big and white and why there are so many of them.'

When the man had said this he took leave of them, and they all went aboard the boat and set sail towards that island, making the sign of the cross and pronouncing benediction.

X As they reached the island, the boat came to rest before they could bring it into port; so Saint Brendan told the brothers not to fear, but to get out of the boat into the sea in order to reach land. They did so, and when they were in the water they took ropes and pulled the boat into the harbour and tied it up well. The island was full of stones; there was no grass anywhere, and there was no sand on the beach, just dry land. Then all the brothers settled themselves to pray in different places, while the abbot stayed on the boat, for he knew well what kind of island it was; but he did not want to tell them, lest they be afraid.

Very early, when day came, he commanded all the priests that they should each sing a mass. He did the same; and when Saint Brendan and all the other brothers had sung their masses in the boat, the brothers started to bring out from the boat the raw meat and fish they had brought with them from the other island, in order to cook it. Then they put a pot on the fire and, when there was a big fire burning underneath and the pot was boiling hard, the whole island began to move like a wave. The brothers ran to the boat in fear, leaving everything behind and devoutly praying the saint to rescue them; and the abbot took them all by the hand and brought them into the boat. When they were all aboard, they rapidly set sail; and the island moved away towards the west. They saw a great fire burning for a distance of two miles, and the holy father explained to them what it was:

'My brothers', he said, 'why are you amazed at the fire which you see coming from the island over there?'

'You are right, sir', they replied, 'we were greatly afraid.'

So he said to them:

'My sons, do not be afraid; for God revealed to me in a vision last night that this island where we have been, and which you see burning, is not an island but the greatest fish in the sea; it is the biggest and longest fish there is, and it is called Jason.'[7]

XI Sailing close to the island where they had been, scarcely had they passed beyond it when they saw to the west not far off, separated from it by a narrow stretch of sea, another island which was full of plants and woods, and every plant and tree there was in flower. They sailed around it looking for somewhere to land, and on the south side of the island they found a stream of fresh water flowing into the sea; so coming into harbour there they tied up the boat and disembarked. Saint Brendan ordered them to drag the boat with ropes as far as they could along the river bank. The river was only just wider than the boat; the abbot alone remained in the boat, and so they dragged it for more than a mile, until they came to a spring from which flowed the water of this river. Then Saint Brendan said:

'See how our Lord Jesus Christ has given us a place to celebrate the Paschal feast of his Resurrection!'
And he added:

'My brothers, even if we had had no other provisions except the water of this river, it would have been all we needed to eat and drink, so much milk and goodness does it contain.'

Over the spring was a tree, very broad and twisted and not very high, which was completely covered with white birds, so that not a leaf or a branch was empty. When the saint saw this, he wondered what it was, and why there were so many birds all together. As he reflected on this, he threw himself to the ground and prayed with tears of devotion, saying:

'O God, you know all things and reveal all secrets and things unknown; you know the anguish of my heart and my desire. I adore you and pray to your majesty, sinner that I am, that you would deign in your mercy to reveal this matter to me, which is so mysterious and which I see with my own eyes. And I know, O Lord, that I am not worthy through my own merits, but that you in your goodness will do this.'

When he had quietly spoken thus, Saint Brendan sat on the ground and watched the birds; and one of the birds flew over from the tree where the others were, its wings sounding like a bell as it flew. The bird came towards where the abbot was sitting and, alighting on the bow of the boat, spread its wings as an expression of delight, fixing its gaze on the holy father with a joyful countenance. The holy father immediately realized that God had heard him and his prayer so, as the bird perched there, he spoke to it, saying:

'If you are a messenger from God, tell me: who are you, and where do you come from? What are all those other birds, and why are there so many gathered together in one place?'
The bird replied:

'O servant of God, we belong to that great company that fell from Heaven with the angel Lucifer, who is the enemy of the human race. We did not sin knowingly of our own accord, and so we are no longer in the place where we were created, but we have been driven out with the host of those who sinned grievously. But because such sin is not in us, God who is our Lord, who is just and true, in his mercy and in his justice and judgement has placed us here for as long as it shall please him. In truth we do not endure suffering of any kind; by the presence of God we can see light, but we cannot separate ourselves from the company of those others who did not humble themselves, but remained obdurate.[8] We wander here and there in different regions of the air under his firmament, and of the earth, like other spirits who are sent here. But on holy days and on Sundays we receive these bodies which you see, and we stay here praising our Creator. Know that a year has passed since you began your voyage, and it will be another six years before you return home; and every year you must celebrate Easter here. And at the end of seven years you will find the place that you are seeking, which you have set your hearts on seeing, the Promised Land of the Saints.'

When it had said this, the bird flew away from the boat and back to its place with the others.

And when it was the hour of vespers, all the birds that were on the tree began to sing with one voice, and beating their wings they said as they sang sweetly:

'Thou, O God, art praised in Sion, and unto thee shall the vow be performed in Jerusalem; O Lord, hear my prayer, and let my cry come unto thee.'

This verse lasted for the space of an hour; and to the abbot and those who were with him the sound of their wings was like a soft song of lament. Then Saint Brendan said to his brothers:

'Eat as much as you like, and let your bodies be fed and satisfied, for your souls have been fed with divine grace.'

After supper, they said compline and then went to bed until the third part of the night; but the abbot did not sleep, but remained awake in prayer, and he called them when it was time for matins. Getting up, they said matins, beginning with this verse: 'O Lord, open thou my lips.' And when they had finished saying matins, all the birds seemed to be saying very softly with their beaks and their wings: 'Praise the Lord, all his angels; praise him, all his powers.' So they spoke in the same way for the space of an hour at vespers; and when it was light, they all began to sing for prime, saying: 'The fear of the Lord be upon us and upon them that fear thee; the fear of the Lord is the beginning of wisdom.' In all their songs they maintained the same tune for the space of one hour; at terce they softly sang this verse: 'Sing psalms to our God, sing psalms to our king; sing praises in wisdom.' At sext they said: 'The Lord make the light of his countenance to shine upon us and have mercy on us.' And at nones they said: 'Behold, how good and joyful a thing it is, brethren, to dwell together in unity.' Thus these birds gave praises to our Lord day and night. Thus Saint Brendan fed his brothers all through the octave of Easter.

And when all the days of Easter were past, he said:

'Let us take our supplies from this spring, even if up to now we have used it only for washing our hands and feet.'

But when he had said this, there appeared the good man who had come to them the other time, before Easter, and had given them food; and he came to them with a boat full of things to eat and drink. When he had unloaded his boat, he spoke to the abbot and the other brothers, saying:

'My brothers, now you have enough to sustain you until the feast of Pentecost; so do not drink of this spring, for it is too strong to drink, as I shall explain to you. Know that anyone who drinks of it immediately falls into such a deep sleep that he sleeps for a day and a night, the space of twenty-four hours; this is the power of the milk within the spring, but outside it is water and not milk, even though it is so white.'

Then he took leave of the brothers, received their blessing, and went away.

And Saint Brendan remained in that place until the octave of Pentecost. On the day of the feast the abbot sang mass with all the others, and then the Steward of Christ's poor came and brought them those things which they needed for the feast and for many days afterwards. As they were eating, this good man said to them:

'You, servants of God, have to make a long journey, and so I advise you to fill all your vessels with water from this river, and take with you as much dry bread as you can carry, and keep it for another year. I will give you as much as your boat can hold and carry.'

So saying, he came back bringing them the biscuit which he had promised; and when the eight days were past, they filled their vessels with water and set off.

Just as the brothers were about to board the boat to depart, a bird suddenly came flying and alighted on the prow of the boat. When the abbot saw this, he got into the boat and told the brothers to wait before they boarded. As they all waited, the bird began to speak with a human voice, and said:

'You should know that you are to stay with us on the holy day of Easter every year for six years; every year you shall keep Maundy Thursday where you were this year, and so also on Holy Saturday; and you shall keep the Easter Vigil where you kept it this year, on the fish called Jason. Wherever you explore and wherever you return, you must do every year as I have told you, and come back to these places. When you leave here, after eight days you will come to an island called the island of the Abbot Ailbe, the servant of God; with him you will keep the feast of the Nativity of our Lord God.'

When it had said this, the bird flew back to its place, and immediately the brothers went aboard the boat, raised the sail, put their hands to the oars, and began to sail rapidly towards the west. And all the birds with one voice began to sing sweetly, saying: 'Hear us, O God our salvation, the hope of all the ends of earth and sea.'

XII Then Saint Brendan and all his companions sailed hither and thither on the sea for the space of three months, and they never found any harbour or island or land of any kind, but only water and sky; and they fasted every third day, or sometimes more often. After three months, there came a day when they sighted an island not far off; but when they approached the shore, there arose a strong wind which drove them away, so that for forty days they sailed continually around this island, never being able to enter harbour, although they were never far off shore. At the end of forty days the brothers were weary, and they agreed to devote themselves to prayer, that God might deliver them from this trial; for they were so overcome with exhaustion that they could labour no longer. So they spent three days in continual prayer and in silence; and the boat moved rapidly by itself until they reached a narrow harbour, wide enough for one boat. There they saw two springs of water, one cloudy and the other clear. The brothers were all much encouraged, and they prepared their vessels to take some of the clear water. But the abbot said to them:

'My sons, do nothing which is improper; take no water or anything else from this island without permission from the old man who lives here serving God. Have no doubt that he will give you plenty, so do not steal it, and do not be tempted to drink water which has been stolen.'

So they disembarked from the boat and looked around, to see in which direction they should go. Then shortly there came to meet them an imposing old man, with hair as white as snow and a handsome, high-coloured face, and a very white beard which reached down to the ground; and when he came near, he knelt devoutly on the ground, before giving the abbot the kiss of peace. When he did this for the third time, Saint Brendan went up to him and, with the other brothers, raised him from the ground; and he gave him his blessing and took him by the hand. And the two abbots walked together in this way for an eighth part of a mile, until they came to a monastery. When Saint Brendan and his brothers reached the gate of the monastery, he stopped and said to the old man:

'Father, whose monastery is this? Who is its head, and where do those who live here come from?'

He spoke many other words to him and asked him many other things, but the old man did not answer any of them; he said not a word, but made clear signs of reply with his hand. So Saint Brendan realized that he was not deaf, but was under a vow of silence; and he called his brethren to him and commanded them to keep silence also, until such time and place as they were allowed to speak, so as not to cause the brothers in that place to break their vow. Shortly after he had given this command, eleven monks came from some way off, carrying crosses and boxes of saints' relics; and they sang hymns and other words, namely a text which says: 'Arise to the Lord, you saints, from your dwellings, and go to meet the truth. Sanctify the place and bless the people, and graciously keep us your servants in peace.' When they had finished singing this verse, the abbot of the monastery gave his blessing to Saint Brendan and his brethren, and led them with him into the monastery and showed them every part of it, saying:

'This is such and such a place, and there is such and such a thing.'

And when he had shown them everything within and without, he had warm water brought and washed the feet of all the brothers, and they sang this verse: 'A new commandment I give unto you, that whatsoever I do unto you, you also should do.' When this was done to the comfort of all, he led them into the refectory and, ringing a bell, made a sign to them with his hand that they should go in and sit at the tables; and they did so. Then he rang the bell again, and shortly there came a brother from the monastery with pure white loaves of bread and fresh roots of plants which had a very sweet taste. One of the brothers from the monastery sat at table with each of the visiting brothers, and to every two brothers was given a whole loaf and two roots. Then the bell was rung again, and a brother brought them drink.

Then the abbot of the monastery encouraged the brothers with a cheerful countenance, saying:
'This drink comes from that spring from which you earlier wanted to take water by stealth to drink. Now you can drink it without fear; it is from the clear spring, so take it in charity and with joy and in the fear of God. As for the other spring which you saw, with cloudy water, it provides water every day to wash the brothers' feet; and it is naturally hot. The loaves of bread which you saw, so white and good, are not made in this monastery; in fact, we do not know where they are made or who brings them to the monastery, but we are sure that this is a gift from God and a grace that he gives to us in his goodness, for he does not abandon his servants. We are twenty-four brothers, and every day we have twelve loaves to eat, one loaf between two brothers; and every Sunday and feast day we receive a loaf per man, so that he may have it for supper together with the strawberries which we gather. But today, even though it is not a feast day, God has sent us a loaf per man because you have come here, and he wanted to send provisions for you. Christ our Lord has fed us in this way ever since the time of Saint Patrick and Saint Ailbe, which is a good eighty years.[9] Truly, our limbs are immune from old age and infirmity. And you should know that on this island we never lack for anything to eat; we never eat anything cooked on a fire; we never suffer from either heat or cold, for the air is very temperate. And when it is the hour to sing

matins and vespers the lamps in the church are always lit, we do not know by whom, and they burn for as long as the office lasts – except that after matins they stay lit until it is day – and the oil in the lamps never runs out.'

When they had drunk three times, the abbot rang the bell, as was his custom, and all the brothers together rose in silence from the table and went ahead of the holy abbots into the church; then the abbots, Saint Brendan and the other, followed them. As they went into the church, twelve other brothers came to meet them, and joyfully genuflected in front of the abbots. When Saint Brendan saw them, he asked:

'Abbot, why did these brothers not eat with us?'

'Because there was not room for them to sit at table with us', the abbot replied, 'but now they are going to eat, and they will be given what God pleases; we are going into the church to sing vespers, because the brothers who are going to eat now will also sing vespers after us.'

After vespers Saint Brendan began to think and speak and look around at how the church was made; and he saw how it was square on every side, and all the altars, vessels, cruets and chalices in the church were all made of purest crystal. There were twenty-four stalls around the church, with the abbot's stall in the middle and two choirs for the brothers on either side. There were seven lamps which had been brought there from the beginning; three stood in front of the high altar, and the other four were divided between the two side altars, two in front of each altar. And he saw that the altars were of pure crystal. The abbot always began the office, and then one choir would recite devoutly to the other, and the other would respond. No one began any chant except the abbot, and none of the brothers dared to leave the church without permission from the abbot. If a brother needed to go out of the church for any reason, he would write what he needed on a wax tablet and show it to the abbot, and the abbot would give his permission. And he saw that no one dared to speak or make any noise in that place, and if anyone wanted to know anything or to seek advice, he would follow this same practice with the abbot.

So they passed the day; and the abbot of the place said:

'It is time to go to supper, while it is still light.'

So they went into the refectory, where they had bread and roots for supper, and water to drink. After supper they went to sing compline, and when the abbot had begun: 'Haste thee, O God, to deliver me', they all knelt down to honour the Trinity. They began this verse: 'We have acted unjustly, we have done iniquity; but you, O Lord, who are our faithful father, spare us. I shall sleep in peace, therefore, and take my rest, for you, Lord, have placed me, singularly, in hope.'

After this they sang the office in due order; and when they had finished the whole office and the benediction, the abbot and all the brothers went out of the church, each to his own cell, and each of the brothers of that place took as his companion one of the visiting brothers. The abbot of the monastery took the abbot Brendan as his companion, and they stayed in the church so that he could show Brendan how God lit the lamps in the church. They spent the night in prayer, all the time that the church was lit, in silence and humility; then the abbot said:

'I have been abbot here for eighty years, doing penance, and never has any better person been here than you and your companions. Truly, we hear the voices of men singing with us when we sing lauds in the morning. We are twenty-four brothers in this place, and none of us speaks during the week except by means of signs with our fingers and hands and eyes; but on feast days we may speak from the end of our mealtime until vespers, but no longer. And since we have been in this place, none of us has ever fallen ill, or suffered any dread or fear from any of the spirits which sometimes go to and fro.'

'We would like to stay here for a year', said Saint Brendan. But the abbot replied:

'That is not permitted you in this place, for it is not what God wills. Do you not remember that I revealed to you what you must do, before you came to this place? Know that you must return with eleven brothers to your own place, where God has prepared the place for your burial; but there are two brothers with you who will not return from this journey. One will remain on an island called the Island of Anchorites, and the other will die a bad death and will be condemned to the pains of Hell.'

As they were talking thus, there came an arrow of fire through a window and, as they watched, it lit all the lamps which were before the altars in the church; then it went straight out again, and the lamps remained lit with a perfectly clear flame. Saint Brendan asked who put out the lamps, and how they were put out for the next day.

'Father', said the abbot, 'come and see this miracle with me.'
And together they went up to the lamps and looked inside them, and there was nothing inside but the flame in the middle; there was no oil or water or wick or flame, from which they could see clearly that this was not a physical fire but a spiritual one. And the saint said:

'How can something burn physically if it has no body? For spiritual creatures are not visible to the physical senses, as we know of the soul, which cannot be seen by the body.'
The holy abbot replied:

'Have you not read in the Bible how, when God came to speak to Moses on Mount Sinai, which is in Armenia, the thorn bush appeared to burn, and he saw the flame from a long way off at night, but the next morning he found nothing, and no trace of fire?'
Day came, and they had not slept all night; and when they had sung mass in due order, Abbot Brendan called his companions and they sought leave to depart, for they wanted to move on from that place. But the old abbot said to them:

'You may not leave now, for you must keep Christmas with us, and all the feasts of the Lord up until the octave of Epiphany.'
So Saint Brendan stayed in that place with his brothers, on the island with the community of Abbot Ailbe.

XIII   When the feasts were over, those holy brothers gave them victuals for the boat, and gave them their blessing and took their leave; and Saint Brendan and his companions boarded the boat, raised the sail and turned the boat towards the west. And having left the port, the boat sailed hither and thither, either under sail or by rowing, until Lent; and they did not know where they were. When it was Lent, they sighted an island close by, and they were full of joy and began to row as fast as they could towards it; for their bread and water had run out, so that they fasted for three days and then had something to eat, and they were very weak and wretched. At the end of the three days they sighted the harbour; and the abbot blessed it and commanded the brothers to disembark from the boat. They did so, and straightaway they found a spring of clear water and many fine plants and roots around the spring, and they saw many different kinds of fish swimming in the river which flowed out of the spring and ran into the sea. Then Saint Brendan said to his brothers:

'God has given you this consolation after your great labours; so now take some of these fish and plants and these plentiful roots, and we shall have enough for supper; and cook the fish with confidence, for God in his goodness has prepared all these things for you.'

They did as the abbot said; but as they were about to take some of the water to drink he said to them:

'My brothers, drink sparingly of this water, and take care not to take too much, although it is so good and clear, lest it upset your stomach, for it would make you sleep more than is good for people like you.'

Some followed the abbot's advice, but others did not; some drank one cup, some two, and others three. Those who drank only one cup were not harmed by it, but those who drank two slept for two days and two nights, while those who drank three cups slept for three days and three nights. When the abbot saw how long and how deeply they slept, he prayed to God for them; and when the days of their deep sleep were past and they woke up, he said to them:

'My brothers, you have lost many hours when you have not been praising God because of the time you have slept; we had better flee this danger lest anything worse should happen to us. For God has given us this food to sustain our lives, but you by your gluttony seem to want to die, and you have done yourselves harm. It is my wish that we should leave this island; so take enough provisions from this place, fish and the other things and water, to last us until Maundy Thursday; and do not drink more than one cup of the water each day, and it will do you no harm.'

So they went gathering plants and roots and caught plenty of fish, and when they had loaded up the boat with what they needed, they went aboard and hauled up the sail and began to sail towards the Ocean, and then towards the north.

XIV Soon a favourable wind arose and lasted for three days; and after three days they found the sea almost completely solidified and frozen over, so that the water appeared motionless, and the brothers were very distressed. The abbot said:

'Ship your oars, and leave the sail up, and let the boat go where God wills, and let him be our helmsman.'

The boat sailed at random for fully twenty days,[10] and then God sent a good wind towards the east. So they raised the sail higher and began to row; they ate every third day.

XV As they were sailing thus one day, a large cloud appeared ahead of them, not far off, and the abbot said to them:

'My sons, do you recognize that cloud? That island is where we were a year ago when we celebrated Maundy Thursday, and that is where the good man lives who is called the Steward of Christ's poor.'

They replied:

'We do not recognize it, but we do remember it.'

So the brothers began to row more vigorously because of the great joy they had; and when the abbot saw what they were doing he said:

'Simpletons, do not wear yourselves out like that; do you not know that God is our navigator and the helmsman of this boat? Leave the oars, and let him do as he wills with the boat and with us; for I am sure that he will bring us to a safe haven.'

No sooner had they approached the shore of the island than the same man came to meet them who had come the previous time, the Steward of Christ's poor; and he took hold of the boat's hawser and brought it gently into the harbour, and they all disembarked praising God greatly. The good man devoutly kissed the feet of all of them, starting with the abbot, and spoke this verse:

'God is wonderful in his saints. The God of Israel will himself give valour and strength to his people; blessed be his name through all eternity.'

Then he helped them all to disembark; and he pitched a tent there, and prepared hot water to wash their feet, and clothed them all in white garments. They had supper there, and remained in that place three days, living and saying the office as they thought fitting to celebrate the Passion of Christ with great devotion.

On Holy Saturday, when they had finished all these things, he said to the brothers:

'My friends, embark in the boat to go on your way, so that on this Easter night you may be in the same place as you were last year. You will stay there until the hour of sext and no longer, doing what you have to do up to that hour, and then return to the boat and sail to that other island, the Island of the White Birds, where you were last year from Easter Day until the octave of Pentecost. Take with you all the things that you need to eat and drink; and I will come to you next Sunday and bring plenty of provisions, so just take enough for eight days.'

So saying, he left them; and afterwards he returned as he had promised, and loaded a small boat of his with bread and water and salt meat and other good things, and brought them to where they were.

Then Saint Brendan gave him his blessing, and they all embarked in the boat and began to row towards the island, as the good man had said; and when they came close to the island they saw their cooking pot which they had left there the year before when they had fled in fright. Then the abbot and all the brothers disembarked from the boat and began to sing the song of the three young men, Ananias, Azarias and Misael, that is the psalm which begins: 'O all ye works of the Lord, bless ye the Lord.' When they had finished reciting this psalm, the abbot said to the brothers:

'Consider in your hearts how God has tamed this beast beneath us, so that he does us no harm.'

Then the brothers went to and fro in the wood, praying devoutly, and so they remained until the hour of matins; and then they gathered together and sang matins and then prime, and then a priest said mass, which lasted until terce. Saint Brendan went on board the boat to sing his mass, and he blessed the lamb, and gave his blessing to all the brothers, saying:

'My brothers, we are keeping Easter here in the same place as last year; let us do everything up to the hour of sext, and then let us set out in the boat, and God will steer it.'

So they did, and as they approached the island and the harbour where they were to go they saw the spring, and the tree with the white birds, all singing with one voice, saying:

'Salvation to our God which sitteth upon the throne', and 'The Lord God hath given us light; appoint a holy day, with festal branches up to the horn of the altar.'

This was the burden of their words, of their beaks and their wings, for the space of half an hour. The abbot and the brothers hastened to disembark from the boat, and unloaded all that they had brought, and placed it in the tent where they had been the previous year, until the octave of Pentecost.

On the octave of Pentecost the good man came with a boat full of dry bread and other things as he had promised on the other island, and he gave them the provisions to take with them. As they were eating, the bird flew over and settled on the prow of the boat, spreading its wings and beating them; and all the other birds made a sound like an organ. When the abbot saw that the bird was watching him, he realized that it wanted to speak to him, and it said:

'Truly, God has provided four places for you to keep the four seasons of the year during the seven years which it will take you to complete your pilgrimage. So you will go, and you will be there at these times, as you have been in this last year which you have already passed: every year you shall spend Maundy Thursday with the Steward of Christ's poor on his island, and you shall spend Easter night on the fish Jason, and you shall stay on this island from Easter until the octave of Pentecost, and every year from Christmas to the octave of Epiphany you shall spend with the Abbot Ailbe in his monastery. And when the seven years are over, you will experience great and wonderful things and will pass through great dangers, and so you will find the Promised Land of the Saints which you are seeking; when you find it, you will stay there forty days and no more, and at the end of forty days God will bring you speedily to your own land, from whence you set out to fulfil your purpose.'

When the bird had spoken thus, straightaway Saint Brendan stood up devoutly, then he threw himself on the ground with all his brothers to give praise and thanks to God their Creator; and when they had completed their prayer, the bird flew back to its place and joined the others.

Then the good man who was the Steward said to them:

'You will remain here until the octave of Easter; I will depart, and will return with the provisions which you will need.'

So he took his leave, and the abbot gave him his blessing, as did all the brothers. When he had gone, the holy father remained there for those days; and when the feast and the octave of Easter were past, Saint Brendan commanded his brothers to prepare to set sail and to fill their vessels with water from the spring. When they had done this they brought the boat down to the sea; and while they were there the good man came with his boat laden with all their provisions, as he had promised. When everything was stowed in the boat, he gave his blessing to them all and took his leave, and returned whence he had come.

XVI Then the holy father and his companions sailed towards the west, and they were in the boat forty days, sailing hither and thither. One day as they were thus sailing at random, there appeared before them in the sea a great beast, very strange to behold, with foam coming out of its mouth; it was moving so fast that the water was all churned up, and it seemed to be coming straight after them to devour them. Seeing this beast, so large and fierce, coming after them so quickly with its mouth open as if to devour them, they were very afraid, and they began to cry out:

'O God, we pray you to help us and deliver us from this evil beast, that it may not devour us.'

Saint Brendan comforted them, saying:

'Men of little faith, have no fear; God who is our aid will surely rescue us from this beast, and from other dangers besides.'

As the beast came nearer and the waves rose up even bigger around them, the boat was threatened and the brothers continued crying out in great fear. So the abbot began devoutly to pray, saying:

'Lord Jesus Christ, who never desert your friends if they turn to you with firm faith, I humbly pray that you will deliver your servants in this boat, as you saved Noah from the flood and David from the hand of the giant Goliath, Jonah from the belly of the fish, Daniel from the lions, Joseph from his brothers and Moses from the hand of Pharaoh.'

When he had said this, another great beast immediately appeared from the west and came right up to the boat, but without touching it; and it attacked the other beast fiercely, and there was a great and hard battle between them. In the end this smaller beast spewed out a great flame of fire from its mouth, and killed the other beast and tore it into three pieces; then it departed and returned whence it had come. When all the brothers saw this, Saint Brendan said to them:

'You have all had a great fright; but what do you think of this thing which God has shown you? You have escaped from a great danger, and have been avenged on the beast which sought to devour you. Great is the mercy of God, so may he always be praised and blessed.'

The next day they sighted an island a long way off, and it was big and beautiful and full of trees. As they approached the shore of that island and disembarked from the boat, they saw one of the pieces of the beast which had been killed by the other. Saint Brendan said to them:

'My companions, do you see that piece of the sea monster which wanted to devour you? Now you will devour it, for it pleases God that you should do so, and accordingly he has cast it up on the shore. Know now that you will stay some time here on this island before you are able to leave, because of the bad weather which is coming and which is already brewing. So I tell you directly, drag the boat further up the shore, and go and find a place where you can pitch the tent for shelter.'

When they had done this, the abbot said to them:

'Go down to the fish which is on the beach and cut off enough for three months' provisions; take it, salt it and store it in the boat, and the rest of it will be eaten tonight by wild beasts.'

So they went, as the abbot had instructed them, after terce, and they stayed until after vespers; and when they had done everything the abbot had told them, they said:

'How can we live or cook anything without water, for we have no water in the boat, and there appears to be no spring here?'

'Do not be concerned about anything', said the abbot; 'is it not harder for God to provide food for us than drink? As he gives you food, so he will also give you drink. Go and explore the island to the south, and you will find a clear spring of water to drink, and plenty of good plants and roots; take as much as you need, and no more.'

They went in the direction the abbot had told them, and found everything just as he had said; and that night the weather turned stormy. And as they went back and forth to fetch water, they found the bones of the fish and nothing more. The weather became so bad with wind and storm that they stayed in that place three months and more. As they talked with the abbot and told him how they had found nothing left of the beast but the bones, he said to them:

'I know that you went to see whether what I had told you was true. Now I will tell you another thing that has not yet happened, but will come about tomorrow, and if you wish you will be able to eat of it: for the sea will cast up a large piece of another very big fish.'

So the next day they went down to the shore and found a piece of a big fish which the sea had cast up during the night; so they took as much of it as they could carry away to eat.

After three months had passed, the abbot said one evening:

'My brothers, tomorrow the weather will be fine, and the next day and the day after that; it will have improved so much that we shall be able to sail safely wherever we think best.'

And it was just as he had said. So after three months and four days the saint had the boat loaded with things to eat and the vessels filled with water; and he had roots and plants brought for himself, because he had not wanted to eat meat or fish or birds ever since he had been made a priest. When the boat was fully laden, they raised the sail and set off towards the north.

XVII   As they were sailing, after two days they sighted an island a long way off, and the abbot said to them:

'Do you see that island which I see in the distance?'

They replied that they did, and he said to them:

'What can you see there?'

'We can see three peoples', they replied, 'that is, three groups of people living on that island. The first group is of little boys, the second is of young men, and the third is of old men.'

The abbot said to them:

'I tell you that one of our brothers will remain on this island with one of these groups.'

So the brothers started asking him:

'Tell us, master, which of us is the one who will remain on this island?'

And as he was talking of other things he saw that his brothers were very sad, so he showed them which brother it was, and said:

'This is the brother who is to remain in this place with one of these groups of people.'

And the brother was very anxious; he was one of those who came after Saint Brendan from the monastery and came aboard the boat, whom the saint did not call when he was on the boat for the first time.

As they approached the island, the boat sailed up on to the shore on its own. The island was very low and flat, so that it did not rise above the level of the sea, and there were no stones or trees or plants or anything else which could be moved by the wind. It was a beautiful, big island, and it was all covered with ripe grapes; and some of the grapes were yellow like topaz, some were purple like garnets, and some were white like snow. The groups of people were separated from each other by about a stone's throw of empty land. Each group was singing very sweetly and softly without moving from their place; and when one was singing the others were silent, but as soon as one had finished singing a verse another would reply, repeating the same verse without any pause. The verse they were singing was: 'The saints will go from strength to strength, and they will see the God of gods in Zion.'

The group of boys was dressed in clothes as white as milk, the group of young men in clothes the colour of garnet, and the group of old men in clothes the colour of topaz; and all their clothes were like deacons' vestments, decorated with wide fringes and stripes.

When they landed, it was the fourth part of the day, and one of the groups began to sing three times as I have described; then they began to sing the psalms, each group singing its verse. And the psalms they sang were these: 'God be merciful unto us'; 'Save me, O God, for thy name's sake'; 'I believed, therefore I spoke', followed by a prayer. At terce they recited these psalms: 'Teach me, O Lord, the way . . .'; 'Haste thee, O God, to deliver me'; 'I believed, therefore . . .', and then the prayer. At sext they sang: 'Her foundations . . .'; 'They that trust in the Lord'; 'I am well pleased . . .', and the prayer. At nones they sang: 'Out of the deep';

'Behold, how good . . .'; 'Praise the Lord, O Jerusalem', and the prayer. At vespers: 'Thou, O God, art praised'; the Benedictus; 'My God, my God . . .'; 'Praise the Lord, ye children', and the five gradual psalms; and as they said these they made the sign of the cross.

When they had finished saying their prayers, there came a great white cloud and covered the whole island, so that the brothers could no longer see these people, although they could hear the sound of their singing. And at the hour of matins they heard the sound of all the groups together singing the psalms: 'Praise the Lord from the heavens', 'Sing to the Lord . . .', 'Praise the Lord in his saints', the Benedictus and the Te Deum. At dawn the island was clear again and emerged from the cloud, and all the groups began to sing these psalms: 'Have mercy upon me, O God'; 'O God, thou art my God, early will I seek thee'; 'Lord, thou hast been our refuge.' At terce they sang: 'Clap your hands, all you people'; 'Haste thee, O God, to deliver me'; 'I am well pleased . . .', and the prayer. Then there appeared a great white lamb which they offered in sacrifice; and they pronounced a blessing over the lamb, and devoutly made their communion. As they were receiving communion one by one they all recited this verse: 'Take this holy body of the Lord and blood of the Saviour for everlasting life.'

When they had all received communion from this blessed lamb, two of the young men had a basket full of the ripe grapes; they brought this covered basket to the brothers and said:

'Take this with you in the boat, for it will be useful to you.'

And when they gave it to them they said:

'Take this fruit from the Island of Strong Men, and give us back our brother, for you should not keep what belongs to another; and then go in peace, and God be with you.'

So Saint Brendan called that brother to him and said:

'Give us your blessing, and then go with these men who are asking for you. And know that your father begot you in a good hour, for you have proved worthy through your good works to dwell with these good people who are so dear.'

The brother devoutly gave his blessing to them all, saying 'I commend you to God'.

And the abbot said:

'My son, do you not remember how many favours God has granted to us on this journey? Go, God be with you, and pray to God for us.'

So he went away with the two young men to join their group; and at the hour of nones the abbot commanded his brothers to prepare their food, and to take one of the grapes from the basket, for he wanted to see and try this thing which was so beautifully coloured. When he saw how big and heavy it was, he was astonished, and said:

'I have never seen or heard of such grapes anywhere in the world.'

The grapes were all the same size and weight, but they were different in the colour of their skin. So he commanded to be brought a clean basin and scales, for he wanted to know how much it weighed and to see what it was like inside. He found that it weighed a pound, and when he broke the skin, which was as thick as oxhide, the juice was like honey, giving off a strong sweet fragrance. He weighed out the grape among them; each one had an ounce, and that ounce was so filling that they had no room to eat anything else that day. They did the same every day until the twelfth day, and for those twelve days they neither ate nor drank anything else; and they were satisfied, and they had always a flavour of honey in their mouths. At the end of the twelve days they had finished the twelve grapes which they had been given.

XVIII As they sailed hither and thither, their food ran out, and Saint Brendan commanded his brothers to dwell in peace and to remain devoutly at prayer, and to fast for three days; and they did so. When the three days had passed, at the middle of the hour of terce a bird came flying towards them. It was very large, bigger and more beautiful than a peacock, and it seemed to come from the direction of the island where they had been with the boat, where they had seen the three groups of people so finely dressed. This bird was carrying in its beak a branch of a tree which was wonderful to behold, for the beauty of its leaves and branches, and for its fruit; for at the end of the branch was a cluster of large bunches of grapes, with twelve grapes in each bunch, all the same size, and all as brightly coloured as precious stones. The bird landed on the boat and placed this branch in the abbot's lap where he was sitting, and then immediately flew away. When he saw this, Abbot Brendan devoutly praised Jesus Christ and, calling his brothers to him, said:

'You see what joy we have? Rejoice and trust in the Lord God, who does not abandon his friends. He has sent you a rich dinner, so praise him and give him thanks to the best of your ability.'

And they did so. The bunches on the branch were all the same, and each grape was as big as an apple, and weighed a pound; and there were twelve bunches, with twelve grapes in each bunch. So the abbot gave each brother his bunch of grapes to eat as he chose, so that they had food for twelve days. And at the end of the twelve days the abbot commanded his brothers that they should fast and pray; and they did so.

At the end of the third day they saw an island close by which was densely covered with trees, all laden with grapes like those they had had to eat; and their fragrance and taste were such that they cannot be described to anyone who has not experienced them. The trees were all weighed down to the ground by the abundance of grapes, and there was not one tree that was not laden with them. The abbot went ashore on his own and told the brothers to wait for him, while he went alone to explore the island, for he wanted to see the source of the fragrance which he smelt from the plants and flowers. There were so many of these fruit trees that they would have filled a paradise, and the birds which were there sang so delightfully and were so lovely to behold that they could not be described; so he forgot to go back to his brothers, who were still waiting for him in the boat and watching to see if he was coming. And all the time there came to their noses a sweet fragrance carried on a light wind, so that they forgot what the abbot had told them about fasting and eating. As the abbot went further into the island he found six beautiful springs from which flowed six streams, and the streams were full of green and fragrant plants, with roots which were long and thick and excellent to eat. When the abbot had thoroughly explored the whole island, he returned to his brothers, bringing with him a branch with the fruit of this island, and he gave it to them, saying:

'My brothers, it is good to stay here; so disembark from the boat and pitch the tent, and take heart and be strengthened in God, and gather the good fruits of this precious island to which God has brought us.'

So they stayed there forty days and forty nights, and they were fed once a day on the grapes and plants and roots. When the forty days were past, they went back to the boat, taking with them as much of the fruit of the trees of the island as they could carry, and so they set sail. But on their journey they encountered a great tribulation.

XIX As they set off they saw a great ugly bird called a griffin coming towards the boat from a long way off, and it seemed ravenous as though it wanted to devour them. It was part bird and part beast and part fish; its mouth and its eyes were wide open, and it appeared full of fury. So the brothers said to the abbot in great terror:

'Father, what shall we do, for this evil beast is coming upon us to devour us?'

'Have no fear of anything', the abbot replied; 'God is and will be our helper; he has defended us many times, and he can do so again, if it is his will.'

The griffin's beak was curved, and so were its claws, and its wings were as sharp as razors. And as they were speaking, another bird came up with a branch in its mouth, and when it was over the middle of the boat it dropped the branch into the abbot's lap; and then it cried out against the other bird and fought against it so fiercely that it overcame and killed it. And when it was dead, the griffin fell into the sea beside the boat, whereupon the good bird returned whence it had come.

XX Then Saint Brendan and his sailor brothers devoutly and humbly praised God; and after a few days they sighted an island, which gave them great comfort. The abbot and his companions quickly reached the island, and it was the Island of the Community of Abbot Ailbe. So they stayed with him as they had before, and kept the feast of Christmas until the octave of Epiphany; and when the festivals were over they took their leave, and received the blessing of Abbot Ailbe and his twenty-four brethren. They embarked in their boat and set out, and they sailed hither and thither on the sea, never resting except in the festival seasons, that is from Easter to Pentecost, and when they were on one of those delightful islands.

XXI Once, on the feast of the apostle Saint Peter, when Saint Brendan was singing mass on the boat, he and his brothers looked and saw that the sea was so clear it was as if there was no water at all, so clearly could they see everything that was on the bottom. One of them looked down and saw a great variety of creatures moving about; some were big and some were small, and it seemed as if he could touch them with his hand. It was like a great city with houses and towers, and all the creatures were holding on to each other, the mouth of one to the tail of the other; and they looked like sheep and goats, pigs, dogs, wolves, oxen, donkeys, lions, griffins, bears, mules, buffaloes, camels, dragons, elephants and deer. And as the abbot was singing mass, they asked him humbly if he would say the mass more quietly, so as not to disturb the animals in the sea. At this the abbot laughed and said:

'I am amazed at how simple you are! You seem to have more fear of those peaceful creatures down there than of him who is Lord of heaven and earth and this water and these creatures and fish. Do not be afraid; you escaped from the evil sea monster which seemed about to devour us, and from the griffin, and from the fish which did not stir when you lit a fire on its back, and from the forty days' storm and all the other great dangers, so you will surely escape from these creatures who are more than five miles away from you.'

And so saying, he began to sing as loudly as he could; and he and several of the brothers praised God and sang the mass at the top of their voices, paying no attention to the creatures in the sea. As soon as they began the mass all the creatures rose up and started moving about under the water, and some of them came up out of the water, like flies on the surface of wine; but none of them touched the boat. There were so many of them that the brothers could see nothing else, but only the sky and these creatures. They all stayed away from the boat, moving about in the water; and when the mass was finished they all disappeared. After this the brothers were another eight days sailing over this sea.

After eight days, when they had crossed the transparent sea, the abbot sang mass; and they sailed another three days, and at the end of the three days they found an island where there was a wood of many bitter plants. Many of the plants were attractive to look at and full of leaves and flowers and fruit, some unripe and others ripe. They had this quality, that they came up out of the ground as soon as the sun rose in the morning, and grew little by little until the hour of nones; then they remained motionless for a while, neither growing nor shrinking, and they were all similar in appearance and in their leaves and their fruit; then as soon as the sun began to go down after the hour of nones, the trees also began to go back under the ground. They continued to shrink little by little until finally, when the sun set, the trees too disappeared under the ground, and there was no trace of where they had sprung up. The other parts of the island were full of lovely sweet-smelling plants; in one place there were beautiful trees of various colours. On the top of each of these trees was an apple, round and a marvellous colour to behold; there were seven of them altogether, and they made a gentle sound like the chimes of a clock with seven bells. Nearby were seven mountains, each of a different metal; and there were seven springs, from each of which flowed a stream, one of water, one of wine, the third of blood, the fourth of oil, the fifth of milk, the sixth of honey and the last of balsam.

XXII   As they sailed hither and thither in the boat, one day after they had sung mass they saw a great upright column in the sea; they decided to go over to it, and it took them three days to get close to it. The abbot looked up to see if he could see the top, but he could not, for he could not see where it ended, and it seemed higher than the firmament. Then they saw that it was surrounded by a net, fixed with a hempen rope wound round it; and the holes in the net were large enough for a boat to pass through. He reflected on this, wondering what it was and why it was there. It was silver in colour and harder than marble, and the column looked like clearest crystal, and its form was like that of a crystal cut in the shape of a pear. Then Saint Brendan said to his brothers:

'Ship the oars, and stow the sail and the mast, and one of you go to the bow and hold on firmly to the knot of the sounding-line, and take one end and fix it to the column.'

The column and net were a good mile high, and the hole in the net extended into the depths; so the abbot said to his brethren:

'Take the boat as best you can through one of the holes, and you will see this marvel of God.'

When they were inside, they looked all around them and saw the sea clearer than glass, so that they could see everything right down to the bottom, as if there were no water there. And looking down at the foot of the column they saw that it was fixed at the base, like the marble columns in a church; and the end of the rope reached to the bottom a long way down. The saint measured one of the holes between the four ropes and found that it was four cubits on each side, for the holes were square; so they sailed all day along the side of the column, and found that each side was fifty cubits. They spent four days doing this. On the fourth day they found a very large chalice of the same substance as the net, and a paten the same colour as the column, in a window in the side of the column facing south; and it was lowered as when the priest lowers the chalice after he has consecrated the wine. The abbot straightaway took it in his hand and looked at it in great wonder, saying:

'God be praised for showing us these great things, which many will believe when we recount them.'

When they had done this, the abbot commanded that a mass should be sung for the Holy Spirit, and then they should all eat; for they had been so absorbed by seeing these things and measuring the column that they had had no thought of eating or drinking. When they wanted to see this thing, they found that the column was made like a pear-shaped stem of crystal; the base on which it stood was finely carved from four stones of four colours; it lacked nothing, either at the base or in anything else. When the night had passed, they sailed towards the north, and passing through one of the holes in the net they raised the mast and fixed the sail; and several of them stood in the bow and held the meshes of the net while the others set up everything in the boat. When they had done all this, God sent them a good wind which quickly brought them in eight days close to the mouth of Hell, towards the north, where the wind called Boreas comes from.

XIII As the wind carried them towards the north, they saw an island close by, covered with large rocks and stones, which was very foul to behold. There were no plants or trees anywhere, but everywhere were blacksmiths' forges and grinding-wheels, hammers and anvils, sickles and iron saws, large gimlets and carpenters' adzes. Beside every forge stood a huge ugly man like a blacksmith, and all these smiths were beating out various tools at their forge, while others sharpened them; and all around were very large furnaces, burning fiercely. When the abbot saw these hideous and terrifying things, he said to his brothers:

'My dear brothers, this is a bad place to stay in; I am so distressed by these things I see that I do not want to go there or even to approach, if God gives us grace.'

At this, there came a great wind which drove the boat close to the island, which was very mountainous where it came down to the sea; and as God willed, the boat passed by safely on a straight course. But as they passed, when they were about a stone's throw away, they heard the sound of huge bellows like a thunderclap, and the beating of many hammer-blows on anvils. When he heard this, the holy abbot made the sign of the cross and protected himself with the cross on all sides, saying:

'O Lord Jesus Christ, deliver us from this island, if it be your will.'

No sooner had he said this than a man from the island came running down towards us.[11] He was an old man with a long beard, and he was all black and naked and hairy like a hedgehog, and he stank of sulphur and petroleum. As soon as he saw these servants of God, he ran back to his forge. The abbot signed himself again with the cross and commended himself to God; then he said to the brothers:

'My sons, hoist the sail higher, and row as hard and as fast as you can, and let us escape from this island, for it is bad for us to stay here.'

Immediately an evil, bearded old man came running down to the shore, holding a huge pair of tongs in his hands, in which he had a great ball of iron, weighing fifty pounds, which was showering sparks like molten iron straight out of the furnace. When he reached the shore, he threw it after the brothers; but as God willed, it did them no harm, but passed close to them, about a mile from the shore. And where it fell into the sea the water began to boil, like a cauldron of meat on the fire. The brothers saw this, and the sparks flying for the distance of a mile; and then they saw all the men of that place come running to the shore as the first one had done, all carrying tongs with a ball of fire, and giving off a foul-smelling smoke which polluted the air. The water made a boiling sound like a huge cauldron. There were so many of them that they were throwing over the top of each other, and then they would go back to their forge and take some more iron and run back down to the sea and throw it after them, so that the whole sea along that coast was on fire. The whole island seemed to be on fire, giving off

great flames and smoke, and it continued burning for three days;
and as the brothers departed they heard a great crying and shouting
from all those people, and a great stench assailed their noses. The
abbot encouraged them, saying:

'Comrades, be confident and have no fear, for the arms of God
are stronger than those of the world. I tell you that we are in the
region of Hell, and this is one of its islands; you have seen
something of its devices, and I intend to watch and pray, so that we
need not fear these evil things.'

When he had spoken thus, they heard a voice crying out in great
anguish:

'O holy father, you who are God's servant and friend, pray for
me, wretch that I am! I am lost, and am held here by force against
my will, and I would gladly come to you but I cannot. I am so
unfortunate, woe is me that I was ever born into this miserable
world, which is so full of deception and tribulation. Here I am
hemmed in on every side, and I do not know what is holding me, or
by what means. Wretched is my life from now on!'

The brothers were all terrified, and called on God's mercy that he
would be gracious to them and not make them go to such an evil
place when they died. Looking towards the island, they saw a naked
man being led to torment, and they heard voices shouting:

'To the fire!', and others, 'to the water!'

Some shouted:

'Grab him!'

Some said:

'Hang him!', and others, 'tie him up!'

Others again said:

'Death, death to all our enemies who are servants of God!'

At that the water of the sea became cloudy and turbulent, and then
it caught fire, throwing up great flames in many places, and flinging
burning coals into the air which then fell back into the sea, and
there was a strong stench of sulphur and petroleum. They did not
know where to go to escape the smoke and the stench, and they
could hear voices saying:

'Roast him, put him in the fire, beat him, cut him, saw him, bind
him!'

XXIV   Another day, as they were departing, there appeared a great
mountain in the sea towards the west, and in that direction there
suddenly appeared clouds from the north; and in the clouds
appeared many different shapes, looking like griffins, bears, pigs,
deer, horses and camels, and a great plume of smoke appeared from
the top of the mountain. They wanted to get away from the place,
but a wind drove them on shore, and the boat struck hard against
the land. The cliff was very high, and there flowed down from the
mountain a river of blood. One of the three brothers who had
remained in the abbot's company wanted to get out of the boat. He
did so, and immediately began to sink to the bottom of the cliff;
and when he got to the bottom, he was caught, and cried out loud:

'O holy father, how wrong I was to leave your company! Now I
am caught and I do not know by whom, for I have no strength to
come back to you.'

The brothers began to move the boat away, wanting to escape from
the shore, and they prayed to God:

'O Lord, have mercy on us sinners!'

The abbot watched the brother who was sinking, and he saw the
poor wretch being roughly carried off by demons to the place of
torment. And he saw him being swallowed up by a dragon with nine
heads and every time being excreted again, and then he was taken
to a place where fire was lit all around him. The abbot said:

'Woe to you, my son! Why were you born? I believe that you have
deserved such a place for your wicked deeds, such is the end to
which I see you have come.'

Then a strong wind sprang up and carried the boat towards the
south; and looking back to the island from which they had come,
they saw in the distance the high mountain completely uncovered
and the summit burning fiercely, and flames rising very high into
the air of heaven and then quickly coming down again still burning,
and the whole scene was like a flaming fire. Seeing this, the abbot
and all his brethren rowed hard towards the south for the space of
seven days, seeing nothing but sky and water.

XXV   After seven days, they saw in the distance a small shape in the sea,
looking like a man seated on a rock in the sea. And there was a cloth
hanging some way in front of him, about the size of a ship's rigging,
hanging from two iron hooks, which flapped ceaselessly in the wind,

so that the man seemed to be beaten by the waves of the sea, like a boat when it is in danger of sinking and the waves beat against it on every side. As they got closer, some of the brothers in the boat said it was not a man but a bird, and others thought it was a small boat. But the abbot, hearing what they were saying, said:

'My brothers, cease this arguing and do not carry on in this way; but steer the boat and go towards the place you have seen, and we shall find out what it is.'

When they got close, they saw that it was a man, naked, misshapen and covered in hair, sitting on a big rock, with the waves of the sea beating upon him on every side, from his head to his feet, so that they often covered him completely; and when the waves receded, they left uncovered the bare rock on which this miserable wretch was sitting. And the cloth which was hanging some distance in front of him flapped repeatedly like a banner in the wind, often striking him in the eyes and on the brow.[12]

When they saw this, they were amazed; and Saint Brendan spoke to him thus:

'Tell me who you are, and why you are here in this place, for it seems as if you are doing a great penance. What have you done to deserve this? Are you dead or alive, and how long do you have to stay like this?'

'I am dead, not alive', he replied; 'I am Judas Iscariot. I killed my father with a stone and lived for a long time with my mother as my wife, without knowing it, and I had many children with her. I was a wealthy merchant, and I falsified my merchandise whenever I could; I clipped the coinage, lent money, cloth and corn at usury, and was a great thief. Then I became an apostle of Jesus Christ, and he made me treasurer of the group and put me in charge of everything we were given. So that I could support the children I had left, he gave me power to take a tenth of everything and send it to my children, and that was what I did. So when Mary Magdalen spent so much on ointment to anoint Christ's head and feet one evening at Simon the Leper's house – for she used an ointment which she bought for three hundred silver coins – I was angry because of the tenth which should have come to me. I planned to recover this tenth which I had been denied, and so I had the idea of deceiving the others and betraying my lord for thirty silver coins. This I did, and thus regained the tenth I had lost. But I meant no harm, and I never expected things to turn out as they did; I thought that with his great wisdom and power he would be able to escape. I was greatly deceived and, when I saw that Jesus Christ was condemned by Pilate and that he would surely be put to death, I was so grief-stricken at what I had done to him that I gave back all the money I had taken, and admitted my guilt in everyone's hearing. But when I saw that it was to no avail, I was so desperate with grief and sorrow that I bought a rope and hanged myself from a tree, as a thief is hanged, and so I died. When I was dead, I was placed here where you see me now.'

Then he added:

'This state in which you see me now is not the one which I deserve, but is given to me as a special grace from God, who does with me as he pleases. Nor is it the place of penance which is my due, but it is a place of pardon and refreshment which is granted to me to the honour of God every Sunday; and as today is Sunday, that is why you have been able to find me here. Truly it seems to me when I am on this rock that I am in Paradise, and I find greater consolation here than in all the delights of the world put together – than in eating, playing, dancing, singing and drinking, or lingering at will in the company of beautiful women, finding buried treasure or being given a position of honour by some great lord. Such is the fear I have of the cruel pains and dreadful torments which I have to undergo, and which I expect to suffer in this coming night, and then without ceasing until the next Sunday or major festival of God and his sweet mother. For his love he gives many such mercies both to the living and to the dead; and so I am here every Sunday, every Christmas until the feast of Epiphany, from Easter Day to the end of the day of Pentecost, and on the four feasts of Saint Mary, who is the fountain of mercies and full of grace, namely the days of her Nativity, her Annunciation, her Purification and her Assumption, and on All Saints' Day. And although as you see me here I do not appear to suffer any other pain, I am burning like red-hot iron in the furnace or like a mass of lead poured into a pot; and when I am taken away from here I am day and night in the middle of that very high mountain you see in the distance.

'In that mountain are Leviathan and his knights, all suffering different torments. I was there when your brother who came with you, and who left the boat so foolishly, was swallowed up. It was because he came into Hell that Hell showed such signs of rejoicing, which was why the fire burnt more fiercely and the flames and smoke and stench burst out; for this happens every time a sinner's soul arrives and is devoured by the dragon. Now I have told you my condition, and the reason for it, and thus I must stay until the Day of Judgement. I am cruelly punished in the depth of Hell together with King Herod and Pilate, and Annas and Caiaphas who made the bargain with me when I betrayed the body of Christ our Lord. And as I see that you are a friend of God, I beseech you in his name, who is the Lord of honour and redeemer of the world, that you would deign to pray for me that I may stay here until tomorrow, and that the devils may not be able to harm me or to take me away to my evil inheritance, which I bought for such a cursed price.'

'As for what you ask me', Saint Brendan replied, 'be it as God wills; this coming night you will suffer no more torment until the sun rises tomorrow.'

Then he asked him: 'Tell me why you are standing on this stone, and what is the purpose of this cloth hanging in front of you, and why it hangs on these two iron hooks.'

He replied: 'I am standing on this stone, which is a great boon to me, because it is a stone which I once put into a ditch where the road was muddy, so that those who passed that way could step on it; this was before I was an apostle of God. This cloth which is in front of me is out of my reach because I once gave such a cloth to a poor leper, when I was the Lord's steward; it was not mine, but belonged to the Lord and his apostles, and that is why I see it from a distance; it does me no good, in fact it sometimes hurts me. And the iron hooks you see on which the cloth is hanging are those I gave to the priests of Solomon on which to hang their seals.'

After he had said this, when evening came, a shadow came up and covered the man and the rock. Then shortly appeared a countless host of demons; and they all surrounded Judas, crying out in complaint:

'O servant of God, leave us now in this place; for because of you we cannot approach this our companion on this rock, and we dare not appear before the face of our master Lucifer without bringing to him his friend Judas, who betrayed the Lord of Lords. Truly, you have deprived us of our confidence to seize him and punish him as we are wont to do; do not come to his aid this night, however much he may beg you.'

The abbot replied: 'It is not I who defend him; but the Lord God has granted him grace this night, that he may be defended from you, and from any more pains you try to inflict on him.'

The demons replied: 'Why do you want to help him, or protect him in the name of God, when you know that he was the betrayer of the Lord?'

He said: 'I command you in the name of the Lord Jesus Christ to do him no harm this night.'

The demons replied: 'How can you invoke the name of the Lord in his aid, when you know that he betrayed him, causing so much evil to follow?'

'I do not defend him contrary to the will of God', replied the abbot; 'what God wills I will, so let his will, not ours, be done.'

He spent the whole night in prayer, and the demons did not dare to touch Judas or to do him any harm. At sunrise the abbot commanded his brothers to row in God's name; and as soon as he had said this and they began their journey, there appeared a great crowd of demons, like baboons, and they covered the whole surface of the sea. And that stretch of sea was called the abyss. The demons shouted harshly:

'You servant of God, our great enemy, go, and a curse be upon you! Cursed be your journey, your going out and your coming in, by land and by sea! Because of you our prince has treated us very harshly this past night, and has had us severely punished, because we did not bring him this accursed wretch who was defended by your prayers.'

The holy abbot replied:

'Your curse can do no harm to me, but only to you; may he who cursed you be blessed,[13] for those who cannot truly bless cannot curse either. So I do not fear your curses.'

The demons said:

'We will double this wretch Judas's punishments for the next seven days, because you have protected him this past night.'

The abbot replied:

'Neither you nor your prince has any authority, but the will of God will be done; and for your arrogance and your threats, I

command you and your prince in the name of Jesus Christ not to
treat him any worse than you are wont to do; and do not dare to
speak any further.'

'Do you speak with the voice of Jesus Christ, the Lord of all
things, that we have to obey you?', the demons replied. 'Does God
will everything that you will?'

'I am the servant of the Lord in all things and in all my words',
said the abbot; 'that is why you must obey me. God alone is the
Lord, and it is by his will that his servants speak and act. It is by the
power of his words, which are holy, that you must obey him, not me;
anything that I command in his name, I do by his commandment,
and it is with his consent that I have this authority.'
So with the abbot thus speaking and the devils complaining, they
followed him until Judas was out of sight; and then the demons
returned to take Judas from his rock, and once they had him in their
power, they carried him off with a great noise to Hell.

XVI   And Saint Brendan and his brothers continued to sail towards the
south, devoutly praising God. On the third day, they saw a small
island to the south a long way off, and as soon as the brothers saw it
they started to row hard towards it. As they approached the island,
Saint Brendan said to them:

'My brothers, do not weary your limbs so much, for you have
exerted yourselves enough since we left our monastery. I tell you
that this Easter, which is now near, it will be seven years since we
left the monastery to seek the Land of Truth and the Promised
Land of the Saints; we shall soon fulfil our purpose, and then we
shall return home safe and sound. We shall find and see Saint Paul
the Hermit, a servant of God and a man of great spiritual contrition,
who has been on this island a full seventy years doing penance. For
the last forty years he has not eaten any food or worn any clothes,
and for the first thirty years he was miraculously fed by a fish which
God sent to him every third day.'

As they approached the shore of the island, they found the cliff so
high that they could not find a harbour for the boat. The island was
a circular mountain, some two hundred paces high, and on the top
of the mountain there were no plants or trees or anything else
except a very large rock, smooth and square on all sides, as long as it
was wide and high. They sailed around the island until they found a

very narrow harbour, so enclosed that the boat's prow could barely enter it. The mountain was very dangerous to climb, and when Saint Brendan saw this, he said to his brothers:

'Wait for me here, and do not go away before I return. It is not lawful for you to come here or to meet the one who lives here without his permission, for he is a servant of God who is here to do penance. He is the Saint Paul I told you of, and since he came here no man has visited him until now. But if it is possible, you will see him along with me.'

So he set off up the mountain, and the brothers waited in the boat.

When Saint Brendan reached the top of the mountain, he looked around him and saw close at hand two caves — that is, dwellings under the ground — one with its door facing east and the other facing west. In front of the cave which faced east was a beautiful clear, circular fountain, with water springing out of the living rock. It was just by the entrance to the cave where the holy servant of God lived, and for the space of a cubit the stream penetrated the rock, which was all perforated with small holes. The bottom of the fountain was hollowed out, and there were twelve very beautiful precious stones, all of different colours. Around the edge of the fountain, not on the bottom, were twelve very strange figures which seemed as if they were of clearest crystal, and they were like the twelve signs of the heaven and the earth. Among them also were some gold stars, brighter than crystal, some of them bigger and brighter than others; and in the middle of the water was a ball of earth, which was fixed and did not move. The twelve figures were in constant motion around the water, making a very sweet sound as they moved.

As soon as Saint Brendan reached the top and approached the entrance to the cave which faced east, there emerged an old man who came to meet him, reciting this verse: 'Behold, how good and joyful a thing it is, brethren, to dwell together in unity.' Saint Brendan understood the meaning of these words which the servant of God spoke, and he went back down and told his brothers to come up the mountain, where they would see strange and wonderful things. When they reached the top of the mountain where the servant of God was, they devoutly exchanged the kiss of peace with one another, and the servant of God exchanged the peace with them one by one, saying kindly: 'Welcome', and calling each one by name. The brothers, hearing these words and seeing his long white hair and beard, were amazed, for he was a very strange sight clothed as he was in his beard and hair which reached down to the ground. His hair and beard were all as white as snow, and reached down to the ground, so that all that could be seen of him were his eyes, mouth, nose and fingernails. He wore no clothes save the hair on his body, like a sheep, and he was very old.

Seeing all this, Saint Brendan became very thoughtful and sad at heart, and he said quietly to himself:

'Woe is me, for I wear a good monk's habit to cover my flesh and keep me warm, and I have many men who wear my habit under my command; and in this state to which God has called me I thought to do penance to be pleasing to God. But now I have found a servant of God who is a man like other men, yet, because of where he dwells and how he is dressed, lives in a quite different condition. Although he is so old and has dwelt for many years on this rock, and has not eaten bread or drunk wine or eaten any food cooked on a fire, he is nevertheless still hale and hearty in body and pure in his soul from vice and sin.'

As he was reflecting to himself on these and other things, the servant of God said to him:

'O holy servant, worthy of reverence, you have cause to be joyful and take comfort in God, seeing and recalling all the wonders and miracles which God has shown you in this voyage of yours. God has indeed shown you and allowed you to see things which he has not revealed to any of the other saints; and yet you say in your heart that you are not worthy to wear a monk's habit and are not sure that you are a friend of God, nor do you consider that you lead a life pleasing to God. This comes from your humility and goodness. So know that you are a true and good monk – and more than a monk, for the majority of monks do not work, but you work hard, labouring all day with your hands on the boat, and praying with your heart and tongue. And you must see to it that others do the same, and concern yourself with keeping your companions in a state of salvation. Do you not know that it is now seven years that you have been sailing back and forth across the sea, undergoing great fear and tribulation, and God has fed and clothed you and your brothers all this time? So your life is good, useful, holy and righteous. And I, wretch that I am, dwell here like a bird on this rock, like an eagle; I am naked and have nothing to cover my flesh except the hair of my head, beard and body, and I know that I am a fearful sight to behold.'

Then Saint Brendan humbly asked him his name, and what order of brothers he had belonged to, and where he was from and how long he had been doing penance in that place. He replied:

'My name is Paul; from the age of three I was brought up in the monastery of Saint Patrick, who was a holy man. I dwelt in that monastery for fifty years, and I was given the job of looking after the cemetery and the monastery cloister; whenever one of the brothers died I helped to bury him. One day, as I was saying my prayers in that place, my superior came to me and told me that a brother had died, and that I was to make a grave to bury him; and he showed me where I should dig the next day. But when evening came, there appeared to me an old man whom I did not know, and he said to me: "My brother, although your superior has told you to dig a grave tomorrow to bury a man who has died, do not do so; for that place belongs to another, though you do not know it." I looked at him and, not recognizing him, said: "Who are you, Father?" "How is it that you do not know me?", he said; "Am I not Patrick, your abbot?" "But I know him, and if I saw him I would recognize him." He said to me: "Paul, know that I am Patrick your abbot, even though you do not recognize me." "How can you be Patrick, since you do not look like him?" I asked. He replied, "Know that I am Patrick, and you do not recognize me because I am dead and not alive; yesterday I departed this life and am no longer in this world. I have found a good place in the next life and can call myself well content. The other brothers all know this. Ailbe shall be the next abbot; he will be a good man, of holy life, and he will be a friend of God." Then he added: "That place where your superior told you to dig a grave is the place where my body will be buried, and others, not you, will dig it. Do not tell anyone else what I am telling you. And I tell you it does not please God that you should stay any longer in this place or go on doing this work. Tomorrow morning, this is what you are to do: after matins, set off early in God's name and go to the sea shore; there you will find a boat all prepared. Embark in it in God's name, and let it take you wherever God wills. In a few days it will bring you, by the power of God, to a place where you are to do a hard and taxing penance; and there you will die, when God wills. It is a very strange and lonely place; it is close to the Earthly Paradise, and you will see many things from the Earthly Paradise which will bring you great consolation in your life. Have no fear, for you will receive consolation and salvation; and there is a good place prepared for you where you will be in the next life." When he had said this, I saw him no more, but I did not observe how he disappeared or where he went; and I remained all that night lost in thought.

'Early the next morning I did as the holy man had told me. I did not delay, but went down to the shore and there found a very small boat with oars and rowlocks all ready. So, in the name of the Father and the Son and the Holy Spirit, I got into the boat, sat down in the middle, and did as the holy father had told me; and the boat set off from the shore. I took an oar and began to row in the direction in which the prow was pointing, which was towards the east. The boat carried me across a sea which was bright green, then bright red, then clearer than crystal; and I was three days in the midst of that crystal-clear sea. Then I came to a high, circular mountain, which extended the eighth part of a mile up into the sky; and that was this place where I am now. The boat entered through a very small narrow opening where it seemed very dangerous to go. Seeing this, I got out of the boat and, commending myself to God, thrust the boat away with my foot. It sailed away from the shore in the direction from which it had come, and it appeared to move very fast. For seven days I explored this island, and on the seventh day I came here to this mountain top and this square stone. When I saw these two caves and this fair fountain, I chose to enter this cave which faces east; and here I have dwelt from that first day until now.

'On the first day that I entered the cave, I stayed there until the hour of nones; then, being hungry, I went outside and looked around, and I saw a small boat approaching in the distance, which did not stop until it came to rest on the shore. There was no human being in the boat, but I could see there was a creature in it, so I went down and found that it was a fish. It was very large, and it had four paws, and it stood upright on its hind paws; in its mouth it had a flint and iron for striking fire, and in its front paws it held a bundle of dry wood and weeds as tinder for lighting a fire.[14] Seeing this, I wondered what it might mean, and as I was wondering the fish came up out of the water without difficulty and started to walk up the shore. When it came to the door of my cave, it threw down its load and, shaking its head and tail as a fish does, it died. So I concluded that God had sent this to me, and that I should strike flame, light a fire and cook the fish and eat it. I set light to the tinder, made a fire and roasted the fish, and cut it into three slices; then I ate the first slice, which was the head, and it was very good to eat. Then I drank some water, but not from the fountain; so this was my fast that day. The next day at nones I ate another slice, and on the third day I ate the tail. On the fourth day, at the hour of nones, I saw in the distance coming across the sea the same small boat, and in it was another fish, with the same things as before; so realizing that this was sent from God I went down and took the fish and cooked it, as I had the first, and I ate it in the same way.

'God fed me in this way for thirty years, and I ate nothing else; and in those thirty years I was never thirsty except on Sundays, so I did not drink. On Sundays at the hour of terce I would see a crystal cup by the fountain, filled with water which ran slowly into it; little by little it would flow out of the square rock, and no other water flowed from it the rest of the week. On that day, when thirty years were past, God sent me food about which I will tell you no more at present.'

So saying, he took leave of them, adding:

'If you wish to explore this island you may do so; otherwise be on your way, for you have more travelling to do. Soon you will fulfil your desires, for which you set out from your monastery. Now I must recite my office and my prayers. God be with you.'

XXVII   After all these things Abbot Brendan did not want to explore the island any further, but he and his brothers returned to the boat and rapidly set sail. As it pleased God, in a few days a wind brought them to an island where they had been before, where there was the pure spring at which they were wont to draw water to fill their vessels for a long voyage. When the feasts of Easter and Pentecost were past, the Steward of the poor, who was with them as usual, said to Saint Brendan:

'Father, embark quickly with your brothers, filling your vessels with water from this spring.'

Then the Steward said:

'I shall be your companion, and I shall lead and guide you where you have to go; for without me you will never be able to find the Land of Truth, the Promised Land of the Saints. Truly I know that it pleases God that I should come with you now, to explain everything to you and to guide you in the Paradise of Delights, that place which God ordained upon earth, in the middle of the world, as a garden for his friends from the beginning of the world. There he placed Adam, the first man, and made him guardian and master of the garden (for he dwelt there), except for one tree which God wanted to save for himself. Indeed, he gave Adam so much of everything else that he could easily have guarded that tree for God; but he did not do so.'

When the Steward had said these words, the abbot embarked with him and his brothers; and as they embarked, all the birds of that island, great and small, came down to the shore. Some flew hither and thither, others settled on the trees, and others on the ground. There were all kinds of birds there, and they all began to sing so wonderfully that the brothers were so joyful and heartened, they could hardly bring themselves to leave the shore. But the good man said to them:

'Hoist the sail and let us set off; and may fortune favour us.'
As soon as they raised the sail, there came a great swarm of snow-white birds; some were like flies, others were like bees, and others like finches. They all flew hither and thither in the air, and they began to sing with one voice like men, women and children, singing this verse very softly: 'The Lord prosper their journey presently, and fulfil their desire, for he is the hope of all the ends of the earth and the farthest reaches of the sea. Let us rejoice in the Lord; exult, you just men, and rejoice, all you of upright heart. Glory be to the Father and to the Son, and to the Holy Ghost, as it was in the beginning, is now and ever shall be, world without end. Amen.'
When they had sung these and other verses, they all fell silent. When this wondrous song was ended, Saint Brendan and those who were with him began to sail rapidly towards the east; and as they went, all the birds left and returned to their places. So they came to the Steward's island, and there the boat sailed straight to the shore of its own accord.

When they reached the port, they began joyfully to sing the Te Deum. When they had sung it all, the Steward disembarked first from the boat, then the abbot, then all the brothers, and they tied up the boat firmly. They spent forty days with the Steward on that island, and he supplied them amply with every good thing; he led them along all the coasts that were in his care, and showed them everything.

While they were with the Steward on his island which was so large and beautiful, Abbot Brendan and his brothers found and saw so many things quite unlike those which are found elsewhere that they can hardly be written down. They found – believe it or not – a road lined with stakes, inlaid with various precious stones all beautifully worked and all different from each other; and the stakes were beautifully decorated with gold and silver. The road was a mile long, with a shallow channel on either side, in which there were frogs wonderful to behold because of the strange patterns on their skin, which made them more beautiful to behold than purple cloth or ample embroideries woven with many golden silk threads, pearls and precious stones. These frogs sang so well, sweetly and harmoniously, that they would not be outdone by the music of the psaltery, half-psaltery or dulcimer. Along the streams cicadas were singing in the grass, and there were lizards, large and small, running here and there, delightful to see because of the patterns on their skin, which cannot be adequately described or written down.

The grass on the verges was so fair and fragrant that it surpassed in beauty and fragrance all our aromatic herbs; the scent of savin, rosemary, mint, violets, roses, cummin or oranges would be as nothing by comparison. The trees along the way were so large and fair and had reached such perfection of height and size that words cannot describe them. They were all covered with flowers of different colours and laden with fruit. On every branch of every tree there was fruit of every degree of ripeness; there were date palms, many varieties of pines, pear trees, chestnuts, plums, peaches, lemons, cinnamon and carob trees. We saw sugar cane, and so many other trees with different kinds of fruit which are not found in Italy that it would be a great labour to recount them all. The crickets in the fields were so fair to behold and so pleasing in their singing that you would never grow weary of hearing them. These and many

other things were along the side of the road. All the trees were full
of birds which sang so sweetly that their song alone would be
paradise enough; if you listened to them, you would have no need
to eat or drink, and no desire to say or do anything else but stay and
listen to their delightful song, and you would care nothing for the
song of our nightingales, blackbirds, larks, finches or linnets.

At the end of the road was a great river, a hundred paces or more
wide. Its water was divided into four streams, each different from
the others, which flowed very fast, so that from a distance it looked
like four pieces of cloth stretched out, each of a different colour.
The first was like water clearer than crystal, and carried along in the
water were precious stones, large and small, of all colours, and
pearls, more numerous than building stones or gravel in our rivers.
The second stream was of dark red wine, very precious for its
fragrance, flavour and clarity, and it too carried along precious
stones like blocks of chalk and marble, and pieces of gold, and fish,
and many animals very strange to see and smell, and other creatures
which are not found in our country. The third was of milk, sweet,
mild and fragrant; in it were pieces of silver, long and large, and
other strange things, living animals in strange shapes which are not
found among us. The fourth stream was of oil, bright yellow, clear,
sweet and strong, and carried in it were pieces of wax and earth of
various colours, and precious stones of every kind and colour, all
minutely cut and very fine for their properties and colour.

Over this river there was a very wide bridge, made of four beams:
the first beam was of crystal, the second garnet, the third pearl, and
the fourth topaz. The beams were paved with twenty-four kinds of
precious stone, each piece measuring a full span. At each end of the
bridge there were two columns, very tall and wide, of four colours:
one was of agate, the second of emerald, the third of sky-blue
sapphire, and the fourth of yellow jacinth. One pair of columns was
crowned with a beam of beautiful garnet, and the other with a beam
of clearest carnelian.[15]

On these beams stood an arch of shining gold. Under the arch the
twelve months of the year were carved in precious stones, as if in a
block of marble; above it were carved the twelve signs of the zodiac,
each with the seven planets in precious stones, and divided into

degrees and hours. On one side the whole of the Old Testament was depicted in precious stones, and on the other side, also in precious stones, the New Testament and all the rulers of the church and the world, that is, all the popes and emperors until the great events that will happen at the end of the world. Under one end of the arch was a figure of the pope, wearing his vestments and seated on a wondrous throne which rested on four living creatures; under the other end was a figure of the emperor, crowned and robed in state, seated on a strange throne which rested on four figures representing the four evangelists.

All these scenes were so wonderfully worked in precious stones, gold and silver, that the flesh of the figures seemed like real flesh, and similarly with their clothing and everything else. The figures were so beautiful and so well carved that they seemed alive; they were so fair to behold that no one would ever weary of looking at them or even remember to eat or drink, such were the qualities and beauty of the stones. The emperor appeared to be looking at the pope and to be talking to him about something. In the middle, at the highest point of the arch, was marvellously depicted a very large throne resting on four living creatures, and a carving of the gracious Lord God as he will appear on the Day of Judgement when he will come to judge the world. The whole scene was made of precious stones, with two figures both alike, placed back to back so that they could be seen by everyone on either side. At the summit of the heavenly realm is a beautiful large double mirror, which has the quality of being able to reflect anyone wherever they may stand to view themselves. This image of the Lord's Heaven has the most beautiful carvings of birds, trees, rays of light and small creatures, such that, if its beauty consisted only of these, they would suffice to give great delight to the body and comfort to the spirit.

On the south side, about a stone's throw away, a crystal column stands in the middle of the river, very broad and tall; on this column is depicted a great wheel, all in precious stones, representing Paradise and all that is in it and how it is arranged. It is such a delight to behold that, if there was nothing else to see in the world, it would suffice to bring comfort and joy. On the north side, a good slingshot away, stands a fair column in the middle of the river, very broad and tall; it is of red marble, encircled with iron and covered with lead. On this column is depicted a great wheel in coarse stones, neither precious nor shining, representing Hell and all that is in it and how it is arranged. It is so dreadful to behold that, if it was the only ugly and frightening thing to be seen, it would suffice, and there neither is nor has been nor ever will be anyone so wicked that, when he saw it, he would not be in fear and trembling of going into Hell.

At the end of this bridge was a castle, well defended by a surrounding wall of shining gems. Its walls were plastered and compacted, with battlements and well-built towers and turrets with commanding views. Its doors were half gold and half silver, inlaid with finely cut precious stones. Its passages, communal quarters and state rooms were beautifully constructed within and without, such that they cannot be adequately described. The living quarters had all the household goods each family could need; there were no people inside the castle, and yet it seemed to be inhabited. I asked what it was called, and the Steward said to me: 'It is called Bel Veder.' The vessels were all made of precious stones, such as jasper, sapphire, emerald, garnet, ruby, jacinth, carnelian, amethyst, alabandine, crystal and paneros.[16] There were wonderful cockerels, bigger than geese and with feathers brighter than peacocks, pheasants, partridges, doves and many other things in great numbers, such that anyone who tried to describe them would seem merely foolish. So I stayed there with the Steward, looking at everything; and at the end of forty days he would not allow me to remain any longer, so I departed.

VIII When the forty days were ended, the Steward led me to the boat and told us all to embark, and he himself gladly came with us. We sailed until it was nearly evening, and then there came a great fog, so dark and thick that we could hardly see each other. Soon there arose a storm with great flashes of lightning and loud bursts of thunder, horrible to hear, so that the brothers were all greatly afraid.

'Do not be afraid of anything', said the Steward.
Then he said to Saint Brendan:
'Do you know what fog this is?'
'No, I do not', he replied.
'Look behind you', said the Steward, 'and tell me what you can see.'

Saint Brendan looked behind and in front, and said:

'I can see nothing but this thick fog, and I can smell a strong, sweet odour which gives me great comfort.'

The Steward replied:

'This thick fog which you see has surrounded this precious island which you have been seeking these past seven years; and because you have stood firm in the faith and have conducted yourselves well throughout this voyage, it is God's will now to grant you consolation. And from what you have seen and undergone, now you can know how great is the lordship and power and wisdom of God. He has done far greater things than these for sinful humanity, who cannot comprehend them because of their sin.

'You have experienced in a small way how it is through many trials and tribulations that we can see Paradise, which is called the kingdom of God. There is no other way to get there, except through many tribulations of the body and the soul; that was the way which was taken by all God's saints, and by him who took our nature and became a man like other men. I know that you have seen many strange things which would hardly be believed if they were recounted, and yet they are great things which are worthy to be believed. And I tell you that all this is as nothing compared to those things which you will see and touch in the noble Promised Land of the Saints, where they are joyful and full of comfort, looking forward to the day when they will see their bodies arise from death to life. Then their glory and their share in Paradise will be complete, which God has promised to give to all his faithful who die in a state of salvation. That is why John the Evangelist said: "Blessed are the dead who die in the Lord, for their deeds follow them for their reward, and they will find them in the other world, which will never come to an end." Soon you will see the proof of the saying of the prophet David, in the verse "Blessed are they that dwell in thy house, O Lord." And God himself, when he was a man, said: "In my Father's house are many mansions." '

After they had been speaking thus for the space of an hour, while the boat continued to sail on through the fog, they emerged and saw a great brightness like the sun. It was yellow like a clear bright dawn, and as they advanced the brightness grew so strong that they were filled with amazement. They could see all the stars in the sky much more sharply than they can be seen anywhere else, and the seven planets moving across the sky appeared in their places with absolute clarity. The light there was so great that there was no need for the sun.[17] They wondered at where this light came from and whether there was another sun in this place, brighter than our sun. The Steward told them:

'The light which shines so brightly here does indeed come from another sun, which is not like the sun which appears among the signs of the zodiac. The sun which gives this light never moves from its place; it is much higher and its brightness is a hundred thousand times greater than that of the sun which moves among the stars. And just as the moon receives light from the sun and so shines with reflected light, not its own, so the sun which shines on your world is the companion of this other sun. As the sun continually shines on the moon, so this higher sun illuminates the sun below, and enables it to shine so fair and bright all the time; and anyone who could rise to the height of the sun which is the companion of the moon would be able to receive some of this higher light. The lower sun cannot fully sustain the brightness of this higher sun, just as the eye of man cannot look directly at the sun. It is because of the light which shines so preciously and powerfully here that everything in this place is so fair and wonderful and great and good. This noble sun is the glorious God, who here reveals something of his power to his saints.'

As we sailed on in the boat, the sky became more fair, the air clearer, and the daylight brighter, and there was the sound of birds singing, their different voices combining to make sweet music. Such was the delight and comfort which the abbot and his brothers received from this, and from the sweet smell of fragrant plants, that their souls almost left their bodies, so rapt were they by what they smelt and heard. The boat continued until it reached the harbour and came to rest by the shore, and they all said the Te Deum, praising God with great reverence.

When they had finished the psalm, they disembarked from the boat, and saw that noble land, more precious than all others for its beauty and the things that were there, its fragrant plants and flowered meadows and fruits. The trees were all full of birds, with plumage which was delightful to see and voices which were sweet,

strong and clear; they sang so well, so sweetly and softly and
harmoniously that it could never be described in words or conceived
by the heart, and could scarcely be written down. They flew from
branch to branch and from tree to tree most delightfully. The birds'
singing and the greenery and the blossom on the trees made it seem
like springtime, and yet the ripe fruit on the vines and the apple
and pear trees made it seem like June. As the brothers explored
these shores they found the whole landscape a mass of different
colours, as if carpets had been spread over it, or purple cloth with or
without gold embroidered in different forms – knots, leaves,
lozenges, trees, birds and other lovely things – depicted on
hangings, on cloths of purple or in paintings on the walls of
churches or palaces, decorating the rooms and halls so as to delight
the heart. [. . .][18]

I saw enormous pomegranates with seeds as big as walnuts, bean
pods a yard long with beans as big as walnuts, cherries as big as
peaches or ordinary apples, roses the size of dinner-plates and
medlars like apples, reeds forty feet tall and as thick as the mast of
a ship, mandrakes as big as a normal man and lobsters the size of a
human being. There were strange creatures of all shapes and sizes;
some had two feet, some three or four or as many as twelve; some
had one head, others two or three, and so on up to twelve; some of
them had hands and others wings, some had feathers and others
bristles, some fur, others skin, yet others a hard shell. Of these
some had forked horns, others crests, others beards; some had one
eye, others two or three, and so on up to twelve. Some of them
sang, others danced; some walked, others jumped or ran.

There were fields which had been ploughed ready for sowing, and
others which had been sown and the shoots were already coming
up; some were full of cotton, some of saffron, others of carnations
and others cardamom, others of rice and other plants very wonderful
to see and smell. I saw many springs of different colours from which
rivers flowed out, branching out into many streams, and carrying
along bright precious stones of many different colours.

They met Enoch and Elijah and many other saints walking up and
down, taking their ease and talking in twos and threes. They were
very handsome to behold and well dressed; they all seemed to be

looking at us, but no one said anything to us except Enoch and Elijah, who were together, both dressed very poorly in what seemed like old sackcloth. They came and greeted me with joy, welcoming us warmly and asking us about ourselves. We told them our whole story, how we had left our homeland and all the things that had appeared to us during the whole journey, both good and bad.

Abbot Brendan asked them who they were and who the people were who appeared in that place. One of them replied:

'We are both prophets; this is Elijah, and I am Enoch. I was in a public place preaching to the people before the Flood, telling them of the end of the world, and how God had commanded Noah to make the ark so that he and his family might be saved from the waters. I preached thus many times, telling them these and many other good things. Then the weather became stormy, and there was thunder and lightning. As I finished speaking, dressed in sackcloth as you see me now, there was a tremendous thunderclap right over my head. I was taken up, I know not by whom, and brought to this place, where a voice said to me: "Stay here until the coming of Antichrist, who will seek to destroy the faith of Christ with words and miracles, with wealth that he will give and torments that he will cause. Then God will send you back to that place, and you will preach your message in the presence of Antichrist, before him and behind him. You will fight against him boldly and confidently; you will refute all that he says, witnessing to God and recalling the Old Testament."'

When he had finished speaking, Elijah said:

'I am that great prophet of whom the Bible says that I spoke many things, at the time when the world was renewed, a long time after the Flood. As I was preaching one day among the people, there came a great flash of lightning and a clap of thunder, and it came and struck me. I was brought at great speed to this noble place, and I was told that I should not leave this place until God sends for me at the time of the false preaching of the son of perdition, the dragon of Babylon, that is Antichrist. He will win the world for himself by many means; many prophets have spoken of him, and so did Saint John the Evangelist in the Apocalypse, which was a vision which appeared to him when he was in anguish at the Last Supper, grief-stricken on hearing that Judas would betray the Lord. So we two have been here ever since, and we shall remain alive and well until the time when we return in these clothes. All this time we have not eaten or drunk or slept; there has been no night, and we have suffered no infirmity or displeasure of any kind. All this is by the will of God and through the properties of these precious things. But if we were to eat or drink then we would need to sleep, which is not good; and no bad or evil thing can exist in this place, but only those things which are good and pure. It is always day here, as you can see, and the weather is always temperate as in spring. It is no hardship for me to be here; it is such a pleasant place, with its pure air, its precious stones and fragrant plants, its flowers and its sweetly singing birds, whose song, as you have heard, is unsurpassed. We shall remain here until the day when we return whence we came. Then we shall no longer be old or weak or mad; not a hair of our head or our body shall be harmed, and we shall have no thought for dressing or undressing or anything else except to take our ease here, walking to and fro and seeing these great marvels which God has made. Since we have been here, many have come and have stayed as long as God willed; you are to stay forty days, and no more. So you may come and go as you please.'

As we walked to and fro, we found two fair valleys and many other delightful places. We found the paths and fields more thickly covered with precious stones, and the hills more rich in pebbles of gold and silver, and azure as fine as sand, than all the stones and dust and sand in our country. We wanted to go and see the tree from which Adam picked the apple, the tree of good knowledge and the tree of life,[19] and other things, but the Steward told us that they were on the other side of the river which flowed clearer than crystal, along with many other great things, more than all those we had seen; and that it was not God's will that we should see them.

We and all the brethren were so comforted, joyful and encouraged at these things that we experienced neither hunger nor thirst, nor sleep, nor anything else which might be irksome to us. One of the brethren did, indeed, drink once from the fair springs which were in that place, not out of thirst, but rather for pleasure and to see what it was like; and the water was quickly converted into sweat, and did not pass through him in any other way. In the same way, for sheer pleasure, they took some of the plants in their hands, and some of the leaves from the trees.

As they walked about they saw a delightful wood, and in the midst of it a great tree standing out above all the other trees, laden with golden apples and with leaves as white as snow. At the top of the tree was a very lovely bird, standing ten feet high, with a tail and crest and feathers like those of a peacock, only this bird was larger than a peacock and its plumage was even more beautiful. This bird began to sing, so clearly and beautifully that their souls almost left their bodies as they listened to it; and the verses of its song were these: 'Who is thy equal, O Lord God? Who is like thee in power? Who can do such great works of power? Thou alone rulest for all eternity.' Then it sang, 'Blessed are they that have seen thee, and that are chosen for thy salvation'. When it had sung these verses, the bird flew across the great river.

Then we came closer to the wood, and there we found trees laden with precious stones, with leaves of silver and gold, and with gemstones on their branches. The other side of the trees seemed to be burning, and there came to our nostrils a fragrance so sweet that we almost fainted; it was like incense, aloes, musk, balsam, amber, rosemary, savin and roses, and like the scent of jasmine. But for all the flames we could not see any smoke. We went round to the side where the flames appeared to be, but we saw nothing but the trees. When we looked up, looking back to the side whence we had come, the flames seemed higher than ever; and we went back to the first side again, and there was no fire there.

Looking again to the other side, we saw an even greater flame, burning very bright and high; and in the midst of it was a broad, straight pillar which seemed to reach the sky; cut into it were steps made of large jewels, like powdered gold, set with pearls and carnelians. Then there appeared an angel, so fair and pleasing in his countenance and clothing that human words can hardly describe it; he had the appearance of a youth of about fifteen. When he was level with the top of the tree which bore the golden apples, he flew up and sang a song so beautifully, with such delightful verses and such a sweet-sounding voice, that it can hardly be described; and yet this is the plain truth. He sang a song of twenty-four verses; it was a love song, such as a young maiden might sing to her lover. When the song was finished, he said:

'This is the song of the soul of the just, which seeks for its bridegroom the Son of God, who is a fair youth, noble, wise, virtuous and bold, courteous, sagacious, rich and full of joy; his qualities can never fail. Today is the last of the forty days which God has granted you to see and smell and touch everything here. So now prepare yourselves to return to your home; and our Lord God would have you know that he will grant you salvation, that is your souls will attain Paradise when they pass from this world; of that you may now be sure.'

Having said these words, he returned whence he had come. When he had vanished and was seen no more, there seemed to issue from all sides of the pillar many honey bees, as large as doves. Nearby was a place where there was a little water in which was a great number of very large frogs; they sat in pairs facing each other, singing more sweetly than any stringed instrument even when it is perfectly tuned. There too were those insects which jump to and fro among the fragrant plants; in the cracks in the ground and among the plants were very large crickets, which sang more sweetly than any stringed instrument which we have, even when it is perfectly tuned. And the insects flew to and fro among the plants, of such lovely colours and so delightful to behold that it was a great joy to see them.

When we had seen these things and were preparing to depart, there came up to us a great flock of sheep as big as oxen, lambs, goats, deer, unicorn, foxes, hares and dogs, all gambolling and grazing together. After all these animals came an equal number of young boys, so fair and so beautifully dressed that they cannot be described, all decorated and garlanded with flowers and gold ornaments, precious stones, pearls and sequins. They all sang more sweetly and delightfully than the most expert singer among us could sing any part of a musical score; because of their youth their voices were those of angels, strong, sweet and clear.

The brethren were so filled with joy and comfort at all these things that they were oblivious of anything else, but just stood there, looking and listening to these precious things, their souls almost abandoning their bodies in an ecstasy of love. So filled and satisfied were they that they had no care for anything else, but simply remained there in silence. When the animals and the children had departed, as God willed, they came to themselves and set out to go further into the island. They came upon seven springs, one next to the other, without any bank of dry land between them. From each flowed a great river; the first was of water, clear as crystal; the second was of wine, the third of milk, the fourth of blood; the fifth was half of manna and half of balsam; the sixth was of pure clear oil, and the seventh was of honey. Nearby were seven large horses, saddled ready to ride, and there stood seven pavilions; and there were seven churches made of seven different precious stones, and in each were carved the seven sacraments. The inside of the first church was all of crystal; the second was of garnet, the third of sapphire, the fourth of topaz, the fifth of ruby, the sixth of emerald, and the seventh was half of coral and half of carnelian. Each church had seven altars with seven candles, and in each there was balsam to burn. In front of the seven churches was a great square, beautifully made with delicate carving in precious stones.

At the far end of the square was a great column of clear chalcedony, wonderfully carved with scenes showing the whole of the Old and New Testaments. At the top of the column was a fair mill-wheel carrying bells; each bell had three clappers, each of a different size, and when the wheel turned it gave out such a delightful sound that anyone who heard it would gladly stay to listen without wanting to eat or drink. Sometimes the sound was like a cymbal or a harp or a guitar; sometimes it was like the chime of a clock, and sometimes it was as if viol, lute and timbrel, wind instruments and psaltery, organ, flute and every other kind of instrument were all playing together in harmony. Its sweet and pleasing sound was so harmonious that it cannot be described; and if there were no other music made by birds or human voices or any other sound in Paradise, it would suffice for the whole world.

The column was three hundred and sixty cubits high, and the square was a furlong – that is an eighth of a mile – across. It was carved with many wonderful things in precious stones, gold and silver; there is nothing good in land or sea which is not depicted there. There were steps leading to the sea, which is clearer than crystal, and so full of fish and many things very strange to recount, such that anyone who described them would be thought a simpleton; and yet this is the plain truth. This was what the prophet David recalled in the Psalm which says: 'So is the great and wide sea also, wherein are things creeping innumerable.' As they walked along the shore of the sea which surrounded this wonderful island, they came to a great river, not too wide, which looked like milk. It was spanned by a bridge, beautifully made with precious stones, gold, silver and carnelian.

We went over the bridge, and at the other end was a delightful shore where there were many wonderful things which are beyond description – indeed we could hardly believe them ourselves. At the far side of this island both the earth and the sea were bright red. We went along the shore until we came to a great bridge, so long that we could not see the end of it, or the shore on the other side. We set out to cross the bridge, and went a long way before we found that it was broken and did not reach the other side. So, realizing that we could go no further, we gave great praises to the Lord, and turned back. Exploring the island in another direction, we found many beautiful fountains and trees laden with fruit. There is neither night nor sunlight there, but the weather is brighter and the air is clearer than the sun; all the stars in the sky were visible all the time, and so were the movements of the sun, moon and planets. Whatever we found there – apples, pears, pine-nuts, grapes, oranges, precious stones and many other things – we could take as many of them as we liked. Such things are more plentiful there than everyday things in our world: there is more fine azure than we have sand, and the precious stones and mountains of gold and silver there are like our mountains of earth, marble and other rocks.

As we explored this shore in both directions, we came to a great river which flowed through the island, dividing it in half; and we could see no bridge over it. Then Saint Brendan turned to his brethren and said:

'My brothers, this river is so wide that we cannot cross it; and, because it divides this island in half, we cannot explore any more of it, or find out how big the whole island is. What is more, God does not wish us to discover what is on the other side. And indeed, we have seen, learnt and touched so many things that we should be well satisfied.'

When he had said this, there came to meet him a handsome young man, finely dressed and very pleasing to behold, wearing ornaments of gold and precious stones, many kinds of flowers and spangles. As he approached, he sang a song which was delightful to hear, and he bore a hawk on his hand. He greeted them with great courtesy, embracing and kissing them with great joy and calling them all by name, with as much familiarity as if they had always been with him. Then he recited these verses from the Psalter: 'Blessed are all they that dwell in thy house, O Lord, for they shall praise thee from generation to generation', and 'Rejoice and be glad, O habitation of Zion, for great in thy midst is the holy one of Israel.'

Then he spoke to Saint Brendan, saying:

'My friend and servant of God, this is that precious and loving island which you have sought day and night for many months and years, enduring great weariness and discomfort and facing many great dangers. And now blessed be God, because you have come through safely, and you have been strong, valiant and firm in your faith that you would be able to fulfil your intention; so God has been gracious to you and has granted your desire. You were not able to find this place any sooner, because God wanted first to show you the many secret and marvellous things which he has created in the western land and sea. You have seen some of these things, yet they are as nothing compared to the others which you have not seen and which are still to come.

'Now you are to return in your boat to your own country from whence you set out, where you dwelt for a long time; there you will complete your penance in honour of the Saviour, who will give you a good reward. You were blessed from the day you were born into this world! By your return to your own country you will serve God and the brothers of your monastery and others, and you will bring them great comfort, both of body and soul. Of all the good and precious things that are on this fair island you may take as many as you want, and load your boat as fully as you please. If you know which are the most precious gems, take as many of them as you can carry and give them to whom you will; they will confirm what you say about all you have seen and discovered on your voyage. For by God's grace you have seen in your lifetime what is in the Promised Land of the Saints and that precious Paradise on earth which God planted at the beginning of the world, when he first created all things.

'This is that garden of delights which he gave to the first man, whose name was Adam, to have charge of it; and when he placed him there, he commanded him to enjoy everything as he pleased, and to rule over it as he wished. Everything was given to Adam except for one very fair tree bearing apples; of that tree God commanded him that he should not touch it or eat its fruit, but that everything else was for him to enjoy as he pleased. But on the very day when God placed him there, Adam sinned and transgressed God's commandment, preferring to obey the plea of his wife Eve, who wickedly deceived him without cause, than to obey the command of the Lord God, who had created him in his own image and likeness and had given him so many good things to enjoy. He was more afraid of offending the woman Eve than God, who was the Lord of both of them and of the whole world. She indeed deceived him very cunningly, with the result that Adam dwelt there with his wife only half a day, from the morning until the ninth hour. After the ninth hour the Lord, knowing Adam's fault, went and rebuked him for what he had done against his commandment; but Adam made excuses, blaming his wife for making him do it. When the Lord saw how Adam had done wrong and did not accept the blame, but rather blamed his wife, saying: "She made me do it", he drove them both out of the garden; and they were naked. When he had driven them out, he clothed them, giving each of them a new fur to wear; and he commanded that thenceforward they should labour and should live by the sweat of their brow and the work of their hands. Then he commanded an angel to guard the place, so that they should not return there and no one else should enter it without permission; and it has been constantly guarded ever since. And it is also defended by a great heat which no one can bear except by a miracle of God. So it is by special grace that God has enabled you to come to this place, and the angel has not prevented you from entering.

'Now I tell you that the day of your departure has come; you must leave this place and return to your monastery, where you will dwell until God calls you to himself in death. Many years after your lifetime these deeds of yours will be told, and this country will be revealed to your successors, especially when the persecution of Christians by Antichrist begins. This great river which you see divides this island in half. Its light is always constant; night never falls, and there is no darkness or disturbance of any kind. By its nature this place is always full of every good thing; it abounds with fruit trees, which bear both unripe and ripe fruit at all times. The light of this island is the light of Christ, not of the sun or the moon; that is why night never falls here.'

Then he added:

'I am one of the servants of God; he has sent me to you, so that you may see me and I may talk to you. In his name I say to you, may it please you to return to your own land, from which you set out with the intention of discovering and seeing those things which you have discovered and seen by the special grace of God. So you can call yourselves content with all these things that you have seen. Look all around you, and you will see that in the whole of this island are all manner of gems; take as many of them as you like. I tell you again, this island is full of precious gems of every colour; take them, for you have full permission to do so, and if you take them they will be useful to you.'

When he had finished speaking, he at once left them, so that they saw him no more. So Saint Brendan told his brethren that they could confidently gather every kind of fruit of the island, and every kind of gem, and could take whichever they wanted; and they did so. Then he took leave of the Steward who was with them, and embarked in the boat with his brethren, and set out in the name of Jesus Christ, sailing towards the west. In a short time they reached the great fog which they had encountered before, and they sailed through it for the space of three days. Then they emerged into the light of the sun, and they no longer saw the other great light; and from then on they experienced night and day. About an hour after they had emerged from the fog, they came to an island called the Island of Delights. They remained there for several days, finding much refreshment, for there are many good, fair and wonderful things there which are not found anywhere else; it is not fitting to describe them, for they would not be believed, but would simply be considered folly. On the fourth day they set out from that place, in the name of God and good fortune; and the boat always encountering good weather, they did not stop until they returned safe and sound to their own country from whence they had set out.

XXIX So it was that blessed Saint Brendan, having received the Steward's blessing, returned with his monks in four days to their own country; and they were all safe and sound, fair, plump and – according to those who saw them – younger than they were when they set out. As soon as they reached the shore of their own country, they began joyously to sing the Te Deum, and then these psalms: 'Behold, how good and joyful a thing it is, brethren, to dwell together in unity'; 'Praise the Lord, O Jerusalem, and praise your God, O Zion'; 'O all ye works of the Lord, bless ye the Lord'; and then the Benedictus. As soon as they began to sing the Te Deum, all the monks in the monastery got up and came out to see who was singing; and immediately they recognized their abbot and the others, and welcomed them graciously and with great reverence. He gave them his blessing, and exchanged the peace with them.

Now may Saint Brendan in his sanctity pray to God for me, and may God give me grace to make a good end of my body and soul; and may he pray for all those who read this his legend, and those who gladly listen to his story, to the honour of God. For he was a good man, a holy and honest religious from the time of his childhood until the day of his death. Amen. Thanks be to God.

6

The Occitan Version

Margaret Burrell

Manuscript and Edition The Occitan prose version of Brendan's voyage is preserved in just one manuscript: Paris, Bibliothèque Nationale de France (BNF), fr. 9759, dating from the fifteenth century. The Brendan material forms part of a compilation of saints' lives entitled *Vidas dels sans e sanctas*, written in an Haut-Languedoc dialect of Occitan. The manuscript is written in two columns on neatly ruled lines, still faintly visible; there are thirty-three lines per column. A diplomatic edition of the Brendan text was published in 1902 by Carl Wahlund. Beneath the lines of the Occitan he inserted the Latin *Vita sancti Brendani episcopi* from BNF, lat. 755, ff. 249ᵛ-253ᵛ. A new edition of the text has been prepared for the present volume. The text is translated here for the first time.[1]

Authorship, Patron and Date The text does not permit any identification of author or patron. The manuscript contains the date 12 June 1211, which serves as a guide to the dating of the text.

Source In Wahlund's view the source of the Occitan Brendan was the abridged version of the *Navigatio* preserved in MS BNF, lat. 755. This manuscript came from the Benedictine monastery of Notre-Dame-de-Montmajor (Bouches-du-Rhône). But Wahlund was also aware of another Latin manuscript, Rome, Biblioteca Vallicelliana, vol. 7, which contains a version very close to that found in the Paris manuscript. The version in the Rome manuscript was edited in 1872 by Cardinal Patrick Moran under the title *Legenda in festo sancti Brendani* (pp. 132-39). But was the Occitan version based on the Paris or the Rome text, or on a common ancestor of both?

---

1. Problems presented by the text, and procedures used in preparing the edition, are discussed in the Textual Notes.

Content and Structure The work begins with a general statement introducing St Brendan, but there is no formal prologue. A division of episodes according to content gives the following structure:

(1)   Introduction
(2)   The initial voyages
(3)   Return visits to familiar places and glimpses of Hell
(4)   The encounter with Judas
(5)   The final voyage, visit to the Promised Land and Brendan's return

Section (1) includes the general introduction, Brendan's desire to see the Promised Land, preparations for the voyage, the episode of the intruding monks and the conditions of the voyage. Section (2) recounts the first island visit, the Easter feast and the visits to the Isle of Birds and a community of silent monks. In section (3) the monks return to the Isle of Birds, then voyage onwards and catch their first sight of Hell. Section (4), the longest, contains the encounter with Judas and with the demons who drag him back to torment. Section (5) is surprisingly brief; Brendan fulfils his desire to visit the Promised Land and returns to his country, where he dies surrounded by his faithful brethren.

The following comments relate to the Occitan version, but they are also relevant to the abridged Latin versions. The omission or abbreviation of episodes found in the *Navigatio* is the most noticeable feature of the Occitan. It opens, like the *Navigatio*, with a statement on Brendan's lineage. He is said to be father superior to 'many' monks (the *Navigatio* specifies three thousand). The following sections (Brendan's desire to see Paradise and 'the relics of the saints' and the account of preparations for his voyage) are considerably abbreviated. There is no equivalent to the story of Barrind. But the election of fourteen monks, Brendan's speech to them, requesting their advice, and their readiness to follow him even at the risk of death are included. As in the *Navigatio*, the monks request only that their journey be undertaken according to the will of God.

The vernacular version mentions the forty-day fast, after which the monks make their way to the coast to build the boat. In the Occitan version they go towards the eastern shore (*pleia oriental*). The island on which the boat is built is called Ahenda in the Occitan text (Aende in the abridged Latin versions). As in the *Navigatio*, three latecomers arrive, but the vernacular version omits Brendan's prediction of their ultimate fate. In the *Navigatio* the wind is initially favourable, a detail not found in the Occitan; in both versions the wind drops after fifteen days. Brendan's encouragement of the fearful monks is similar in both versions, but the Occitan omits their ignorance of the direction in which they are sailing.

The account of the first landfall is similar in both versions, although very abbreviated in the vernacular (which does, however, mention the dog as messenger, the beautiful hall, Brendan's warning to the monks to be on their guard against temptation and the table spread with bread and fish). But the nature of the temptation, the Ethiopian boy holding a bridle in his hand and the fate of the tempted monk are omitted. The Isle of Sheep episode in the *Navigatio* is much abbreviated in the Occitan, which includes the celebration of the feast of Easter, but makes no reference to the Great Fish (see, however, the note to the place name Velluer).

Although briefer in the vernacular, the Paradise of Birds episode is similar in both versions. The occupants are identified as angels who fell along with Lucifer, although his name is not mentioned in the Occitan text. The vernacular version of the canonical hours sung by the birds is close to that of the abbreviated Latin texts. The visit to the island of St Ailbe includes references to the crystal vessels, the monks' eighty years of residence, the silence they maintain, the continuous burning of the lamps and Brendan's request to remain there; but, unlike the *Navigatio*, provides little explanation for what happens.

Other island visits are virtually omitted in the Occitan, apart from a brief return to the Paradise of Birds, where the voyagers are informed of the cyclical nature of their journey. Other adventures of the monks before the Judas episode are dealt with in two lines expressing the impossibility topos: the many marvels experienced by Brendan would be boring to relate. The vernacular version gives few details of the volcanic island and makes no mention of the disappearance of the third monk.

The fullest and most faithful representation of the *Navigatio* is found in the Judas episode. Judas is not allowed to enumerate his torments, but Brendan's powerful intervention is given its full worth. The episode of St Paul the Hermit is not reproduced in the vernacular text and the account of the visit to the Promised Land is very brief. Brendan duly sees the Promised Land and the relics of the saints. In the Occitan version his return to his monastery and his death are related very briefly.

The Author's Purpose The Occitan prose version adheres so closely to the two abbreviated Latin texts that it is likely that the author's purpose was to a great extent merely that of translation. Like the two Catalan versions, the Occitan text adds the figure of St Brendan to the corpus of saints provided by the *Legenda aurea* tradition.[2]

---

2. I wish to thank those who have helped me with advice and comments: Robert Sanderson for his computer-enhanced text, Peter Ricketts for pointing out some errors in my preliminary draft, Glynnis Cropp and Roy Harris for their help with difficult passages. Special thanks are due to Glyn Burgess for his encouragement and patience. Any remaining errors are entirely my own.

[*ccxʳ*] Lo benaurat Sant Branda nat foc de mot noble linatge e baro de mot gran abstinencia e en vertut mot resplanden. Payre foc de motz monges e de mans[1] segon que es dich. El volc encercar e strutar[2] las partz e las fis de la mar Oceana. (4)

Sant Branda de tota la sua congregacio elegic .xiiii. frayres e intrero a l'oratorii parla[r] amb els. E dis lor:

'Senhos meus, mot etz amatz per Nostre Senhor, per que jo ves demandi cosselh que me acosselhetz en so que jo ves enqueri. Car la mia cogitacio es anar d[e]vas Terra de Promissio; e desiri mot veser las reliquias dels sans que aqui son; aconsolatz mi si.n tenics en be.'[3]

E donc els, tantost conoguda la voluntat del sant baro, quays per una bocha totz disseron:

'Senher payre, la nostra[4] voluntas e resposta es ayssi coma tu vols, e hem apparelhatz de anar am tu entro a la mort ment[r]a[5] vida nos sostenga. Una causa nos tant solament demandam: quant aysso sia fach a la voluntat de Jhesu Christ.' (17)

E Sant Branda manda aquels de junar .xl. dies ans que els d'aqui moguesson. E passatz .xl. dies, preseron comiat dels fayres e pesson de anar vas la pleia oriental a una illa que era de Sant Branda, hon avia un monestier de[6] [*ccxᵛ*] de Sant Branda, e aquela yla avia nom Ahenda. E aqui els steron .iij. dies e .iij. nuechs. E aqui comenseron de far una barcha no gayre granda mas mot laugeyra; e agron la facha dyns .xl. dies e cubriron de cuers de buous crus, e ajusteron de la part de foras totas las juncturas dels pels am claus. E meseron en a aiguela[7] so que necessari lor era a us de vida humana; e agueron albre e vella e so p[er]tany[8] a barcha. (27)

E Sant Branda amb aquels .xiiii. frayres mas se en la barcha am lo nom de Nostre Senhor; mas abans que d'aqui moguesson vengron .iij. frayres del orde de Sant Branda. E disseron li:

'Senhor, nos volem anar am tu, coma paressat avem de morir en peligrinatge e de seguir tu aytant coma tu velras estar la von anar vols.'

E coma lo sant de Dieu conogues la voluntat daquels dis:

'Sia fach filh ayssi coma vols.'

E aquels pogeron en la barcha e comenseron a navegiar la velas stendudas anant la hon lo ven menar los volia. (36)

The blessed Saint Brendan was born of very noble lineage and was a lord of great self-restraint and a shining example of virtue. He was father superior of many monks and monastic houses,[1] according to what is said. He wished to seek out and explore the regions and boundaries of the Ocean sea.[2]

Saint Brendan selected fourteen brothers from his entire community and they entered the oratory to discuss the matter. He said to them:

'My lords, you are greatly loved by our Lord, so I ask your advice that you might counsel me on the matter I put before you.[3] For my intention is to go to the Promised Land and I have a great desire to see the relics of the saints there; tell me if you approve of this.'
As soon as they knew the saintly man's wish, they said with one voice:

'Lord father, our wish and response is to do as you will and we are ready as long as life sustains us to accompany you until we die. One thing only we ask of you:[4] that it be done by the will of Jesus Christ.'

Saint Brendan instructed them to fast for forty days before they set out. Once forty days had passed, they took leave of the brothers and decided to go towards the eastern shore,[5] to an island which belonged to Saint Brendan, where a monastery of Saint Brendan stood and the island was called Ahenda.[6] They stayed there three days and three nights and there began to build a boat, which was not very big but very light; and they had it ready within forty days, covered it with skins of raw ox-hide and sealed all the external joints of the skins with nails. They put into it what they needed for human life; they had a mast, sails and everything necessary for the boat.

Saint Brendan in the name of our Lord entered the boat with the fourteen brothers; but before they departed, three brothers of Saint Brendan's order came there. They said to him:

'Lord, we wish to come with you, for we are prepared to die on pilgrimage and to follow you for as long as you wish and go wherever you wish.'
When the holy man of God knew what they desired, he said:

'My sons, let it be as you wish.'
They got into the boat and, with the sails hoisted, began to sail

E apres .xv. dies passatz lo ven cessa que neguna part ni a autra anar no pogueron, per que los frayres agueron pahor que no dures aquela bonanansa, mas Sant Branda los cofforta e lor dis:

'No agiatz pahor, car Dieus es Nostre Ajudador. Layssatz la vela stenduda e fassa Dieus de nos so que li plassa, coma nos hem sirvens seus.'

E anan sercan las suas meravilhas; ayssi steron .xl. dies en la mar ses aribar a terra. (44)

E passatz los .xl. dies, apparech lor una part de la yla de septenccio auta mot e plana d'albres. E donc coma els s'acostesson a la riba viron una rocha ayssi facha coma mur e viron rius d'ayga davalar d'aquela rocha que.s confunian en la mar. Empero els no podian aqui trobar lor[9] port ni loc edonc la barcha pogues penre terra; e los frayres eron costretz fort de set e donc coma els anesso entorn d'aquela yla, al ters jorn troberon port que es appelat Pedra Foradida[10] e davaleron en terra. E tantost venc a els un gran qua qui no ladra ni sona mot; e Sant Branda dis als frayres:

'Bon mesatge nos ha trames Nostre Senhor; e donc podem conoysser que en aquesta yla es abitabla de alcunas creaturas.'

E lo ca gira son cap e pessa s'en de anar; e los frayres siguiron lo entro a un bel hostal e intreron dins l'ostal. E viron una bela sala apparelhada de citis e de honratz lietz. Adonc Sant Branda dis a sos frayres:

'Gardatz vos que Sataretz[11] vos engan, coma jeu veg que d'aquels .iii. frayres que apres (.ii.) vengueron, ja a pres un frut[12] vil e mal a sos ops. Pregatz per la arma da [ccxi] quel coma la carn liurada es en poder de Satanas.'

Sant Branda manda als frayres si tenien res de manjar que magesson a taula. Un frayre anec avan per la sua mayo e troba una taula parhada am belas toalhas e pa de meravilhosa blancor e peys cueg en motas guisas. E donc els mangeron e begueron e loreron[13] Dieu; apres lo maiar, dis Sant Branda:

'Frayres, repausatz nos nos[14] ayssi; lietz apparelhatz datz [r]epons als vostres membres.'

E ayssi steron aqui .iij. dies. Empero manda Sant Branda als frayres que re que fos de tota aquela yla no traguesson; e torneron s'en a la barcha anant per la mar. (73)

wherever the wind wished to take them.

After fifteen days the wind died down and they could go no further in any direction. This made the brothers fear that the sea would continue calm, but Saint Brendan comforted them, saying:

'Fear not, for God is our Saviour. Leave the sails hoisted and let God do with us what he pleases, for we are his servants.'

They went in search of his wonders and so spent forty days at sea without reaching shore.

After the forty days had passed, there appeared to the north a high, flat island covered in trees. As they sailed along the coast, they saw a cliff like a wall and they saw waterfalls streaming down the rock and mingling with the sea. Yet they could not find any harbour or place where they could put the boat ashore; the monks were sorely afflicted with thirst and continued to sail around the island and on the third day they found a landing-place which was called 'The Hollow Rock', and there they disembarked. Presently there came to them a large dog, which neither barked nor made a sound; and Saint Brendan said to the monks:

'Our Lord has sent us a good messenger; now we may know that this island is habitable by some creatures.'

The dog turned its head as if to go away; the monks followed it to an attractive dwelling which they entered. Within they saw a beautiful hall, prepared with hangings and fine beds. Then Saint Brendan said to the monks:

'Take care lest Satan trick you, for I foresee that of those three monks who came later, one has already partaken of forbidden fruit for Satan's evil purpose. Pray for his soul, for his body is given into the power of Satan.'

Saint Brendan bade the monks to bring food which they could eat at the table. A monk came forward as his steward and discovered a table spread with beautiful cloths, and bread of amazing whiteness and fish cooked in many ways. They ate, drank and gave praise to God; after the meal, Saint Brendan said:

'Brothers, let us take our rest here; give your limbs repose in these beds ready prepared.'

They stayed there for three days. Then Saint Brendan instructed the monks that they should take nothing away from that island; they returned to the boat and sailed on.

Viron una autra yla, de laqual yla yssien motas fons e aqui els prengueron terra, e era dia en loqual Nostre Senhor fec la cena am ses discapols.[15] Per que steron aqui tro als di sapdes a pren;[16] pueys meseron se per la yla, e troberon gran ramatz de bestial. E donc Sant Branda dis als frayres:

'D'aquest bestial podetz penre coma Nostre Senhor los ha prepausatz per so que pre[n]gam e fassam Pascha.' (81)

La Pascha facha, meseron se en mar e vengron en una autra yla en laqual troberon una bela fon e un albre de gran altesa ple de motz ausels e totz blancz. Coma am mistatz ayssi reminar e albre e los ausels, un d'aquels vola e comensa a parlar a Sant Branda e li dis:

'No.t meravilhes, sant payre, de nos. Car sapias que nos hem d'aquela gran ost dampnada del antic qui passa lo mandamen de Dieu. Mas nos no peccam ni cossentiz al precat mas per so stam ayssi; quant no demandam ajutorii ni refregeri al Senhor, coma n'anem los autres trabucar. Mas per so coma lo Senhor nos crehano[17] volc que anessem aqui, e donc aquels autres aneron; e volc nos far tanta de gratia que non soffririan pena, mas tremans nos en aquest loc hon stam ocioses per diversas partz de l'ayre sotz lo fermamen de las planetas, ayssi volant coma los autres speritz; e a nos mandat lo Senhor Dieus que en lo dia dels Dimenges lausem lo Creator nostre; he ayssi ho fam. E tu am los teus frayres as stat un an en ton viatge e encaras as anar per aquesta mar .vi. ans; e passat .vi. ans vendras en la Terra de Promissio, hon hem los sans de Dieu del Vielh Testamen.' (99)

Quant aysso hat dich aquel ausel comenset de volar als autres; e donc coma la hora de vespas vengues, comenseron totz aquels ausels que en l'ayre eron quays a una vetz de cantar firian am los becz las lors alas disens: 'A tu Senhor Dieus secons cant en Sion e a tu sera reduda la promissio en Jerusalem,' e tota via torneron las demanc disens paraulas. E totas aquestas [ccxi[v]] cansas finadas, lo sant baro comensa a dire: 'Senhor Dieus, tu obriras las meuas aurelhas.'

E depueys ausiron quels ausels disseron: 'Lausatz Dieus, totz los angels seus, e lausatz Dieu, totas las vertutz d'aquels.' E coma l'alba comensa de resplandir els comenseron de cantar: 'La resplandor de Nostre Senhor, Dieus, sia sobre nos.' Semblanment, disseron a hora de tercia cantans: 'Al rey nostre cantatz.' E a la sexta hora canteron e disseron: 'Vet vos coma es bona causa habitar e star los germans en

They sighted another island, from which many springs flowed and landed upon it, and it was the day on which our Lord celebrated the last supper with his disciples. For that reason they stayed there until the sabbath day came; then they explored the island and found a large herd of animals. Saint Brendan then said to the monks:

'You may take some of these animals, for our Lord has put them here so that we may take some and celebrate the feast of Easter.'

Once the Easter feast was over, they put to sea and came to another island on which they found a beautiful spring and a tree of great height, full of pure white birds. As they admired the wondrous tree and its birds, one of the birds flew down and began to speak to Saint Brendan, saying to him:

'Be not amazed at us, holy father. Know that we are from that large army of devils who once transgressed God's command. Ours was not sin, nor did we yield to his pleading, but instead we dwell here; since we neither asked for help nor sought refuge with our Lord, we fell from grace along with the others. Yet, because our Lord had created us, he wanted us to come here, and then some others came; he has given us this much grace in that we suffer no hardship, but sends us here where we have leisure to fly like other spirits through the different parts of the firmament and the planets. The Lord our God has commanded us to praise our Creator on Sundays and this we do. You and your brothers have been a year on your journey and still have six more years to be at sea; and after six more years you will come to the Promised Land, where dwell the saints of the Old Testament.'

When he had said this, the bird took wing to fly back to the others; since the hour of vespers had come, all the birds in the air began at once to sing, while striking their wings with their beaks: 'To you, Lord God, let praises be sung in Sion and to you will be given homage in Jerusalem,' and they continued their responses.[7]
When these hymns were ended, the saintly man began to say:

'Lord God, open thou my ears.'
Then they heard the birds say: 'All his angels praise God, and praise him for all these powers.' As dawn was beginning to break, they began to sing: 'May the splendour of our Lord God be upon us.' Similarly, at the hour of tierce, they sang: 'Sing to our King.' At the hour of sext, they sang these words: 'Behold what a good thing it is

un loc.'[18] E ayssi de dia e de nueg las aviis retins e donanon lausor a Nostre Senhor, per la bona odor que dels ausels yssia e del dos cant e plasent que disian, stech Sant Branda entro a Pantacosta. (116)

Pueys partit d'aqui e venc a una yla hon atrobec un monestier de monges qui fazian lo servizi de Dieu; aqui avia una gleya quatradal[19] auta coma longa. Havia hy .ii. alas que eron totas de bel cristal, e los vayssels que en la gleya sirvian eron totz de cristalh, se es la panan e lo calser e los terrases e candalabres e encenses; los frayres aquestz avian tan gran cilenci entre els que no parlanon; am sagals alcunas vetz demostranon so que volian. Sant Branda pres a una part lo prior d'aquels e demandec li l'estamen del monestier; e aquel am gran reverentia respos:

'Senher payre, davant lo meu senhor Jhesu Christ confes que .lxxx. ans son passatz depueys que nos venguem en sta viala e de tot aquest terma[20] humana votz no ausi exceptat quant cantant entre nos la lauzor a Dieu, quans respon lo Sant Sperit per boca d'angel una mot nobla paraula, que nos amonesta que perseveramment irem e starem en r[e]pons dels angels.'
E Sant Branda li dis:
'Senhor prior, plassa te que nos demorem asyssi am tu?'
Respos lo prior:
'No.s cove coma tu sabes be que revelat es per Nostre Senhor so que fic Dieus; car a tu cove que tornes al loc don moguist solament am .iiij.[21] frayres e no pus.'
Ementre que ambidos parlanon un rach de (s)fuot intrec per una fenestra e amortec los ciris que stano davant l'autar. Empero ja fos que semblant era que fosson apagatz non erem pas, coma lo lum demorava en los ciris e per nul temps aquels no s'amortavon, aus stavon ayssi cremant dia e nueg. Sant Branda vic la tota una nueg davant l'autar e al mati demandec al prior licencia que s'en volia anar. El prior li dis:
'Tu celebraras la nativitat de Nostre Senhor ayssi cro a la Piffania.' (146)

Se partic d'aqui Sant Branda e meseron se en mar; el ven mena los en loc hon viron l'Ala dels Ausels tant que [ccxii] a la yla vengueron e ausiron los ausels que cantavon e disian:
'Salutz al Senhor Nostre sobre la sua cadieyra.'
Adoncz la una d'aquels venc a Sant Branda e dis li:

to dwell and live as brothers in one place.' Thus night and day the
birds uttered resounding praises to our Lord, and because of the
fragrant smell which came from the birds, and of their sweet and
pleasant song, Saint Brendan stayed there until Pentecost.

Then he departed that place and came to an island where he found
a monastery of monks who were engaged in the service of God;
there was a cathedral church, as lofty as it was long. Here there
were two altars which were both of beautiful crystal, and the vessels
which were used in the church, namely the paten, the chalice, the
plates, the candelabra and the censers, were entirely of crystal. The
monks maintained the utmost silence among themselves so that no
one spoke; occasionally they used signals to indicate what they
wanted. Saint Brendan took the prior to one side and asked about
the establishment of the monastery, and he most reverently replied:
    'Lord father, before my lord Jesus Christ, I declare that eighty
years have passed since we came here to this island, and in all that
time I have not heard a human voice except when in our
community we sing the praises of God and when the Holy Spirit
replies through the mouth of an angel, encouraging us in a noble
speech to maintain our determination and response to the angels.'
Saint Brendan said to him:
    'My lord prior, are you content that we stay here with you?'
The prior replied:
    'It is not permitted; though you well know that it has been
revealed through our Lord what God has decreed: except for the
four brothers, you must return to the place whence you set out.'
While they were both speaking, a shaft of fire entered through the
window and extinguished the candles which were standing in front
of the altar. After that, the flame, which seemed to have been
extinguished, was not really so, since the light remained in the
candles and at no time did they go out but stayed burning night and
day. Saint Brendan spent the entire night in front of the altar and in
the morning asked permission to sail away. The prior said to him:
    'You will celebrate the birth of our Lord here until Epiphany.'

Saint Brendan then left there and put out to sea; the wind
conveyed them to the place where they sighted the Isle of Birds;
they came to the island and heard the birds singing these words:
    'Salvation to our Lord who sits upon his throne.'

'Sapias, sant de Dieu, que en la ciutat de Velluer celebraras la Pascha e auras motz grans e diverses perilhs; pueys vendras a Terra de Promissio que demandes pueys tornara Dieus en la tua terra.'

E Sant Branda quant ausit aysso redec gracias a Dieu Nostre Senhor. Motas tribulacios e diversas de meravilhas vic Sant Branda anant per la mar Oceanana lasquals serian long de comptar. (157)

Assayadament li apparech una montanhia mot auta que quays al mieg del cel tocava e aqui avia mot gran fum sus aut en lo sobira loc de la montanhia; e no agron stat longament que la barcha venc sobre riba terra. E viron aquela montanhia descuberta de la part desus que gitavo mot grans spiras de flamas de fuoc que tocavon tro al cel, e en descepesc[22] davalec aquel fuoc per lo mon aval cremant cro sus en la mar. Per que Sant Branda volent se partir d'aquel mal loc. (164)

No gayre luehn de la terra en forma d'ome cremat e negre e so querrat, e sesia sobre una podes; e yvia[23] un drap de li davant el que peniava entre .ij. forges de ferre e lo drap aquel no tenguan. E los frayres que am Sant Branda eron disseron quant ho vigron de luehn que era nau que stava abocada. Els autres disseron que era peys mort; e donc coma els s'apropiesson aquel home els lo troberon que sesia sobre la peyra de fort lege forma; els homes[24] de la mar bategeron lo tro sus al cap. E coma los homes sen partian paria la peyra e el tot e lo drap que davant aquel per los huelhs e per lo fron e a las nadadas tirans aquel yssic. Sant Branda comensa aquel a demandar qui era e per qual colpa era pausat aqui e per qual merit aytal pena sostenia. E aquel respos:

'Jeu soy lo mort, mal nat Judas, que non hyey per meritz meus aquest loc, mas per la gran misericordia de Jhesu Christ es donat a mi aquest loc per penitencia. E sapias que jeu stant ayssi en aquesta peyra que sia en penas, e que aia totz delietz per raso de la temor dels turmens que me cove a soffrir; coma jeu cremi ayssi coma massa de plom regialada en ola, de nueg e de dia en mieg d'aquel mon que veses. Aquel mon es Infern qui gitana las suas plagas tos temps devorant las armas dels non piatadoses peccadors. Ara veramen e un pauc de reffrigeri ayssi e totz Dimenges de las unas vespras tro [ccxii[v]] als autres e en la nativitat de Jhesu Christ entro al dia de pericio e de Paschas entro a Patacosta; e en la Purifficacio de la Verges Maria he jeu aquest refrigeri que i sofero.n[25] infern e venc ayssi en aquest loc; e pueys soy turmentat en lo plus prion de

Then one of them came to Saint Brendan and said to him:

'Know this, saint of God, that you will celebrate Easter in the city of Velluer[8] and you will experience many great and diverse dangers; then you will come to the Promised Land, which you have sought for, and then God will restore you to your own land.'

When Saint Brendan heard this, he gave thanks to our Lord God. Saint Brendan endured many tribulations and witnessed diverse marvels in the course of his journey across the Ocean sea, which would take a long time to recount.

Suddenly there appeared a mountain so high that it soared up into the sky, and from the highest peak there came a fiery smoke; it was not long before the boat came to shore. They saw exposed the top of the mountain which threw out long tongues of flame and fire, reaching right up to the heavens and then the fire falling right down to the depths of the sea. For this reason Saint Brendan wanted to leave that evil place.

Not far from the land, he caught sight of something like a blackened and burnt figure sitting on a rock; in front of him he had a cloth hanging from two iron spikes, and he was not holding the cloth. The monks who were with Saint Brendan, when they saw it from afar, said that it was a boat which had capsized. Others said that it was a dead fish, but as they approached the man they found him sitting on a very large rock; the waves of the sea beat upon him, struck him full on the head. As the waves retreated, the rock appeared in its entirety and the cloth which was in front of him flapped against his eyes, his forehead and his nostrils. Saint Brendan began by asking him who he was and for what crime he had been put there, and why he endured such punishment. He replied:

'I am the late misbegotten Judas. I am not here in this place because of any merit of mine, but through the great mercy of Jesus Christ this place is given me for my penance. Know that I stay here on this rock so that I may be punished, and yet here I have the uttermost delight by comparison with the dread of the torments which I must endure. Night and day I burn like a lump of molten lead in a pot, in the middle of that mountain you see. This is the mountain of Hell which throws out its fiery bolts, continually consuming the souls of unrepentant sinners. I have indeed a brief period of respite here every Sunday, from vespers to the following

la habitacio dels demonis am Erodes e am Anna e am Cayphas. E per amor d'aquel Payre Sant, jeu conjuri per lo redemptor del mon que deias pregar lo meu Senhor Jhesu Christ que jeu aia poder de star ayssi tant solament entro dema lo solelh yssit, per so qu'els demonis no tumenton mi en lo anament que.n no.m²⁶ porton en la mala heretat que jeu compriey per lo mal pres que Jhesu Christ agui.'

E lo sant baro dis:

'Sia fach a la voluntat del Senhor.' (198)

Adonc li demandec Sant Branda qui.n drap era aquel que davant sos huelhs peniava. E Judas respos:

'Aquest drap que tu veses doniey jeu a un lebros quant anava am lo Senhor meu Jhesu Christ; empero jeu no hyey negun refugi per aquest, ans dona a mi gran albregament coma lo drap no foc meu ni lo hagui de bon just. Los forcons de ferre en que pendi jeu doniey jeu en present als sacdotz del tompl.²⁷ La peyra en sich pausiey jeu en un clot en una carrieyra publica, per que mielhs ne passesson los caminans; e aquo fesi jeu dabans que fos discipol del Senhor.'

E donc coma fos venguda la hora de vespras, vengron en un gran moltitut de diables cridan:

'Departis te de nos, sant de Dieu, que no nos podem apropiar de nostre conpanho entro que tu de.l te partiscas davant. Ni detras lo nostre princip Satanas mas no ausam apersequj[r] ni retener²⁸ entro que el aia lo seu ama Judas Scariot.'

El sant baro respos, Sant Branda respos lor:

'Jeu no soffren a vos autres ni en barch ni contrast que lo enemic de Dieu vos apropietz; mas jeu hyey pregat Nostre Senhor Jhesu Christ que li alargue l'espaside las penas entro demo mati. E lo Senhor a me autreiat no per los meus meritz, mas per sa gran merce e misericordia²⁹ que el stia ayssi tota aquesta nueg entro al mati; per que vos mandi de part del meu Senhor Jhesu Christ que.l laysses anar.'

Els demonis cridant am gran vos disseron:

'Cossi pot esser que Jhesu Christ nil seu poder aiude ni done refugi de gratia a aquest que es stat traydo seu ple de mals e de iniquitatz?'

'Jeu vos mandi,' dis Sant Branda, 'aprop d'aquel qui la sua gratia e merce sten sobre quis vol que vos autres no.l toguetz ni negun mal no li fassatz.'

evening, and from the day of the birth of Jesus Christ until the day of Epiphany, and from Easter until Pentecost; and on the day of the purification of the Virgin Mary I have this respite so that I do not suffer in Hell but come here to this place. And afterwards I am tormented in the lowest depths of the demons' lair along with Herod, Annas and Caiaphas.[9] For the love of God the Father, I implore you by the redeemer of the world to beg my Lord Jesus Christ that I may have leave to stay here until sunrise tomorrow, so that the demons do not torment me as usual or carry me away to the painful fate which is my reward for the evil bargain I made over Jesus Christ.'

The noble saint said:

'May the Lord's will be done.'

Saint Brendan then asked him whose was the cloth which was hanging before his eyes. Judas replied:

'This cloth which you see here I gave to a leper when I was with my Lord Jesus Christ; but I do not have any respite because of it, rather it was given to me as a torment,[10] since the cloth was not rightfully mine. The iron spikes on which it hangs I gave as a gift to the priests of the temple. The rock on which I sit, I placed in a ditch on a public highway to assist the passers-by; and this I did before I was a disciple of the Lord.'

Since the hour of vespers had now come, there arrived a large crowd of demons, shouting:

'Be gone from us, saint of God, because we cannot approach our companion until you have departed hence. We dare not appear in the presence of or return to our master, Satan, until he has his own beloved Judas Iscariot.'

Saint Brendan, the noble saint, replied to them:

'I will not allow you on board the boat nor will I bargain with the enemy of God; but I pray our Lord Jesus Christ that he may grant him respite from his punishment until tomorrow morning. May the Lord grant me this not because of my merit but out of his great mercy and grace, that he may stay here tonight until morning; so I command you in the name of my Lord Jesus Christ to let him go.'

The demons cried out at the top of their voices:

'How can it be that Jesus Christ has any power to give aid or respite to the one who, filled with evil and malice, betrayed him?'

'I command you', said Saint Brendan, 'for the sake of him whose

E ayssi foc complit que tantost s'enpoieron los demonis in Infern. E al mati meneron lo sen mot ajustadamen; el torneron a la penas de [*ccxiii^r*] crusels hon stava dabans e stara de fi en fi per tos temps. (232)

Sant Branda am los seus companhos venen sa vas la plassa meridiana e anan vas en la barcha la hon Nostre Senhor la volia guidar; anan ades am ven ades am autre e ades anan a destra ades a sinistra. Troban e vesen motas meravilhas que qui las volia totas dire tornarian a enueg. E cascun jorn glorifficavon e lausavon Dieu en totas causas e per totas causas. Quant hat anat ayssi .vii. ans per la mar volc Nostre Senhor que aribes en Terra de Promissio; e pres terra e aqui visitava de las reliquias dels sans. Aqui en aquela terra jasian sans. (241)

Pel torn de qu'en venc en la terra del seu monestier; e recampta e dis aquestas causas lasquals en la oceana mar avia vistas e aqui stant no fos longa sa vida. Ans los pres Nostre Senhor garnitz dels sagramens divinals so es del cors de Dieu que humalment recebec en las mas dels seus discipols. Mot gloriosament s'en anec a Jhesu Christ. (247)

Finic a .xii. dies de jun en l'an de la Incarnacio de Jhesu Christ .m.cc.xi. (249)

grace and mercy is all powerful, that you and the others do not touch him or do him any harm.'

It so happened that the demons returned immediately to Hell. In the morning they led him back there without a word; they returned him to the cruel punishments which he suffered before and will suffer for evermore.

Saint Brendan sailed towards the south with his companions and they went in the boat wherever our Lord wished to direct them; they sailed on, sometimes with the wind from one direction, at other times from another, sometimes to the right, sometimes to the left. They met with and witnessed so many marvels that whoever would wish to recount them all would become a bore. Each day they praised and glorified God in and for all things. When they had been at sea for seven years, our Lord wished them to reach the Promised Land; they landed and visited the relics of the saints. Saints lay buried in that land.[11]

Thereafter he returned home to his monastery; he related those things which he had seen on the Ocean sea and he did not live long there. Our Lord took him, fortified by the sacraments of the Church, which he received humbly from the hands of his disciples. In great glory he went to Jesus Christ.

Finished on the twelfth day of June in the year of the Incarnation of our Lord, 1211.

7

The Catalan Version

Margaret Burrell

Manuscript and Editions There are two extant Catalan versions of the Voyage of St Brendan, a longer one (Escorial, Bibliotheca San Lorenzo N.III.5, ff. 223ᵛ-226ʳ) and a shorter one (Vic, Biblioteca Episcopal 174, ff. 512ᵛ-522ʳ). The longer version is so similar in structure and detail to the Occitan version that its inclusion here would be redundant. The shorter version has therefore been selected for this volume because of its idiosyncratic treatment of some of the episodes. Both versions are in prose. The Vic manuscript is written on paper in a fourteenth-century script and decorated with alternating capitals in blue and red. Some of the chapter headings are also marked by elaborate finials in blue ink (for further details see Massó i Torrents 1902, 241-43). The manuscript was transcribed and published by Nolasc Rebull in *Jaume de Voràgine, Llegenda Àuria* (1976, 808-14). Rebull's text has been corrected here after viewing the manuscript in the *atelier* of the Monestir Sant Pere de les Puelles in Barcelona.[1] A new edition of the text has been prepared for the present volume. The text is translated here for the first time.[2]

Authorship, Patron and Date The text does not permit identification of the author or patron. Geneviève Brunel (p. 241), who designates it as V, states that the manuscript is 'sans doute de la première moitié du xvᵉ siècle'. After describing the physical appearance of the manuscript, she lists its contents, beginning with a 'liste des Vies de saints contenues dans le manuscrit, suivant l'ordre de l'année liturgique' (p. 242). This list contains nearly all the saints in

---

1. I am indebted to the sisters of the convent for their generosity in allowing me to see the manuscript in its damaged state.
2. Problems presented by the text, and procedures used in preparing the edition, are discussed in the Textual Notes.

the *Legenda aurea*, though their ordering differs slightly. This is followed by 'toute une série de Vies de saints qui n'appartiennent pas au corpus de la *Legenda aurea*' (p. 242), amongst whom she lists 'sent Brenda' (p. 243). Brunel concludes this part of the description of the contents by saying: 'Cette série s'achève avec la Dédicace de l'Eglise, chapitre final de la compilation latine (f. 584d)' (*ibid.*).

Structure and Contents Like the Occitan version this work begins with a general statement introducing St Brendan, but it has no formal prologue or dedication to a patron. Dividing the episodes according to content gives the following structure:

(1)   Introduction
(2)   The initial voyages
(3)   Judas
(4)   The Promised Land
(5)   The loss of the monks
(6)   Brendan's return via Persia and Jerusalem

Section (1) includes the introductory episodes, namely the general introduction, Brendan's proposal to see the Promised Land, the building of the boat, the episode of the intruding monks and the conditions of the voyage. Section (2) recounts their first island visit (where one of the monks is tempted by Satan), the Crystal Isle, the Easter feast and the Isle of Birds. The order in which these episodes are related is different from that in the Occitan version and the longer Catalan version. Section (3) contains the encounter with Judas and the conversation with the demons sent to bring him to his punishment. Section (4) is the visit to the Promised Land, located on an island called Deliciosa. Section (5) recounts the loss of two of the monks who are carried off by birds, and section (6) concludes Brendan's voyage with a detour to the Dead Sea, Persia and Jerusalem before he returns home, where he dies.

Like the Occitan version, the shorter Catalan version is remarkable for its omission and abbreviation of many of the episodes in the *Navigatio*. Brendan's intention to see the Promised Land is baldly stated, as is his wish to have the fourteen monks accompany him. The preparations for the voyage are similar in other versions, as is the episode of the intruding monks, although one has to note the scribal error concerning the arithmetic of three plus fourteen becoming eighteen. There is no Isle of Sheep episode and the Easter feast occurs on an island. The visit to the Crystal Isle is similarly abbreviated, and the Isle of Birds episode is very brief; the tree on which the birds sit, unlike that in other versions, is barren and leafless. Only one canticle of the birds is mentioned and their purpose seems merely to tell Brendan of the seven-year voyage he must undergo. The encounter with Judas gives details which are similar to those in the Occitan version, and in an interesting contrast the next episode recounts the visit to the Promised Land.

But it is in this episode that the first mention of the King of Persia occurs. The entire episode can be divided into separate narrative events: the island they have reached is called Deliciosa and its paradisial properties are well described; then there is a statement about the length of time St Brendan stayed there and about the written account of all the marvels he found which he composed for the King of Persia; then there are the many fish seen by Brendan in the stream, leading him to call the island the Branch of Paradise. This is followed by another mention of white birds which sing in harmony, and finally a voice informs Brendan that the island is called the Branch of Souls. There is obviously considerable conflation of episodes here. The presence of the birds and the identification of the place as the Branch of Souls suggest this may originally have been part of the detail of the Paradise of Birds episode. The presence in the next episode of more birds, this time predatory and menacing, is unique to this version.

The final episode is the most startling. St Brendan succeeds in finishing his voyage and returns to his homeland, but he makes a considerable detour, described with much fantastic detail, some of which seems to echo other medieval texts. The uncertain nature and identity of the two men guarding cattle in the woodland remind one of the Hideous Herdsman episode in Chrétien de Troyes's *Yvain*, and the men branded with the sign of the cross recall the fervour of crusading epics. The visit to the ruler in Persia (now called the emperor rather than the king) and the guide to Jerusalem are reminiscent of the journey of Charlemagne to Jerusalem and Constantinople in the *Pèlerinage de Charlemagne*. Just why Brendan visits Persia and the emperor is not clear, but the diversion of the hitherto standard account of Brendan's exploits into the realms of secular fantasy makes this version interesting and unique.

The Author's Purpose Given the late date of this version and the elements of the fantastic outlined above, it is likely that the author simply wanted to recount a familiar story, whilst striving to make it more interesting by some inventive amplification. The additions serve to make St Brendan an even greater figure of wonder, and the whole account, brief as it is, is more an exercise of the author's imagination than a faithful vernacular rendering of the *Navigatio* tradition.

[*dxii*^{*v*}] Lo abat sent Brenda nasque de molt noble linatge e fo baro de fort
gran abstinencia, e pare de .d.¹ mongos. Aquest sent Brenda volgue
sercar les pars e les fins de terres encontrades de la mar Oceana. E
tria amb ell .xiiii. frares; e dix-los:

'Amichs frares, jo he proposat de anar en Terra de Promissio, e
volria que.m saguissets.'

E ells tots respongueren:

'Pare sant, nos som tots apparallats de saguir tu en tot loch fins a
la mort.'

E sent Brenda mana aquells dejunar .x. dies, abans que d'equi
pertissen. E, pessats los dits .x. dies, ells prengueren comiat per
anar en plaga oriental. E vengueren en una illa qui avia nom Ende, e
aqui estigueren .iii. dies. E entratant, ells agueren una nau sotil e
molt leuguera, e ancuyraren-la de cuyrs de bous e maseren-hi
vianda assats. E puys reculliren-se. E vengueren a ells .iii. frares qui
estaven en aquella illa e digueren que ells volien anar ab ells en lo
peragrinatge. E sent Brenda reeb els e foren ab aquests be .xviii.
frares. E apres, maseren la nau en la mar ab guiyament de Deu sens
vela e sens timo; e axi anaren .xv. dies per la mar sa e la, axi com los
corrents e los vents los menaven. E a veguades avien molt vent e a
veguades no.n avien gents, e desigaven que pusquessen venir en
algun loch hon pusquessen refrescar d'aygua. (22)

E con agueren axi anat per .xl. dies, ells vengueren en una illa de
part de septentrion qui era fort alta e tota plena d'arbres; e vaeran
aqui molts bells rius d'aygues qui corrien per la roca avall. E
trobaren aqui bon port e axiren tots en terra, e tantost vengue
envers ells un ca molt suament e ximpla. E lavors sent Brenda dix al
frares:

'Bon missatge nos a trames Nostre Senyor Deu Jhesuchrist.
Anem derrera aquesta bestia e saguim-la.'

E lavos [*dxiii*^{*r*}] lo ca se mes primer e ell apres, he vengueren en hun
bell alberch on entraren dedins e vaeren aqui sitis e lits molt richs.
E sent Brenda dix als seus frares:

'Guardats-vos que Satanas no us engan, car veig que dels .iiii.
frares qui apres nos vengueren ja la hu ha mengat hun fruyt mala als
seus ops. E pregats Deu per la sua anima, car lo cors d'equell ja es
liurat a Sathanas.' (37)

E partiren-se d'equi hon eran los sitis e los lits. He entraren en una

The abbot Saint Brendan was born of very noble lineage; he was a nobleman of great self-restraint and the father of five hundred monks. This Saint Brendan wanted to explore the regions and lands bordering the Ocean sea. He selected fourteen brothers to go with him; and he said to them:

'My dear brothers, I have proposed to go to the Promised Land and want you to accompany me.'

They all replied:

'Holy Father, we are all prepared to follow you anywhere until we die.'

Saint Brendan instructed them to fast for ten days before they departed. Once these ten days had passed, they took their leave to journey to the eastern shore. They came to an island which was called Ende, where they stayed for three days. Meanwhile they got a boat, flimsy and very light, covered it with oxhide and put into it a quantity of food. Then they retired. And there came to them three[1] brothers who were on that island and who said that they wished to accompany them on the pilgrimage. Saint Brendan accepted them and altogether there were eighteen monks. After that, they put to sea in the boat without sails or rudder, entrusting themselves to God. They were on the sea, going hither and thither, for fifteen[2] days, as the winds and currents took them. Sometimes there was a strong wind, sometimes none, and they prayed that they might come to some place where they could restock with fresh water.

When they had gone thus for forty days, they came to an island in the north which was very high and full of trees; and there they saw many beautiful streams of water which flowed down the rock. They found a good place to land there and everyone disembarked; immediately there came towards them a very mild and gentle dog. Then Saint Brendan said to the monks:

'Our Lord Jesus Christ has sent us a good messenger. Let us go behind this dog and follow it.'

With the dog in front and them behind, they came to a pleasant house into which they entered and saw there very rich hangings and beds. Saint Brendan said to his monks:

'Take care lest Satan tricks you, for I foresee that one of the four monks who came after us has today eaten a forbidden fruit to do Satan's work.[3] Pray to God for his soul, for his body is already delivered into the power of Satan.'

altra case hon trobaren les taules meses ab molt belles tovalles e ab
bell pa e de bon peix, per que ells faeren oracio a Nostra Senyor
Deu e benehiren la taula e pensaren de menjar. E quant agueren
menjat e bagut ells se ajustaren e faeren gracies e laors a Nostre
Senyor Deu, e puys ells anaren en lo palau hon eran los lits e
dormiren aqui per .iii. dies e .iii. nits que no despertaren; e apres
ells se levaren e cuydaren-se que no aguessen dormit sino una nit.
E sent Brenda dix-los:

'Guardats-vos que nagu de vosaltres no trasque d'aci alguna
cose.' (48)

E puys ells se reculliren en lo nom de Jhesuchrist e navaguaren tot
lo die. E al vespra ells vengueren en una altra illa e sent Brenda dix
a sos companyons:

'Devallem açi e mengem, car vuy es lo dijous de la cena de
Nostre Senyor Jhesuchrist.'

E axi ells romangueren aqui fins al vespra de Pasqua. E aqui ells
trobaren gran folchs de bastiars, co es d'ovelles e de bous, e sent
Brenda dix-los:

'Reebets d'equest bestiar les coses qui son a nos necessaries per
la Pasqua.'

E aqui ells celebraren la Pasqua. (59)

E apres ells partiren d'equi e navaguaren tant fins que vengueren
en una altra illa hon avia huna bella font hon trobaren un arbre de
meravellosa virtut. E aqui avia hun monestir hon estaven mongos
negres, e entraren dedins lo monestir e vaeren aqui dos altars de
bell cres[*dxiii^v*]tall e duas lanties qui cremaven aqui. E totes
quantes coses hi avia a servey del altar e de la missa totes eran de
bell crestall; e d'aquests mongos negres era lo lur scilenci que a
penes parlaven. E sent Brenda demana al prior de liu estament e
aquell repos e dix:

'Pare sant, sapies que .lxxx. anys ha que jo son en aquesta illa
que james null hom no he vist sino los meus frares e tu e tos
companyons, e no parlam entre nos de naguna res sino per senyals
dels dits de les mans.'

E sent Brenda li demena si convenia a ell estar aqui ab ells e lo prior
li dix:

'No cove que tu abits açi, car mes mar e mes coses as encare a
sercar e a veura que no as vist. E puys tornaras la d'on venguist e

They left the place where the hangings and the beds were and entered another building, where they found tables spread with beautiful cloths, delicious bread and good fish; they prayed to our Lord God, blessed the table and prepared to eat. When they had eaten and drunk, they gave praise and thanks to our Lord God. Then they went to the palace where the beds were and slept there for three whole days and nights before waking. When they did get up, they thought they had slept only one night. Saint Brendan said to them:

'Make sure no one takes anything from here.'

Then they assembled in the name of Jesus Christ and sailed on for the whole day. At nightfall, they came to another island and Saint Brendan said to his companions:

'Let us stop here and eat, for today is the Thursday before the Last Supper of our Lord Jesus Christ.'

So they remained there until the vespers of Easter. They found there large flocks of animals, namely sheep and cattle, and Saint Brendan said to them:

'Take from this flock what is necessary to us for Easter.'

And there they celebrated the Easter feast.

Then they left there and sailed until they came to another island, where there was a beautiful spring; there they found a tree of wondrous qualities. There was a monastery there where black-robed monks dwelt. They entered the monastery and saw two altars of beautiful crystal and two lanterns burning there. Everything used on the altar and for the mass was made of beautiful crystal. Among the black-robed monks there was silence, so that they hardly spoke at all. Saint Brendan asked the prior about the place and he replied:

'Holy Father, know that in the eighty years which have passed since I came here I have seen no man apart from my brothers, yourself and your companions, and we do not speak amongst ourselves save by making signs with our fingers and hands.'

Saint Brendan asked him if he could remain there with them and the prior said to him:

'You cannot dwell here, for you have still more seas to roam and more things to see than you have yet seen. Then you will reach the place from which you came and that will be your grave.'

aqui sera la tua sapultura.'
E quant vench al mati, sent Brenda dix al prior que anar-se'n volia, e lo prior li dix que anas en bona ventura:

'Mas açi te cove tornar, e estaras aqui ab nos la festa de Sincogesma, e estaras hi fins les octaves sien passades.' (81)

E lavos sent Brenda s'en parti e vench-se'n en una illa molt luny d'equi qui avia nom Paradis dels oucells. E com ell se acostas al port d'equella illa, ells vaeran gran multitut d'aucells qui cantaven en hun arbre qui no avia fulles ne flores ne nagun fruyt. E tots los aucells dehien cantant:

'Beneyt sia lo Senyor Nostre qui seu en la sua cadira axi com anyell.'

E hun d'equells aucells vingue a la lur nau e dix a sent Brenda lo temps que li era predestinat de navaguar per la mar, co es. '.vii. anys complits e puys vendras a Bellver², e celebraras aqui la Pasqua; e passats los .vii. anys, tornar-te'n as en aquesta terra.'

E quant aço ague dit l'aucell, torna-sse'n a sos companyons al arbre sech. (94)

E sent Brenda comensa de navaguar, e anaren tant per la mar, fins que vaeran en la mar une forma d'oma qui sehia sobra una pedra; e estave-li devant hun drap de li, que penjave [*dxiiijᵗ*] entre dues forques de ferra. E dementra que ells lo vehien de luny, alguns dels frares dehien que aquella cose era nau, e los altres dehien que era auçell e que era boca de peix. E quant ells se foren acostats en aquell loch, ells vaeran l'ome qui sehia sobra una pedra, e era de leya e terrible figura; e les ondes de la mar farien-lo per lo cap e per tot lo cors. E quant les ondes de la mar se departien d'equens, aparia aquella pedra tota nua hon sehia aquell infael. E sertanent lo drap que denant aquell era estes, a veguades lo feria per los huylls e per la care, a veguades tirave aquell açi. E sent Brenda comensa a aquell a demenar qui era, ne per qual cose estave aqui ne per quins merits sofferia aytal penitencia. E aquell respos:

'Sapies que jo son lo maleyt Judes Escariot qui per los meus merits estich en aquest loch, e per la misericordia de Jhesuchrist m'es atorgat aquest loch per penitencia; e per la indulgencia de Jhesuchrist e per la sua resurectio m'es atorgat de estar açi los digmenges, per so car Jhesuchrist en aytal die ressucita. E es-me semblant que quant son açi que sia en paradis avent tots los delits

When morning came, Saint Brendan told the prior that he wished to go. The prior bade him farewell, and said:

'But you must return here; you will be with us for the feast of Quinquagesima,[4] and then you will be here until the octave has passed.'

Then Saint Brendan departed and came to an island far from there called the Paradise of Birds. As they approached the coast of this island, they saw a great multitude of birds singing in a tree, which had no leaves, flowers or fruit. All the birds sang:

'Blessed be our Lord who sits on his throne like a lamb.'

One of the birds came to their boat and told Saint Brendan how long he was predestined to sail over the sea, namely 'seven full years, then you will come to Bellver and you will celebrate Easter there; after seven years, you will return to that land.'

When the bird had said this, it went back to its companions on the barren tree.

Saint Brendan continued onwards, and they travelled over the seas until they saw in the sea the shape of a man sitting on a rock; he had in front of him a linen cloth hanging from two iron spikes. While they beheld this sight from afar, some of the brothers said it was a boat, others that it was a bird and yet others the mouth of a fish. When they had approached that place, they saw sitting on a rock a man whose appearance was ugly and terrible; the waves of the sea battered him right over his head and his body. As the waves ebbed, the rock on which the wretched man was sitting came clearly into view. And indeed the cloth in front of him sometimes flapped over his eyes and face and sometimes pulled him this way and that. Saint Brendan began to ask him who he was, for what reason he was there and why he merited such penitence. He replied:

'I am the ill-begotten Judas Iscariot who deservedly dwells in this place, and through the great mercy of Jesus Christ I am granted this place as a penance; and by the indulgence of Jesus Christ, and through his resurrection, I am permitted to stay here on Sundays, since Jesus Christ was resurrected on that day. It seems to me that when I am here I am in Paradise with all earthly delights, especially because of the anguish caused by the torments which are my lot, for I burn forever like a lump of molten lead in the middle of this

del mon, e axi per rao de las penas dels turments qui.m son esdevenidors, car jo tostemps crem axi coma pessa de plom sus al mig d'equella muntanya que vesets; la qual muntanya es infern qui gita les sues flames tostemps, devorant les animes dels peccadors. E ara, axi com dit t'é, jo he açi verament rapos tots digmenges de les unes vespres fins a les altres, e an la Nativitat de Jhesuchrist fins al dia de Parity, e de Pasqua, e de Pasqua fins a Sincogesma, e an la Purificacio de la Verge Maria e an la Assumpcio. E, aprés, jo son turmentat el lo lus pregon d'infern ab Arodes e ab Pons Pilat e ab Cahifas. E per ço jo.t prech per lo redemptor Jhesuchrist que tu vulles preguar ell que jo age licencia de estar açi solament fins l'endema lo sol axit, per ço que lo diables no.m tur[*dxiiij*ᵛ]mentem en lo teu aveniment ne.m porten a la dolorosa aretat que jo compri per lo preu de Jhesuchrist que.n agui.'
E sent Brenda dix:
   'La voluntat de Nostre Senyor Deu sia feta.' (130)

E lavors sent Brenda li demena quin drap era aquell qui denant li estave. E ell respos:
   'Aquest done jo a hun lebros, quant jo era ab lo Senyor de tot lo mon; mas no.n he per ell nagun refrigeri, ans me done molt enpatxament per quant no era meu. E les forques de ferra en que esta doni jo als saserdots del templa, e la pedra en que estich mesi jo en hun loch hon avia hun forat en un carreta publica sots los peg dels trespassants, ans que jo fos dexeble del Salvador.'
E apres quant la hora de vespres fos venguda vengueren una gran multitud de diables cridant e dient:
   'Parteix-te d'aci, sent Brenda de Deu, car nos no.ns podem acostar a aquest nostre companyo fins que tu de ell te partesques, ne denant la care del nostre princep no guosariem tornar fins li retam aquest amich seu.'
Als quals sent Brenda respos:
   'Jo no deffen pas a vos altres que a ell no us acostets, mas Jhesuchrist ha atorguat a ell aquesta nit fins al mati.'
A qual digueren los diables en qual manera lo nom de Jhesuchrist es invocat sobra ell, com ell sia traydor seu. E sent Brenda li dix:
   'Jo us man en lo nom de Nostre Senyor que vosaltres no li fassats mal fins al mati.'
E axi fo fet. (152)

mountain you can see; this is the mountain of Hell which throws out at all times its fiery flames, consuming the souls of sinners. Here, as I have told you, I have indeed a brief respite every Sunday from one vespers to the next, and also on the day of the birth of Jesus Christ until the day of Epiphany,[5] and at Easter, from Easter until Quinquagesima, and on the day of the purification of the Virgin Mary and on the feast of the Assumption. Afterwards, I am tormented in the deepest part of Hell with Herod, Pontius Pilate and Caiaphas. I beg in the name of Christ the Redeemer that you are willing to pray to him that I may have permission to stay here until sunrise tomorrow, so that the demons do not torment me at your coming nor carry me away to the painful destiny which is my price for the evil bargain I made over Jesus Christ.'

Saint Brendan said:

'May the will of our Lord God be done.'

Then Saint Brendan asked him whose cloth it was which was before him. Judas replied:

'I gave this to a leper when I was with the Lord of this world; but I do not have any respite because of it, instead it gives me a lot of trouble, since the cloth was not mine. The iron spikes on which it hangs I gave to the priests of the temple, and the rock on which I sit I placed in a ditch on a public street to assist the passers-by, before I was a disciple of the Saviour.'

Since the hour of vespers had now come, there arrived a large throng of demons, shouting:

'Be gone from here, Saint Brendan of God, for we cannot approach our companion until you have departed from here, nor dare we return to our prince without this friend of his.'

To which Saint Brendan replied:

'I am not preventing you from approaching him, but Jesus Christ has granted him respite until tomorrow morning.'

At that, the demons asked how the name of Jesus Christ was invoked on Judas's behalf, since he was a traitor. Saint Brendan said to them:

'I command this in the name of our Lord that you do him no harm until the morning.'

And thus it was done.

E apres sent Brenda ab sos companyons navegua tota la part
meridiane, loant e glorificant Nostre Senyor Deu en totes coses. E
en axi que.s estigueren .vij.anys complits fins que.s fo vengut a la
Terra de Promissio, en una illa qui es dita Deliciosa. E an aquella
illa avia aytal odor que, si totes les bones odors del mon eran el ella,
axi com d'almesc e aygua-ros e ambre encare, no serien res envers
aquelles odors e virtuts d'on tot lo bosch d'equella illa era tot ple,
car aqui avia diversos liris, roses, violes e d'altres maravelloses flors
qui retien aqui [*dxv^r*] gran verdor e molt maravellosa odor. E avia
aqui arbres ten alts que envides podia hom veura les simes. E les
fulles d'equells arbres eran de granesa de dos palms, plenes de
fruyts e totes be olents e flayrants, axi que no paria craedor la bona
odor que.n axia. E antora la illa no trobariets hun fust ten gran com
lo dit qui no rates bona odor, e les fulles dels arbres eran de color
d'aur, luents e d'amts resplandien axi com estels. E per lo mia
d'equells arbres corria hun molt gran riu clar e luent, e açi lo fons
del riu avia moltes pedres precioses qui en aquell resplandien. E
sent Brenda estigue en aquella illa .viii. dies, co es del hun
digmenga fins al altre, per veura les coses de la illa. E feu escriure
totes aquellos maravelles e les altres que avia trobades, per tal que
ho pogues recomptar al rey de Percia, quant seria en sa terra tornat.
E estant sent Brenda riba aquell riu, ell vahe aqui molt peix e dix a
sos frares que no crehia que en aquella illa agues naguna cose vivent
sino peix, 'car nagu de vos no y a pugut alre veura'. Per que dix que
crehia que aquella illa fos dita Ramey de Paradis. E estant axi, ells
vaeran aucells volar tots blanchs del gran de hun colom. E aquells
aucells posaren en aquells arbres e comensaren a cantar hun cant
molt dolc e molt saboros. E aquest cant fahien los aucells .iiii. hores
del die, e estigueren fins a hora de tercia, e puys volaren per
diverses partides. E lavos sent Brenda se agenolla e pregua Deu qui
li digues demostrar qual illa era aquella. E huna veu li dix que
aquella illa era del Ramey de les Animes, co es d'equells qui avien
ahuda alguna poca fe en Deu e que ell dagues saber que .lxiii.
rameys eran de paradis e aquesta illa dix que era lo manor ramey. E
lavors sent Brenda glorifica lo nom de Jhesuchrist. (187)

E apres ell se reculli en la mar ab la sua companya e naveguaren
tant [*dxv^v*] fins que vaeran huna illa. E abans que ells fossen en la
illa ells vaeren caure pedres del aer ten grans com hun quintal. Mas
les pedres no.s acostaven a la nau, ne ells no.s volgueren acostar a la

After that, Saint Brendan and his companions sailed towards the south, praising and glorifying our Lord God in all things. So they travelled for seven full years until they came to the Promised Land, to an island called Deliciosa. On that island there was such a scent that all the beautiful scents in the world, such as musk, rose-water and amber, would be nothing compared with the scents and the properties with which the vegetation of that island was filled, for there were different kinds of lilies, roses, violets and other wonderful flowers which grew there in green profusion amidst marvellous perfumes. And there were trees of such height that one could hardly see their tops. The leaves of these trees were as wide as two palm-widths, full of fruit and smelling sweetly, so that one could not believe the sweet scent which came from them. On the whole island you would not find a piece of wood as big as a finger which did not give forth a sweet smell, and the leaves of the trees, which were the colour of gold, were as glittering and radiant as stars. In the middle of these trees there flowed a very broad stream, clear and sparkling, and in the bed of the stream were many glittering precious stones. Saint Brendan stayed on that island for eight days, that is, from one Sunday to another, in order to see the features of the island. He made a written copy of all these marvels and of the others which he had found, so that they could be recounted to the King of Persia, when he journeyed to his land. While Saint Brendan stood by that stream, he saw there many fish and said to his brothers that he did not believe that anything lived in this stream except fish, 'for none of you has been able to see anything else'.

For that reason, he said he thought the name of that island was the Branch of Paradise. While they were there, they saw white birds in flight, the size of doves. These birds alighted in the trees and began to sing a song of sweet and gentle harmony. The birds sang this song for four hours a day, until the hour of tierce when they flew off in different directions. Then Saint Brendan knelt down and prayed God to tell him what the island was. A voice told him that the island was the Branch of Souls, that is, of those who had only a little faith in God, and that he should know that there were sixty-three branches of Paradise and that the island was the lowest branch. Then Saint Brendan glorified the name of Jesus Christ.

illa; ans naveguaren .xx. dies complits, fins que ells axiren en una riba hon avia hun boscatge. E no y pogueren veure bestia ne naguna cose vivent sino hun riu de molt bella aygua. E dementra que ells estaven en la riba del riu, vench hun aucell molt gran denant sent Brenda, e pres hun frare de quells seus e porta.l s'en (e puys). E puys vench altra aucell e porta ss'en altra frare; e aquell die perde sent Brenda dos homens. (198)

E vist aço, sent Brenda reculliren-se tots en la nau e naveguaren .xl. dies fins que foren en la Mar Morta. E d'aqui ells vaeran la terra ferma; e axiren en terra e anaren sa e la per saber qual terra era aquella. E anant per lo boscatge ells trobaren .ij. homens qui guardaven bestiar e demenaren-los quins homens eran. E ells parlaren en lur lenguatge mas nagu no.ls entania. E hun frare qui era gramatich vahe que ells avien lurs brassos cremats ab lo senyal de la creu. Parla a ells en lati e aquells digeren-li en lati que.ls saguissen e que.ls mostrarien la terra. E ana tant sent Brenda saguint aquells dos pastors fins que vingueren en Persia hon era l'emperador, lo qual quant lo vahe fo molt alegra e dona a sent Brenda aur e argent assats; mas ell no liy volgue pendra. E l'emperador dona-li hun cavaller qui.l sagui fins que foren en la terra de Jherusalem. E d'aqui sent Brenda se'n vench en sa terra e aqui recompta tot son esser e les meravelles que vistes avia. E apres pochs dies ell se'n ana a Deu. (214)

After that, Saint Brendan set sail with his company and they sailed until they sighted an island. Before they set foot on the island, they saw falling from the sky rocks as big as quintal. Although the rocks did not reach the boat, the monks did not wish to draw near the island; instead they sailed for twenty full days until they came to a shore where there was a wood. They could see no animals, nor any other living thing, except a stream of very beautiful water. While they stood on the edge of the stream, there came a very large bird before Saint Brendan; it took one of the brothers and carried him away. Then came another bird which carried away another brother; that day Saint Brendan lost two men.

When he saw this, Saint Brendan reassembled them all in the boat and they sailed for forty days until they were in the Dead Sea. From there they saw dry land; they disembarked and went to and fro to find out what land it was. As they made their way through the woodland they found two men guarding cattle and asked what sort of men they were. The men spoke in their own language and no one understood them. One brother with a knowledge of languages saw that they had their arms branded with the sign of the cross. He spoke to them in Latin and they told him in that language that the monks should follow them and they would show them the land. Saint Brendan followed the two shepherds until they came to Persia, where the Emperor was. When the Emperor saw him, he was overjoyed and gave Saint Brendan a great deal of gold and silver; but he refused to accept it. The Emperor gave him a knight, who followed him until they were in the land of Jerusalem. From there Saint Brendan went to his own country, where he recounted the whole story of his journey and the marvels he had seen. After a few days, he went to God.

8

The Norse Version

Andrew Hamer

Manuscript, Edition and Translation All that remains of the Norse version (*Brandanus saga*) of the *Navigatio* is preserved on a single damaged leaf of a vellum manuscript which, most probably, originally contained eight leaves: fragment 68 in the Norwegian National Archive (Norsk Riksarkiv). Most commentators are agreed that the manuscript was written during the thirteenth century,[1] although it is dated to the fourteenth century in an important survey of Old Norse vernacular saints' lives.[2]

The surviving translation corresponds to the Latin of Selmer's edition between §6, l. 56 and §11, l. 35.[3] The fragment was edited by C.R. Unger (1877), and translated into German by C. Wahlund (1900).

Authorship and Date The Norse translation was possibly made before the thirteenth century[4] and certainly before 1300, at a time when the Icelandic and Norwegian languages were still very similar. This, together with the brevity of the extant text, makes it difficult to localize.

Boyer believes it to be Icelandic, while Unger states cautiously that the manuscript was 'perhaps written in Norway' (p. xi); Halvorsen[5] and Lilli Gjerløw[6] merely refer to the 'West Norse

---

1. See Unger 1877, I, xi; E.F. Halvorsen 1957, col. 201; R. Boyer 1989, 41.
2. O. Widding, H. Bekker-Nielsen and L.K. Shook 1963, 304.
3. Accordingly, to provide a continuous text, I have inserted my own translation of the Latin *Navigatio* at points where the manuscript is damaged and the Norse text lost. The reconstructed lines are printed in italics.
4. Boyer claims that 'a close palaeographic study proves that the translation was certainly older' [than the thirteenth century], *ibid*.
5. Halvorsen, col. 200.
6. 'Brandanus', *Kulturhistorisk Leksikon for nordisk Middelalder* 22 vols (Copenhagen:

language (*mál*)'.

One or two spellings indicate phonological developments known to have taken place in Norwegian but not in Icelandic; this suggests that *Brandanus saga* was written by a Norwegian. Although no definite claim can be made as to the provenance of the translation, the slight evidence in favour of Norway is as follows:

(i) Loss of [n] between two consonants: *vaz* (= [*vats*]), gen. sg. of *vatn* 'water' (Old Icelandic *vatns*);[7]

(ii) Loss of initial [h] before [r]: *rædder* (twice), masc. nom. pl. adj. 'afraid' (Old Icelandic *hr-*).[8]

Translator's Method and Style Even from such fragmentary remains it is possible to gain some impression of the translator's method. Halvorsen (201) states that the translation follows the Latin 'fairly closely' (*temmelig nøye'*), although he notes that the translator has a tendency to abbreviate. For Boyer, 'this translation is very faithful to the original'.

The translation is indeed reasonably faithful to the sense of the original, but it is certainly not literal. Some of the translator's changes seem to be attempts to add vividness to the story. For example, the sheep, which in the original follows the monks as if tame (*quasi domestica*), follows them in the Norse translation like a dog (*sem rakci*). Other changes appear to have been made on stylistic grounds; for example, the change of direct speech to indirect. Where speeches are preserved, their interruption after a few words by a second reference to the speaker, with another verb of speaking, is a familiar feature of saga-style, e.g. 'Then Brendan spoke (*mælte*) to the monk: "Now receive the *corpus domini*", he said (*qvað*), "because you must now . . .".'

The translator does abbreviate, and at times this results in the loss of important information. For example, when the monks are given a favourable breeze, the Norse omits an implicit reference in the Latin to the guiding mercy of God: 'So that they might not have to labour beyond what their strength could endure.' On the other hand, some of the abbreviations are improvements, as when the plodding *diuersos greges ouium unius coloris, id est albi* ('various flocks of sheep of one colour, that is white') is rendered simply by *sauði marga oc sniohuita* ('many snow-white sheep').

Rosenkilde and Bagger, 1956-78), II (1957), cols 199-200 (col. 199).
7. D.A. Seip 1931, 178 and 131, no. 3.
8. Jan Terje Faarlund 1994, 43.

Here the translation would have been closer to the Latin if the sheep had simply been described as 'white'. But it is worth pointing out that the translator uses the same colour term when describing the birds (*fuglum sniohuitum* – dative and plural), thus capturing well the sense of the Latin (*auibus candidissimis*). In the *Norwegian Homily Book*,[9] the same word is used to describe the clothing of another messenger of God, the angel who rolls the stone from Christ's tomb (Matthew 28: 3), where the Vulgate text has *vestimentum ejus sicut nix.*[10]

The translator apparently worked by reading and reflection rather than translating sentence by sentence. According to the Latin text, the monks find large flocks of completely white sheep (§9, l. 10), which are later described as being larger than oxen (§9, l. 42); the Norse, sensibly enough, mentions at the same time both of the remarkable qualities of the sheep, their colour and their size.

At two points the translator adapts the narrative to suit his Scandinavian audience. The first of these concerns the description (*petrosa* – 'rocky') of the sea-monster Jasconius, which the monks mistake for an island (§10, l. 5). The Norse translation, *skeriutt* ('full of skerries'), makes reference to a feature that would have been familiar to anyone who knew the Norwegian or Icelandic coastlines: rocky outcrops that are submerged at high tide. The second adaptation occurs in the passage which recounts how Brendan saves the soul of a sinful monk (§7, l. 4ff.) The saint drives out of the monk an evil spirit which is described at the moment of its exorcising as 'howling with a loud voice', and as asking him why he is expelling it from its home (*ululantem uoce magna ac dicentem: 'Cur me, uir Dei, iactas'*). In the Norse the evil spirit howls *sem vargr* ('like a wolf / werewolf / criminal') and asks the saint: 'Why do you drive (*rækr*) me away?' The collocation of the noun *vargr* and the verb *reka* was familiar to a Norse audience: the law-code *Grágás* makes reference to the way in which an outlaw shall be pursued *sem menn víðast varga reka* ('as men drive out criminals / wolves far and wide'). It is the fate of the *vargr* to be driven out. In departing from his original in order to make use of this collocation of *vargr* and *reka*, the translator of the *Navigatio* does the same as another Norse translator, the thirteenth-century Norwegian who translated Marie de France's *Bisclavret.*[11]

---

9. Dated *c.*1200 by Gustav Indrebø 1966, *39.
10. The Norwegian reads: *í snehvitum clæðum* – 'in snow-white clothing' (Indrebø, 82).
11. Hamer 1994, I, 312-13.

. . . munkenum þvi likast sem fyrir bornum. En þa stoþ Brændanus vpp oc var a bœnum sinum allt til dags. Enn vm morgunenn eptir gengu þeir oc gœrþu þionostu sina oc dualþoz þar .iii. daga, enn hvern dag var þæim borþ buet sem hinn fyrsta dag. Enn þann dag er þæir foru i brott, þa varaði enn hælgi B. brœðr sina við, at þæir skylldu ekci taka þess i brott, er þar var. Þa svoroðu þæir aller senn:

'Faðir', qvaðu þæir, 'vili eigi guð þat, at ver spillem for varri.'
Þa mælti B. við þa:

'Her er nú broðir varr, sa er ek hefi yðr sagt ifrá, hann hefir bæisl eitt i serki sér gœrt af silfri.'
Enn sa enn væsli munkr dualði ekci ok fell þegar til fota Brandanus oc mælti:

'Faðir', qvað [hann], 'ek syngoþvmz, firirgef mer oc bið firir salu minni, at . . .'

. . . [mun]kenum oc þaut sem vargr oc mælti við B.:

'Þu guðs maðr, hui rækr þu mik brott heðan ór minu herby[r]gi, þui er ek hefi buet i .vii. vetr?'
Hinn hælgi B. svaraði:

'Ek byð þer, fiande, i guðs nafni, at þu gœr engum manne mæín ne skaða ne villu til domadags.' (20)

Þa mælte B. við munkenn:

'Tak nu', qvað hann, 'corpus domini, þui at nu skalltu lata lif þitt, oc her skal grafa þik. Enn broðer þinn annarr, sa er fylgþi þer hegat, hann skal fara i hælviti.'
Enn siþan tok hann bæði sk[r]ipt oc husl með mikille iðran synða sinna, oc andaðiz þegar. Enn at augsiandum þæim ollum þa komu ænglar guþs i moti sal hans oc hofðu hana með ser. Enn B. oc hans menn foru til skips sins. (28)

Enn er þæir komu a skip, þa kom þar maðr einn vngr, oc hafði laup fullan braðs oc konnu fulla vaz, oc mælti við þa:

'Taker fórn þessa af þræli yðrum; þer hafer langt at fara, aðr enn þer hittet þat er þer vilir; eigi skal yðr skorta vatn ne brauþ heðan i fra[1] til pasca.'

. . . the monks just as though before children. But then Brendan arose, and was at his prayers right through to daybreak. And on the following morning they went and held their service, and they remained there for three days; on each day a table was prepared for them as on the first day. But on the day when they travelled onward, the saintly Brendan warned his brothers that they should not take away anything which was there. Then they all replied, saying:

'Father, God does not wish that we should desecrate our mission.' Then Brendan said to them:

'Here now is our brother of whom I have previously told you; he has a bridle made of silver in his shirt.'

That wretched monk did not delay, but instantly fell at Brendan's feet and said:

'Father', he said, 'I have sinned. Forgive me, and pray for my soul, *that it may not perish.'*

And without delay they all at the same time fell to the ground, praying to God for the brother's soul. And when the monks got to their feet, and the aforementioned saintly father raised up the brother, they saw a small black man spring out of his shirt, and he howled like a wolf and said to Brendan:

'You, man of God, why do you drive me away from my dwelling here, in which I have lived for seven years?'

The saintly Brendan replied:

'I command you, devil, in God's name, that you do no man harm or injury or ill from now till Doomsday.'

Then Brendan spoke to the monk:

'Now receive the *corpus domini*', he said, 'because you must now lose your life, and you shall be buried here. But as for your other brother, who accompanied you here, he shall go to Hell.'

And afterwards he received both confession and absolution, with great penitence for his sins, and immediately afterwards he died. And in the sight of all of them God's angels then came to receive his soul and led it away with them. And Brendan and his men went to their ship.

And when they embarked, there appeared a young man who bore a basket full of bread and a jug full of water, and he said to them:

'Receive this offering from your servant. You have far to travel before you find that which you desire. You shall not lack bread or water from now till Easter.'

Enn þæir toku þat brauþ oc vatn oc foru siðan i haf oc ato eigi optarr enn annanhuern dag; enn þæir foru hingat oc þingat oc vissu eigi, huert þæir skylldu. (36)

Þa var þat þui næst vm dag einn, at þæir sa ey eina skamt ifra ser, enn þa kom þæim byrr, oc siglðu þæir til þæirar æyiar. Þa bauð hinn hælgi B. þæim at ganga vpp a land af skipi. ... gekc ... sem ... með ...
'... her [fœ]rum ... [dy]ri dagr.'
Enn þeir varo þar til paska aptans. (42)

Þæir sa þar sauði marga oc sniohuita oc stora sem ygxn. Þa mælti hann við brœðr sina:
  'Takit einn savð.'
Enn þeir gœrþu sva. Enn þegar er þæir hofðo bundit hann, þa fylgþi hann þæim sem rakci. Þæir toku oc lamb eitt, oc er þeir hœfðu sua gœrt, þa kom þar maðr einn oc færþi þæim laup fullan hvæitibrauðs oc marga aðra luti, er þæir þurftu, oc fell til fota B. oc mælti:
  'Huaðan kom mer þat faðir, at ek skyllda fœþa B. með minu ærfiðe?'
Enn B. tok i hond honum oc mælti: 'Sonr! guþ hefir ættlaðan oss þenna stað, at ver skolum hallda vpprisu dag.'
Þa svaraði sa maðr:
  'Brandane faðir', qvað hann, 'her skolu þer vera til pascha, enn pascadag skolu þer messu oc óttvsong hafa i æy þæiri, er þu matt nu siá heðan.'
Þa tok sa maðr oc bió þæim alla pascavist oc færþi þæim til skips, enn siðan mælti hann við hinn hælga B.:
  'Skip yðart ma eigi bera mæira at sinni, enn er .viii. dagar eru gengnir, þa skal ek senda yðr œrenn mat til huitasvnnodags.' (61)

Þa svaraði hinn hælgi B.:
  'Huat mattu vita² til þess, huar ver erum þa?'

And they took the bread and water and then put to sea, and did not
eat more often than once a day. And they voyaged hither and thither
and did not know where they might be.

Next, it happened one day that they saw an island a short distance
from them, and then a breeze favourable to them sprang up and they
sailed to that island. Then the saintly Brendan commanded them to
go ashore from the ship. *He, however, left the ship after them. And when they
started to walk about the island, they saw water in abundance, full of fish,
running from various springs. And the saintly Brendan said to his brothers:*
    *'Let us hold divine service here, and render a spotless offering to God,
because today is Maundy Thursday.'*
And they remained there until the eve of Easter.

They saw many sheep there, snow-white and as large as oxen. Then
he said to his brothers:
    'Take one sheep.'
And they did so. And as soon as they had leashed it, it followed them
just like a dog. They also took a lamb; and when they had done so a
man came there, and brought them a basket full of wheaten bread,
and many other things which they needed. He fell at Brendan's feet,
and said:
    'How does it come about, father, that I should feed Brendan by
my labour?'
And Brendan took him by the hand and said:
    'Son! God has destined for us this place where we are to celebrate
the day of resurrection.'
Then the man answered:
    'Father Brendan', he said, 'you shall remain here until Easter; but
on Easter Day you are to celebrate Mass and evensong on that island
which you can now see from here.'
Then the man set to and prepared for them all their Easter food, and
conducted them to the ship. And afterwards he said to the saintly
Brendan:
    'Your ship cannot carry more at present, but when eight days have
passed I shall send you enough food to last until Whit Sunday.'

Then the saintly Brendan replied:
    'What might you know about where we shall be then?'

Þa svaraði sa hinn hælgi maðr:

'I nott oc i morgen til miðs dags þa skolu þer uera i ey þeiri, er nu farit þer til, enn siþan skolu þer fara til annarar æyiar skamt frá þæiri i vestriþ, en su er kallat paradisi fugla, oc skolu þer þar vera, til þess er niu netr eru fra huitsunnodegi.'

Enn B. spurði, hui sauðir þæir enir myklo oc fæito gengo þar. Hann svaraði:

'Þessa sauþi mól[kar] . . . aðrer . . .'
. . . til ar[a] . . . [monn]um at ganga . . . landz. (72)

Su ey var skeriutt oc ekci gras i oc litill skogr, oc engi var sandr i þæiri æy. Þæir voru þar þa nott oc sungu ottosong oc baðu fagrlega bœnum sinum. B. vissi, huar þæir voru komnir, en þæir vissu ekci til. Enn vm morguninn eptir þa bauð hann huerium þæira munka sinna, er prestar voru, at syngia messu, oc sialfr hann. Þa er þæir hofðu messu sungit, þa toku þæir mat sinn oc letu i katla oc festu vpp oc gœrþu vndir ælld. (79)

Enn er vella tok, þa rærðiz æyen vndir þæim, þui likast sem bara, oc þæir vrðo sua ræddir, at þæir runno til skips, sem þæir fara mattu oc . . . Enn hann græip i hond þæim oc kipti i skip til sín. Enn katlar þæira oc matr vrðu epter þæim i æ[y]inni. Enn æy su for brott i haf vt. Enn er æy su var komen .ii. vikur fra þæim, þa sa þæir enn elldinn brænna. Þa mælti hinn hælgi B. við þá:

'Kynlict þykcir yðr, hui æý þessi ferr sua?'

Þa suoroðu þæir honum:

'Oss þykkir einka kynlekt, oc rædder eru ver um for æyiar þessar.'

Þa suaraði B.:

'Bœrn min, verit eigi rædder, guþ syndi mer i nótt, huat þat

Then the holy man answered:

'Tonight and tomorrow until midday you shall be on the island to which you are now travelling; but afterwards you shall travel to another island a short distance from it to the west, and that one is called the Paradise of Birds. And you shall be there until nine nights after Whit Sunday.'

But Brendan asked why such large and fat sheep were there. He answered:

'These sheep *no one milks, nor does winter weather distress them, but they are always in pastures, night and day, and for that reason are bigger here than in your lands.'*

They set off to the ship, and having received a blessing, began their voyage again.

When they arrived at the other island, however, and before they could reach a harbour, the ship began to run aground. The saintly Brendan commanded the brothers to go from the ship into the sea, and this they did. And they dragged the ship with ropes on both sides, until they came into a harbour. That island had many skerries, there was no grass on it, and little woodland, and there was no sand on the island. They spent that night there, sang evensong, and said their prayers fittingly. Brendan knew where they were, but the others did not. And on the following morning he commanded all of his monks who were priests to sing mass, and he did so himself. When they had sung mass, they took their food, placed it in a pot, covered it and lit a fire beneath it.

And when it started to boil, the island moved beneath them, just like a wave, and they were so frightened that they ran to the ship as fast as they could, *entreating the saintly father to protect them.* And he seized them by the hand and drew them to him on the ship. But their pot and food remained behind them on the island. And the island moved away on the sea. And when the island was two miles away from them, they could still see the fire burning. Then the saintly Brendan said to them:

'Does it seem extraordinary to you that this island should move in this way?'

Then they answered him:

'We think it extremely strange and we are terrified by this island's movement.'

Then Brendan answered:

'My children, do not be afraid. Last night God revealed to me

iartegnir; þat er eigi eý, er ver bioggum i, þat er fiskr, sa er mestr er i hæiminum, oc ferr at leita at sporði sinum oc villdi koma ollu saman sporði oc hofði, oc má eigi, sua er hann mykill, enn hann heitir a bok Jaskonius.' (95)

Nu reru þæir til æyiar þæirar, er hinn goðe maðr visaði þæim til, sa er þæim fekc mate[nn] . . .
    '. . . oss.' (98)

Oc var træ eitt hia kelldunni einkar hat, oc mykit lauf á. Þat tré var skipat með fuglum sniohuitum ollum, sua at huerr kuistr var hulðr. Þa þotte þæim einka kynlekt, hui þat mundi gegna. Þa fell hann a knebeþ oc bað drotten varnn gratande, at hann skylldi honum þær iartegnir syna. Þa er hann hafði lokit bœn sinni, þa flaug einn fugl or þui tre oc til B. oc blœkti vengium sinum oc fagnaði honum sua. Enn sa fugl settiz a stafnenn hia B. oc mælti Brandanus við fuglenn:
    'Ef þu ert gvðs œrendreki, þa seg þu mer, huat fuglum þer eruþ.'
Þa suaraði fuglenn:
    'Ver fellum ofan', quað hann, 'ór himnum . . . (108)

what it means. It is not an island upon which we landed; it is the largest fish in the world. It seeks after its own tail, wanting to bring its tail and head together. But it cannot, because it is so large. And in a book it is called Jasconius.'

Now they rowed to the island which the good man had shown them, the one who gave them the food. *And they began to search the perimeter of the island for a harbour. Sailing onward, opposite the island's southerly zone they discovered a small stream pouring into the sea, and there they brought their ship to land. They went ashore from the ship, and the saintly Brendan commanded them to drag it with ropes as far as they could up the bed of the river. Indeed, the river was just as wide as the ship. The aforementioned father sat in the ship, and they proceeded in this way for a mile, until they had come to the source of the river. Then the saintly Brendan said:*
'Behold, our Lord Jesus Christ has given us a place in which to remain for his holy resurrection.' And he added: 'If we had no provisions other than this spring, I believe it would be sufficient for food and drink for us.'

And there was a tree beside the spring, extremely tall, with thick foliage. The tree was filled with birds, all snow-white, so that every twig was covered. They thought this extremely strange, wondering what it might mean. Then he fell on his knees and, weeping, prayed our Lord that he would explain those miracles. And when Brendan had finished his prayer, one bird flew to him out of the tree, flapped its wings and in this way welcomed him. The bird settled on the prow beside Brendan, who said to it:
'If you are a messenger of God, tell me what sort of birds you are.'
Then the bird replied:
'We fell down from Heaven', it said . . .

9

English Versions

W.R.J. Barron

I: The *South English Legendary* Version

Whatever the ultimate origin of the English Voyage of Saint Brendan, the three versions which survive are all related to each other. Two are presented here: the prose version included in Caxton's *Golden Legend*, first printed in 1484, and the earliest, which occurs in a massive compendium of similar material in verse, the *South English Legendary*.

The South English Legendary is a compilation of saints' lives arranged in the order of their commemoration in the church calendar (*sanctorale*), interspersed at appropriate points with accounts of the chief festivals of the liturgical year (*temporale*), using major events of Old and New Testament narrative to explore central truths of Christianity. Earlier Ælfric (*c*.955-*c*.1020), in his two series of *Catholic Homilies* and his *Lives of the Saints*, provided a similarly structured exposition of doctrine exemplified in the lives of saints, heroes and martyrs of the faith. But whatever his work may have contributed to an English homiletic tradition available to both clergy and laymen in the vernacular, the immediate model for the *South English Legendary* (*SEL*) is most likely to have been in continental tradition, which had recently reached its classic formulation in Jacobus de Voragine's *Legenda aurea* (1261-76). Its condensed versions of saints' legends for the complete liturgical year interspersed with *temporale* pieces, prompted by the Lateran Council's concern for the religious instruction of the laity, was to be enormously popular throughout Europe for centuries to come.[1]

But there is little textual evidence of any substantial dependence of the English collection upon the *Legenda*. The issue is complicated by the apparently disordered state of the oldest of the surviving *SEL*

---

1. More than a thousand manuscripts are said to be still extant (Burgess and Strijbosch 2000, pp. 27-30).

versions, Oxford, Bodleian Library MS Laud. Misc. 108 (*c*.1300), variously interpreted by analysts. Opening with *temporale* texts, it contains only some two-thirds of the *sanctorale* items found in characteristic *SEL* collections, interrupted by a misplaced prologue and by disparate material, religious and secular, and it includes a number of unique saints' lives. Its idiosyncratic state has been interpreted as representing an early stage in a progressive process of compilation. An alternative view sees in its disorder some traces of what later manuscripts establish as the standard *SEL* textual order, implying disruption of a pre-existent structure. Others interpret the physical make-up of the manuscript as suggesting that its components may originally have circulated as independent booklets and that the compiler experimented with various orderings related to the liturgical year before the prologue implying a strict calendrical order became available to him.[2]

These issues are more than merely technical since if the Laud text, as generally assumed, represents a formative stage in the evolution of the *SEL*, they may suggest the underlying purpose of the compilation, the audience for which it was intended and the cultural context from which it emerged. Though Laud. Misc. 108 initially resembles a miscellany, the later emergence of traces of calendar order, possibly reflecting the incipient influence of the *Legenda aurea*, suggests that it too was intended to be a *liber festivalis*. All later manuscripts of the *SEL*, despite manifold variations in scope, content and order of components, are organized on that liturgical principle. Early commentators assumed that the collection was produced by a religious order, perhaps for the use of nuns, or by friars as an adjunct to popular preaching. However, use in the context of formal church services seems unlikely in view of the wide variations in the length of individual legends, ranging from 58 to 2,478 lines; use in preaching is equally improbable since didactic purpose is largely subverted by narrative interest.

Neither function need rule out clerical authorship any more than the *liber festivalis* structure excludes a lay audience. The lives of laymen were ordered, out of church as well as in, by the familiar cycle of the liturgical year, and the prominence of English legends as well as the occasional substitution of a local saint suggests an appeal to popular tastes. Inherent interest rather than liturgical importance may account

---

2. The views condensed here are respectively those of Carl Horstmann (1887, p. x), M.E. Wells, 'The *South English Legendary* in its Relation to the *Legenda aurea*', *PMLA*, 51 (1936), pp. 337-60, and T.R. Liszka, 'MS Laud. Misc. 108 and the Early History of the *South English Legendary*', *Manuscripta*, 33 (1989), pp. 75-91.

for the inclusion of the Brendan legend, which is already present in Laud. Misc. 108 and features prominently in the *SEL* tradition.

Manuscripts, Editions and Translations Of the more than 60 surviving manuscripts which contain the *SEL* in whole or part, Brendan figures in 18 (Burgess and Strijbosch 2000, pp. 67-70). In addition to its appearance in complete editions of the *SEL* by Carl Horstmann (EETS, OS 87 (London, 1887) and D'Evelyn and Mill (EETS OS 235-36 (London, 1956), 244 (1959), it has been separately edited by Thomas Wright in *St. Brandan: A Medieval Legend of the Sea in English Verse and Prose*, Percy Society 14 (London, 1844), reprinted by Denis O'Donoghue, *Brendaniana* (Dublin, 1893), by Horstmann in *Archiv für das Studium der neueren Sprachen und Literaturen*, 53 (1874) and by Martha Bälz, *Die ME Brendanlegende des Gloucesterlegendars* (Berlin, 1909). Selections were published by George Sampson in *The Cambridge Book of Prose and Verse* (Cambridge, 1924) and the complete Brendan was translated by Jessie Weston in *The Chief Middle English Poets* (London and Boston, 1914).

Date and Place of Origin No precise date for the origin of the *SEL* can be determined, not least because the collection, though it may well have had a model (probably continental), shows signs of having evolved in stages. That evolutionary period is variously dated between 1250 and 1288[3] and in the earliest manuscripts, dated *c.*1300, St Brendan is already present. Since his liturgical importance is marginal, Brendan's presence in a work with at least the colouring of a *liber festivalis* may throw some light on the identity and intentions of the compilers. The language of the earliest manuscripts, strongly marked with characteristics of dialects of the south-west Midlands, has suggested that it originated in that area, possibly in Worcester whose cathedral library was rich in relevant source material and whose localized saints and scholars figure prominently in the earliest texts (Görlach 1974, pp. 32-37).

Authorship and Source In the circumstances of the age in which the *SEL* evolved it is probably pointless to look for an individual author. Even attempts to identify a particular religious community as its sponsor or patron – Ramsey Abbey which, with its rich stock of

---

3. See Görlach 1974, pp. 37-38, and T.J. Heffernan, 'Additional Evidence for a More Precise Date of the *South English Legendary*', *Traditio*, 35 (1979), pp. 345-51 (p. 345).

liturgical manuscripts produced another famous collection of saints' lives; or an order of mendicant friars compiling material for popular preaching (Görlach 1974, pp. 24, 49) – rest on questionable assumptions about the character and purpose of the compilation. Evidence of interaction between monasteries of the south-west Midlands and local gentry in the diffusion of vernacular literature suggests the cultural climate and widens the implied audience, but concrete proof is lacking.[4]

The form in which the Brendan legend was most likely to be available in such institutions was the widely diffused *Navigatio sancti Brendani* from which the great majority of vernacular versions derive – including, by general assumption, the English Brendan (Schirmer 1888, p. 56). There has been some suggestion that the *SEL* compiler supplemented his Latin source with details from the Anglo-Norman version (Bälz 1909, pp. v-xii). But since the latter also derives from the *Navigatio* significant textual variations are rare and, under analysis, offer no proof of a secondary source other than the imagination of the English redactor. His inventions, mostly commonplace, agree only coincidentally with similar variations in the Anglo-Norman text, reflecting similar methods of abridgement and a common didactic purpose, yet without reproducing any of Benedeit's distinctive artifice (Lavery 1984, pp. 28-29). Though both English and Anglo-Norman poets have a liking for episodes which invite didactic comment, the former borrows none of the latter's formulaic elaborations, falling back instead on expressive commonplaces, brief and repeated, often merely clichés, to fill out a line or serve the needs of the alliterative verse.

Content and Structure With only trifling variations from manuscript to manuscript, the Brendan section of *SEL* outlines the saint's voyage with balance and economy in some 730 lines whose irregular septenary couplets and insistent alliteration do not seriously inhibit the

---

4. See Derek Pearsall, 'The Origins of the Alliterative Revival', in *The Alliterative Tradition in the Fourteenth Century*, ed. by B.S. Levy and P.E. Szarmach (Kent, Ohio, 1981), pp. 1-24, and P.R. Coss, 'Aspects of Cultural Diffusion in Medieval England: The Early Romances, Local Society and Robin Hood', *Past and Present*, 108 (1985), p. 36. 'If we posit the same kind of audience for the legendary as he [Coss] has done for the romances, then we have a work written initially for regional gentry and perhaps secular clergy, and designed either for individual reading or for reading in the chamber, rather than as entertainment of the hall or public instruction in church' (Annie Sampson, 'The *South English Legendary*: Constructing a Context', *Thirteenth Century England*, 1 (1986), pp. 185-95 (p. 194).

narration. Its general fidelity to the Latin *Navigatio* is apparent from an outline analysis:

(1) Brendan learns from abbot Barynt of an island where lies the Promised Land (1-80)

(2) Setting sail with fourteen companions, he visits various islands sighted on the voyage (81-342)

(3) The voyagers revisit the islands in turn, celebrating on each a feast of the Christian year, are attacked by dangerous beasts and fish, and sail close to infernal islands (343-513)

(4) Continuing their voyage, they encounter Judas and Paul the Hermit (514-663)

(5) Revisiting the various festal islands, the voyagers are given a glimpse of the Promised Land before returning to Ireland, where Brendan dies (664-733).

This balanced tripartite division of the voyage, framed by shorter sections establishing and achieving its goal, conceals, however, some radical departures from the pattern of the *Navigatio*. The author deals economically with the repeated visits to islands where the annual feasts are celebrated. Repetition of similar details on each occasion is avoided, but the Judas episode, with its lively verbal exchanges, is fully rendered. More significantly, whole episodes of the *Navigatio* are entirely omitted: the visit to St Enda and the retreat to Brandon Mountain, which delay the start of the voyage (§§III-IV); the death of a monk tempted to theft, whose soul is saved by his confession (§VII); the voyagers' drinking of the soporific well, whose waters induce various periods of slumber (§XIII), their encounter with the Coagulated Sea (§XIV), and their landing on the island of the Three Choirs (§XVII), all vaguely suggesting spiritual meanings which the English redactor may not have felt able or willing to make explicit. So also the episode of the Crystal Column (§XXII), whose obscure significance may not have seemed to justify the difficulty of conveying its technical complexity in alliterative verse. The practical effect of these omissions in a comparatively brief redaction is to increase the onward drive of the narrative towards the goal of the voyage while leaving its basic didactic purpose, the pursuit of a spiritual mission through exotic perils under divine guidance and protection, and implicit educative function unharmed. If, however, the author of the *Navigatio* intended an overall allegorical interpretation of Brendan's voyage – since pilgrimage is frequently used in Christian didacticism to express the passage of the soul through the perils of a sinful world towards the refuge of the Promised Land – these episodes may have a concomitant meaning whose loss would damage the significance of the whole.[5] The pragmatic English redactor, concentrating on narration to the virtual exclusion of commentary, shows no awareness of any such significance in his material

Genre and Audience In a different formal context, such a long and perilous mission in pursuit of some spiritual goal, some Holy Grail of idealistic aspiration, would be readily recognized as an episode of romance. But the formal accidents of the romance genre, over-emphasized by modern critics, seem comparatively superficial in relation to the fundamentals of the romance mode, in particular that aspiration towards an ideal which characterizes both romance and saint's life. The ideal may be social in one case, spiritual in the other, yet often expressed in identical adventures carried to similar extremes and by protagonists of the same type. 'Any impression that only the former is fit subject for romance and the latter a pietistic intrusion is a modern misconception; medieval readers, accepting them as parts of the same essential unity, needed no elaborate commentary to appreciate their interrelationship.'[6] It is scarcely surprising if contemporary readers saw the knight errant and the saintly pilgrim as fellow travellers, their adventures equally tinged with the romance of distant lands, exotic settings, perils and hardships endured for the sake of a supreme ideal.

Just as clerical training did not bar medieval clerics from appreciation of the social values expressed in the chivalric literature of which they were both copyists and authors, so contemporary laymen were clearly appreciative of the interest of religious literature; spiritual salvation was the concern of all. So it is equally possible to imagine the *SEL* being read to a religious community in the refectory or to a

---

5. Even at the non-allegorical level, the *Navigatio* has been interpreted as showing a structural complexity, three layers of narrative each dealing with the theme of death and rebirth, of which the English redactor shows no awareness. See Carp 1984, pp. 127-42.

6. W.R.J. Barron, *English Medieval Romance*, Longman Literature in English Series (London and New York: Longman, 1987, p. 80). A characteristic example of the dual protagonist is the hero of *Guy of Warwick*, who spends the first half of the romance in chivalric adventures and the second on a pilgrimage of atonement in which his prowess is deployed in defence of the weak. His exemplary status is acknowledged in the *Speculum Guy de Warewyke*, a treatise of basic religious instruction such as might be credited to some saintly figure, which is nonetheless associated with the romance in the popular literary compendium of the Auchinleck manuscript (ibid., pp. 74-80; see also D.T. Childress, 'Between Romance and Legend: "Secular Hagiography" in Middle English Literature', *Philological Quarterly*, 57 (1978), pp. 311-22).

gathering of laymen in the hall of some local patron of the order. The one audience might have greater appreciation of the liturgical observances, the monastic usages, the hermit figures of Brendan's voyage, the other of the appeal of a traveller's tale ranging over remote regions not entirely unknown from established tradition; both would surely feel the perennial appeal of improbable incidents anchored in reality by association with a respected representative of Christian antiquity.[7]

The Author's Purpose It is not necessary to assume that the English redactor consciously favoured the laymen in his audience merely because he has omitted episodes of the *Navigatio* which would lend themselves to theological or learned commentary. Even in those episodes, and indeed throughout, the Latin author has not developed any didactic or exegetical commentary on his material. What the poet has done is to favour entertainment, not by any absolute discrimination between incident and meaning, since in a didactic age the one would not be inherently more appealing than the other, but by the rapidity and clarity of his narration, avoidance of excessive or confusing detail, the use of speech to heighten the immediacy of the action. He seems to have aimed at a tale well told, leaving its inherent message of man's search for salvation, the multiple forms of temptation in a perilous world, and the inevitability of punishment for sin to speak for itself.[8]

---

7. The enormous success of the *SEL*, demonstrated by the number of surviving texts and their temporal and geographical spread, suggests an audience wider than the professional clerics for and by whom the initial compilation may have been made. That its varied components catered to specialist interests is evidenced by the way in which the Chronicle attributed to Robert of Gloucester drew upon it for such historical material as the lives of the English saints: Athelwold, Edward the Martyr, Edward the Confessor and Thomas à Becket (Görlach 1974, pp. 40-45).
8. The following text of the *SEL* Brendan is reproduced, by kind permission of the Bodleian Library, University of Oxford, from Bodleian MS Ashmole 43. A few lines lacking there have been supplied from Corpus Christi College, Cambridge, MS 145, as edited by Charlotte d'Evelyn and Anna J. Mill (EETS, 235 (London, 1956)). These recovered lines are not included in the line numbering here, to facilitate comparison with the edition of the Brendan text of Ashmole 43 by Carl Horstmann (in *Archiv für das Studium der neueren Sprachen und Literaturen*, 53 (1874), 17-48). Emendations, indicated here by asterisks in the margin, are discussed under the corresponding line number in the Textual Notes, where the editorial principles applied are indicated.

Seyn Brendan, þe holi mon,   was ȝend of Irlonde.   *
Monek he was of harde lyue,   as ich vnderstonde,
Of vastynge and penaunce inou;   abbot he was þere   *
Of a þousend monekes   þat vnder him alle were.
   So þat it byuel in a day,   as our Lordes wille was,   5
Þat Barynt, anoþer abbod,   to him com bi cas.
Seyn Brendan him bisoȝte anon   þat he scholde him vnderstonde
And telle of þat he hadde iseie   aboute in oþer londe.
Þis godemon, þo he hurde þis,   sikynge he made inowe,   *
And bigan to wepe in grete þoȝte,   and vel adoun iswowe.   10
Bitwene is armes, Seyn Brendan   þis holi mon up nom,
And custe him and cride on him   vorte is wit aȝen him com.
"Fader," he sede, "par charite,   oþer red þou most take;
Huder þou come vor our solas,   and noȝt such deol to make.
Tel ous wat þou hast iseie   as þou hast aboute iwend   15
In þe muchel se of Occian,   as our Lord þe haþ isend."
   Nou is þe se of Occean   grettost and mest also,
Vor heo geþ aboute al þe world   and al oþer sees goþ þerto.
So þat Barynt, þis olde man,   riȝt at is herte gronde,   *
Al wepynge gan him telle   wat he hadde ifounde.   20
He sede, "Ich hadde a godsone   – Mernoc was is name.   *
Monek he was, as we beþ,   and mon of gret fame,
So þat is herte him ȝaf to wende   in a priue stude and stille
Þer he miȝte alone be   to seruy God to wille.
So þat, by myn leue, he wende   and alone him drouȝ   25
To an ile ver in þe se   þat delitable was inouȝ,
Biside þe mountayne of stones   þat couþ is wel wide.   *
So longe þat þis gode monek   in þis ile gan abide
Þat he hadde of monekes   vnder him monyon.
   "Anon so ich hurde telle þus,   þuderward ich wende anon;   30
So þat in a vision   our suete Lord him kende,
Þat aȝen me, as ich to him com,   þre iorneys he wende.
So þat we dude ous in a scip   and estward euene drowe
In þe se of Occian,   wiþ torments inowe.   *
Toward þen est so ver we wende   þat we come ate laste   35
In a stude swiþe derk,   and clouden ous ouercaste;
Al an tide of þe day   we were in derkhede.
Ate laste our suete Lord   verrore ous gon lede
So þat we seie an ilond;   þuderward our scip drouȝ.
Briȝt it is as þe sonne;   ioie þer was inouȝ,   40

The blessed Saint Brendan came from Ireland.[1] He was, so I understand, a monk leading a strict life of much fasting and self-denial; he was abbot there over a thousand monks who were all under his authority.

It so happened one day, as was the will of our Lord, that another abbot, Barynt, chanced to come to him. Saint Brendan presently requested him that he would recollect and recount what he had seen here and there in other lands. The worthy man, when he heard this, gave many sighs, began to weep in great distress, and fell down in a swoon. Saint Brendan took the saintly man up in his arms, and kissed him and called his name until he came to his senses again.

'Father', he said, 'for pity's sake, you must behave differently; you came here for our pleasure, and not to make such lamentation. Tell us what you have seen as you have travelled about upon the great sea of Ocean, as our Lord has ordained for you.'[2]

Now Ocean is the widest and also the largest of seas, for it encircles the whole world and all other seas join with it. Accordingly, this old man, Barynt, from the very bottom of his heart, weeping greatly, began to tell him what he had experienced. He said:

'I had a godson – his name was Mernoc.[3] He was a monk, as we are, and a man of high repute, until his heart moved him to go to a secluded and quiet place where he could be alone to serve God as he wished. And so, with my consent, he set out and journeyed alone to an island far away in the sea which was most delightful, close by the stony mountain which is known far and wide.[4] This good monk remained in that island so long that he had many monks under him.

'As soon as I heard tell of this, I at once went thither; of which our dear Lord informed him in a dream, so that, as I journeyed towards him, he travelled three days journey to meet me. We accordingly went on board a ship and voyaged directly eastwards upon the Ocean tide in great hardship.[5] We journeyed eastwards so far that we came at last to a very gloomy region, and clouds covered us; we were in darkness for a whole period of the day. Our dear Lord finally guided us so far that we sighted an island towards which our vessel made its way. Bright as the

Of tren and herbes þicke it stod,   biset in ech side,
Of presious stones ek   þat scynde briȝt and wide.
Ech herbe was vol of floures   and ech tre vol of frut;
Bote it were in Heuene sulf,   nas neuer more dedut.
Þerinne, with ioie inou,   wel longe we gonne wende,   45
Þei it lute wule ous þoȝte;   we ne miȝte fynde non ende
So þat we come to a water,   cler and briȝt inou,
Þat euene framward þen est   toward þe west drou.
We stode and bihulde aboute,   vor we ne miȝte noȝt ouer wende.
    "Þer com to ous a ȝong mon,   swiþe vair and hende;   50
He wilcomede ous vaire euerichone   wel mildeliche and suete,
And anempned ech is riȝte name   and wel vaire ous gon grete,
And sede: 'Ȝe aȝte Ihesu Crist   þonky wel wiþ riȝte,
Þat sceweþ of is priuete ȝou   so muche, and of is miȝte.
Þis is þat lond þat he wole ȝut,   ar þe worldes ende,   *   55
His dernelynges an erþe ȝyue   and hider hi scholleþ wende.   *
Þis lond is half in þis side,   as ȝe seþ wel wide,
And biȝonde þe water þe haluendel,   as bi þe oþer side;
Þat water ne mowe ȝe passe noȝt   þat oþer del to se.
And her ȝe habbeþ alle ȝer   meteles ibe,   60
Þat ȝe ne ete ne dronke noȝt,   ne slepte noȝt wiþ our eie,
Ne chele ne hete ne fredde ȝe noȝt,   ne no nyȝt ȝe ne seie.
Vor þis is Godes priue stude,   and þoru him is þis liȝt;   *
Þeruore it worþ euer her day   and neuer nyȝt.
Ȝif mon aȝen Godes heste   nadde noþing mysdo,   65
Hereinne he hadde ȝut bileued   and is ofsprung also.
Ȝe ne mowe her no leng bileue;   aȝen ȝe mote fare,
Þei it þenche ȝou lute wule   ȝe habbe ibe her ȝare.'
    "So þat he broȝte ous in our scip   and wel uaire is leue nom;
And þo we were hamward in þe se,   we nuste war he bicom.   70
Aȝenward he wende aȝen our wille;   it ous ofþoȝte sore inouȝ.
Aȝen to þis oþer monekes   þis scip wel euene drou.   *
Þis monekes ourne aȝen ous,   þo hi myȝte ous ise,
And sori were and wroþ inou   þat we hadde so longe ibe.
We sede þat we hadde ibe,   wiþ gret ioie and feste,   75
Byuore þe ȝates of Parays   in þe Lond of Biheste,   *
Þat our suete Lord haþ bihote   hem þat he loueþ her,
Þer is euere day and neuer nyȝt,   and þe leme euer cler.   *
'Certes,' queþe þis monekes,   'wel we mowe ise
Bi þe suote smul of ȝou,   þer ȝe habbeþ ibe.' "   80

sun it is; there was great pleasure there from trees and plants standing very thickly clustered on every side, and also from precious stones brightly shining far and wide. Every plant was full of flowers and every tree full of fruit; never was there greater delight, unless it were in Heaven itself. Therein, with great contentment, we went roaming a long while, although it seemed to us a little time; we could find no boundary until we came to a river, most clear and bright, which flowed from the east directly towards the west. Since we could not cross over, we stopped and looked around.

'There came to meet us a young man, very handsome and polite. He welcomed us one and all most graciously and pleasantly, calling everyone by his proper name, and greeted us most courteously, saying: "You ought by rights to thank Jesus Christ greatly, who shows you so much of his secret place and of his power. This is that land which, at some future time before the end of the world, he will give to his beloved upon earth and they shall come here. The land is half on this side, stretching far and wide as you see, and the other half lies beyond the river, along the other bank; you may not cross the river to view that other part. And here you have been without food for a whole year, in which you neither ate nor drank anything, nor closed your eyes in sleep, nor did you experience cold or heat, nor have you seen any darkness. For this is God's secret place, and this light proceeds from him; and so it is always daylight here and never night. If mankind had not done any wrong, contrary to God's commandment, he would still have been herein and his descendants too. You can no longer remain here; you must go back, though it seems to you but a little while you have been present here."

'Accordingly, he conducted us to our ship and took his leave most courteously; and when we were on the sea homeward bound, we knew not what became of him. He departed against our will; it grieved us very greatly. The ship drew quite close to the other monks again; when they caught sight of us, the monks ran to meet us and were grieved and very angry that we had been away so long. We told them that we had been in great contentment and delight before the gates of Paradise in the Promised Land which our dear Lord has promised to those here whom he loves, where it is always day and never night, and the light is always bright.

"Truly", said these monks, "this we can tell by your sweet savour, that you have been there."'

Þo Seyn Brendan ihurde þis,   in þoȝte he stod wel stille;
He þoȝte fondi more herof,   ȝif it were Godes wille.
He wende among is monekes   and twelf out he nom
Þat he truste mest to of alle,   wen eny neode com.
Þis twelfue he clupe in conseil,   and in priuete hem sede: 85
"Ich þenche do a priue þing,   þerof ȝe mote me rede:
To seche þat lond of biheste,   ȝif God wolde ous þuder lede.
Seggeþ wat ȝour conseil is,   to do so gret a dede!"
"Leue fader," þe oþer sede,   "our wille we habbeþ vorsake,
Our frend and al our oþer good,   and clanliche to þe itake;   90
And wen our dede is on þe,   ȝif þou wolt þat it be,
We scholle vawe wiþ þe wende,   our Lordes grace to se."
     So þat hi uaste fourti dawes,   and gret penance dude also,   *
And bede ȝerne our Lordes grace   þulke viage to do.
Hi let hem make a strong scip,   and aboue it al bicaste   95
Wiþ bole huden, strong inouȝ,   and nailede þerto vaste,
And seþþe ipiched al aboute,   þat þe water in ne come.
Hi wende to hor breþeren   and wel vaire hor leue nome,
And seþþe in our Lordes name   to scipe hi wende anon.
Hor breþeren, þat bihynde were,   sori were echon.   100
And þo hi were ȝut in þe scip,   after þer come two
And bed hem vaste þat hi moste   þen wei wiþ hem go.
"Ȝe mowe wel," Seyn Brendan sede,   "ac or oþer schal ate ende
Repenti ar he come aȝen,   and al quic to Helle wende."
     Worþ him wende þis holi mon   wuder our Lord him sende;   105
And þis twei monekes þat come last   also wiþ hem wende.
In þe grete se of Occean   vorþ hi rewe vaste,
And truste al to our Lordes grace,   and noþing nere agaste.
Þe wynd drof hor scip al after wille;   þe wynd was good inouȝ.
As þe wynd hem drof, wel euene   uorþ est hor scip drouȝ,   *   110
Euene aȝen þat þe sonne arist   a Mydsomeres Day.   *
Non nuste of hem war he was,   ne no lond ne say.
Euene est fourti dawes   þe wynd hem drof vaste,   *
So þat hi seie in þe norþ side   a gret ile ate laste,
Of harde roche and gret inouȝ,   aboue þe se wel hei.   115
     Þre dawes hi wende þeraboute   ar hi miȝte com þerney;
A lute hauene hi founde,   a lond hi wende þere.
Hi wende aboute as mopismen   þat nuste war hi were.
Þer com gon a wel vair hound,   as it were hem to lere;   119
At Seyn Brendan's vet he vel adoun,   and made hem vaire chere.

When Saint Brendan heard this, he stood quite still in reflection; he intended, if it were God's will, to find out more about this matter. He went among his monks and selected twelve in whom he trusted most of all when any trouble came.[6] He called these twelve together and said to them in private:

'I intend to do something in secret on which you must advise me: to seek out the Promised Land, if God should guide us there. Say what your advice is on undertaking such a great deed.'

'Dear father', said the others, 'we have renounced our free will, our friends and all else we possess, and utterly committed ourselves to you; and since what we do depends upon you, if you wish it to be so, we will gladly go with you to witness our Lord's providence.'

Accordingly, they fasted forty days and did severe penance also, and earnestly prayed for our Lord's grace to undertake that voyage. They had a stout boat made ready for them and had it covered all over with very stout bull-hides firmly nailed to it and then coated all over with pitch, so that the water could not get in. They went to their brethren and very courteously took their leave, and then, in the name of our Lord, went immediately on board ship. Their brethren, one and all who remained behind, were sad. And when they were already in the boat, two came after them and earnestly prayed that they might make the journey with them.[7]

'You may indeed', said Saint Brendan, 'but one of you shall in the end regret it before he returns, and go to Hell still living.'

The saintly man set out whither our Lord directed him; and the two monks who came last went with them also. They rowed out swiftly upon the great sea of Ocean, trusting wholly in our Lord's grace, and were in no way daunted. The wind drove their boat just as they wished; the wind was very favourable. As the wind drove them, their boat moved very steadily away eastwards, straight towards where the sun rises on Midsummer Day.[8] None of them knew where he was, nor sighted any land. For forty days the wind drove them swiftly due east, until at last they saw to the north a great island of stout rock and very large, towering up from the sea.

Three days they sailed around it before they could get close to it; then they found a little haven, where they went ashore. They wandered about like men bewildered who knew not where they were. A very handsome dog came running up as if to guide them; it dropped down at Saint Brendan's feet and fawned upon them affectionately.

"Beu freres," quaþ Seyn Brendan, "ȝe ne dorre noþing drede;
Ichot þis is a messager, þen riȝte wei ous to lede."
Þis hound ladde þis holi mon to an halle, vair inouȝ,
Gret and starc and swiþe noble; wel euene in he drouȝ.
Þe monekes founde in þis halle bord and cloþ isprad, 125
And bred and fisc þerup inouȝ; þer nas non þat nas glad.
Hi sete adoun and ete vaste, vor hem luste wel þerto.
Beddes hi seie, ȝare ymad ar hor soper were ido;
After soper to bedde hi wende to reste hem as þe wise.
    Þo hi hadde alle islept inouȝ, sone hi gonne arise 130
And wende aȝen to hor scip, as hi hadde er ibe.
And in þe se wel longe hi were ar hi miȝte eny lond ise.
Þo seie hi bi þe oþer side an ile, vair inouȝ,
Grene and wiþ a wel vair lese, þuderwar hor scep drouȝ.
Þo hi come into þisse vaire londe and bihulde aboute wide, 135
Þe vairest scep þat miȝte be hi seie in ech side; *
A scep was grettore þen an oxe, and wittore ne miȝte be.
Gret ioie hi hadde in hor herte, þis vaire scep to se.
    Þo com þer go a wel vair man, and grete hem wiþ vaire chere,
And sede: "Ȝe beþ her icome, as ȝe neuer er nere. 140
Þis is icluped þe Lond of Scep, vor scep wel vaire her beþ,
Muchele and wite and gret inouȝ, as ȝe al day iseþ.
Vairore hi beþ þen ȝoure scep and grettore vniliche,
Vor muri weder her is inouȝ, and lese good and riche;
Her nys neuer wynter non, ne non hei ifounde, 145
Ac hi eteþ þe erbes also nywe as hi springeþ of þe gronde.
Me ne gadereþ noþing of hor mylc, þat hi scholde þe worse be.
Vor þis þing, and mony oþer, þe bet hi mowe iþe.
To a stude ȝe scholleþ henne wende, þoru our Lordes grace,
Þat is Foulen Parais, a wel ioyuol place 150
Þer ȝe sculle þis Ester be, and Witsontid also.
Wendeþ vorþ a Godes name, þat þis viage were ido."
    Seyn Brendan and is breþeren to scipe wende anon,
And rewe uorþ in þe se, in tempest monyon,
So þat hi seie bi þe one side an ile, gret inouȝ. 155
Hor scip, þoru our Lordes grace, þuderward euene drouȝ.
Þo hi come almest þerto, up roches it gan ride,
Þat it ne miȝte to þe ile come, ac bileuede biside.
Þis monekes wode up to þis ile, ac Seyn Brendan noȝt.
Þis monekes gonne make hor mete of þat hi hadde ibroȝt; 160

'Dear brethren', said Saint Brendan, 'you need not fear anything; I believe this is a guide to lead us the right way.'

The dog led the saint to a most beautiful hall, large and stoutly made and most magnificent; he went straight in. In this hall the monks found the table set up and the cloth spread, and thereupon much bread and fish; all were glad at that. They sat down and ate quickly, for they greatly longed for it. They saw beds already prepared before their supper was ended; after supper they went to bed to rest themselves like sensible men.

When they had all slept long enough, they arose quickly and took to their boat again, where they had been previously. And they were at sea a very long time before they caught sight of land. Then they sighted in the opposite direction a very lovely island, green and with most beautiful pasture, towards which their boat made its way. When they landed in this lovely land and looked around far and wide, they saw on every side the finest sheep there might be; each sheep was larger than an ox, and none could be whiter. They had great joy in their hearts, seeing these lovely sheep.

Then there came walking there a most handsome man and, greeting them graciously, said:

'You have arrived where you have never been before. This is called the Land of Sheep because there are very fine sheep here, many and very large and white, as you see repeatedly. They are finer than your sheep and larger beyond compare, for here there is very pleasant weather and good, lush pasture; here there is never any winter, for here no hay is found, but they eat herbs as fresh as they spring from the ground. Nor is any of their milk taken, lest they might be the worse for it. For this reason, and many others, they can thrive the better. You shall go from here, by our Lord's grace, to a most pleasant place which is the Paradise of Birds, where you shall remain this Easter and Whitsuntide also. Set forth, in God's name, that this voyage may be accomplished.'

Saint Brendan and his companions at once went on board, and rowed swiftly out to sea through many a tempest until they saw on one hand a very large island. Their boat, by the grace of our Lord, moved directly towards it. When they had almost arrived there, it ran upon the rocks so that it could not reach the island, but came to rest nearby. The monks landed upon the island, but Saint Brendan did not. The monks began to prepare their meal from what they had brought; they made

Hi made hem fur and zode hem fisc   in a caudron vaste.
Ar þis visc were isode inouȝ,   hi were somdel agaste,
Vor þo þis fur was þoruhot   þe ile quakede anon   *
And wiþ gret eir hupte al up   – þis monekes dradde echon,
And þe wei toward hor schip   ech after oþer nom;   165
God leuest, hem þoȝte, he was   þat sonest þuder com.
      Hi bihulde hou þis ile   in þe se wende vaste,
And as quic þing hupte up and doun   and þat fur fram him caste;
He swam more þen to myle   þe wule þis fur ilaste.
Þis monekes seie þat fur longe,   and were sore agaste;   170
Hi cride ȝerne on Seyn Brendan   wat þat wounder were.
"Beþ still" quaþ þis holi mon,   "uor noȝt ȝe habbeþ fere;
Ȝe weneþ þat it be an ile,   ac ȝe þencheþ amys;
Hit is a visc of þe grete se,   þe meste þat þer is.
Iascony he is icluped;   he fondeþ nyȝt and day   *   175
To pulte is tail in is mouþ,   and vor grettnesse he ne may."
      Vorþ hi rewe in þe se   euene west wel uaste,
Þre dawes ar hi seie lond   – hi were somdel agaste.
Þo seie hi a wel vair lond,   of floures þicke inouȝ;
Wel glade hi were þo hi seie   þat hor scip þuder drouȝ.   180
In þis vair lond hi wende   lengore þen ich ȝou telle,
So þat hi founde in a stude   a swiþe vair welle.
Bi þe welle stod a tre,   brod and hei inouȝ.   *
Foules, swiþe wite and vaire,   so þick were in ech bouȝ
Þat vnneþe eny lef   me myȝte þeron ise,   185
Þat it was ioie and blisse inouȝ   to loke on þis tre.
Seyn Brendan vor ioie wep   and sat adoun akne
And bed our Lord to scewe him   wat such cas myȝte be.
      Þo fley þer up a lutel fowel   and toward him gan te;
As a viþele is wyngen verde   þo he bigan to fle;   190
Mergore enstrement neuer nas   þen is wyngen were.
He bihuld Seyn Brendan   wiþ wel vaire chere.
"Ich hote þe," quaþ Seyn Brendan,   "ȝif þu art messager,
Þat þu segge me wat ȝe beþ   and wat ȝe doþ her."
Ac þei it þoȝte aȝen kunde,   þis fouwel ansuerede anon: 195
"We were," he seide, "somtyme was,   angles in Heuene echon.
Ac, as sone as we were imad,   our maister was to prout,
Lucefer, fram is vaire stude   þat he vel sone out,
And wiþ him also monyon,   euer as hor misdede was.
And we velle also adoun   – ac vor non mysdede it nas,   200

themselves a fire and cooked fish for themselves in a stout cauldron. Before the fish were sufficiently cooked, they were somewhat alarmed, for when the fire was quite hot the island presently began to shake and with great violence sprang right up – the monks were all terrified, and one after another made their way towards their boat; he who got there first thought himself favoured by God.

They watched how the island moved swiftly through the sea and, leaping up and down like a living thing, threw the fire off him; he swam more than two miles while the fire remained. The monks watched the fire for a long time and were sorely afraid; they anxiously questioned Saint Brendan as to what the strange creature might be.

'Be calm', said the saint, 'for you have nothing to fear; you believe that it is an island, but you judge wrongly; it is a fish of the open sea, the largest that there is. It is called Jasconi; it tries night and day to thrust its tail into its mouth, but cannot because of its size.'

They rowed out into the ocean, going very swiftly due west for three days before they saw land[9] – they were somewhat fearful. Then they sighted a very lovely land, quite thick with flowers; they were very glad when the saw that their ship was approaching it. They journeyed into this lovely land further than I can say, until in a certain place they came upon a very beautiful spring. Beside the spring stood a tree, very broad and tall. On every branch were very lovely white birds, so crowded one could scarcely see a leaf upon it, so that it was a great joy and delight to gaze upon the tree. Saint Brendan wept for joy and knelt down upon his knees and implored our Lord to reveal to him what such a sight might mean.

Then a little bird flew up and came towards him, its wings moving like a fiddle as it took flight; never was there a merrier instrument than were his wings.[10] It looked upon Saint Brendan with a most pleasant gaze.

'If', said Saint Brendan, 'you are a messenger, I command you to tell me who you are and what you are doing here.'
And though it seemed contrary to nature, the bird instantly replied:

'Once upon a time', he said, we were one and all angels in Heaven. As soon as we were created, our leader, Lucifer, was so proud that shortly he fell from his favoured place, and many others with him, all because of their misbehaviour. And we too fell down – but that was not because of any wrongdoing, nor because we were in any way

Vor noþing þat we ensented   to is foule vnriȝte,
Bote soulement vorte scewe   our suete Lordes myȝte.
Ne we beþ her in pyne non   ac in ioie inou we beþ
And somdel ney our swete Lord,   and is myȝte we seþ.
And bi þe erþe we fleþ aboute   and bi þe lufte also,   205
As gode angles and luþer ek   riȝt is vorte do;
Þe gode vorte do men good,   þe luþer luþerhede makeþ.
And þe Soneday, þat is day of reste,   such fourme we takeþ,
Þe fourme of such wite foweles   as þu myȝt her ise,
And honoureþ God þat ous made,   her up þis brode tre. *   210
    "Twelf monþe it is ipassed   þat ȝe gonne verst out wende,
And al þis six ȝer ȝe scholle vare   ar ȝe bringe þis viage to ende.
Vor, wanne ȝe habbeþ ipassed þis seue ȝer,   our Lord ȝou wole sende
An siȝt of þat ȝe habbeþ isoȝt   ate seue ȝeres ende.
Ech ȝer ȝe scholleþ her wiþ ous   holde ȝoure Ester feste,   215
As ȝe nou doþ, vorte ȝe come   to þe lond of biheste."
Nou was þis an Ester Day,   þat al þis was ido.
Þis fowel nom is leue at hem   and to is felawes wende also.
    Þis foweles, þo it tyme was,   bygonne hor euesong –
Mergore song ne myȝte be,   þei God himsulf were þeramong.   220
Þis monekes wende to bedde and slepe,   þo hor soper was ido;
And þo it was tyme of matyns   hi arise vp þerto.
Þis foules songe ek hor matyns   wel riȝt, þo it was tyme,
And of þe sauter sede vers,   and seþþe also prime,
And vndarne seþþe, and mydday,   and afterward seþþe non;   225
And ech tyde of þe day songe   as Cristenemen scholde don.
    Þis monekes were in þe londe   eiȝte wuke also,
Vorte al þe feste of Ester was   and of Witsonetid ido.
Þo come ate Trinyte þis godemon   to hem þar,   229
Þat spac wiþ hem in þe Lond of Scep   and ladde hem aboute þar.
He chargede hor scip swiþe wel   wiþ mete and drinke inou,
And nom is leue wel hendeliche   and aȝenward him drou.
Þo Seyn Brendan was in þe scip,   and is breþeren also,
Þis fowel þat spac wiþ him er   wel sone com him to.
He sede: "Ȝe habbeþ her wiþ ous   þis heie feste ibe;   235
Gret trauail ȝou is to come   ar ȝe efsone lond ise.
Ȝe scholleþ after seue monþes   fynde an vair ile,
Þat Abbey icluped is,   henne it is mony a myle.
Ȝe scholleþ myd holi men be   þis Mydwynter þere;
Ȝour Ester ȝe scholleþ holde þer,   as ȝe duden toȝere,   240

consenting with his wicked misdeeds, but simply to display the power of our gracious Lord. Nor are we in any torment here, for we are in great bliss and quite close to our dear Lord, and we behold his power and majesty. And we fly about the earth and in the sky also, as is proper for good angels, and evil also, to do; the good angels in order to do good to men, the evil to commit wickedness. And on Sunday, which is the day of rest, we assume this shape, the shape of white birds such as you can see here, and here upon this broad tree honour God who made us.

'A year has now passed since you first set out, and you shall journey fully six years to come before you bring this voyage to an end. For when you have passed seven years, our Lord will send you, at the end of seven years, a vision of that which you have sought. Every year you shall keep your Easter festival here with us, as you are doing now, until you come to the Promised Land.'
Now it was an Easter Day when all this came to pass. The bird took its leave of them and returned to its companions.

When it was time, the birds began their evensong – merrier singing could not be, though God himself were present there. When their supper was finished, the monks went to bed and slept; and when it was time for matins they arose for that purpose. The birds too, when it was time, sang their matins very fittingly and repeated verses of the Psalter, and afterwards the service for prime also, and for tierce afterwards, and sext, and afterwards nones; and at each canonical hour of the day sang as Christians should do.[11]

The monks remained in the land eight weeks in the same way, until the whole festival of Easter and of Whitsunday was ended. Then at Trinity came to them there the saintly man who had spoken with them in the Land of Sheep and guided them there. He loaded their boat very fully with much food and drink, and took his leave very politely and departed. When Saint Brendan was in the boat, and his companions also, the bird which had spoken to them earlier very shortly came to them. He said:
'You have been here with us during this solemn festival; great hardship is to come upon you before you see land again. After seven months you shall reach a lovely island which is called Abbey, many a mile hence.[12] You shall be with holy men there this Christmas; you shall keep your Easter where you did this year upon the great fish's

Vp þe grete visches rugge,   as þin monekes were in fere,
And ȝour Ester wiþ ous,   riȝt as ȝe nou were." *
    Seyn Brendan a Godes name,   and is breþeren echon,
In þe se of Occean   vorþ hi wende anon.
Þe wynd hem harled up and doun   in peril monyon;   245
So weri hi were of hore lyue   þat hem ne roȝte wuder gon.
Þis four monþes hi wende in þe se   in swiþe gret turment,
Hi ne sei noþing bote þe se   and þe firmament.
Þo seie hi ver fram hem   an ile as it were;
Hi cride ȝerne on Ihesu Crist   þat hi moste ariue þere.   250
Ȝut, after þat Seyn Brendan   verst þis ile isei, *
In þe se he wende fourti dawes   ar he miȝte come þerney.
Hem þoȝte þat hor lif was loþ   – þe monekes were agaste;
Hi cride ȝerne on Ihesu Crist   and his help bede vaste. *
    A lutel hauene, swiþe streit,   hi founde ate laste,   255
Vnneþe hor scip com þerinne;   hor ancre þer hi caste.
Þis monekes wende þer alond   – wel longe er hem þoȝte. *
Hi wende and bihuld aboute, and þonkede God þat hem þuder broȝte,
So þat hi seie twei vaire wellen; þe on was swiþe cler,
And þe oþer wori and þicke inouȝ.   Þis monekes eode ner,   260
To drynke of þis vaire well;   Seyn Brendan it isei:
"Wiþþoute leue of oþer men   ne come ȝe noȝt þerney,
Of olde men þat herinne beþ;   vor myd gode wille
Hi wolleþ parti þerof myd ȝou   – and þeruore beþ ȝe stille!"
    A uair old mon, and swiþe hor,   aȝen hem com gon;   265
He wilcomede hem vaire inouȝ,   and Seyn Brendan custe anon.
He nom and ladde him bi þe hond,   al bi a uair wey,
Aboute in mony a muri stude,   and seþþe into an abbey.
Seyn Brendan bihuld aboute   and escte wat it were,
And wat manere men were wiþinne,   and ho wonede þere.   270
Stille was þis olde man   and ne ȝaf him non vnsuere.
Þo sei he come a uair couent,   and a crois biuore hem bere
Wiþ taperes in eiþer side   – monekes it were echon,
Reuested in uaire copes;   aȝen hem hi come gon,
Wiþ procession vaire inouȝ.   Þe abbod bihynde com,   275
And vaire custe Seyn Brendan   and bi þe hond him nom *
And ladde him and is monekes   into a noble halle,
And sette hem adoun a rank   and wesc hor vet alle.
Of þe wori welle he wesc hor vet,   þat hi er iseie.   279
    Into þe freitor he ladde hem seþþe   and sette hem þer heie,

back, where your monks were terrified, and your Easter with us just as you have now been.'

Saint Brendan, and his companions one and all, at once set forth, in the name of God, upon the Ocean tide. The wind drove them hither and thither in many a perilous plight; they were so weary of their way of life that they cared not where they went. Four months they voyaged in very great hardship, seeing nothing but the sea and the sky. Then, far away from them, they sighted what seemed as if it were an island; they called earnestly upon Jesus Christ that they might land there. Nevertheless, after Saint Brendan first sighted this island, he voyaged forty days upon the sea before he could get near it. Their life seemed hateful to them – the monks were terrified; they called earnestly upon Jesus Christ and prayed urgently for aid.

In the end they discovered a little haven, very narrow, so that their boat could barely enter; there they dropped anchor. The monks went ashore there – it seemed to them very long before they could do so. They walked about and looked around, thanking God who had brought them there, until they saw two fine springs; the one was very clear, and the other very turbid and muddy. The monks approached to drink from the clear spring; Saint Brendan saw that and said:
 'Do not go near it without the permission of someone, of elders who are in this place; for they are ready to share some of it with you – and so be at peace.'

An old man, handsome and very venerable, came walking towards them; he welcomed them most graciously, and at once kissed Saint Brendan. He took him by the hand and led him along by a pleasant path, conducted him around in many a delightful place, and afterwards into an abbey. Saint Brendan gazed around and asked what it might be, and what manner of men were therein, and who lived there. The old man was silent and gave him no answer. Then he saw approaching a splendid company, and a cross borne before them with candles on either side – they were one and all monks, vested in fine choir-robes; they came walking towards them in most splendid procession. The abbot came after and kissed Saint Brendan graciously and, taking him by the hand, led him and his monks into a noble hall and, seating them all in a row, washed the feet of all of them. He washed their feet with water from the muddy spring which they had seen earlier.

Imedled wiþ is owe couent;   and þo hi were alle isete
Þer com on and seruede hem   and vette hem alle mete.
A vair wit lof he sette   biuore two and two;
Wite moren as it were of erbes   he sette biuore hem also –
Swetere þing ne miȝte be;   hi ne knewe it noȝt on.   285
Of þe clere well þat hi seie,   þis monekes dronke echon.
"Beþ nou glade," þe abbod sede,   "and drynkeþ nou inouȝ
In charite of þulke welle   þat ȝe wolden er wiþ wouȝ;
Hit is betere to drinke in charite,   wen it is ȝou ibroȝt
[Þanne þeofliche istole   þanne ne helpeþ it ȝou noȝt.
Þis bred of wan ȝe eteþ nou,   we nuteþ wanne it is;
Ac a strong man it bringþ us eche day,   to oure celer iwis.
We nuteþ noȝt, bote upe God,   wanne it is ybroȝt] – *
Vor hoso douteþ Ihesu Crist,   him ne schal faili noȝt.   290
    Four and twenti freres we beþ here,   and wen we beþ alle isete,
Twelf suche loues ech day   me bringeþ ous to mete.
Ate feste of eche holi day,   and wenne it Soneday is,
He bringeþ ous foure and twenti loues,   þat ech monek haþ his;
And ech frere of þat he leueþ   wite to is soper.   295
Vor ȝou it is today idoubled,   as ȝe seþ nou her;
Vor our couent nys noȝt her,   ac haþ muchedel vnete.
So þat our Lord, þoru is grace,   ech day send ous mete.
Seþþe Seyn Patrikes day,   and Seyn Ailbi also,   *
We habbeþ ibe her vour score ȝer,   þat nomon com ous to;   300
Euereft our Lordes grace iued   ous haþ echon.
Þis weder is euer mury her;   sekenesse nys her non.
And wanne we scholleþ do our seruise,   our Lord tend our liȝt,
And our taperes ne beþ noþe lasse,   þei hi berne day and nyȝt."
    Hi arise up and to chirche eode,   þo hi hadde alle iȝete;   305
Twelf oþer monekes ate quer   hi mette toward þe mete.
"Hou is þis?" quaþ Seyn Brendan.   "Wi nere noȝt þes wiþ ous?"
"Leue fader," þe abbod sede,   "it mot neode be þus;
Þer nelleþ bote vour and twenti monekes   in our freitor be ido,
And wen ȝe were þer wiþ ous,   þes ne miȝte noȝt also.   310
Þe wile we singeþ euesong,   þes scholleþ sitte and ete;
Hor euesong hi scholleþ seþþe synge,   wen hi habbeþ iȝete."
    Seyn Brendan bihuld hor vaire weued;   him þoȝte it was al,
Weued, calis, and cruet,   al pur cristal.
Seue taperes in þe quer   þer were, and nammo,   315
And four and twenti seges also,   to wan hi scholde go;

Afterwards, he led them into the refectory and seated them there honourably, intermingled with his own community; and when they were all seated a man came and served them and brought them all food. He placed a fine white loaf before each pair; he also set before them white roots, of herbs as it were – nothing could be sweeter; not one of them recognized what it was. Each of the monks drank from the clear spring which they had seen.

'Be content now', said the abbot; 'and now drink copiously and gratefully from that spring whose water you wrongfully desired earlier. It is better to drink with gratitude when it is brought to you than that you should take it thievishly as you had intended. This bread which we are eating, we do not know where it comes from; an unknown man brings it every day, brings it, in fact, to our store-room. We do not know, unless by the grace of God, whence it is brought – for whoever honours Jesus Christ, to him nothing shall be lacking.

'We are four and twenty brethren here, and when we are all seated at table twelve such loaves are brought to us every day for our meal. At the celebration of every festival, and when it is Sunday, he brings us four and twenty loaves so that each monk has his own; and whatever part of it each brother leaves, he keeps for his supper. For you today it is doubled, as you see here and now; for our community is not all here, and has left much uneaten. And so our Lord, out of his grace, sends us food each day. Since Saint Patrick's day and Saint Ailbi's too, we have been here four score years without anyone coming to us; our Lord's grace has ever since fed us one and all. The weather here is always pleasant; there is no sickness here. And when we are to celebrate our service, our Lord lights our lights, and our candles are no shorter, though they burn day and night.'

When they had all eaten, they arose and went to church, meeting twelve other monks in the choir, coming in for the meal.

'How is this?' said Saint Brendan; 'why were these not with us?'

'Dear father', said the abbot, 'it must needs be thus; only four and twenty monks may be seated in our refectory, and when you were there with us, these could not be so also. While we sing evensong, these shall sit and eat; they will sing their evensong afterwards, when they have eaten.'

Saint Brendan gazed at their splendid altar; it seemed to him that everything, altar, chalice, and other vessels, was entirely of clear crystal. There were seven candles and no more in the choir, and also

Vor þer were four and twenti monekes,   þat euerich hadde his;
And þe abbodes sege was   amydde þe quer iwis.
      Seyn Brendan escte þe abbod þo: "Sei me, leue broþer,
Hou holde ʒe so wel silence   þat non ne spekeþ wiþ oþer."   320
"Our Lord it wot," þe abbod sede,   "we habbeþ her ibe
Vor score ʒer in suche lyue   as þou miʒt her ise,
Ac þer nas neuereft among ous alle   ispeke a none wise
Ar þis tyme non oþer word,   bote our Lordes seruyce.
Ne we neuereft nere in feblesse,   ne sik, of ous noʒt on."   325
      Þo Seyn Brendan hurde þis,   uor ioie he wep anon.
"Leue fader," he sede, "uor Godes loue,   mote we bileue here?"
"Þou wost wel," quaþ þis oþer,   "ʒe ne mowe in none manere;
Ne haþ our Lord iscewed wel   al þat þou schalt do,
And come ʒut to Irlond aʒen,   and þi twelf breþeren also?   330
And fram þe to þe Ile of Ankres   þe þretteþe schal wende,   *
And þe fourteþe to Helle al quic   and be þer wiþþouten ende?"
      Þo com þer in a fury arwe   at an fenestre anon,
As þei he fram Heuene come,   and þe taperes tende echon,
And aʒenward flei, riʒt as he com,   bi þulke fenestre þere.   335
Þis taperes barnde longe inouʒ   and noþe wors nere.
"Lord Crist," quaþ Seyn Brendan,   "ich wondri in my þoʒt
Hou þis taperes berneþ þus   and ne wonyeþ noʒt."
"Nastou noʒt," quaþ þe abbod,   "in þe Olde Lawe ifounde   *
Hou Moyses sei a þorn berne   fram þe croppe to þe gronde,   340
And þe swiþer þat þis þorn brende   þe grener þe leues were?
Ne wenestou noʒt þat our Lord be   her as miʒti as þere?"
      Þis monekes were togadere þus   vorte Mydwynter was ido;
Hit was after Twelfþe Day   ar hi partede atwo.
Anon to Seyn Hillare Day   Seyn Brendan vorþ wende,   345
Wiþ is monekes, in þe se,   þoru grace þat God hem sende.
Hi rewe up and doun in sorwe inouʒ;   þe se hem caste heie.
Vorte ver in Leynte fram þulke tyme,   no lond hi ne seie;
So þat aboute Palme Soneday   hi bihulde aboute vaste.
Hem þoʒte hi seie ver fram hem   as a cloude ate laste;   350
Þis monekes wondred þerof,   wat þe cloude were.
"Beþ stille" quaþ Seyn Brendan;   "er ʒe habbeþ ibe here.
Þis is oure gode Procuratur,   þat muche good ous haþ ido
In þe Foulen Parays,   and in þe Lond of Schep also."
      So þat hor scip ate laste   toward þis ile drouʒ;   355
A Scere Þorsday hi come þuder,   wiþ trauail and sorwe inouʒ.

four and twenty seats to which they were to go; for there were four and twenty monks and each one had his own; the abbot's chair was actually in the middle of the choir.

Saint Brendan then asked the abbot:
'Do tell me, dear brother, how you maintain silence so well that no one ever speaks to another'
'Our Lord knows', said the abbot, 'we have been here four score years in such a way of life as you may observe here, and never by any means before this moment was there uttered among us all any word other than worship of our Lord. Nor were we ever in ill-health or unwell, not one of us.'

When he heard this, Saint Brendan at once wept for joy.
'Dear father', he said, 'for the love of God, may we remain here?'
'You know well', said the other, 'you cannot by any means remain. Has not our Lord clearly revealed everything you must do and then return to Ireland again, and your twelve brethren also. And the thirteenth shall go from you to the Island of Anchorites, and the fourteenth shall go to Hell alive and remain there for ever.'

Then suddenly there came in at a window a flaming arrow, as if it came from Heaven, and lit all the candles, and flew out again at the window, just as it had entered. The candles burned a long time and yet were not less.
'Lord Christ!' said Saint Brendan, 'I marvel at heart how these candles burn like this and do not grow shorter.'
'Have you not learnt from the Old Testament', said the abbot, 'how Moses saw a thorn-bush burning from top to bottom; and the longer the thorn burned the greener were the leaves? Do you not believe that our Lord is as powerful now as then?'

The monks remained together in this way until the Christmas season was ended; it was after Twelfth-day before they parted company. Immediately after Saint Hilary's Day Saint Brendan set out, with his monks, upon the sea, by the grace that God gave them.[13] They rowed hither and thither in great distress, tossed high by the sea. From that time until late in Lent, they sighted no land; until about Palm Sunday they gazed anxiously about them. At last it seemed to them they saw very far away from them something like a cloud; the monks were greatly surprised at that, wondering what the cloud might be.
'Be calm,' said Saint Brendan; 'you have been here before. This is

Þis gode Procuratur com aȝen hem glad,   and wilcome hem anon
And custe Seyn Brendanes vet   and þe monekes echon,
And seþþe hem sette to þe soper,   vor þe day it wolde so;
And seþþe he wesc hor alre vet,   hor Maunde to do.   360
Hor alre Maunde hi hulde þere,   and þere hi gonne bileue
A Gode Friday allonge day   vorte an Ester Eue.
An Ester Eue hor Procuratur   bed hem hor scip take
And þe holi Resurexcion   up þe fisches rug make;
And aftur þe Resurexcion   hem het euene te   365
To þe Foulen Parays,   as hi hadde er ibe.
     Þis holi men hem wende uorþ,   and our Lordes grace nome   *
So þat to þe grete fische   þulke day hi come,
As a lond þat houede;   hor caudron hi founde ek þere,
As hi bileuede it vp is rugge   in þe oþer ȝere.   370
Louerd Crist, þat such a best   houy scholde so stille,
And soffri men þerup gon   and do al hor wille!
Þis monekes up þis fisches rugge   bileuede al longe nyȝt,
And songe matyns and euesong,   and seþþe, þo it was liȝt,
Anoward is rugge songe   masse echon;   375
And euer was þis muchel best   so stille so eny ston.
As þis Resurexcion   wiþ gret honur was ido
And þis monekes hadde isonge   hor massen also,
Aboute vndarne of þe day   to hor schip þen wei hi nome;
And to þe Foulen Parays   þulke day hi come.   380
     Anon so þe foules iseie hem come,   hi gonne to synge echone
Aȝen hem wiþ gret melodie,   as it were vor þe none.
And þulke þat spac wiþ hem er   aȝen hem sone drouȝ –
Þe soun of is wyngen muri was;   he welcomede hem vaire inouȝ.
"Ȝe auȝte," he sede, "our Lord Crist   honouri myd þe beste;   385
He purueieþ ȝou vour studes,   to habbe inne ȝoure reste
Wiþ ȝoure gode Procuratur,   ȝoure Maunde to do,
And seþþe þe Resurexcion   up þe fisches rugge also,
And wiþ ous her þis eiȝte woukes   uorte after Witesoneday,
And to Mydwynter vorte Candelmasse   in þe ile of þe abbay.   390
And in þis grete se of Occian   in gret peril ȝe scholle wende,
In trauail, al þe oþer tyme,   vorte þe seue ȝeres ende;
And seþþe þat Lond of Biheste   God wole þat ȝe se,
And þerinne in ioie inouȝ   vourti dawes be.
And to þe contrei þat ȝe beþ of   seþþe ȝe scholleþ wende,   395
Al eseliche, wiþoute anuy,   and þer ȝour lif ende."   *

our generous Provider who has done us so much kindness in the Paradise of Birds and also in the Land of Sheep.'[14]

And so at last their boat drew near the island; they arrived there, with great effort and distress, on Maundy Thursday. The generous Provider came happily to meet them and at once welcomed them, and kissed the feet of Saint Brendan and each of the monks, and then set them down to supper as the hour required; and afterwards he washed the feet of all of them to fulfil the rites of Maundy Thursday.[15] They all kept their Maundy there, and there they remained all day long upon Good Friday until the eve of Easter. On Easter Eve their Provider bade them take ship and keep their Feast of the Holy Resurrection upon the back of the fish; and he bade them go, after the Resurrection festival, straight to the Paradise of Birds where they had previously been.

These holy men set out and, aided by the grace of our Lord, that same day came upon the great fish which rose up as if it were an island; there they also found their cauldron, as they had left it upon its back the previous year. Lord Christ, that such a creature should lie so still, and allow men to walk upon it and do everything they wished! The monks remained upon the fish's back the whole night long, and sang matins and evensong, and later, when it was light, they all sang mass upon its back; and all the time this great fish was as still as any stone. When the Feast of the Resurrection had been celebrated with great reverence and the monks had sung their mass as well, about mid-day they took the path to their boat; and that same day they reached the Paradise of Birds.

As soon as the birds saw them coming, they all began to sing with great melody as if it were in order to greet them. And the same one which had previously spoken with them immediately approached them – the sound of his wings was pleasant; he greeted them most courteously:

'You ought,' he said, 'to honour in the highest our lord Christ; with your generous Provider, he provides for you four places in which to take your rest, to celebrate your Maundy rites, and then your Resurrection rites also upon the fish's back, and here with us the eight weeks right up until after Whit Sunday, and from Christmas until Candlemas in the island of the abbey.[16] And upon the great sea of Ocean you shall voyage in great peril and in pain all the rest of the time until the end of seven years; and thereafter God wills that you should see the Promised Land, and then remain there in great bliss for

Þis holi men bileuede þer   vorte þe Trinyte.
Hor Procuratur com þo to hem,   þat was euer in pleynte.
He broȝte hem mete and drynke inouȝ   as he hadde er ido,
And chargede hor scip þerwiþ,   and let hem wende so.   400
    Þis holi men hem wende vorþ,   as God hem wolde sende;
Vor Godes grace was wiþ hem,   þe bet hi myȝte wende.
As hi wende vp an tyme,   in gret tempest inouȝ,
A gret fisch hi seie and grisliche   þat after hor scip drouȝ.
Brenninde fom out at is mouþ   and at is nese he caste —   405
Þat water was herre þen hor schip   biuore hem at eche blaste.
He wolched after as an hous,   and pursiwede hem vaste;   *
Wiþ is breste so uaste he scef   þe monekes were agaste,
And cride ȝerne on Seyn Brendan,   and on Ihesu Crist also.
After þe schip so uaste he scef   þat he com almest þerto.   410
As he hem hadde almest oftake,   and hi ne tolde noȝt of hor lyue,
Anoþer fisc out of þe west   þer com swymme wel blyue,   *
And encontred þis luþer fisc   and smot to him vaste,
And uorclef is foule bouk   in þre parties ate laste;
And þen wei as he com er   wel euene aȝen he drou.   415
Þis monekes þonkede Ihesu Crist   and were joyuol inouȝ.
    So longe wende þis holi men   in þe se aboute so
Þat hi were ofhongred sore;   hor mete was al ido.
Þo com þer fle a lutel fowel   and broȝte a gret bouȝ
Vol of grapes swiþe rede,   and wel euene to hem drouȝ.   420
Þis grapes he tok Seyn Brendan;   þis gode mon somdel louȝ.
Þerby hi lyuede fourtene nyȝt   and hadde alle mete inouȝ.
Þo þis grapes were ido,   hi were ofhongred sore.
By þe one syde hi seye an yle,   and mete þerinne more;
Þe ile was uol of vaire tren,   and so þicke euerich bouȝ   425
Of suche grapes as hi hadde er   þat to gronde it drouȝ.
Seyn Brendan wende upon þis yle,   and of þe grapes nom uaste
And bar into þe schip to libbe by,   þat fourti dawes ilaste.
    Sone þerafter þer come a grip fle   vaste in þe se,
And asailed hem uaste and hor scip,   and fondede hem to sle.   430
Þis monekes cride deluolliche,   and ne tolde noȝt of hor lyue.
Þo sei hi come þe lutel foul   toward hem wel blyue
Þat in Foulen Parays   so ofte hem hadde irad.
Þo Seyn Brendan sei him come,   he was somdel glad.
Þis lutel fowel smot to þis grip,   and nom is dunt wel heie;   435
Þe verste dunt þat he him ȝaf,   he smot out eiþer eie.

forty days. And thereafter you shall voyage to the country to which you belong, quite pleasantly, without difficulty, and end your life there.' These holy men remained there until Trinity Sunday. Their Provider, who was always well supplied, then came to them. He brought them much food and drink as he had previously done, and loaded their boat with it, and so let them depart.

These holy men set forth wherever God wished to send them; since God's grace was with them, they were able to voyage more surely. As they voyaged on one occasion, in a most violent storm, they saw a large and hideous fish which came after their boat. It spewed out burning spume from its mouth and from its nose – at every spout the liquid was higher above them than their boat. He came wallowing after like a house, and pursued them swiftly, thrusting with his chest so fiercely that the monks were terrified, and called earnestly on Saint Brendan and upon Jesus Christ also. He rushed after the boat so furiously that he almost reached it. When he had almost overtaken them, and they reckoned their lives worth nothing, another fish came swimming very swiftly from the west and attacked the fierce fish and struck at him vigorously, and finally split his foul carcass into three pieces;[17] and at once moved off again the same way he had come. The monks thanked Jesus Christ and were very glad.

These saintly men voyaged about the ocean in this way so long that they were exceedingly hungry; their food was quite finished. Then a little bird came flying and brought a large spray full of very red grapes, and approached quite close to them. He bore the grapes to Saint Brendan; the saint laughed a little. On them they subsisted for two weeks and all had plenty of food. When these grapes were finished, they were exceedingly hungry. In one direction they saw an island, and in it more food; the isle was full of lovely trees, and every branch was so full of such grapes as they had previously had that it drooped to the ground. Saint Brendan landed upon the island, and quickly took some of the grapes and carried them on board ship to live upon, which lasted for forty days.

Shortly thereafter, a griffin came flying swiftly over the sea, and attacked them and their boat fiercely, trying to kill them. The monks cried out in fear, accounting their lives of little worth. Then they saw coming towards them very swiftly the little bird which had so often helped them in the Paradise of Birds. When Saint Brendan saw it coming, he was very glad. The little bird struck at the griffin, and

Þis luþer best sone he slouȝ   þat he vel dun in þe se –
Þing þat God wole habbe iwust   ne schal noþing asle.
     Þis holi men wende in þe se   aboute her and þere;
And in on of þe four studes   þe vour festes euer hi were.   440
A tyme, a Seyn Petres Day,   gret feste myd hor tonge
In þe se hi made of Seyn Petur,   and hor seruyce songe.
Hi come in a stude in þe se,   so cler þe se hi founde
Þat hi sei in ech half   clerliche to þe gronde;
Hem þoȝte þe grond iheled was   wiþ fisc al at an hepe,   445
Þat hi ne seie non oþer grond,   bote as hi were aslepe.
Þis monekes bede Seyn Brendan   þat he softe speke
Þat he ne aweite noȝt þat fisc,   leste hi hor scip tobreke.
"Wat is ȝou?" quaþ Seyn Brendan;   "warof beþ ȝe adrad?
Vp þe maistres rugge of alle fisches   ȝe habbeþ imad ȝou glad,   450
And anoueward is rug fur imad,   and doþ fram ȝere to ȝere!"
Þis holi mon þe loddore song,   uor þe none as it were.
     Þe fisches sturt up uor hor song,   as hi awoke of slepe,
And come al aboute þe schip   al at one hepe;
So þicke hi flote bi ech half   þat non oþer water me ne sei,   455
And bisette þis scip al aboute,   ac hi ne come noȝt þer ney.
So þicke hi were aboute þis schip,   and siwede it euer so,
Þe wule þe holi mon is masse song,   uorte it was al ido.
And þo þe masse was al ido,   ech wende in is ende.
Muche wonder me may ise,   hoso wole aboute wende!   460
     Þat wynd was strong and stif inouȝ,   and drof þat schip wel uaste.
As ver as hi wende seuenyȝt,   þe clere se ilaste,
Þat hi seie in þe se as clerliche   as hi scholde alonde –
Gret wonder hadde þis gode men   and þonkede Godes sonde.
Þo com a souþerne wynd   þat norþward hem drof uaste,   465
Riȝt euene norþ, hi nuste wuder   – þat eiȝte dawes ilaste.
     Þo seie hi, ver in þe norþ,   a lond, derk inouȝ,
Smokie as it smythes were;   þuderward hor scip drouȝ.
Þo hurde hi of bulies   gret blowynge þere,
And gret betynge and noyse inouȝ,   as it þonder were.   470
Þo was Seyn Brendan sore agast;   he blessede him anon faste. *
Þo com þer out a luþer wiȝt,   wel grisliche ate laste,
Þoru suart and brennyng al;   up hem his eien he caste, *
[And turnde him in anon aȝen   – þis monkes were agaste.]
Þis luþer þing made a cri   þat me miȝte ihure wide.
     Þo come þer such screwen mo,   wel þicke bi eche side   475

delivered his blow very fiercely; at the first stroke he gave him, he struck out both eyes. He quickly slew the evil creature so that it fell down into the sea – the creature whom God wishes to keep safe nothing shall kill.[18]

These holy men sailed about hither and thither upon the ocean; and for the four festivals they were always in of the four places. On one occasion, on Saint Peter's Day, they made a great celebration for Saint Peter with their voices upon the ocean, and sang their service.[19] They came to a region of the sea where they found the water so clear that on every side they could see right to the bottom; it seemed to them that the bottom was covered with fish so crowded together that no other ground was visible, all as if they were asleep. The monks urged Saint Brendan to speak softly so as not to arouse the fish, lest they might damage the boat.

'What is the matter with you', said Saint Brendan; 'what are you afraid of? You have made yourselves at ease on the back of the greatest of all fish, and built a fire upon his back, and do so year after year!' The saintly man sang the louder, as if on purpose.

At their singing the fish leapt up, as if waking from sleep, and came all around the boat all in a shoal; they swam so close together on all sides that no water whatever could be seen, and surrounded the boat on all sides, yet they did not come near it. They were closely packed around the boat in this way, and continually followed it during the time the saintly man sang his mass until it was quite finished. And when the mass was quite ended, each went its own way. Whoever shall travel widely may see many marvels!

The wind was very strong and fierce, and drove the boat most swiftly. As far as they sailed in a week, the water remained clear, so that they saw things in the sea as clearly as they could on land – the good men were greatly amazed and gave thanks for divine providence. Then came a southern wind which drove them swiftly northward, directly due north, they knew not whither – eight days it continued.

Then, far to the north, they sighted a very dark land, as smoky as if it were a smithy; their boat headed in that direction. Next they heard a great puffing of bellows there, and a great pounding and much noise, as though of thunder. Then Saint Brendan was greatly afraid; he immediately crossed himself devoutly. In the end there emerged an evil creature, most hideous, quite black and burning all over; he turned

Wiþ tongen and wiþ homeres,   brenynde monyon.   *
To þe bremme hi ourne of þe se,   toward þe schipe anon.
Þo hi ne miȝte come no ner,   hi gonne ȝolle uaste,
And hor oweles, al brennynde,   after þis men hi caste,
Þat me ne miȝte noþing bote fur   ise noþer ihure;   480
Þe se, as it uel adoun,   þoȝte ek afure.
Euerich caste upon oþer   þis oweles al an hei
And aboute þe scip ek in þe se,   ac þer ne com non ney.
Ate laste hi turnde hem aȝen,   þo hi ne spedde noȝt þere;
And al þat lond þoȝte of hem ek   as it afure were;   485
And al þe se þeraboute   barnde and smokede uaste.
Strong was þe stench and þe smoke   and wel long ilaste.
Þo þe monekes were so ver   þat hi ne miȝte ise nammore,
Hor ȝellyng ȝut hi hurde,   þe screwen wope so sore.
"Hou þyncþ ȝou?" quaþ Seyn Brendan.   "Was þis a muri pas?   490
We ne wilneþ come þer nammore,   uor an ende of Helle it was,
And þe deuelen hopede wel of ous   habbe iheued a good cas,
Ac, ihered be Ihesu Crist,   hi caste ambes-as."
   Þe souþerne wynd laste ȝut   and drof hem euer vorþ
So þat hi seie an hei hul   ver in þat norþ,   495
Cloudi and brennynge smoke   – muche wo was þere.
Þe lye of þe fur stop up an hei   as it a wal were;
Ȝif þer was muche wo in þen oþer,   þer was wel more.
On of is monekes bigon þo   to wepe and ȝelle sore,
Vor is tyme was þo icome   þat he ne miȝte no leng abide.   500
He hupte him out amydde þe se,   out of þe schip biside,
And orn him uaste upon þis water   toward þis fure,
And cride and ȝal deluolliche,   þat deol it was to hure.
"Alas!" he sede, "my wreche lif;   uor nou ich seo myn ende.   504
Wiþ ȝou ichabbe in ioie ibe,   and I ne may no leng wiþ ȝou wende.
Acorsed be heo þat me bar,   and þe tyme þat ich was ibore,
And þe fader þat me byȝat,   uor nou icham uorlore!"
Aȝen him þe deuel com anon,   and nome þen wreche vaste
And defoulede him stronge inouȝ,   and amydde þe fur him caste.
Þo vond he þat Seyn Brendan   him sede þo he out wende;   510
Him failede grace, hou so it was,   is lif vorto amende.
So stronge barnde þis montayne   þat hi noþing ne seie,
Þe ȝut hi were ver þerfram,   bote fur and lie.
   Þo turnde þe wynd into þe norþ   and souþward hem drof vaste; *
In þulke side strong inouȝ   seuenyȝt þe wynd ilaste.   515

his eyes upon them [and immediately turned away – the monks were terrified]. That evil creature gave a cry that could be heard far and wide.

Then there emerged more such devils, thronging on every side, many with flaming tongs and hammers. They immediately ran to the seashore, towards the boat. When they could not get near it, they began to yell loudly, and hurled their hooks, all aflame, after these men, so that nothing could be either seen or heard but flames; as it descended, the very sea seemed afire. Each, one after another, flung all the hooks up high and into the water all around the boat, but none came close to it. In the end, when they had no success there, they turned away; and that whole region seemed to them as if it were also on fire; and the sea all round about burned and smoked fiercely. The stench and the smoke were intense and lasted a very long time. When the monks were so far off they could no longer see it, they still heard their yelling, the wretches wept so bitterly.

'What do you think?' said Saint Brendan. 'Was that not a lucky escape? We will no longer go there, for it was an outskirt of Hell, and the devils had high hopes of us, of having a lucky chance, but, Jesus Christ be praised, they drew a blank.'[20]

The southern wind still continued and drove them ever onwards until, far to the north, they sighted a high hill, clouded and burning with smoke – there was great misery there. The flame of the fire rose up on high as though it were a wall; if there had been much misery in that other place, there was much more there. One of his monks then began to weep and lament bitterly, for his hour had come when he could no longer survive. He leapt out of the boat into the water, the open sea beside it, and ran swiftly upon the waters towards the fire, shouting and yelling so bitterly that it was most grievous to hear:

'Alas!' he said, 'for my miserable life; for now I foresee my fate. I have been happy to be with you, and I can no longer go with you. Accursed be she who bore me, accursed be the hour when I was born, and the father who begat me, for now I am damned.'
The devils at once advanced upon him, and firmly seizing the wretch and abusing him very severely, flung him into the midst of the flames. Then he discovered the truth of what Saint Brendan had said to him when he set out: however it befell, he lacked grace to amend his way of life. So fiercely did the mountain burn that, while they were still far from it, they could see nothing but fire and flame.

So longe hi wende euene souþ   þat hi seie aten ende
An harde roche in þe se,   and þe se þerouer wende;
Þerouer þe se caste ilome,   and ofte he was al bar.
Þo hi come þis roche ney,   of oþer hi were iwar;
Anoueward þe roche hi seie sitte,   wen þe se wiþdrouȝ,   520
A wrechedde gost, naked and bar,   in miseise inouȝ.
Aboue him was a cloþ iteid   myd twei tongen vaste,
Þe neþer ende tilde to is chynne;   oueral þe wynd it caste
Þat, wan þat water him wiþdrouȝ,   þat cloþ þat heng so heie,   *
Bet, as þe wynd it bleu,   þen wreche amydde þe eie.   525
Þe wawes bete ek of þe se   biuore and bihynde;
Wrecchedore gost þen he was   ne dorte nomon fynde.
     Seyn Brendan him bad a Godes name   to telle him wat he were,
And wat he hadde God mysdo,   and wat he dude þere.
"Icham," he sede, "a deluol gost,   þe wrecche Iudas   530
Þat uor panewes our Lord solde,   and an erþe myd him was.
Þis nys noȝt my riȝte stude,   ac our Lord doþ me grace
To habbe her my Parays,   as ȝe seþ, in þisse place;
Vor no godnesse þat ichabbe ido,   bote our Lordes milce and ore,
Vor I ne myȝte habbe so muche pyne   þat I nabbe ofserued more.
Vor in þe brennynge hul   þat ech of ȝou isay,   536
My riȝte is to be and brenne   þerinne nyȝt and day,
Þer ich was þis oþer day   þo ȝoure broþer þuder com,
And was into pyne ilad   and wel sone hadde is dom.
Þeruore Helle was glad inouȝ   þat he made þe grete lie,   540
Vor ioie þat he was icome,   þat ȝe so ver iseie –
So he deþ wen eny soule   verst is þuder icome.
Þoru our Lordes heie milse   icham anon þenne inome,
Vor icham her eche Soneday;   and fram þe Saterdayes eue
Vorte it be þen Soneday eue,   her ich schal bileue.   545
And at Mydwynter ek,   vorte Twelfþe Day be ido;
And fram bigynnynge ek of Ester   vorte Witesoneday also;
And our Ledi festen ek,   vor vol of milce heo is.
And al þe oþer tyme of þe ȝere   in Helle icham iwis,
Wiþ Pilates and Herodes,   Anne and Cayphas –   550
Bote ich may corsi þe tyme   þat ich euer ibore was.
Ac ich bidde ȝou, vor þe loue of God,   þat ȝe fondi in alle wise
Þat ich bileue her al nyȝt   vorte þe sonne arise,
Þat ȝe wite me fram þe deuelen   þat comeþ sone after me."
     Seyn Brendan sede: "Þoru Godes grace,   we scholleþ wite þe.

Then the wind shifted into the north and drove them swiftly southwards; all that week it persisted very strongly in that direction. They voyaged due south until they finally sighted a rugged rock in the sea, and the sea washing over it; the sea repeatedly washed over it, and often it was quite uncovered. When they neared the rock, they became aware of someone; when the sea drew back, they saw, sitting atop the rock, a miserable soul, stripped and naked, in great distress. Above him a cloth was fastened with two long thongs, the lower end raised to his chin; the wind blew it about so that, whenever the water retreated, the cloth which hung on high, as the wind blew it, struck the wretched creature right in the eye. The waves of the sea too beat on him fore and aft; a more wretched soul than he was no one could find.

Saint Brendan begged him in God's name to tell him who he might be, and what he had done to offend God, and what he was doing there.

'I', he said, 'am a sorry soul, the vile Judas who sold our Lord for money, and was with him upon earth. This is not my rightful place, but our Lord does me the kindness of having my Paradise here in this place, as you see; not for any good deed that I have done, but out of our Lord's mercy and grace, for I do not have so much pain that I have not deserved more. For it is my due to be in the flaming Hell which each of you saw, and to burn therein night and day, where I was yesterday when your brother arrived there, and was led away to punishment and very quickly met his doom. Hell was so happy on that account that it raised that great blaze which you saw so far off, for joy that he had come – so it does when any soul first arrives there. Through our Lord's divine mercy I am immediately removed from there, for I am here every Sunday; and from the Saturday evening until the evening of Sunday comes I have to remain here. And at Christmas too, until Twelfth-day is over; and also from the beginning of Easter until Whitsunday as well; and also at the festivals of our Lady, for full of mercy she is. And at all other times of the year I am indeed in Hell, with Pilate and Herod, Annas and Caiaphas – so I may well curse the hour that ever I was born! But I beg you, for the love of God, that you should contrive by every means that I may remain here all night until the sun rises, and that you protect me from the fiends who will shortly come for me.'

Saint Brendan said:

'By God's grace, we shall protect you. Tell me now what is that cloth which hangs so high there?'

Tel me nou wat is þat cloþ   þat so heie hongeþ þar."   556
"Þo ich was an erþe," quaþ Iudas,   "and our Lordes panes bar,
Þis cloþ ich ȝaf an mesel;   uor myn owe it nas noȝt,
Ac it was myd our Lordes panewes,   and myd our breþeren, iboȝt.
Ac vor ich it ȝaf vor Godes loue,   nou it is me byuore;   560
Vor me ne schal noþing do uor him   þat schal be uorlore.
And uor it was of oþer monnes,   as myn inwit vnderstod,
It doþ me, þei it honge here,   more harm þen good,
Vor it bat in myn eien sore   and doþ me harm inouȝ.
Her me may ise wuch it is   to ȝeue of oþer mannes wiþ wouȝ,   565
As wolleþ mony riche men   myd vnriȝt alday take
Of poure men her and þer   and almesse suþþe make.
Þat hi doþ uor Godes loue   ne schal noȝt be vorȝete,
Ac to pyne it schal hem turne,   as hi scholleþ þanne iwite.
Þe tongen also," quaþ Iudas,   "þat ȝe seþ honge an hei,   570
Prestes is ich ȝaf an erþe,   þeruore hi beþ me ney;
Vor clanliche me schal al þing fynde   þat me deþ uor is loue.
Þe ston vp wam ich sitte,   þat makeþ me sitte aboue,
In a wei ich fond him ligge   þer no ned nas to ston;
Ich caste him in a deop dich   þat me þer myȝte ouer gon. *   575
Vewe gode dede ichabbe ido   of wam ich mowe telle,
Ac non so lute þat I ne fynde   her oþer in Helle."
    Þo it was eue þen Soneday,   þe deuelen come blaste
Vorte lede to Helle þis seli gost   – hi cride and ȝolle vaste.   579
"Wend henne," hi sede, "þou Godes mon!   Þou nast noȝt her to done.
Let ous habbe our felawe   and to Helle him lede sone,
Vor we ne dorre noȝt oure maister ise,   vorte we him habbe ibroȝt.
Wend fram him, vor hit is tyme   and ne let þou ous noȝt."
"I ne lette ȝou noȝt," quaþ Seyn Brendan,   "ne wite ȝou noȝt her, *
Ac doþ our Lord Ihesu Crist,   þat is of more power."   585
"Hou darstou," þe deuelen sede,   "byuore him nempne is name?
Ne bitraide he him and solde ek   to deþe wiþ gret schame?"
Seyn Brendan sede: "In is name,   ich hote ȝou, as ich may,
Þat ȝe touche him noȝt tonyȝt,   ar tomorwe day."
Grisliche þe deuelen ȝolle þo,   and aȝenward gonne fle.   590
Iudas þonkede pytosliche   þat deol it was to se.
    Amorwe, so sone so it was day,   þe deuelen come blaste;
Grisliche hi cride and ȝolle   and chidde also uaste.
"Awei!" hi sede, "þu Godes mon;   acorsed be þe stounde
Þat þou come ower heraboute,   and þat we her þe ifounde!   595

'When I was on earth', said Judas, 'and was the bearer of our Lord's purse, I gave this cloth to a leper; for it was not my own, but it was bought with our Lord's money and that of our brethren. But because I gave it for the love of God, it now hangs before me; for nothing one may do for him shall be wasted. And, as I understand, because it was someone else's, it does me more harm than good even though it hangs here, for it strikes painfully upon my eyes and does me much injury. Here one may observe what it is to give away the property of others wrongfully, as many rich men will continually take unjustly from poor people in various places and then give it away as alms. What they do for love of God shall not be forgotten, but it will become a torment to them, as they shall subsequently discover. The thongs also', said Judas, 'which you see hanging up there, upon earth I gave them to priests, and for that reason they are close by me; [21] for a man shall regain fully everything he does for his love. The stone on which I am sitting, which causes me to sit higher, I found lying in a path where no stone was needed; I threw it into a deep ditch so that people might cross over there. I have done few good deeds of which I can now boast, but none so slight that I do not regain it here or in Hell.'

When it was evening on the Sunday, the devils came breathing fire to take that wretched soul to Hell – they wailed and howled loudly.

'Go hence, you man of God!' they said. 'You have no business here. Let us take our fellow inmate and carry him off to Hell immediately, for we dare not set eyes on our master until we have brought him. Leave him be and do not hinder us, for it is time.'

'I am not hindering you', said Saint Brendan, 'nor blaming you in this matter, but our Lord Jesus Christ, who is of greater authority, does so.'

'How dare you', said the devils, 'pronounce his name before him? Did he not both sell him and also betray him to a most shameful death?'

Saint Brendan said:

'In his name, I command you, as I am able, that you do not touch him tonight, before dawn tomorrow.'

The devils howled hideously then, and went fleeing homewards. Judas gave thanks so pathetically that it was pitiful to see.

Next day, as soon as it was light, the devils came breathing fire; they howled and wailed horribly and railed just as furiously.

'Away, you man of God', they said; 'accursed be the hour when you came anywhere near us, and when we came upon you here! Our master

Our maister ous haþ itormented   grisliche al longe nyȝt,
And strong inouȝ, vor we ne broȝte   wiþ ous þis luþer wiȝt.
Ac we wolleþ ous wel awreke   – up himsulue it schal go;
Vor we scholle þis six dawes   þeruore doubli is wo."
Þis wrechede gost quakede þo   þat reuþe it is to telle.   600
Þis deuelen nome him grimliche   and bere him to Helle;
Ac Seyn Brendan hem vorbed,   in our Lordes name,
Þat he nadde uor þulke nyȝt   neuer þe more schame.
    Seyn Brendan and is monekes   in þe se vorþ wende
Ȝut þre dawes euene souþ,   as our Lord hem sende.   605
Þe verþe day hi seie an yle   al bi souþe an hei.
Seyn Brendan siȝte sore   þo he þis yle isei.
"Poul," he sede, "þe heremyte,   is in þe yle þat ich ise;
Þer he haþ wiþoute mete   fourti ȝer ibe."
Þo hi come to þisse yle,   in hi wende echon.   610
Þis hermyte, þat was so old,   aȝen hem com anon.
His her to his fet tilde,   of berd and of heued,
And helede al aboute is bodi;   þer nas bar noȝt bileued.
Non oþer cloþes nadde he on;   is lymes were al hore.
    Seyn Brendan him bihuld,   and bigan to sike sore.   615
"Alas," he sede, "ichabbe so ȝare   in stude of monek ibe,
And nou in lyue of angel   an mon ich ise!"
"Be stille!" quaþ þis hermite;   "God deþ wel bet bi þe,
Vor he scewe þe more þen eny oþer   of is priuete.
Vor a monek lyueþ bi þe suench   of is owe honde,   620
And þoru our Lordes grace   þou lyuest, and þoru is sonde.
And in þe Abbei of Seyn Patric   monek ich was iwis,
And of is chirchei a warden,   þer is Purgatorie is.
A day þer com a mon to me;   ich ecste wat he were.
'Icham,' he sede, 'þin abbod;   of me naue þou fere.'   625
Non oþer þen Seyn Patric   myn abbod is," ich sede.
'No ich it am,' quaþ þis oþer;   'þe ne dar of me noȝt drede.
Tomorwe aris sone daies;   to þe se þou most wende.
A schip þou schalt fynde ȝare,   as our Lord þe wole sende.
Do þe uorþ in þulke schipe   in þe se wel wide   630
And it wole lede þe in þe stude   þer þou schalt abide.'
    "Sone amorwe ich aros   to don is holi bone;
Vorþ ich wende to þe se;   þe schip ich fond wel sone.
Mid me ich let þat schip iworþe;   wel euene uorþ it wende;   *
Þen seueþe day to þis ile   our swete Lord me sende.   635

has cruelly tortured us all night long, and most severely, because we did not bring this wicked creature with us. But we will avenge ourselves thoroughly – it shall fall upon his own head; for the next six days we will redouble his suffering on that account.'

The miserable soul so trembled then that it is painful to relate. The devils seized him fiercely and carried him off to Hell; but Saint Brendan forbade them, in our Lord's name, from inflicting any further humiliation on him during that night.

Saint Brendan and his monks set forth upon the sea, voyaged three more days due south, as our Lord directed them. The fourth day they sighted an island towering up due south. Saint Brendan, when he saw the island, sighed bitterly. He said:

'The hermit Paul is in the island that I see there; he has been there forty years without food.'

When they reached this island, they all went ashore. The hermit, who was very old, immediately came to meet them. The hair of his beard and head reached down to his feet, and concealed his body all round; no part of it was left bare. He had no other covering; his features were all hoary with age.

Saint Brendan gazed at him, and began to sigh bitterly.

'Alas', he said, 'I have been so long in monastic orders, and now I see a man in the form of an angel!'

'Be silent!' said the hermit. 'God favours you greatly, since he shows you more of his mysteries than anyone else. For a monk lives by the labour of his own hands, and you live by the grace of our Lord and through his dispensation. And I was, in fact, a monk in the Abbey of Saint Patrick and a keeper of his church where his Purgatory is. One day a man came to me; I asked him who he might be. "I am your abbot", he said; "have no fear of me." "No one other than Saint Patrick is my abbot", said I. "No, I am he", said the other; "you need have no fear of me. Tomorrow, arise early in the day; you must go to the seashore. You will find a boat ready prepared, which our Lord will send you. Set forth in that boat upon the wide sea, and it will convey you to the place where you shall dwell."

'Early next day I arose to do his saintly bidding; setting out for the seashore, I very quickly found the boat. I let the ship go forth with me; it set out immediately; the seventh day our dear Lord brought me to

Anon so ich was out of þe schip, þen wei aȝen it nom
As euene as it miȝte drawe, riȝt as it huder com.
Elynge, ich eode her al one and confort nadde non
So þat vp is hinder vet an hotur þer com gon;
Myd is vorþer vet he broȝte an furire and an ston   640
Vorte smyte me fur þerof, and of fisc good won.
Þis hotur wende anon awei; ich made me fur wel uaste,
And seþ me fisch a Godes name þat þre dawes ilaste.
So þat euer þe þridde day þis hotur to me drouȝ
And broȝte me mete, þat ichabbe þre dawes on inouȝ.   645
    "Water of þis harde ston, þoru our Lordes sonde,
Þer sprong eche Soneday, to drynke and wesche myn honde.
Þo ichadde þritti ȝer in þis lyue ibe,
Þis welle him gan verst to scewe, as þou miȝt her ise.
Bi þis welle ichabbe ilyued fourti ȝer nou and on.   650
And fifti ȝer ich was old þo ich gan huder gon,   *
So þat of an hondred ȝer and twenti þerto
Bi þis tyme icham old, our Lordes will to do;
And my deþ ich abide her wen God hyme me wole sende,
Wen God wole þat ich to him come and of þis world wende.   655
And nym wiþ þe of þis watur, þat þou hast neode to;
And wend uorþ uaste in þe se, uor þi wei nys noȝt ido,
Vor þou schalt ȝut in þe se fourti dawes fare,
And þanne þou schalt þin Estur holde, as þou hast ido ȝare.
And þenne þou schalt wende uorþ to þe Lond of Biheste;   660
And þer þou schalt fourti dawes bileue ate meste,
And to þin owe lond aȝen þou schalt wende so."
Þis godemen wiþ deol inouȝ partede þus atwo.
    Þis holi men hem wende uorþ in þe se wel uaste
Fourti dawes, euene souþ, þe wule Leynte ilaste.   665
To hor gode Procuratur an Ester Eue hi come;
Wiþ hem he made ioie inouȝ, as he dude er ilome.
He ladde hem to þis grete visch, þuder hi come an eue.
Þis Estur nyȝt vorte amorwe þer hi gonne bileue;
Þer hi songe hor matyns and hor masse also.   670
Þis fisch bigon to meouy him, þo þe masse was ido,
And bar þis monekes uorþ wiþ him, and swom uorþ wel uaste
In þe grete se wel grisliche – þis monekes were agaste.
A wonder þing it was to mete, hoso it hadde iseie:
A so gret best aboute wende, as al a contreie!   675

this island. As soon as I had left the ship, it set off again as directly as it could go, just as it had come here. Sad at heart, I came here all alone and had no consolation until an otter came running on his hind feet; between his forefeet he brought a steel and a flint-stone with which to strike fire for myself, and a good supply of fish. The otter soon departed; I very quickly made myself a fire and, in the name of God, cooked fish for myself which sufficed for three days. Subsequently, every third day the otter came to me and brought me food, so that I have enough for three days.[22]

'By our Lord's dispensation, every Sunday there sprang out of the solid rock water to drink and wash my hands in. This spring which you can see here first began to appear when I had been thirty years in this way of life. I have lived beside this spring now for forty-one years. And I was fifty years old when I came here, so that I am now, at this moment, a hundred and twenty years of age, obedient to our Lord's will; and I here await my death when God chooses to send it, when my God wills that I should come to him and depart from this world. And take with you some of this water, whatever you have need of; and set forth quickly upon the sea, since your journey is not finished, for you shall voyage upon the sea forty days more, and then you shall keep your Easter, as you have previously done. And then you shall set forth for the Promised Land; and there you shall remain at most forty days, and then you shall return to your own land.'
In this way these holy men separated with great grief.

These saintly men immediately set forth upon the sea, voyaged due south for forty days while Lent lasted. On the eve of Easter they reached their good Provider; he made great rejoicing with them, as he had often done before. He accompanied them to the great fish, where they arrived in the evening. The night of Easter until the following day there they remained; there they sang their matins and their mass also. When the mass was ended, the fish began to stir and bore the monks away with him, swimming away very swiftly in the open sea most frighteningly – the monks were terrified. For anyone who saw it, it was a wondrous thing to experience: so huge a creature, like a whole province, moving about! He conveyed all the monks to the Paradise of

To þe Foulen Parays   þis monekes he ladde echon
And sette hem vp þer al hol and sound,   and wende aȝen anon.
       Þo þis monekes þuder come,   wel ioiuol hi were.
Vorte after þe Trinyte   hi bileuede þere,
Vor hor Creatur þulke tyme   broȝte hem mete inouȝ,   *   680
As he hadde er ofte ido,   and to hor schip it drouȝ,
And wende uorþ myd hem   as our Lord him sende.
Riȝt euene toward þen est   fourti dawes hi wende.
Þo þis fourti dawes were ago,   hit gan to hauli vaste,
And wel derk myst þer com also   þat wel longe ilaste.   685
"Beþ glade," quaþ þis Procreatur,   "and makeþ gret feste,
Vor ichot we beþ nou ney   þe lond of biheste."
       Þo hi come out of þis derke myst   and myȝte aboute ise,
Vnder þe vairest lond hi were   þat miȝte an erþe be;
So cler and so liȝt it was   þat þer was ioie inouȝ.   690
Tren þer were, vol of frut,   wel þicke euerich bouȝ.
Þicke it was biset of tren,   and þe tren þicke bere,
Þe applen were alle ripe inouȝ,   riȝt as it heruest were.
Fourti dawes in þis lond   aboute hi gonne wende;
Hi ne miȝte fynde in non half   of þis lond non ende.   695
Hit was euermore day,   hi ne founde non nyȝt;
Hi ne wende fynde in no stude   so muche clerte ne liȝt.
Þe eir was euer in o stat,   nouþer to hot ne to cold –
Bote þe ioie þat hi founde   ne may neuer be itold.
       So þat hi come to a uair water;   hi nolde noȝt ouer wende,   700
Ac ouer hi miȝte þat lond ise,   vair wiþþouten ende:
Þo com þer gon a ȝongliche man,   swiþe vair and hende;
Vairor man ne miȝte be   as our Lord hem gan sende.
He wilcomede hem ech by nome,   and custe hem echon,
And honourede vaire Seyn Brendan,   and nom is hond anon.   705
"Lo," he sede "her is þat lond   þat ȝe habbeþ isoȝt wide,
And longe, uor our Lord wolde   þat ȝe longe scholde abide,
Vor ȝe scholde in þis grete se   is priuetes ise;
Chargeþ ȝoure schip wiþ þis frut,   vor ȝe ne mowe no leng her be.
Vor þou most to þin owe londe   aȝenward anon wende,   710
Vor þu schalt sone of þis world   – þi lif is ney þen ende.
Þis water þat ȝe her iseþ   deleþ þis lond atwo;
Þis half ȝou þencþ vair inouȝ,   and a ȝondhalf it is also.
A ȝondhalf ne mowe ȝe come noȝt,   uor it nys noȝt riȝt.
Þat frut is euer iliche ripe,   and þat lond iliche liȝt.   715

Birds and landed them there quite safe and sound, and immediately departed again.

The monks were very content when they arrived there. There they remained until after Trinity Sunday, for their Provider brought them plenty of food during that period, as he had often done previously, and carried it aboard their boat; and he sailed out with them wherever our Lord directed him. Forty days they voyaged straight and true towards the east. When the forty days were past, it began to hail furiously, and there came also a very dark mist which lasted a very long time.

'Be happy', said the Provider, 'and make great rejoicing, for I believe that we are now near the Promised Land.'

When they emerged from this dark mist and could see around them, they were in the fairest land that could be upon earth; it was so clear and bright that there was great rejoicing. The trees there were full of fruit, very thick on every branch. It was thickly planted with trees, and the trees bore heavily, the apples were all fully ripe, just as if it were autumn. They roamed about this land for forty days; nowhere could they find on any side a limit to this land. It was always light, they experienced no darkness; they never found in any place so much brightness and light. The climate was always the same, neither too hot nor too cold – but the delight that they experienced there can never be recounted.

In the end they came to a fine river; they could not cross over, but they could see the land on the opposite side, lovely beyond measure. Then there came walking a youthful man, very handsome and polite; no one could be more handsome than he whom God sent there. He greeted everyone by name, kissing each of them, and showed courteous respect to Saint Brendan and at once took his hand.

'See', he said, 'here is that land for which you have sought far and wide, and for a long time, since our Lord wishes that you should long remain, so that you should see his mysteries in this great ocean; load your ship with this fruit, since you may remain here no longer. For you must shortly return again to your own land, since you shall soon depart this world – your life is near the end. This river which you see here divides this world in two; this side seems to you very lovely, and it is so also on the further side. You may not enter the other half, for it is not fitting. The fruit there is always equally ripe, and the land equally

And wen our Lord ech maner men   to him haþ idrawe,
And ech maner men iknoweþ him   and beþ vnder is Lawe,
Þis lond he wole þenne scewe,   toward þis wordles ende,
Hem þat beþ next icore him,   ar hi henne wende."
　　　Seyn Brendan and is felawes   of þis frut nome vaste,   720
And of preciouse stones,   and into hor scipe caste;
And vaire and wel hor leue nome,   þo þis was al ido.
And wiþ wop and deol inouȝ,   partede þus atwo
And wende hamward in þe se,   as our Lord hem sende;
And wel sonere come hom   þen hi outward wende.   725
　　　Hor breþeren, þo hi come hom,   ioyuol were inouȝ.
Þis holi mon Seyn Brendan   sone to deþe drouȝ,
Vor neuereft after þulke tyme   of þe world he ne roȝte,
Bote as a man in anoþer world,   and as he were in þoȝte.
He deide in Irlonde sone   after þulke stounde.   730
Mony myracle me haþ   uor him seþþe ifounde.
An abbei þer was seþþe arered   as is bodi was ido.
Nou Gode ous bringe to þulke ioie   as is soule wende to.

bright. And when our Lord has drawn to himself all manner of men, and when men of all kinds know him and are under his Law, then, nearing the end of the world, he will reveal this land to those who are most dear to him, before they depart hence.'

Saint Brendan and his companions quickly took some of the fruit, and some of the precious stones, and placed them in their boat; and, when all this was done, they graciously and fittingly took their leave. And with much weeping and sorrow, they parted company and voyaged homeward on the sea, as our Lord directed them; they came home much more quickly than they had voyaged out.

When they arrived home, their brethren were very happy. The saintly man Saint Brendan shortly drew near to death, for he never after that time cared anything for the world, but was like a man in another world, and as if he were meditating. He died in Ireland shortly after that time. Many miracles have since been experienced because of him. An abbey was later built where his body was laid. Now God bring us to that state of bliss to which his soul has gone.

II: Caxton's *Golden Legend* Version

The legend of Brendan's voyage was firmly established in the English tradition by its inclusion in one of the most prestigious products of Caxton's Westminster press, the *Golden Legend*, continuously reprinted between 1484 and 1527 and revived in 1878 in a Holbein Society facsimile.

The *Golden Legend* is, like the *South English Legendary*, a compilation of saints' lives rooted in continental tradition but much varied in the process of transmission. The most influential exemplification of that tradition, Jacobus de Voragine's Latin *Legenda aurea* (1261-76), proved enormously popular, providing preachers and teachers with abbreviated lives of Biblical figures, apostles, martyrs, saints legendary and apocryphal, arranged in the order of the ecclesiastical calendar from Advent onwards. The early dates of many of the surviving manuscripts, which are exceptionally numerous, show that its dissemination all over Europe was rapid (Görlach 1974, p. 22).[1]

In the spirit of the age, copyists evidently felt free to vary the original structure, to make selections from it and to add lives of local saints familiar to their particular audience. The life of St Brendan was not part of the standard *Legenda* text, but a small number of manuscripts contain a section on him (Burgess and Strijbosch 2000, pp. 27-28). The redactors of various vernacular versions took the same liberty; the most popular, Jean de Vignay's *Légende Dorée* (*c*.1333), exists in more than one version, numerous manuscripts and early printed editions.[2] From it, in 1438, was derived an English version, conventionally known as the *Gilte Legende*, which survives in only a handful of texts, no two alike in the number and order of their items. The initial redactor seems to have made some use of the Latin

---

1. For an integral, if somewhat outdated, edition see *Legenda aurea Jacobi a Voragine*, ed. J.G. Graesse (Dresden, 1846; 3rd edn, Breslau: Koebner, 1890); for more recent studies, see S.L. Reames, *The Legenda aurea: A Reexamination of its Paradoxical History* (Madison: University of Wisconsin, 1985) and B. Fleith, *Studien zur Überlieferungsgeschichte der lateinischen Legenda aurea*, Subsidia Hagiographica 72 (Brussels: Société des Bollandistes, 1991).

2. For details see C. Knowles, 'Jean de Vignay, un traducteur du XIVe siècle', *Romania*, 75 (1954), 353-83.

Legenda, while a later hand added a number of lives of English saints, including Brendan.[3]

Unfortunately, lack of an edition of the *Gilte Legende* has inhibited judgement of its relationship to other legendaries. Caxton's prologue makes clear that he took the bulk of his material from de Vignay's *Légende Dorée*, drawing upon the *Legenda aurea* for five lives omitted by the French translator. Much of the material common to all the versions he might have taken without the labour of translation from the 1438 version, but his debt to it is limited to fifteen lives of English saints, suggesting that he only discovered the collection late in his work. The presumption must be that it was the source of his life of St Brendan. Three of the *Gilte Legende* manuscripts share a group of lives, additional to the basic content of the redaction, mostly lives of English saints whose precise origin is unknown but which have been identified as 'basically de-versified lives from the *South English Legendary*'.[4]

Editions and Translations Caxton's version of the Brendan legend was first printed in 1484, in his *Jacobus de Voragine, The Golden Legend*; the section entitled 'The Lyfe of Saynt Brandon' is found in ff. 394[v]-398[v]. This work was reprinted with varying foliation in 1498, 1503, 1510, 1512 and 1527. In 1520 the section devoted to St Brendan appeared in separate print under the title *Here Begynneth the Lyfe of Saynt Brandon* (London: Wynkyn de Worde). Wynkyn de Worde's edition was reproduced in 1844 by Thomas Wright in his *St Brandan: A Medieval Legend of the Sea*. Wright's text was reprinted by Denis O'Donoghue in his *Brendaniana: St Brendan the Voyager in Story and Legend* (pp. 380-93). In 1878 a facsimile edition of Caxton's *Golden Legend* was published by Frederick S. Ellis under the title *Jacobus de Voragine, The Golden Legend, Done Anew*. In 1892 Ellis published a modernized version under the same title. This modernized version was reprinted in 1913 by Martha Shackford and in 1970 by Morris Bishop.

Authorship and Date Caxton is the author of the *Golden Legend* not only – in a sense very acceptable to the Middle Ages – as compiler and translator, but also in a revolutionary initiative as its printer and

---

3. On the versions and texts of the *Gilte Legende* see Auvo Kurvinen, 'Caxton's *Golden Legend* and the Manuscripts of the *Gilte Legende*', *Neuphilologische Mitteilungen*, 60 (1959), 353-75 and Richard Hamer, *Three Lives from the Gilte Legende*, Middle English Texts 9 (Heidelberg: Carl Winter Universitätsverlag, 1978), pp. 26-33 [Nicholas, George, Bartholomew].
4. Hamer, p. 20; see also P. Butler, *Legenda Aurea, Légende Dorée, Golden Legend* (Baltimore: Murphy, 1899), p. 83.

publisher. The young William Caxton (1422?-91) was apprenticed to a London mercer whose guild controlled the Merchant Adventurers Company, which in the fifteenth century dominated trade with the Low Countries and often acted in diplomatic negotiations between the English crown and the regional ruler, the Duke of Burgundy. Its members imported the *de luxe* manuscripts, often richly illuminated, which were produced in Flanders, and later the books printed there. In 1469, when the new art of printing had not yet reached Flanders, Caxton had begun a translation of the *History of Troy*, later to be the first book published in English. In 1471, having participated in the work of the press newly established at Cologne, he resumed the translation, set up his own press at Bruges, and printed it in a volume dedicated to Margaret, sister of Edward IV and wife of Charles Duke of Burgundy. Returning to England in 1476, he established his press in the precincts of Westminster Abbey where, up to his death in 1492, he produced some one hundred editions, many compiled, translated and edited by himself: Boethius's *Consolation of Philosophy* in Chaucer's translation, Chaucer's own *Parliament of Fowls*, *Troilus and Criseyde* and *Canterbury Tales*, Malory's *Morte d'Arthur*, Higden's *Polychronicon*, two volumes of the *Chronicles of England*, books of manners, morals and popular science, and works of Gower and Lydgate.

Of all his publications, the *Golden Legend* is the longest, the only one on the largest paper size, some 600,000 words in double columns on 449 leaves, and lavishly illustrated with woodcuts. The enormous labour of translation took about fifteen months between July 1482 and 20 November 1483. The latter date appears on the first edition, and has been interpreted as that of its printing, but it is now generally accepted as recording completion of the translation, printing occupying the later part of 1484.[5]

Content, Structure and Source Caxton was characteristically a conscientious editor; where more than one source was available to him, he would conflate the wording of both, producing a stylistic elaboration in keeping with the aureate diction of the age. In addition, he would often interject comments based on his travels and personal experience. His treatment of the life of St Brendan in these respects cannot be clearly judged in ignorance of the immediate source from which he drew his material. Without being able to establish which manuscripts

5. On the dating, see G.D. Painter, *William Caxton* (London: Chatto and Windus, 1976), p. 143. A convenient biographical outline is supplied by N.F. Blake, *William Caxton and English Literary Culture* (London and Rio Grande, Oh.: Hambledon Press, 1991), pp. 1-18.

of the Latin, French and earlier English texts Caxton had available to him, there must be a possibility that he derived his material from one of the rare *Legenda aurea* manuscripts, all inedited, which contain a life of Brendan. But the probability that his source was one of the *Gilte Legende* additions identified as prose redactions of lives from the *South English Legendary*, by 1438 the most renowned and widely available of English legendaries, is strengthened by structural and other resemblances between his version and the *SEL* Brendan.

The sequence of episodes in Caxton's life of Brendan, the series of islands visited and re-visited, is that of the *SEL* version. All the more significant, therefore, is the absence of precisely those episodes whose absence in the *SEL* distinguishes it from its source in the *Navigatio*: III-IV, VII, XIII-XIV, XVII, XXII. Without identification of the particular version of the 1438 prose available to Caxton, the nature of his redaction cannot be fully judged. Analysis of those surviving prose texts which contain added lives of English saints shows that 'some twenty *SEL* legends were rewritten ("unrhymed") to supplement the original *Gilte Legende*, and the majority of these "additional legends". . . were then used by Caxton'.[6] Traces of the origin of his life of Brendan in an alliterative text are not obtrusive in Caxton's version, no doubt due to transmission through the 1438 prose redaction. Despite the fact that Caxton sometimes loosely paraphrases the earlier prose, their association is indicated by a large number of concrete details and turns of phrase common to both. Though some single lines and even complete couplets of the *SEL* survive in the *Gilte Legende*, they are not sufficient to connect it with a particular version of the earlier legendary.[7]

Patron and Audience The survival of his Westminster press over more than twenty years and its continuation under his apprentice, the Alsatian Wynkyn de Worde, when others became bankrupt, owed much to Caxton's tireless energy, but also to his good judgement in the choice of projects and patrons. He addressed individual volumes to royalty and nobility, but also to classes of reader, gentlemen and merchants, to whom particular works might be expected to appeal. The *Golden Legend* was addressed to Willam Earl of Arundel, at his

6. M. Görlach, *The South English Legendary, Gilte Legende and Golden Legend*, Braunschweiger Anglistische Arbeiten 3 (Braunschweig: Technische Universität Carolo-Wilhelmina zu Braunschweig, Institut für Anglistik und Amerikanistik, 1972), p. 103.
7. See Görlach, pp. 61-63. Some significant correspondences are cited in the Notes to this version.

request according to Caxton's prologue. His reward in this case was a bi-annual gift of game, a buck in summer and a doe in winter; but his real return on the volume lay in the possibility that the earl would 'take a reasonable quantity of them' to give as gifts. Caxton's profit lay not in his patrons' pockets but in the prestige their names could lend his publications in the eyes of lesser men.

The Author's Purpose The large format in which the *Golden Legend* was printed, comfortably readable only on a lectern, suggests that Caxton envisaged clerical institutions as potential purchasers. But in an age when clerics knew how to exploit all the techniques of rhetoric, literature, music and art for the propagation of the faith, the scope and variety of Caxton's narrative served exegesis without excluding entertainment attractive to laymen. Its success in both functions launched the *Golden Legend*, rapidly reprinted, and with it Brendan, upon the wider world of books.[8]

---

8. The text of Caxton's Life of Saint Brendan is here reproduced from the facsimile edition of the *Golden Legend* by F.S. Ellis (London: Holbein Society, 1878) with the addition of some glosses for unfamiliar terms, the substitution of modern punctuation, capitalization, sentence division and paragraphing to facilitate reading, and the following textual modifications: expansion of the ampersand as *and*, distinction between *u* and *v*, *i* and *j*, and the use of modern word division in such forms as *where as*, *a londe*, *a ferde*, *to gyder*, etc.

Saynt Brandon the holy man was a monke and borne in Yrlonde. And there he was abbotte of an hows wherein were a thousand monkes; and there he had a ful strayte (*strict*) and holy lyf in grete penaunce and abstynence, and he governed his monkes ful vertuously. And thenne, within shorte tyme after, there came to hym an holy abbot that hyght (*was called*) Beryne (*Barrind*) to vysyte hym, and eche of them was joyeful of other. And thenne Saynt Brandon beganne to telle to th'abbot Beryn of many wonders that he had seen in dyvers londes. And whan Beryn herde that of Saint Brandon he began to syghe and sore wepte; and Saint Brandon comforted hym the beste wyse he coude, sayeng:

'Ye come hyther for to be joyeful with me, and therfore for Goddes love leve your mornynge and telle me what mervaylles ye have seen in the grete see Ocean that compasseth al the world aboute, and alle other waters comen out of hym whyche renneth in al the partyes of th'erthe.'[1]

And thenne Beryn beganne to telle to Saynt Brandon and to his monkes the mervaylles that he had seen, ful sore wepyng, and said:

'I have a sone,[2] his name is Meruoke (*Mernoc*) and he was a monke of grete fame (*repute*), whiche had grete desyre to seke aboute by shyppe in dyvers contrees to fynde a solytarye place wherin he myght dwelle secretelye out of the besynesse of the world, for to serve God quyetly with more devocion. And I counceylled hym to sayle into an ylonde ferre (*far*) in the see besydes the monteyn of stones whiche is ful wel knowen, and thenne he made hym redy and saylled thyder wyth his monkes. And whan he came thyder he lyked that place ful wel, where he and his monkes servyd our Lord ful devoutelye.'

And thenne Beryn sawe in a vysyon that this monke Meruok was saylled right ferre eestward in the see more than thre dayes sayllyng.[3] And sodeynlye to his semyng (*it seemed to him*) there cam a derke cloude and overcoverd them, that a grete parte of the day they sawe no lyght; and, as our Lord wolde, the cloude passed awey and they sawe a ful fayre ylonde and thyderward they drewe. In that ylonde was joye and myrthe ynough, and the erthe of that ylonde shyned as bryghte as the sonne. And there were the fayrest trees and herbes that ever ony man sawe, and there were many precyous stones shynyng bryght, and every herbe there was ful of floures and every tree ful of fruyte, soo that it was a gloryous syght and an hevenly joye t'abyde there.

And thenne there came to them a fayre yonge man and ful curtoysly he welcomed them al and called every monke by his name, and said that they were moche bounde to preyse the name of our Lord Jhesu, that wold of his grace shewe to them that gloryous place where is ever day and never nyght; and this place is called Paradyse Terrestre.[4] But by this ylonde is another ylonde wherin no man may come. And this yonge man said to theym:

'Ye have ben here halfe a yere wythoute mete, drynke, or slepe.' And they supposed that they had not ben there the space of halfe an houre, so mery and joyeful they were there. And the yonge man tolde them that this is the place that Adam and Eve dwelte in fyrst, and ever shold have dwellyd here, yf that they had not broken the commaundemente of God. And thenne the yonge man broughte them to theyr shyppe ageyn and sayd they myght no lenger abyde there; and whan they were al shypped, sodeynlye this yonge man vanysshed aweye out of theyr syght.

And thenne wythin shorte tyme after, by the purveaunce of our Lord Jhesu, they came to th'abbey where Saynt Brandon dwellyd. And thenne he with his brethern receyved them godely and demaunded them where they had ben so longe, and they said:

'We have ben in the Londe of Byheest (*promise*, i.e. *the Promised Land*) tofore the yates (*gates*) of Paradys, whereas is ever day and never nyght.'

And they sayden al that the place is ful delectable; for yet al theyr clothes smellyd of that swete and joyeful place.

And thenne Saynt Brandon purposed (*planned*) sone after for to seke that place by Goddes helpe; and anone beganne to pourveye (*make provision*) for a good shyppe and a stronge and vytaylled (*provisioned*) it for seven yere. And thenne he toke his leve of alle his brethern and took twelve monkes with hym;[5] but or (*before*) they entred into the shyp they fastyd fourty dayes and lyved devoutelye, and eche of them receyved the sacramente. And whan Saynt Brandon wyth his twelve monkes were entred into the shyppe, there came other two (*two more*) of his monkes and prayed hym that they myght sayle with hym; and thenne he sayd:

'Ye may sayle with me but one of you shalle goo to Helle or ye come ageyn.'
But not for that (*nevertheless*) they wold goo wyth hym.

And thenne Saynt Brandon bad the shypmen to wynde up the saylle and forthe they saylled in Goddes name, so that on the morowe they were out of syght of ony londe. And fourty dayes and fourty nyghtes after they saylled platte (*due*) eest; and thenne they saw an ylelonde ferre fro them and they saylled thyderward as faste as they coude. And they sawe a grete rocke of stone appere above alle the water, and thre dayes they saylled aboute it or they coude get into the place; but at the laste by the pourveaunce of God (*divine providence*) they fonde a lytel haven and there wente alonde everychone.

And thenne sodeynlye came a fayre hounde and fyl doun at the feet of Saynt Brandon and made hym good chere in his manere. And thenne he bad his brethern be of good chere:
'For our Lord hath sente to us his messager to lede us into somme good place.'
And the hounde broughte hem into a fayr halle where they fonde the tables spredde, redy sette ful of good mete and drynke. And thenne Saynt Brandon sayd graces, and thenne he and his brethern satte doun and ete and dranke of suche as they fonde; and there were beddes redy for them wherin they toke their reste after theyr longe laboure.

And on the morne they retorned ageyn to theyr shyppe, and saylled a longe tyme in the see after or they coude fynde ony londe, tyl atte laste by the purveaunce of God they sawe ferre fro them a ful fayre ylone ful of grene pasture, wherin were the whytest and grettest sheep that ever they sawe; for every shepe was as grete as an oxe. And sone after cam to them a goodly olde man, whiche welcomed them and maad them good chere, and sayd:
'This is the Ylonde of Sheep, and here is never colde weder, but ever sommer, and that causeth the sheep to be so grete and whyte; they ete of the beste grasse and herbys that is owhere (*anywhere*).'
And thenne this olde man toke his leve of them, and bad them saylle forthe ryght (*due*) eest, and wythin shorte tyme, by Goddes

grace, they shold come into a place lyke Paradys wherin they shold kepe theyr Estertyde.

And thenne they saylled forthe, and cam sone after to that londe; but by cause of lytel depthe in somme place, and in somme place were grete rockes, . . .[6] But at the laste they wente (*landed*) upon an ylonde wenyng (*thinking*) to them (*themselves*) they had ben saufe, and maad theron a fyre for to dresse (*prepare*) theyr dyner, but Saynt Brandon abode stylle in the shyppe. And whan the fyre was ryght hote and the mete nyghe soden (*cooked*), thenne this ylonde began to moeve, wherof the monkes were aferde, and fled anone to shyppe and lefte the fyre and mete behynde them, and mervaylled sore (*greatly*) of the moevyng. And Saynt Brandon comforted them and sayd that it was a grete fysshe named Jasconye, which laboureth nyght and day to put his tayle in hys mowthe, but for gretenes he may not.

Ane thenne anone (*immediately*) they saylled weste thre dayes and thre nyghtes or they saw ony londe, wherfore they were ryght hevy (*sad*). But sone after, as God wolde, they sawe a fayre ylonde ful of floures, herbes and trees, wherof they thanked God of his good grace. And anone they went on londe; and whan they had goon longe in thys they fonde a ful fayre welle, and therby stood a fayre tree ful of bowes, and on every boughe satte a fayr bryde (*bird*), and they satte so thycke on the tree, that unnethe (*scarcely*) ony leefe of the tree myght be seen. The nombre of them was soo grete and they sange so merely that it was an hevenly noyse to here; wherfore Saynt Brandon knelyd doun on his knees and wepte for joye and made his prayers devoutelye to our Lord God to knowe what thyse byrdes mente (*signified*).

And thenne anone one of the byrdes fledde fro the tree to Saynt Brandon, and he with flykeryng (*fluttering*) of his wynges made a ful mery noyse lyke a fydle, that hym semed he herde never so joyeful a melodye.[7] And thenne Saynt Brandon commaunded the byrde to telle hym the cause why they satte so thycke on the tree and sange so meryly. And thenne the byrde said:
    'Somtyme (*formerly*) we were aungellys in Heven but whan our mayster Lucyfer fyl doun into Helle for (*because of*) his hygh pryde and we fyl with hym for our offencys (*sins*), somme hygher and

somme lower after (*according to*) the qualyte (*nature*) of the trespaas. And by cause our trespaas is but lytel therfore our Lord hath sette us here out of al payne, in ful grete joye and myrthe after his plesyng, here to serve hym on thys tree in the beste manere we can. The Sonday is a day of reste fro al worldly ocupacyon, and therfore that day alle we be made as whyte as ony snowe for to preyse our Lord in the beste wyse we may.'

And thenne thys byrde sayd to Saynt Brandon, that
   'It is twelve monethes passed that ye departed fro your abbey, and in the vii yere herafter ye shal see the place that ye desyre to come to; and al this seven yere ye shal kepe your Ester here wyth us every yere, and in the ende of the seventh yere ye shal come into the Londe of Byheste.'
And thys was on Ester Day that the byrde sayd thyse wordes to Saynt Brandon; and thenne this fowle flewe ageyn to his felawes that satte on the tree, and thenne al the byrdes beganne to synge evensonge so meryly that it was an havenly noyse to here. And after sowper Saynt Brandon and hys felawes wente to bedde and slepte wel; and on the morne they aroos bytymes and thenne those byrdes beganne matyns, pryme and houres, and al suche servyce as Cristen men use to synge. And Saynt Brandon with his felawes abode there viii wekes tyl Trynyte Sonday was paste, and they sayled ageyn to the Ylonde of Sheep and there they vytaylled them wel, and sythe (*then*) toke theyr leve of that olde man and retorned ageyn to shyppe.

And thenne the byrde of the tree came ageyn to Saynt Brandon and sayd:
   'I am come to telle you that ye shal sayle fro hens into an ylonde wherein is an abbey of xxiiii monkes,[8] whiche is fro thys place many a myle, and there ye shal holde your Crystemasse, and your Ester wyth us, lyke as I tolde you.'
And thenne this byrde flewe to his felawes ageyn.

And thenne Saynt Brandon and his felowes saylled forth in the occyan. And sone after fyl a grete tempeste on them, in which they were gretely troubelyd longe tyme and sore forlaboured (*exhausted*). And after that they fonde by the purveaunce of God an ylonde whyche was ferre fro theym; and thenne they ful mekely (*humbly*) prayed our Lord to sende them thyder in sauftee, but it was fourty dayes after or they came thyder, wherfore alle the monkes were so wery of that trouble that they sette lytel prys by theyr lyves, and cryed contynuelly to our Lord to have mercy on them and brynge them to that ylonde in saufte. And by the purveaunce of God they came at the laste into a lytel haven, but it was soo strayte (*narrow*) that unnethes (*scarcely*) the shyp myghte come in; and after they came to an ancre, and anone the monkes wente to londe.

And whan they had longe walkyd aboute, at the laste they fonde two fayre wellys (*springs*); that (*the*) one was fayr and clere water and that other was somwhat trowbly (*turbid*) and thycke (*cloudy*). And thenne they thanked our Lord ful humbly that had broughte hem thyder in saufete; and they wold fayne have dronken of that water, but Saynt Brandon charged them they shold not take wythoute lycence.

'For yf we absteyne us a whyle our Lord wyl pourveye for us in the beste wyse.'

And anone after came to them a fayr olde man wyth hoor (*grey*) here and welcomed them ful mekelye (*humbly*) and kyssed Saynt Brandon, and ledde them by many a fayre welle tyl they came to a fayre abbey where they were receyvyd wyth grete honour and solempne processyon wyth xxiiii monkes al in ryall copes of clothe of golde and a ryal crosse was before them. And thenne the abbot welcomed Saynt Brandon and hys felawshyp and kyssed them ful mekely, and toke Saynt Brandon by the honde and ledde hym with his monkes into a fayre halle and set them doun arewe (*in order*) upon the benche. And the abbotte of the place wysshe alle theyr feet wyth fayre water of the welle that they sawe before,[9] and after ladde them into the fraytour (*refectory*) and there sette them emonge his covente (*community*).

And anone there came one by the purveaunce of God which servyd them wel of mete and drynke; for every monke had sette before hym a fayre whyt loof and whyte rootys and herbys whyche were ryght delycyous, but they wyst not what rotes they were. And they dranke of the water of the fayr clere welle that they sawe before whan they came fyrst alonde, which Saynt Brandon forbadde them.

And thenne th'abbot came and chered (*welcomed*) Saynt Brandon
and hys monkes and prayed theym ete and drynke for charyte.

'For every day our Lord sendeth a goodelye olde man that
coveryth thys table and setteth our mete and drynke tofore us; but
we knowe not how it cometh, ne we ordeyne (*order*) never no mete
ne drynke for us and yet we have been lxxx yere here and ever our
Lord – worshypped mote he be – fedeth us. We ben xxiiii monkes
in nombre and every feryal (*ordinary*) day of the weke he sendeth to
us xii loves, and every Sonday and festeful day xxiiii loves, and the
brede that we leve at dyner we ete at sowper; and now at your
comyng our Lord hath sente to us xlviii loves for to make you and
us mery togyder as brethern. And alweye twelve of us goo to dyner
whyles other twelve kepe the quere, and thus have we don this lxxx
yere; for so longe have we dwellyd here in thys abbey. And we came
hyther out of th'abbey of Saint Patrikes in Yrelonde, and thus as ye
see our Lord hath pourveyed for us, but none of us knoweth how it
cometh but God allone, to whome be gyven honour and lawde
(*praise*) world withouten ende. And here in thys londe is ever fayre
weder and non of us hath ben seek sythe we came hyther. And
whan we goo to masse or to ony other servyce of our Lord in the
chirche, anone (*immediately*) seven tapres of waxe been sette in the
quere and ben lyght at every houre of servyce, and never waste ne
mynysshe (*lessen*) as longe as we have been here, which is lxxx yere.'

And thenne Saynt Brandon went to the chirche wyth the abbotte of
the place, and there they sayd evensonge togyder ful devoutely.
And thenne Saynt Brandon loked upwarde towarde the crucyfyxe,
and sawe our Lord hangyng on the crosse which was made of fyn
crystalle and curyously wroughte. And in the quere were xxiiii
seetys for xxiiii monkes and the seven tapres brennyng; and
th'abbottes sete was made in the myddes of the quere. And thenne
Saynt Brandon demaunded of the abbotte how longe they had
kepte that scilence that none of them spake to other, and he sayd:

'Thys xxiiii yere we spake never one to another.'
And thenne Saynt Brandon wepte for joye of their holy
conversacion.

And thenne Saynt Brandon desyred of the abbotte that he and his
monkes myght dwelle there stylle with hym. To whome th'abbot
sayd:

'Syr, that may ye not do in no wyse, for our Lord hath shewed to you in what maner ye shal be guyded tyl the vii yere be fulfylled; and after that terme thou shalt with thy monkes retorne into Yrlonde in saufte, but one of the ii monkes that cam last to you shal dwel in the Ylonde of Ankers (*hermits*), and that other shal goo quyck (*alive*) to Helle.'

And as Saynt Brandon knelyd in the chirche, he sawe a brythte shynyng aungel come in at the wyndowe and lyghted alle the lyghtes in the chyrche, and thenne he flwe our ageyn at the wyndowe unto Heven.[10] And thenne Saynt Brandon mervaylled gretely how the lyght brennyd so fayr and wasted not. And thenne the abbotte sayd that it is wryton that Moyses saw a busshe al on a fyre and yet it brennyd not,

'And therfore mervaylle not herof, for the myghte of our Lord is now as grete as it ever was.'

And whan Saynt Brandon had dwellyd there fro Crystemasse Even tyl the Twelfthe Day was passed, thenne he toke hys leve of the abbot and covente, and retorned wyth hys monkes to hys shyppe, and saylled fro thens wyth his monkes toward the abbaye of Saynt Illaryes;[11] but they had grete tempestys in the see fro that tyme tyl Palme Sonday. And thenne they came to the Ylonde of Sheep, and there were receyved of the olde man, whyche broughte them to a fayre halle and servyd them. And on Sherthursday (*Maundy Thursday*) after souper he wesshe theyr feet and kyssed them, lyke as our Lord dyd to hys dyscyples, and there abode tyl Satyrday, Ester Even. And thenne they departed and saylled to the place where the grete fysshe laye; and anone they sawe their cawdron upon the fysshes backe which they had lefte there twelve moneth tofore. And there they kepte the servyce of the Resurrexyon on the fysshes backe; and after they saylled that same day by the mornyng to the ylonde whereas the tree of byrdes was. And thenne the sayd byrde welcomed Saynt Brandon and alle his felawshyp, and wente ageyn to the tree and sange ful meryly.

And there he and hys monkes dwellyd fro Ester tyl Trynyte Sonday as they dyd the yere before, in full grete joye and myrthe; and dayly they herde the mery servyce of the byrdes syttyng on the tree. And thenne the byrde tolde to Saynt Brandon that he shold retorne ageyn at Crystemasse to the abbay of monkes, and at Ester thyder ageyn, and the other dele (*part*) of the yere, labour in the occean in ful grete perylles, and fro yere to yere tyl the seven yere be accomplysshed.

'And thenne shal ye come to the joyeful place of Paradys and dwelle there xl dayes in ful grete joye and myrthe; and after ye shal retorne home into your owne abbey in saufete, and there ende your lyf, and come to the blysse of Heven, to whiche our Lord boughte (*redeemed*) you wyth his precyous blood.'
And thenne the aungel of our Lord ordeyned alle thynge that was nedeful to Saynt Brandon and to hys monkes in vytaylles and al other thynges necessarye. And thenne they thankyd our Lorde of his grete goodnes that he had shewed to them ofte in their grete nede, and thenne saylled forth into the grete see Occyan, abydyng the mercy of our Lord in grete trouble and tempestys.

And sone after cam to them an horryble fysshe whyche folowed the shyppe longe tyme, castyng soo moche water out of hys mowthe into the shyppe that they supposed (*feared*) to have ben drowned; wherfore they devoutely prayed God to delyver them of that grete perylle. And anone after came another fysshe gretter thenne he out of the west see, and faughte wyth hym, and atte laste clave (*split*) hym into thre pyeces, and thenne retorned ageyn. And thenne they thanked mekelye (*humbly*) our Lord of theyr delyveraunce fro this grete perylle; but they were in grete heuynesse by cause their vytaylles (*provisions*) were nyghe spente. But by the ordenaunce of our Lord there came a byrde and broughte to them a grete braunche of a vygne ful of red grapes by whyche they lyved fourtene dayes. And thenne they came to a lytel ylonde, wherin were many vygnes ful of grapes; and they there londed and thanked God, gadred as many grapes as they lyved by xl dayes after, alwey sayllyng in the see in many storme and tempeste.

And as they thus sayled, sodeynly cam fleyng toward them a grete grype (*griffin*), which assayled them and was lyke to have destroyed them. Wherfore they devoutely prayed for helpe and ayde of our Lord Jhesu Cryste. And thenne the byrde of the tree of the ylelonde where they had holden theyr Ester tofore came to the grype and smote out bothe his eyen, and after slewe hym. Wherof they thanked our Lord, and thenne sayled forth contynuelly tyl

Saynt Peter's Day; and thenn songen they solempnely their servyce in t'honour of the feste. And in that place the water was so clere that they myght see al the fysshes that were aboute them, wherof they were ful sone aghast. And the monkes counceylled Saynt Brandon to synge noo more, for al the fysshes laye thenne as they had slepte. And thenne Saynt Brandon sayd:

'Drede ye not, for ye have kepte by two Esters the Feste of the Resurrexyon upon the grete fysshes backe, and therfore drede ye not of thyse lytel fysshes.'

And thenne Saynt Brandon made hym redy and wente to masse and had his monkes to synge the beste wyse they coude. And thenne anone al the fysshes awoke and came aboute the shyppe so thycke that unnethes (*scarcely*) they myght see the water for the fysshes; and whan the masse was done al the fysshes departed so as they were nomore seen. And seven dayes they saylled alweye in that clere water.

And thenne there came a south wynde and droof the shyppe northward, whereas (*so that*) they sawe an ylonde ful derke and ful of stynche and smoke And there they herde grete blowyng and blastyng of belowes; but they myght see noo thynge, but herde grete thonderyng, wherof they were sore aferde and blessyd them (*crossed themselves*) ofte. And sone after there came one stertyng (*rushing*) out al brennyng in fyre and stared ful ghastlye on them with grete staryng eyen, of whom the monkes were aghaste; and at his departyng fro them he made the horryblest crye that myght be herde. And sone ther came a gret nombre of fendes (*demons*) and assayled them with hokes and brennyng yron mallys (*hammers*), whiche rannen on the water, folowyng their shyppe faste in suche wyse that it seemed al the see to be on a fyre. But by the plesure of our Lord they had no power to hurte ne greve (*injure*) them ne theyr shyppe; wherfore the fendes began to rore and crye, and threwe theyr hookes and malles at them. And they thenne were sore aferde and prayed to God for comforte and helpe, for they sawe the fendes al aboute the shyppe, and them semed thenne al the ylonde and the see to be on a fyre. And with a sorowful crye al tho fendes departed fro them and retorned to the place that they came fro. And thenne Saynt Brandon tolde to them that this was a parte of Helle, and therfore he charged them to be stedfaste in the feythe, for they shold yet see many a dredeful place or they came home ageyn.

And thenne came the south wynde and droof theym ferther into the northe, where they sawe an hylle al of fyre and a foule smoke and stynche comyng fro thens; and the fyre stood on eche syde of the hylle lyke a walle al brennyng. And thenne one of his monkes began to crye and wepe ful sore, and sayd that his ende was comen, and that he myght abyde no lenger in the shyppe, and anone he lepte out of the shyppe into the see. And thenne he cryed and rored ful pyteously, cursyng the tyme that he was borne and also fader and moder that bygate hym, by cause they saw no better to his correccion in his yonge age:

'For now I must goo to perpetuel peyne.'

And thenne the sayeng of Saynt Brandon was verefyed that he sayd to hym whan he entryd. Therfore it is good a man to do penaunce and forsake synne, for the houre of dethe is incerteyn.

And thenne anone the wynde torned into the northe and droof the shyppe into the southe, whiche saylled seven dayes contynuelly. And they came to a grete rocke stondyng in the see, and theron sat a naked man in ful grete myserye and payne, for the wawes of the see had so beten hys body that alle the flesshe was gone of, and noo thynge lefte but synewes and bare bonys. And whan the wawes were goon, there was a canvas that hynge ouer hys heed whyche bete hys body ful sore wyth the blowyng of the wynde; and also there were two oxe tonges,[12] and a grete stone that he satte on, whyche dyd hym ful grete ease. And thenne Saynt Brandon chargyd hym to telle hym what he was, and he sayd:

'My name is Judas that solde our Lord Jhesu Cryst for xxx pens, whiche sytteth here thus wretchedlye; how be it I am worthy to be in the grettest payne that is, but our Lord is so mercyful, that he hath rewarded me better thenne I have deserved, for of ryght my place is in the brennyng Hell. But I am here but certeyn tymes of the yere, that is, fro Crytemasse to Twelfth Day, and fro Ester tyl Whytsontyde be paste, and every festeful day of our Lady, and every Satyrday none tyl Sonday that evensonge be doon. But all other tymes I lye stylle in Helle in ful brennyng fyre, with Pylate, Herode, and Cayphas; therfore acursed be the tyme that ever I knewe hem.'

And thenne Judas prayed Saynt Brandon to abyde stylle there al
that nyght, and that he wold kepe hym there stylle, that the fendes
shold not fetche hym to Helle. And he said:

'With Goddes helpe thou shalte abyde here alle this nyght.'

And thenne he asked Judas what cloth that was that henge over his
heed, and he sayd it was a clothe that he gave to a lepre, whiche
was boughte wyth the money that he stale fro our Lord, 'Whan I
bare his purs, wherfore it dothe to me ful grete peyne now, in
betyng my face wyth the blowyng of the wynde. And these two oxe
tonges that hange here above me, I gafe them somtyme to two
prestys to praye for me; them I boughte wyth myn owne money,
and therfore they ease me by cause the fisshes of the see gnawe on
them and spare me.[13] And this stone that I sytte on laye somtyme
in a desolate place where it eased no man; and I toke it thens and
leyed it in a fowle waye (*muddy path*) where it dyd moche ease to
them that wente by that waye, and therfore it easeth me now, for
every good dede shal be rewarded and every evyl dede shal be
punysshed.'

And the Sonday, ageynst even (*towards evening*), ther came a grete
multytude of fendes blastyng and roryng and bad Saynt Brandon
goo thens that they myght have theyr servaunte Judas:

'For we dare not come in the presence of our mayster but yf we
brynge hym to Helle with us.'

And thenne sayd Saynt Brandon:

'I lete (*prevent*) not you to do your mayster's commaundemente;
but by the power of our Lord Jhesu I charge you to leve hym thys
nyght tyl to mororowe.'

'How darest thou helpe hym that so solde his mayster for thyrty
pens to the Jewes, and caused hym also to deye the moste shameful
dethe upon the crosse?'

And thenne Saynt Brandon charged the fendes by Hys Passyon that
they shold not noye (*torment*) hym that nyght. And thenne the
fendes wente theyr weye roryng and cryend towarde Helle, to their
mayster the Grete Devyll. And thenne Judas thanked Saynt
Brandon soo ruthefully that it was pyte to see. And on the morne
the fendes came wyth an horryble noyse, sayeng that they had that
nyght suffred grete payn by cause they broughte not Judas, and
sayden that he shold suffre double payn the vi dayes folowyng, and

they toke thenne Judas tremblyng for fere with them to payne (*torment*, i.e. *Hell*).

And after Saynt Brandon saylled southward thre dayes and thre nyghtes, and on the Fryday they sawe an ylelond. And thenne Saynt Brandon began to syghe and sayd:

'I see the ylonde wherin Saynt Poule th'Ermyte dwellyth, and hath dwellyd there xl yere wythout mete and drynke ordeyned (*provided*) by mannes honde.'

And whan they came to the londe, Saint Poule came and welcomed them humbly. He was olde and forgrowen (*overgrown (with hair)*), so that no man myght see his body; of whome Saynt Brandon said wepynge:

'Now I see a man that lyveth more lyke an aungel thenne a man; wherfore we wretches may be ashamed that we lyve not better.'

Thenne Saynt Poule sayd to Saynt Brandon:

'Thou arte better thenne I, for our Lord hath shewed to the moo of his prevytes (*secrets*) thenne he hath doon to me, wherfore thou oughtest to be more praysed than I.'

To whom Saynt Brandon sayd:

'We ben monkes and must labour for our mete, but God hath provyded for the suche mete as thou holdest the (*consider yourself*) plesed, wherfore thou arte moche better than I.'

To whome Saynt Poule sayd:

'Somtyme I was a monke of Saynt Patrykes abbey in Yrelonde, and was wardeyn of the place whereas men entre into Saynt Patrykes Purgatorye. And on a day there came one to me and I askyd hym what he was, and he sayd: "I am your abbot Patryke, and charge the that thou departe from hens tomorne erly to the see syde; and there thou shalt fynde a shyppe into whiche thou muste entre, whiche God hath ordeyned for the, whos wylle thou must accomplysshe." And so the nexte day I aroos and wente forthe and fonde the shyppe, in whiche I entred, and by the purveaunce of God was I brought into this ylonde the seventh day after. And thenne I lefte the shyppe and wente to londe and there I walked up and doun a good whyle. And thenne by the purveaunce of God there came an otter gooyng (*walking*) on his hyndre feet and brought me a flynte stone and an yron to smyte fyre wyth in his two fore clawes of his feet, and also he had aboute his necke grete plente of

fysshe, whiche he caste doun before me and wente his waye.[14] And
I smote fyre and made a fyre of styckes and dyd sethe (*cook*) the
fysshe, by whyche I lyved thre dayes. And thenne the ottyr came
ageyn and brought to me fisshe for other iii (*three more*) dayes; and
thus he hath done this li yere thorugh the grace of God. And there
was a grete stone, out of whiche our Lord made to sprynge fayr
water, clere and swete, wherof I drynke dayly; and thus have I lyved
one and fyfty yere. And I was fourty yere olde whan I came hyther,
and am now an hondred and xi yere olde and abyde tyl it please our
Lord to sende for me; and yf it plesyd hym I wold fayn be
dyschargyd of thys wretched lyf.'

And thenne he bad Saynt Brandon to take of the water of the welle
and to carye into hys shyppe:
    'For it is tyme that thou departe, for thou hast a grete journeye
to doo. For thou shalt sayle to an ylonde whiche is fourty dayes
sayllyng hens, where thou shalt holde thyn Ester lyke as thou hast
doon tofore, whereas the tree of byrdes is. And fro thens thou
shalte sayle into the Londe of Byheest and shalte abyde there
fourty dayes, and after retorne home into thy contre in saufete.'
And thenne thyse holy men toke leve eche of other, and they
wepte bothe ful sore and kyssed eche other.

And thenne Saynt Brandon entryd into his shyppe and sayled xl
dayes evyn southe in ful grete tempeste. And on Ester Even cam to
theyr procuratour, whiche maad to them good chere as he had
before tyme. And from thens they came to the grete fysshe wheron
they sayd matyns and masse on Ester Day. And whan the masse was
doon the fysshe began to meve and swamme forth faste into the
see, wherof the monkes were sore agaste whiche stode upon hym,
for it was a grete mervayl to see suche a fysshe as grete as alle a
contre for to swymme so faste in the water; but by the wylle of our
Lord this fysshe sette al the monkes alonde in the Paradys of
Byrdes all hole and sounde, and thenne retornyd to the place he
came fro. And thenne Saynt Brandon and his monkes thankyd our
Lord of theyr delyveraunce of the grete fysshe, and kepte theyr
Estertyde tyl Trynyte Sonday lyke as they had doon before tyme;
and after this they took theyr shyppe and saylled eest xl dayes.

And at the fourty dayes ende it began to hayle ryght faste, and therwyth came a derke myste whiche lasted longe after, whyche feryd Saynt Brandon and hys monkes and prayed to our Lord to kepe and helpe them. And thenne anone came theyr procuratour and bad them to be of good chere for they were come into the Londe of Byheest. And sone after that myste passed aweye, and anone they sawe the fayrest contre eestward that ony man myght see, and was so clere and bright that it was an hevenly syght to beholde, and al the trees were charged wyth rype fruyte and herbes ful of floures. In whyche londe they walked fourty dayes, but they coude see none ende of that londe. And there was alweye day and never nyghte, and the londe attemperate, ne to hote ne to colde. And at the laste they came to a fayr ryver, but they durste not goo over, and there came to them a fayre yonge man and welcomed them curtoysly and called eche of them by his name, and dyd grete reverence to Saynt Brandon and sayd to them:

'Be ye now joyeful for thys is the londe that ye have soughte; but our Lord wyl that ye departe hens hastelye and he wyl shewe to you more of hys secretes whan ye come ageyn into the see, and our Lord wyl that you lade your shyppe wyth the fruyte of thys londe and hye you hens, for ye may no lenger abyde here. But thou shalte sayle ageyn into thyn owne contree, and sone after thou comest home thou shalt deye. And thys water that thou seest here departeth the world a sondre, for on that other syde of thys water may no man come that is in thys lyf. And the fruyte that ye see here is alle waye thus rype every tyme of the yere; and alwey it is here lyght as ye now see, and he that kepeth our Lordes hestys at al tymes, shal see thys londe or he passe out of thys world.'

And thenne Saynt Brandon and his monkes toke of that fruyte as moche as they wolde, and also toke with them grete plente of precyous stones, and thenne toke theyr leve and wente to shyppe wepyng sore by cause they myght no lenger abyde there. And thenne they toke theyr shyppe and came home into Yrelonde in saufete, whome theyr brethern receyved wyth grete joye gyvyng thankynges to our Lord whiche had kepte them al that seven yere fro many a peryl and brought them home in saufete, to whome be yeven honour and glorye world without ende, amen. And sone after this holy man Saynt Brandon wexe (*grew*) feble and seek and had but lytel joye of thys world, but ever after, his joye and mynde was in the joyes of Heven. And in shorte tyme after, he beyng ful of vertues departed out of thys lyf to everlastyng lyf, and was worshypfully buryed in a fayr abbey whiche he hymself founded, where our Lord shewyth (*manifests*) for thys holy saynt many fayr myracles. Wherfore lete us devoutely praye to thys holy saynt that he praye for us to our Lord that he have mercy on us, to whome be gyven lawde (*praise*), honour and empyre (*power*), world withouten ende, amen.

NOTES

The translation of the Latin *Navigatio* by John J. O'Meara is not accompanied by notes.

The Anglo-Norman Version

All textual references are to the edition by I. Short and B. Merrilees (Manchester: Manchester University Press, 1979).

1. In l. 11 ('En letre mis e en romanz'), translated as 'put into writing in the vulgar tongue', the term *letre*, interpreted here as 'writing', could mean 'Latin'. If so, the author would seem to be indicating that he composed two versions of his tale, one in Latin (*letre*), and the other in the vernacular (*romanz*).

2. The real St Brendan was not of royal birth. The author of the *Navigatio* provides more details than Benedeit concerning his family and place of birth (see above, p. 26).

3. In the opening lines of the *Navigatio* the author alludes similarly to the figure of 'nearly three thousand monks' (p. 26), a figure which may well correspond to reality.

4. In the *Navigatio* (p. 26) Mernoc is said to be Barrind's son rather than his godson.

5. The expression *le Salt Brandan* (l. 164) translates literally as 'Brendan's Leap', but *salt* may be a misinterpretation of Latin *saltus* 'meadow', which occurs in the *Navigatio* in the expression *saltus virtutis Brendani* (translated by O'Meara simply as 'Clonfert', p. 26, l. 5). In the *Navigatio* the phrase which corresponds to *le Salt Brendan* is *sedes Brendani* 'Brendan's Seat'. *Selmer* (84) identifies the place concerned as Brandon Mountain on the Dingle Peninsula, whereas in *Short and Merrilees* (82) it is identified as Brandon Head.

6. Abiram and Dathan, along with Korah, were involved in a rebellion against Moses. They were punished when the earth opened and swallowed them up (Numbers 16: 1-33).

7. Line 414, which appears in *Short and Merrilees* as 'Ne sai s'osat, mais poi l'en dist', is translated here as 'I do not know how helpful he was, but he did say a little about it'. The line is difficult to interpret. Emending *ne sai soasat* in the manuscript to *ne sai s'osat* and interpreting the verb *oser* as 'to be forthcoming', Short and Merrilees translate as 'I do not know if he was forthcoming?', but he

told him little about it' (84). The present interpretation is based on the emendation of *ne sai soast* to *ne sai s'os at*; 'I do not know how helpful he was'; the expression *aveir os* 'to be useful / helpful' occurs in l. 636 ('Qui fait uns duiz, qui lur ad os', l. 636). The term *poi* in l. 414 has also been interpreted here as 'a little' rather than 'little'.

8. The sea creature is clearly a whale. In the *Navigatio*, it is called Jasconius (p. 35, etc.). In l. 471 Benedeit first calls it simply a 'pessuns de mer' ('a marine fish'), but later refers to it as *li jacoines* (l. 837). In the *Navigatio*, Brendan states that this fish is 'the foremost of all that swim in the ocean' (p. 35), and in Benedeit's version we read that 'the Divine King made this creature before any other beast in the sea' (ll. 477-78). In Genesis, the whale appears to be the first of God's creatures to be created: 'And God created great whales and every living creature that moveth' (1: 21).

9. The *miserere* is Psalm 51, one of the penitential psalms: 'Have mercy upon me, O God, according to thy loving kindness.'

10. This reference to the discovery of herbs, which would supply both food and medicine for the monks, adds a touch of realism to the tale. A voyage of this kind would doubtless have had a herbalist amongst its crew. See the note to ll. 801-02 in *Short and Merrilees*, 86.

11. Line 914 ('Sil fuïssent mil e cinc cenz') is translated here as 'even if there had been fifteen hundred of them in the boat'. The manuscript reading (*cil furent mil e cinc cenz*) seems to indicate that the only danger to the monks was from the monster's teeth, of which there were fifteen hundred. Short and Merrilees (21) find this unsatisfactory and emend *cil furent* to *sil fuïssent*; they therefore interpret the line as 'One thousand and five hundred men would have fled before it'. The interpretation adopted here retains the verb *estre* by emending *furent* to *fussent* rather than to *fuïssent* (from *fuïr* 'to flee') and takes the figure of fifteen hundred as a hypothetical and exaggerated reference to the number of men in the boat, i.e. no matter how many men Brendan's boat had contained, the monster would still have posed a tremendous threat.

12. At this point the *Navigatio* has an episode entitled 'The Island of the Three Choirs' (pp. 49-51). This is followed by 'The Island of Grapes' episode, in which a bunch of grapes is dropped into Brendan's lap by a large bird (pp. 51-52).

13. There is a similar magic boat in Marie de France's *Guigemar*, which transports the hero across the water with no visible pilot (ll. 151-208).

14. Cf. Revelation 21: 19-20: 'And the foundations of the wall of the city were garnished with all manner of precious stones. The first foundation was jasper; the second, sapphire; the third, a chalcedony; the fourth, an emerald; the fifth, sardonyx; the sixth, sardius; the seventh, chrysolyte; the eighth, beryl; the ninth, a topaz; the tenth, a chrysoprasus; the eleventh, a jacinth; the twelfth, an amethyst.'

15. In the Bible, Palestine is often referred to as a land running with milk and honey (Exodus 3: 8, 17; 13: 5; 33: 3, etc.). This passage in Benedeit's version has no equivalent in the *Navigatio*. Is Benedeit depicting Brendan as a new Moses,

leading the chosen ones to the Promised Land? (see *Ruhe and others*, 22-25). We can note that, when addressing the three latecomers, Brendan cites two biblical figures who rebelled against Moses (see above, note 6).

The Dutch Version

1. Cf. Numbers 22: 21-35.

2. Cf. Psalm 51: 15.

3. Brendan's burning of the book may have been influenced by a passage in Jeremiah 36, in which King Jehoiakim burns a scroll containing the prophecies of Jeremiah.

4. Brendan's conversation with a giant's skull is found only in the Comburg version. According to Strijbosch, it did not occur in O or in the German versions. The direct source is unknown, but there are striking parallels in the *Vita Brendani* as well as in the legends of St Malo (Maclovius, Machutus) and the desert saint Macharius.

5. The notion that in the afterlife Christians are more severely punished for their sins than unbaptized people seems to derive from the Second Letter of Peter (2 Peter 2: 20-22).

6. In the corresponding line in H (v. 339) the monster is said to look *ghelijc een merminne* 'like a mermaid'.

7. Line 373 in C (=H v. 356 *op die zee*) can mean both 'on (the surface of) the sea' and 'along the sea coast'. In the German prose version P the souls are walking round a lake and this probably reflects the original version; the Middle Dutch version may derive from a mistranslation of Middle High German *see* 'lake' by Middle Dutch *zee* 'sea'.

8. In the Dutch and German versions the *Leverzee* ('Liver Sea') corresponds in most cases with the Coagulated Sea of the *Navigatio* and other versions. Medieval geographers situated it in the far north. The fabulous underwater magnet stone was sometimes located in this sea.

9. In v. 614 of version C this cave is located in *eenen tempel hiere* ('here in a temple'?), which makes no sense. The corresponding passage in H (v. 597) mentions *enen ghespletenen stene* 'a split rock'.

10. In the German versions two old men are sitting in the porch. They are Enoch and Elias who, having been taken to heaven while still living, were believed to be awaiting the Last Judgment in or at the entrance of the Earthly Paradise.

11. The toponym *Vaserijn* is hard to explain. In the corresponding passage in H there is a missing line. In the German version, forms such as *Narrasin* and *Nazareth* are found.

12. Line 1658 of version C refers to *letteren steenijn* 'letters of stone' in the walls, whereas H (v. 1594) and the German versions mention precious stones covering the walls.

13. The name *Walscherande* in C, v. 1820 (H *Walschrande*), probably derives from German *Waltschrat* indicating an evil wood demon.

14. *Spiegel historiael* is the title of the vast world history by the thirteenth-century Flemish poet Jacob van Maerlant, based on Vincent of Beauvais's *Speculum historiale*. Like Vincent, Maerlant is doubtful of the credibility of the *Navigatio sancti Brendani*.

The German Version

1. In the Gotha MS (g), the name is spelt *Brandon*; the Heidelberg MS (h) has *Brande*.

2. MS h has *alle samstage zu nacht* ('every Saturday night').

3. Other versions mention nine years, as is the case later in MS g.

4. The word 'tree', used in other versions, seems more appropriate.

5. MS g has *vallen* ('fall'), possibly in error for *wallen* ('roar'). The monster in this episode is probably is a *scylla*, which is described in the natural history book known as *Physiologus*, a widely used source of information on stones, plants and animals.

6. On the Liver Sea see the Dutch version, note 8.

7. The words in italic, lacking in MS g because of a hole in the page, have been translated from MS h. The stone referred to is the 'Magnet Mountain', a phenomenon feared by seafarers for centuries because it was said to wreck ships by attracting them, thus causing them to be wrecked, or by pulling the nails out of the ship.

8. The number of chairs in MS g is fifteen; other versions have cedar trees instead of chairs.

9. This episode employs many stock motifs relating to the earthly paradise, taken from biblical, Irish and medieval continental tradition: the surrounding darkness, the precious stones, the spring with four streams, the high wall, the presence of Enoch and Elias and the permanently good weather. The theft of the bridle is a reminder of the Fall of Man, which was initiated by the taking of an apple in paradise.

10. MS g reads *vnd mit yme wol fünff welte* ('and with him five worlds'). Both readings refer to the division of history into six ages. The sixth age began with Christ's death at the Crucifixion and it will end with the Last Judgement.

11. This second adventure in the 'Liver Sea' probably constituted a single episode with the one occurring earlier in the original twelfth-century text of the *Reis*.

12. This reading is taken from MS h. The wording of MS g, *Ir stelent vns den zoume vor dem paradise* ('you robbed us of the bridle in front of the paradise'), makes no sense.

13. In other versions Brendan does not lose his *Kugelhut* ('monk's cowl'). This episode does not occur in the Dutch versions of the *Reis*.

14. Cf. Psalm 66: 2: *Deus misereatur nostri, et benedicat nobis*.

15. The motif of the hermit on a piece of turf probably derives from the Irish *Immram Máele Dúin*, in which there is an episode concerning a hermit living on a sod of Irish earth. This motif does not occur in the *Navigatio*.

16. Other versions mention *Nazareth*, *Vaserijn* or *Narrasin*. It is not clear which city was originally meant.

17. MS g has *bellen* ('to bark'), which is probably a corruption of *wellen* ('to swell').

18. Other versions mention flaming birds.

19. The reading of MS g, *vornan an die stüre* ('forward at the rudder'), betrays a very limited knowledge of ships.

20. The story of the apostle Thomas, who refused to believe that Christ had risen from the dead, is found in John 20.

21. MS g has the curious words *wellen schottern*. The phrase is translated from MS h: *waldschrantzen* ('wood goblins', kobolds'), which corresponds to the name 'Walserands' mentioned in other versions. As is evident from Brendan's question and the explanation given later in the text, the meaning was not completely clear to the author of the version in MS g.

22. This episode probably describes 'the world beneath us' about which Brendan read in the book which he burnt at the beginning of the story. The text suggests that this world beneath us is inhabited by human beings, the Antipodeans. The hot place where the voyagers get stuck may be the zone of heat which was supposed to separate the known inhabited world from the place of the Antipodeans.

23. MS g seems to imply that Saint Brendan and his crew asked for help. MS h, however, reads *Und sprach, ob er inen zu hilf wölte komen* ('And [the dwarf] asked whether he [the hermit] was willing to come to their aid'). The description of the place seems to refer to the end of the world and the waters over the wood may be inspired by the biblical waters above the firmament. It is not entirely clear which figures are represented by the dwarf and the hermit. This episode and the next do not occur in the Dutch versions of the *Reis*.

24. In other versions this man is not described as a monk, but as an old grey-haired man. This figure has been compared with the German hero Hildebrand, with whom he shares in fact only very superficial traits.

25. MSS h and b have *Hilsprang*. In other versions one finds *Haylbran* (A), *Hildebrant* (I), *Helspran* (M) and *Helspram* (N).

The Venetian Version

1. Personal and place names are given in the form used in the English translation of the *Navigatio*. The often garbled forms used by the Venetian writer are given only in the few instances where they are of interest in their own right.

2. Lapisilis: a conflation of the Latin 'iuxta montem lapidis, nomine Deliciosam'; *deliciosam* is rendered in the following phrase as 'very sweet and delightful'.

3. The Venetian text erroneously translates as 'which we must give to those who will come . . .'; its Tuscan derivative partially corrects this to 'which God gave to those who will come . . .'

4. Here and in the next paragraph the Venetian text changes from first to third person narration. In this translation, the first person is kept throughout Barrind's narrative. For similar inconsistencies later in the text see note 11 below.

5. Venetian *coca*, followed by the Tuscan text (*cocca*); the type of ship is not named in the *Navigatio*. The *coca* or *cocha* ('cog') was a type of merchant ship which was widely used by the Venetians from the thirteenth century onwards.

6. Here, and again in §§XI and XVII, the liturgical verses, mostly from the Psalms, are cited in Latin by the Venetian author. They are rendered here, wherever it has been possible to identify them, with equivalent liturgical versions in English, from either the Book of Common Prayer or the King James Bible.

7. Jason: the Venetian author has confused the *Navigatio*'s Jasconius with the name of the archetypal navigator of classical mythology.

8. The Italian adapters are understandably confused about the status of these souls; this statement in the Venetian text (followed by the Tuscan) corresponds to the bird's explanation in the *Navigatio* that 'God has separated us from sharing the lot of the others who were faithful'.

9. The Venetian text says eight hundred years; the Tuscan corrects this to eighty, as in the *Navigatio* (and as the abbot himself says later in this chapter).

10. Venetian 'twenty miles'; but the Tuscan corrects to 'twenty days', as in the *Navigatio*.

11. The momentary lapse into first-person narrative at this point is a feature of the new passages added in the Venetian text. It is used more extensively (but still not consistently) in the description of the two paradisal islands with which the text ends.

12. The Venetian text states illogically that the cloth repeatedly struck the travellers in the face, rather than Judas. The Tuscan version abbreviates the description, omitting this detail.

13. A reversal of the *Navigatio*: 'The man whom you curse is blessed.'

14. The text says 'hind paws' at this point; the sense, such as it is, appears to require this correction. In the *Navigatio* an otter comes to the hermit with a fish in its mouth and carrying fuel for a fire in its paws.

15. The precious stones identified here evidently derive from the description of the heavenly Jerusalem in Revelation 21: 18–21. A similar list is given in the description of the tableware in the castle of Bel Veder on the next page.

16. Paneros: a precious stone reported by Pliny (*Historia Naturalis*, XXXVII. 178) to have magical properties, including that of overcoming infertility in women.

17. The source of this passage is again in Revelation (21: 23); but its development in the next paragraph, with the analogy between physical and spiritual light, has some points in common with Dante's use of light imagery in the *Paradiso*.

18. There is a lacuna in the Venetian text at this point which the Tuscan version, where this passage is not reproduced, does not help to fill. The resulting passage is rather disjointed, but not significantly more so than other descriptive passages where the text appears to be complete.

19. 'Tree of good knowledge': the Venetian writer's incomplete or abbreviated recollection of Genesis 2: 9: 'also the tree of life [. . .], the tree of the knowledge of good and evil.'

The Occitan Version

Wahlund's diplomatic edition of BNF, fr. 9759 does not deal with some of the problems involved in the expansion of the abbreviations or possible confusion with regard to punctuation. Though most of the manuscript is easily legible, there are obscure passages. The use of high-quality digital scanning and image-enhancement by computer has permitted examination of troublesome passages with a 500% increase in magnification. This has isolated individual letters, so enabling us to examine the ductus and to interpret what the scribe has written with a high degree of accuracy. There has been some bleed-through of ink from the reverse side which has affected the clarity of the script. Since this present study has been published to allow access to hitherto untranslated vernacular texts, the provision of the Occitan text is intended for general interest rather than for detailed linguistic comment. Careful consideration has been given to every occasion on which the present reading differs from Wahlund's diplomatic edition, but the differences have not been signalled in the Notes. I am indebted to the staff of the BNF who permitted me to see the original manuscript despite its availability in microfilm. This new edition has minimized the corrective use of square and round brackets to regularize the text and has in most cases presented the scribal text which, despite its orthographic variants, permits ease of translation. The obscure passages, which defy careful scrutiny and which even the evidence of the Latin text does not elucidate, are discussed in the Textual Notes.

Script The scribal letter-formation is mostly consistent. The minims are usually stroked with a line slanting to the right for -i- and have a hook to the left on the outside stroke of final -n and -m. The semivowel -y- has a large hooked circumflex over it. There is a possibility of confusion between -c- and -t- in some intervocalic and final positions, and these have also been commented on in the Notes. Similarly, there is the potential for confusion between -b- and -v-, though in most instances the scribe makes a careful distinction by slanting the first stroke of the -v- firmly to the left. The scribe's use of capitals and punctuation is erratic, though there are clear capitals when they are intended as paragraph markers. Numbers, except for *un* and *una,* represented respectively as .i. and .i̅., have been retained in their roman form.

In the ultimate position at the end of a word *z* can be either as marked, a *z*, or a sideways *m*, depending on the sense. There is no difference in the ductus of the letters, and they appear mainly in verb forms.

Abbreviation is limited to the stroked *-p-* for *per* or *par*, the hooked *-p-* for *pro*, the occasional vocalic hook as a superscript for *-ir-*, *-er-* or *-re-*, and the consistent horizontal superstroke over the preceding vowel to indicate *-n* or *-m*; similarly, *que* is nearly always represented as *q* with the horizontal superstroke, as Wahlund's diplomatic edition makes plain. Orthography and elision are, however, inconsistent. There are omitted consonants, such a *fayres* for *frayres*; inaccuracies such as *epons* for *repos*, and variants such as *senher* and *senhos* for the more usual *senhor*. Since the sense of the text is apparent without correction of these variant forms, they have been kept in the text.

Elision is likewise inconsistent. A phrase has been elided by means of red dots placed beneath the redundant material; elsewhere black dots are used for elision, as well as a single stroke through the letter or letters to be elided.

The punctuation of the text is erratic. Firm period points occur within phrases, such as *de tota la sua congregatio . elegit...*, while there are long sentences without any marked break. The use of gold, blue and red colouring to emphasize initial letters occurs sometimes to mark the beginning of a new episode, sometimes to mark the beginning of a speech.

Textual Notes

The following abbreviations will be used in the notes: W = Wahlund's edition; H = the meaning given in Honnorat's dictionary; L = the meaning given in Levy's dictionary. There is one persistent difference between this edition and that of Wahlund: he has consistently read an internal *o* where the manuscript often clearly has *e*, with no possibility of confusion. Such is the case when he reads *iouos* where the manuscript has *joues*. Other instances will be briefly mentioned in the notes to each variant reading. Where relevant, the readings of N.III.5, the Catalan manuscript in the library of San Lorenzo del Escorial, here designated as Esc, and of the Catalan manuscript 174 from the Biblioteca Episcopal in Vic, here designated as Vic, will be given for comparison.

1. *mans*: the MS reads *ms*; W *monestiers* (diffidently). Esc has *mes*.

2. *strutar*: W has a question mark after this reading, but the MS has a clearly stroked *-t.-* Perhaps the copyist was anticipating the second *-t-*. H and L have the verb *escrutar* 'rechercher'. Esc reads *escrutar* and Vic *sercar*.

3. *sin tenics en be*: this could be *temcs*, especially since the *-i-* is not stroked. But the syntax requires a 2nd person plural verb and a compromise has been reached between the MS and the suggestion of W who doubts the MS and has tentatively proposed *sin tenetz*. Esc has *sian tenuts en be on*.

4. *nostra*: the MS reads *vostra*, with the same letter formation as in the following *voluntas*. Sense requires the 1st person plural.

5. *menta*: in the MS the final *-a* is clearly part of the word. W reads this as *nient a*, which he presumably interprets from the Latin *sive ad vitam sive ad mortem*, but the syntax seems difficult to unravel. If *menta* is read as a shortened

version of *enmentre*, then the sentence reads otherwise. Esc reads *e mentre*. Vic has *fins a la mort*, with no following phrase. W also reads the repetiton of *nos* as *nos* followed by *uos* though the consonants are clearly the same.

6. The redundant *de* may be a scribal reminder of the place in the text.

7. *aiguela*: W *aquela*, though the tail of the consonant moves firmly left.

8. *soptany*: W has *So que p(er)tany?* but the MS reading is unequivocal. By the ductus of the letters, it is apparent that the scribe considered this to be one word. It has been suggested that the Latin *so que pertinent* is the origin of the phrase. This phrase duplicates the previous 'so que necessari lor era' of the same line. Esc has 'arbre e vele e ço que pertayn a barcha', which supports this duplication and Vic has nothing which corresponds to this passage.

9. *lor*: W omits this entirely, though it is clear in the MS.

10. *foradida*: W *foradada*, though the MS has a clear *i* separated from the curve of the preceding *d*. Esc has *foradada*.

11. *Sataretz*: W has read this as *satanatz*, as it was intended to be, judging from the later *satanas*. But the MS is clear: the letters following the *-a-* are *-retz*. In a footnote, W suggests that the following *vos*, which clearly has initial *v-*, should be read as *nos*, an abbreviation of *no vos*. The meaning is clear, however, without the absent negative.

12. *frut:* There is clearly an initial *-f-* followed by three minims and a final *-t*. W has *fuic* and suggests *furt* in a footnote, which continues the sense of the Latin *unum suasum furtu pessimo*, 'one succumbed to a most terrible theft'; but Vic clearly has *mengat hun fruyt mala* and the reading *frut* seems probable. Esc has *ha pres .i. foruyt molt mal e vil a sos obs*. We have omitted the numeral *.ii.* as this seems to be redundant to the meaning of both the two Latin versions and the Catalan transcriptions.

13. *loreron:* W *et oreron*, but the MS consistently has *e* without a following *-t*, and the consonant is clearly *-l*. H has *orar* 'to praise', which could be here conflated with Latin *laus*.

14. *nos nos:* W reads this as *uos ues*, though the vowels are clearly both *o* in the MS. We have chosen this reading for the purposes of translation, as a 1st person plural verb, with a redundant *-t-* making the reading *repausam*, with the sideways *-z-*.

15. *ses:* W *sos*; before *steron* the MS has *m* with an elision stroke through it.

   discapols: W *discipols*, though the MS, unclear in part, definitely has two base strokes for the following vowel and not the one required by an *-i-*.

16. *als di sapdes:* the text here is indistinct: W has brackets around both *-s-*, though the text allows *sapdes* for 'sabbath'; *apren:* the MS has a thick single stroke for the final consonant; it could be *-n* or *-c*.

17. *crehano:* W *creham*, though *nos* is the object rather than the subject of the verb.

18. *habitar*: MS *hitar*, with a flat stroke over the *-i-*; W reads this as *h'itar*, which gives Vulgar Latin *habitare*: before the *en un loc*, there is *fl* in the MS: W suggests an elided *st*; it could be an elided *f-*, though there is a following *-l*. It could be a suppressed repetition of *star*, the scribe having begun the first two letters and then elided them by a sidestroke.

19. *gleya quatradal*: W *qatra//da t[a]*, influenced by the Latin *quadrata tam*. If the MS reading is kept, the word could also be a form of *quatedral* 'cathedral'.

20. *terma*: W *t'ms*, as an elision for *tems*; but the final letter is clearly *-a* and is formed in the same way as the final *-a* in the following word.

21. *.iiij.*: W reads this as *mi* though the Latin has the number of the intruding monks here. The MS has earlier given the number of intruding monks as three.

22. *descepesc*: MS has *dexepex*; W *dexepc'* with a note suggesting *dexenden*; *cro* for *tro*.

23. *podes e yvia*: W *podeseynia* with a query for the word *desendia*. Judas sits on a rock (*petrum*), with the MS *o* for *e*.

24. *homes*: W has a note suggesting *hondas*; the scribe has the same word for man, *(h)ome* as wave, *(h)onda* in this passage.

25. *i sofero.n*: W has *isgh en*, though doubts his reading and suggests tentatively *que isc de*.

26. *que.n no.m*: W has not expanded the first elision and has suggested *nom* for the second. The scribe may have written an unnecessary superscript stroke over the first word while thinking of the second.

27. *sacdotz del tompl*: the MS has *sa`cdotz*, obviously a version of *sacerdotz del temple*. W has *templ'*, though the initial consonant is clearly *c-*, followed by *-o*.

28. The syntax of this section is difficult: the verb forms seem aberrant in meaning, but the reading of Esc, *no gosaz aparexer ne retornar*, has assisted in the translation of the passage.

29. *misericordia*: W *una*, though suggests *misericordia* in a footnote: the MS has *mia* with a superstroke above all three letters.

Commentary

1. If *ms* with the superstroke above it is a plain expansion, it would be (i) *mans*, which H gives as 'ordres', in the plural, or (ii) *mans, mas* (H 'maison'). Both translations are possible and, combined, give the English translation 'monastic houses'. See the later mention of Ahenda, where Brendan has another establishment.

2. Peter Ricketts first drew my attention to this translation.

3. *jo ves enqueri*: this has been translated as 'the matter I put before you' to avoid repeating Brendan's plea, 'that which I seek of you'.

4. There are three possible ways of punctuating this passage: there is (i) the one we have chosen: *entro a la mort menta vida nos sostenga. Una causa vos tant solament demandam,* which changes the meaning of the second sentence to 'We

ask one thing only of you'; (ii) there is a reading where *Menta* is read as a conjunction – the *vida* thus becomes part of the jussive subjunctive clause and would translate literally as 'meanwhile may one thing sustain life for us'; (iii) there is the reading of the phrase as *entro a la mort ment a vida*, which retains the force of the Latin *ad vitam sive ad mortem tecum ire* but keeps the jussive subjunctive clause. The punctuation of the passage has only a light stroke after 'mort'.

5. In geographical terms, it seems strange that the monks should be setting off from an eastern beach in order to travel west, and indeed W's Latin text has *contra occidentalem plagam*. Esc has *la playa oriental*, Vic *en plaga oriental*. The Occitan versions are consistent in their insistence on the eastern orientation.

6. *Ahenda*: the Latin text names the island as Enda, Esc has *Aenda* and Vic *Ende*.

7. The text is not clear, as there is considerable bleed-through: this translation has been adapted from the *Navigatio*.

8. *Velluer*: W reads *velluer* and notes that the scribe has misread this from the Latin *in dorse bellue* and has made this a place name.

9. *Erodes, Anna, Cayphas*: Herod is obvious as an inhabitant of hell and the other two here are Annas and his son-in-law Caiaphas, both high priests and both involved with the trial of Christ.

10. *albregament*, H has *bregar* 'tourmenter', which would give the nominal form *bregament*. There is possibly scribal confusion between *albergamen* 'lodgings', *aleugament* 'alleviation' and *bregament* 'torture'.

11. *sans*: this is the only version to have this qualifying phrase. Esc finishes the sentence with *jahien* and the Latin versions refer only to the *terram repromissionis*.

The Catalan Version

Textual Notes

1. The numerals have been regularized in this transcription, as the scribe's use of points on either side of the numeral is erratic.

2. *a Bellver*: this has been read as a place name following the reading in the Occitan version, where the city of Velluer has been interpreted by Wahlund to be a misreading from the Latin *in dorse bellue*.

Commentary

1. Numbers are inconsistently written in the text. By the arithmetic, and the mention of four intruding monks in the subsequent section, it is clear that there should be another numeral in the text here.

2. The scribe has written xv here instead of xl.

3. This seems to be a truncation of the version in the Occitan text, 'ja a pres un frut vil e mal a sos ops'. Both *fruyt* and *ops* are masculine, yet *mala* is a feminine form.

4. Quinquagesima is the Sunday before Lent.

5. The manuscript has *al dia de parity e de pasqua*, and Rebull has omitted the first period of time. Esc has *aparici*, BNF 2759 *pericio*. The appearance of Christ to the Gentiles in the persons of the Magi is celebrated on January 6, as Epiphany.

The Norse Version

1. MS *meðan þer*. The emendation is Unger's, on the basis of the Latin: *ab isto die usque in pascha*.

2. MS *vita vita*.

The *South English Legendary* Version

Among the manuscripts of the *South English Legendary* which include St Brendan it might seem best to choose a text as close as possible to the roots of the English tradition. Despite being written in a hand of the second half of the fourteenth century, Bodleian Library, Oxford MS Laud. Misc. 108 is generally judged to offer evidence of an early stage in the evolution of the collection (Görlach 1974, 88-90); but the Brendan section is seriously defective, lacking lines 68-243. Accordingly, the text is here reproduced, by kind permission of the Bodleian Library, University of Oxford, from another Bodleian manuscript, in a hand unlikely to be later than 1330 (Görlach 1974, 74 and n. 13), Ashmole 43, where it occupies folios 71^v – 80^v. In order to provide a readily readable text, modern punctuation, paragraphing and capitalization have been supplied; contractions, including the ampersand, have been silently expanded; and the erratic word-division of the original has been regularized.

In addition to occasional lines dropped or added, the *SEL* texts show constant variation in minor matters of expression, substituting one syntactical structure for another, interchanging synonyms, abandoning or strengthening alliterative patterns without significant alteration of meaning. Emendation of the chosen text, Bodleian Library MS Ashmole 43 – indicated by asterisks in the margin and identified below by the relevant line numbers – has therefore been limited to readings material to the narrative. The manuscripts consulted for the purpose are identified as follows:

A Oxford, Bodleian Library, Ashmole 43
B Oxford, Bodleian Library, Bodley 779
C Cambridge, Corpus Christi College, 145
H London, British Library, Harley 2277
L Oxford, Bodleian Library, Laud. Misc. 108

A full list of *SEL* manuscripts which include Brendan is given on pp. 377-8.

Textual Notes

1 was ȝend of Irlonde] A ȝend *om.*; B was ȝond in erlond; C was ȝend of Irlonde; H was ȝund of Irlande; L was here of ovre londe.

3 abbot] A monek; B abot; C abbod; H abbod; L abbot. The reference to Brendan's visitor as *anoþer abbod* in line 6 confirms the reading here.

9 sikynge he made inowe] A he *om*.; B he *om*.; C sikinges made inowe; H sikinges he makede; L sichingues he made.

19 riȝt at is herte] A riȝ at is herte; C riȝt at is herte.

21 Ich hadde] A ichabbe; B ich hadde; C iche hadde; H Iᶜ hadde; L he hadde.
    Mernoc] A Meruot; B Mermot C Mernok; H Mernoc; L Mernok.
The forms of C, H and L, supported by the *Navigatio* and other versions, suggest that the form in A is the result of two common scribal errors.

27 mountayne] A moutayne; B mountayn; C monteyn.

34 torments] A tormentſ; B turmens; C tormens; H turmentz.

55 worldes] A wordles; B worldis; C worles; L worldes.

56 dernelynges] A deruelynges; B derlingus; C deruelynges; H durlings; L dernelinges. The editors of C print the manuscript form but assume a probable error for *deorlinges*.

63 þis is Godes] A is *om*.; B þis is godus; C þis is godes; H þis is; L þis is ore.

72 wel euene] A we euene; B ful euene; C wel euene; H wel; L wel.

76 Parays] A parays; C parais.

78 euere day] euere *om*.; B euer day; C euere day; H euere dai.

93 penance] A penauce; C penance.

110 uorþ est] A uorþ west; B est norþ; C est norþ; H est forþ. The reading of line 113 and the reference to the sunrise in 111 confirm the eastern direction of the voyage at this point.

111 a Mydsomeres] A a *om*.; B amydsomerus; C a Mid Someres.

113 Euene est] A euene est; B est norþ; C euene est norþ; H euene forþriȝt.

136 scep] A scip; B chep; C ssep; H scheep.

163 Vor þo] A þo *om*.; B þo; C for þo; H ffor þo.

175 Iascony] A Iastony; B Jascom; C Iascony; H Iastoni. The forms in the Latin (*Jasconius*) and Anglo-Norman (*li jacoines* – not a proper name but a common noun meaning 'fish' (<Ir. *Iasc*, 'fish')) confirm the forms with *c* so often scribally confused with *t*.

183 Bi] A in; B in; C bi; H in. The reading of the Latin text (*super illum fontem*) suggests that the tree more naturally stands beside rather than in the spring.

210 brode tre] A brode *om*.; B brode tre; C brode tre; H brode treo.

242 ȝour Ester] A our Ester; B ȝoure Ester; C ȝoure Ester; H ȝoure Ester.

251 þis ile isei] A ile *om*.; C þis ile ysey; H furst þis yle; L þis yle furst yseiȝ.

254 his help] A his *om*.; B his help; C is help; H his help; L is help.

257 wel longe er hem þoȝte] A wel longe er hem þoȝte; B wel longe hem þouȝte her; C wel longe hom þoȝte er; H hem þoȝte er; L heom þouȝte er. The rhyme pattern seems to support the reading of A.

276 bi þe hond] A þe *om*.; B by þe hond; C bi þe hond; L bi þe hond.

289 The four lines inserted between 289 and 290, lacking in A, are here supplied from C and edited in conformity with the rest of the text.

299 Seyn Ailbi] A S. Ailbi; B sent albon; C abbey & seint; H St. Ailbi.

331 þe Ile of Ankres] A of *om.*; B ile of acres; C þe ile of ancres; H þe ylle of ankres; L þe yle of ankres.

339 quaþ þe abbod] A þe *om.*; B quaþ þe abot; C quaþ þe abbot; H quaþ þis abbot; L quath þe abbod.

367 Lordes grace nome] A grace *om.*; B goddus grace; C godes grace nome; H godes grace; L louerdes grace.

396 wiþoute anuy] A wiþ anuy; C wiþoute anuy; L with oute trauail.

406-7 The order of these two lines, reversed in A, has been corrected here.

412 com swymme] A com swymme; B com swymmende; C com s[w]ymmynge; H suymminge; L cam swymme.

471 anon faste] A faste *om.*; B wel faste; C wel uaste; H him blescede faste; L him wel faste.

473 The line following, lacking in A, is here supplied from C.

476 tongen] A togen; C tongen; H tangen; L tongen; a contraction mark has evidently been omitted in A.

514 souþward] A souward; C souþward; H souþward; L south-ward.

524 Þat, wan þat water] A wan þat *om.*; B whanne þe water; C wanne þe water; H þ' þe water; L ȝwane þat water.

575 þat me þer myȝte] A þat me *om.*; B þat men myȝt; C þat me miȝte; L þat men miȝten.

584 ne wite ȝou;] A ne ne wite ȝou; B ne wite þou; C ne wite ȝou. The redundant *ne* in A is presumably a scribal reduplication.

634 wel euene uorþ] A wel euene norþ; C wel euene forþ; L wel euene forth. Though Horstmann in his *Archiv* edition reads *uorþ*, the form of the initial letter in A is clearly *n*.

650-51 In A the order of these two lines is reversed.

680 Vor hor Creatur] The form *creatur* as given in A is here retained as a feasible foreshortening of *procuratour*, the reading of B, C, H and L.

Commentary

1. The *SEL* version omits the details of Brendan's ancestry given in the *Navigatio*, ancient Irish society presumably having less interest for its mixed audience of laity and clergy.

2. The *SEL* redactor, or an intermediary, has interpreted the *Navigatio*'s *oceano* (§I) as the great stream of Ocean thought by the Greeks to encircle the disc of the earth, the open ocean as distinct from the closed sea of the Mediterranean.

3. In common with most of the vernacular versions, the *SEL* text treats Mernoc as Abbot Barynt's godson rather than '*filiolus meus*', as in the *Navigatio* (§I), probably in deference to the abbot's clerical status.

4. The *SEL* redactor, or an intermediary, has interpreted the *Navigatio*'s *insulam iuxta montem lapidis, nomine deliciosam* as descriptive terms rather than the name of the island. Cf. the Venetian version's 'an island near a mountain called Lapsilis, which is very sweet and delightful' (§I).

5. The English redactor shows some confusion as to the direction of Brendan's voyage. Here, in Barynt's narration of his journey in search of Mernoc, they set off eastwards though the *Navigatio*'s 'westwards' (§I) seems more appropriate to a voyage from Ireland upon the open ocean. The apparent error may, however, have been part of the tradition since it recurs in the Venetian version, though there it may merely reflect the maritime republic's preoccupation with the Levant.

6. The *SEL* Brendan selects twelve companions where the *Navigatio* specifies fourteen (§II), possibly to evoke comparison with the Apostles or, less probably, in anticipation of the total made by the addition of the two latecomers who, in this version, join the party.

7. The decision to omit the *Navigatio* episode (§VII) in which one of three latecomers is doomed to die for theft had apparently been taken by the redactor (or his exemplar) by this point, since their number is here reduced from three to two.

8. In Brendan's voyage, as in that of Barynt and Mernoc, the initial departure is eastwards, despite the *Navigatio*'s specification (§VI) of westwards. The Anglo-Norman text formulation that an east wind drove the voyagers westwards (ll. 211-12) may suggest a source for the confusion within the tradition.

9. By this point the *SEL* version seems to have resolved its initial confusion as to the direction of the voyage, joining other texts in giving it as due west.

10. Where the *Navigatio* (§XI) compares the flight of the bird to the ringing of a bell (*tintinnabula*), echoed in some vernacular versions, the English redactor seems to have thought of it primarily in terms of movement, the wings moving like the bow of a fiddle.

11. The *SEL* versions omits, here and elsewhere, the quotations of psalms, versicles, etc. given in the *Navigatio*. They could only have been paraphrased in its verse form as in the octosyllabics of the Anglo-Norman text where they are also omitted.

12. The *SEL* redactor, or his exemplar, has apparently confused the monastic form of the community on this island with the island itself in naming it Abbey. In other vernacular versions, as in the *Navigatio*, it is *insula que vocatur familie Ailbei* (§XII).

13. Saint Hilary's Day, named after Hilarius, a doctor of the church and fourth-century Bishop of Poitiers, falls in the calendar of the English Church on January 13.

14. The office of guide and supplier of provisions to Brendan and his companions is variously interpreted in individual versions. The *Navigatio* calls him *procurator* (§XV), here translated 'steward'; the Anglo-Norman treats him as the messenger (*mes*, l. 405) of God, elsewhere referred to in terms of his fidelity to the divine will (*le Deu fedeil*, l. 580). The term employed in the *SEL* version, rooted in Roman military administration, developed various overtones of meaning relevant to its context there: MED *procuratour* n. (a) One who acts or speaks for another; a representative or spokesman; (b) a person sent as an official representative, a messenger; (d) the steward or manager of a household; (e) the business manager or administrator of a church, college, or an abbey; (f) a provider.

15. Maundy Thursday, the Thursday next before Easter, commemorates the institution at the Last Supper of the ceremony in which eminent laymen or ecclesiastics wash the feet of poor persons as Christ washed those of his disciples. The term itself derives from O. Fr. *mandé*, Lat. *mandatum*, commandment.

16. Candlemas, the feast of the purification of the Virgin Mary, celebrated with a great display of candles, falls on February 2 in the English Church calendar.

17. The *SEL* version interprets both combatants as fish; the *Navigatio*, having called the first *bestia immense magnitudinis* (§XVI) treats the other in the same terms. The Anglo-Norman calls the first *uns marins serpenz* (l. 905), the second *altre beste* (l. 927), as does the Venetian version.

18. The moralistic commentary pervasive in other versions, largely omitted in the *SEL*, is occasionally replaced by this kind of aphoristic summation, exploiting the epigrammatic qualities of the verse medium. For further examples, see ll. 289f., 460, 565-69.

19. The feast of St Peter in the English Church (and of St Peter and St Paul in the Roman Catholic Church) falls on June 29.

20. The expression *hi caste ambes-as* refers to dice games in which the throwing of two ones, a double ace, the lowest possible score, represents bad luck, misfortune in general. See MED *ambes-as* n.; (b) *casten* ~, have bad luck, lose out, fail.

21. The *SEL* redactor, or his exemplar, has not understood the means by which the cloth is suspended before Judas. In the *Navigatio* (§XXV) they are described as *duas furcellas ferreas* 'two small iron fork-shaped supports' originally given by Judas to the priests of the temple to support cooking-pots. The English substitutes thongs or strips, possibly reflecting a contemporary confusion of forms: MED *tonge* n (1), 2 (e) a strip or thong on a cloth [may belong to, or be confused with *thong*]. The Venetian says they were hooks originally given to the priests of Solomon to hang their seals upon (§XXV); the

Anglo-Norman avoids the problem by omitting them altogether and letting Judas wear the cloth wrapped around him.

22. The nature and function of the helpful otter evidently puzzled vernacular redactors. The Latin (§XXVI) says the animal brought a fish in his mouth and a bundle of firewood in his forepaws, from which the hermit made a fire with flint and iron of unstated origin. The Anglo-Norman substitutes a bundle of dried seaweed for the firewood but omits the means of lighting it (ll. 1553-74). The Venetian, for which the otter is a fish, nevertheless gives it a boat to transport it, four paws to carry wood and walk upon, while the flint and iron are put in its mouth, and its own body serves as the hermit's food. (§XXVI).

Caxton's *Golden Legend* Version

1. The naming of the sea as Ocean, as well as its characterization in classical terms, supports the accepted relation of Caxton's text to the *SEL* version. See under *SEL* above, n. 2

2. The adherence of Caxton's version to the relationship specified in the *Navigatio* rather than the baptismal one substituted in the *SEL* may represent the reading of the *Gilte Legende* intermediary or Caxton's eclectic approach to the textual tradition possibly known to him in other versions.

3. Though Caxton's version follows the *SEL* in the eastward direction of Mernoc's voyage there is no absolute proof of dependence since the same reading is found in other vernacular texts. See under *SEL* above, n. 5

4 The explicit identification of the Earthly Paradise with Eden and its association with the Promised Land (two neighbouring islands rather than one island divided by a river as in the *SEL* and the *Navigatio*) may be independent elaborations on Caxton's part.

5. The numbers of Brendan's companions and of the latecomers who join them, dictated by omission from the *SEL* of later episodes (see above under *SEL*, nn. 6, 7) are necessarily reproduced by Caxton whose version lacks the same episodes.

6. There is an obvious lacuna at this point where the *SEL* version reads: '... so that it [the ship] could not reach the island'. See above, p. 291.

7. Though Caxton follows the *SEL* version in comparing the fluttering of the bird to a fiddle, he logically reinterprets movement in terms of sound in keeping with other versions.

8. Caxton, or the *Gilte Legende* redactor, has corrected the *SEL*'s error in naming the island after the abbey sited there. See above under *SEL*, n. 12.

9. Though the *SEL* version agrees with the *Navigatio* (§XII) in specifying that the foot-washing is done with water from the muddy spring, Caxton or his exemplar has substituted water from the clear one – logically but neglecting the intended symbolic contrast.

10. The *SEL* version closely follows the *Navigatio* (§XII) in having the candles lit by the passage of a flaming arrow. The substitution here of a shining angel

suggests scribal error in the process of transmission rather than any interpretative change.

11. The substitution here of the abbey of Saint Hilary for the *SEL* reference to Saint Hilary's Day both establishes a connection between the versions and suggests an error in the (possibly complex) process of transmission.

12. An obvious error in transmission has transformed the 'thongs' of the *SEL* version into 'tongues', presumably through misinterpretation of the initial 'þ', an obsolescent character at the end of the fifteenth century.

13. In an attempt to make sense of the 'tongues' earlier substituted for 'thongs' in *SEL* by identifying them as 'ox tongues', a contemporary delicacy, the *Golden Legend* version now adds a rather ridiculous explanation as to how they might protect Judas by serving as an alternative prey for the fish who gnaw him.

14. The details of the provisions supplied by the otter provide another demonstration of the relationship of Caxton's text to the *SEL* version. See above under *SEL*, n. 22.

BIBLIOGRAPHY

This Bibliography covers works on the Brendan legend referred to in the present volume, plus items of general interest for a study of the legend. For more extensive bibliographical material see Glyn S. Burgess and Clara Strijbosch, *The Legend of St Brendan: A Critical Bibliography*. Dublin: Royal Irish Academy, 2000.

(i) Collective Volumes

Heist, W.W. 1965. *Vitae sanctorum Hiberniae ex codice olim Salmanticensi nunc Bruxellensi*. Brussels: Société des Bollandistes. An edition of the *Codex Salmanticensis*, containing two versions and a fragment of the *Vita* (pp. 56-78, 324-31, 413).

Moran, Patrick F. 1872. *Acta sancti Brendani: Original Latin Documents Connected with the Life of Saint Brendan, Patron of Kerry and Clonfert*. Dublin: Kelly. Contains editions of a number of Brendan texts including the *Vita Dubliniensis* (pp. 1-26) and the *Navigatio sancti Brendani* (pp. 85-131). Also contains (pp. 132-39) the *Legenda in festo sancti Brendani*, which forms the basis of the Occitan version.

O'Donoghue, Denis. 1893. *Brendaniana: St. Brendan the Voyager in Story and Legend*. Dublin: Browne and Nolan. Reprinted under the title *Lives and Legends of Saint Brendan the Voyager*. Felinfach: Llanerch Publishers, 1994. Contains the text and translation of the First Irish Life (pp. 104-78), a translation of sections 11-29 of the *Vita Dubliniensis* (pp. 182-269) and an English translation of the *Navigatio sancti Brendani* (pp. 104-78).

Plummer, Charles. 1910. *Vitae sanctorum Hiberniae: partim hactenvs ineditae ad fidem codicvm manuscriptorvm recognovit prolegomenis notis indicibvs instrvxit*, 2 vols, Oxford: e typographeo Clarendoniano, repr. 1968. Contains an edition of the *Vita* known as the *Vita Oxoniensis* (I, pp. 98-151), and of the Latin text seemingly based on Benedeit's Anglo-Norman version and known as the *Vita secunda* (II, pp. 270-92).

Plummer 1922. *Bethada náem nÉrenn: Lives of Irish Saints, Edited from the Original MSS. with Introduction, Translations, Notes, Glossary and Indexes*. 2 vols, Oxford: Clarendon Press; repr. London: Sandpiper Books, 1997. Includes an edition and translation of the Second Irish Life (I, pp. 44-95, II, pp. 44-92) and of *Dá apstol décc na hÉrenn / The Twelve Apostles of Ireland* (I, pp. 96-102, II, pp. 93-98).

Stokes, Whitley. 1890. *Lives of Saints from the Book of Lismore, Edited with a Translation, Notes, and Indices.* Oxford: Clarendon Press (Anecdota Oxoniensis); repr. (translations only) Felinfach: Llanerch Publishers, 1995. Includes an edition and translation of the First Irish Life (pp. 99-116, 247-61).

(ii) Editions and Translations

N.B. Editions which form the basis of the translations in this volume are indicated by an asterisk.

(a) The *Navigatio sancti Brendani*

Jubinal, Achille. 1836. *La Légende latine de S. Brendaines, avec une traduction inédite en prose et en poésie romanes, publiée d'après les manuscrits de la Bibliothèque du Roi, remontant aux XI*, *XII* et *XIII* siècles.* Paris: Techener.

O'Meara, John J. 1976. *The Voyage of Saint Brendan, Journey to the Promised Land: Navigatio sancti Brendani abbatis.* Mountrath, Portlaoise: Dolmen Press Atlantic Highlands, also New Jersey: Humanities Press, 1976 (limited edition), 1978 (first trade edition), 1981 (paperback edition); repr. Gerrards Cross: Colin Smythe, 1991.

Schröder, Carl. 1871. *Sanct Brandan: ein lateinischer und drei deutsche Texte.* Erlangen: E. Besold.

* Selmer, Carl. 1959. *Navigatio sancti Brendani abbatis from Early Latin Manuscripts.* Notre Dame, Indiana: University of Indiana Press; repr. Blackrock, Co. Dublin: Four Courts Press, 1989.

Tuffrau, Paul. 1925. *Le Merveilleux Voyage de saint Brendan à la recherche du paradis: légende latine du IX* siècle.* Paris: L'Artisan du Livre.

Webb, J.F. 1965. *Lives of the Saints.* Harmondsworth: Penguin Books. Reprinted in 1983 under the title *The Age of Bede.*

See also Moran 1872, pp. 85-131, and O'Donoghue 1893, pp. 104-78.

(b) The Anglo-Norman Version

Bartoli, Renata, and Fabrizio Cigni. 1994. *Benedeit, Il Viaggio di san Brendano* (Parma: Pratiche Editrice).

Lemarchand, Marie-José. 1986. *Benedeit: El viaje de San Brandán.* Madrid: Siruela.

Marchand, Jean. 1940. *L'Autre Monde au Moyen Age, voyages et visions: La Navigation de Saint Brendan, Le Purgatoire de Saint Patrice, La Vision d'Albéric.* Paris: De Boccard.

Michel, Francisque. 1878. *Les Voyages merveilleux de saint Brandan à la recherche du paradis terrestre: légende en vers du XIIe siècle, publiée d'après le manuscrit du Musée Britannique*. Paris: Claudin.

Ruhe, Ernstpeter, Barbara Beck, and Stephanie Lippert. 1977. *Benedeit: Le Voyage de saint Brendan*. Munich: Wilhelm Fink.

Sherwood, Margaret M.1918. *Le Voyage de saint Brandan: Anglo-Norman Poem of the Twelfth Century*. New York: n.p.

* Short, Ian, and Brian Merrilees. 1979. *The Anglo-Norman Voyage of St Brendan*. Manchester: Manchester University Press.

Short and Merrilees 1984. *Le Voyage de saint Brendan par Benedeit*. Paris: Union Générale d'Editions.

Waters, Edwin G.R. 1928. *The Anglo-Norman Voyage of St. Brendan by Benedeit, a Poem of the Early Twelfth Century*. Oxford: Clarendon Press; repr. Geneva: Slatkine, 1974.

(c) **The Dutch Version**

Bonebakker, Ernst. 1894. *Van Sente Brandane: Naar het Comburgsche en het Hulthemsche Handschrift*. Dissertation, Leiden. 2 vols. in 1, Amsterdam: Binger.

Brinkman, Herman, and Janny Schenkel. 1997. *Het Comburgse handschrift: Hs. Stuttgart, Württembergische Landesbibliothek, Cod. poet. et phil. 2° 22*. 2 vols. Hilversum: Verloren.

Brinkman 1999. *Het handschrift-Van Hulthem: handschrift Brussel, Koninklijke Bibliotheek van België 15.589-623*. 2 vols, Hilversum: Verloren.

Draak, Maartje. 1949. *De reis van Sinte Brandaan*. Amsterdam: Meulenhoff, repr. 1978.

* Gerritsen, Willem P., Soetje Oppenhuis de Jong, eds, and Willem Wilmink, transl. 1994. *De Reis an Sint Brandaan: Een reisverhaal uit de twaalfde eeuw*. Amsterdam: Prometheus/Bert Bakker, paperback version 2000. Also paperback version, Utrecht and Antwerp: Het Spectrum, 2003.

(d) **The German Version**

Bayerschmidt, Carl, and Carl Selmer. 1955. 'An unpublished Low German Version of the *Navigatio sancti Brendani*', *Germanic Review*, 30, 83-91.

Benz, Richard. 1927. *Sanct Brandans Meerfahrt: Das Volksbuch erneuert* (with an introduction by Karl von Balz). Jena: Diederichs; Cologne, repr. Dornach, 1983.

Bodemann, Ulrike, and Karl A. Zaenker. 1993. *Historienbibel/Sankt Brandans Meerfahrt: Heidelberg, Universitätsbibliothek, Cod. Pal. germ. 60. Farbmikrofiche-Edition.* Munich: Lengenfelder (a microfiche ed. of MS h).

Dahlberg, Torsten. 1958. *Brandaniana: Kritische Bemerkungen zu den Untersuchungen über die deutschen und niederländischen Brandan-Versionen der sog. Reise-Klasse. Mit komplettierendem Material und einer Neuausgabe des ostfälischen Gedichtes.* Göteborg: Elander.

Fasbender, Christoph, and Reinhard Hahn. 2002. *Brandan: Die mitteldeutsche Reisefassung.* Heidelberg: Jenaer Germanistische Forschungen.

Geck, Elisabeth. 1969. *Die Seefahrt des Sankt Brandan: Faksimiledruck nach der Originalausgabe von Anton Sorg, Augsburg um 1476 (Ex. Mainz, Stadtbibliothek, Inkunabel 322).* Wiesbaden: Pressler.

Hahn, Reinhard. 1998. 'Ein neuer Zeuge der oberdeutschen Redaktion von Brandans Reise (P)', *Daphnis*, 27, 231-61.

Rotsaert, Marie-Louise. 1996. *San Brandano: Un antitipo germanico.* Rome: Bulzoni.

Sollbach, Gerhard E. 1987. *St. Brandans wundersame Seefahrt: Nach der Heidelberger Handschrift Cod. Pal. Germ. 60.* Frankfurt a.M: Insel Verlag.

See also Schröder (in Collective Volumes above), pp. 125-52, 163-92.

(e) The Venetian and other Italian Versions

Galy, J. 1973. *Navigatio sancti Brendani, édition critique de la version italienne contenue dans le ms. 1008 de la Bibliothèque Municipale de Tours.* Doctoral thesis, 2 vols, University of Nice.

* Grignani, Maria Antonietta. 1975. *Navigatio sancti Brendani, La Navigazione di San Brandano.* Milan: Bompiani, 2nd ed. 1992, 3rd ed. 1997 (an edition of the Venetian version).

Novati, Francesco. 1892. *La Navigatio sancti Brendani in antico veneziano.* Bergamo: Istituto Italiano di Arti Grafiche; repr. Bologna: Arnaldo Forni, 1973 (an edition of the Venetian version).

Raugei, Anna Maria. 1984. *La Navigazione di San Brendano, versione italiana del ms. Bologna, Bibl. Univ. 1513.* Fasano di Puglia: Schena (the Bologna version).

Waters, Edwin G.R. 1931. *An Old Italian Version of the Navigatio sancti Brendani.* London: Humphrey Milford (an edition of the Tours manuscript).

(f) The Occitan Version

Wahlund, Carl. 1902. 'Eine altprovenzalische Prosaübersetzung von Brendans Meerfahrt', in *Beiträge zur romanischen und englischen Philologie: Festgabe für Wendelin Foerster*. Halle: Niermeyer, pp. 175-98; repr. Geneva: Slatkine, 1977.

(g) The Catalan Version:

Rebull, Nolasc. 1976. *Jaume de Voràgine: Llegenda àuria*. Olot: The Author. The Catalan version is found on pp. 808-14.

(h) The Norse Version

Unger, C.R. 1887. *Heilagra Manna Sogur: fortællinger og legender om Hellige maend og Kvinder*. 2 vols, Christiania: B.M. Bentzen. The *Brendanus saga* is found on pp. 272-75.

Wahlund, Carl. 1900. *Die altfranzösische Prosaübersetzung von Brandans Meerfahrt, nach der Pariser Handschrift Nat.-Bibl. fr., 1553* (Uppsala: Almqvist & Wiksell; repr. Geneva: Slatkine, 1974). Contains a translation into German of the Old Norse version under the title 'Ein norw.isl. Brendan-Fragment' (pp. xliv-xlviii).

(i) The *South English Legendary* Version

Bälz, Martha. 1909. *Die me. Brendanlegende des Gloucesterlegendars, kritisch herausgeben mit Einleitung*. Berlin: Mayer and Müller.

D'Evelyn, Charlotte, and Anna J. Mill. 1956-59. *The South English Legendary, Edited from Corpus Christi College Cambridge MS. 145 and the British Museum MS. Harley 2277 with Variants from Bodley MS. Ashmole 43 and British Museum MS. Cotton Julius D.IX*. 3 vols, EETS, OS 235-36, 244. London: Oxford University Press (for the Early English Text Society). The Brendan section is found on pp. 180-202.

Horstmann, Carl. 1874. 'Die altenglische Legende von St. Brendan aus Ms. Asmol, 43. fol. 71b', *Archiv für das Studium der neueren Sprachen und Literaturen*, 53, 16-48.

Horstmann 1887. *The Early South-English Legendary or Lives of Saints*. EETS, OS 87. London: Early English Text Society. The Brendan section is found on pp. 220-40.

Sampson, George. 1924. *The Cambridge Book of Prose and Verse in Illustration of English Literature from the Beginnings to the Cycles of Romance*. Cambridge: Cambridge University Press (extracts, pp. 345-48).

Weston, Jessie L. 1914. *The Chief Middle English Poets: Selected Poems Newly Rendered and Edited, with Notes and Bibliographical References*. London, Calcutta and Sydney: Harrap (complete verse translation). The Brendan section is found on pp. 57-72.

Wright, Thomas. 1884. *St. Brandan: A Medieval Legend of the Sea, in English Verse and Prose*. London: The Percy Society, 1844. Reprinted in O'Donoghue (see Collective Volumes above), pp. 359-79.

(j) Caxton's *Golden Legend* Version

Caxton, William. 1483. *Jacobus de Voragine, The Golden Legend*. Westminster, 1483. Reprinted. 1498, 1503, 1510, 1512, 1527. Contains a section entitled 'The Lyf of Saynt Brandon'. The volume is foliated and folio references vary according to edition (1483, ff. 394v-398v, 1512, 361r-365v, 1527, 363r-367r).

Caxton 1520. *Here Begynneth the Lyfe of Saynt Brandon*. London: Wynkyn de Worde (Caxton's text).

* Ellis, Frederick S. 1878. *Jacobus de Voragine, The Golden Legend, Done Anew*. London: Holbein Society. A facsimile of Caxton's version.

Ellis 1892. *Jacobus de Voragine, The Golden Legend of William Caxton, Done Anew*. 3 vols, London: Kelmscott Press. Contains a modernised version of Caxton's text (vol. 3, pp. 1128-40).

(iii) Studies

Anderson, Alan O., and Marjorie O. 1961. *Adomnan's Life of Columba*. London: Nelson; rev. ed., Oxford: Clarendon Press, 1991.

Ashe, Geoffrey. 1962. *Land to the West: St. Brendan's Voyage to America*. London: Collins.

Babcock, William H. 1922. *Legendary Islands of the Atlantic: A Study in Medieval Geography*. New York: American Geographical Society.

Baring-Gould, Sabine. 1868. *Curious Myths of the Middle Ages*. London, Oxford and Cambridge: Rivingtons, 2nd ed., 1866, 2nd ed., 1868, new ed., London: Longmans, Green and Co., 1881, re-issued, 1901.

Bartoli, Renata Anna. 1992. 'L'Epopée irlandaise de saint Brendan en terre d'oc', in *Contacts de langues, de civilisations et intertextualité: IIIᵉ congrès international de l'Association Internationale d'Etudes Occitanes, Montpellier, 20-26 août 1990*. 3 vols, Montpellier: Université Paul Valéry, 1992, III, pp. 795-803.

Bartoli 1993a. *La Navigatio sancti Brendani e la sua fortuna nella cultura romanza dell' età di mezzo*. Fasano di Puglia (Brindisi): Schena.

Bartoli 1993b. 'Itinerari e percorsi dei volgarizzamenti romanzi della *Navigatio sancti Brendani*', in *Omaggio a Gianfranco Folena*. 3 vols, Padua: Editoriale Programma, I, pp. 281-93.

Bayard, Jean-Pierre. 1988. *La Légende de saint-Brendan, découvreur de l'Amérique: légende du IXe siècle, d'après la traduction romane de Achille Jubinal, version en français moderne, introduction et commentaire*. Paris: Guy Trédaniel.

Benedict, Robert D. 1882. 'The Hereford Map and the Legend of St. Brandan', *Bulletin of the American Geographical Society*, 24, 321-65.

Bieler, Ludwig. 1976. 'Two Observations concerning the *Navigatio Brendani*', *Celtica* (Myles Dillon Memorial Volume), 11, 15-17. Reprinted in Wooding 2000a, pp. 91-93.

Bieler 1979. *The Patrician Texts in the Book of Armagh*. Dublin: Dublin Institute for Advanced Studies.

Borsje, Jacqueline. 1996. *From Chaos to Enemy: Encounters with Monsters in Early Irish Texts. An Investigation Related to the Process of Christianization and the Concept of Evil*. Steenbrugis, in Abbatia S. Petri; Turnhout: Brepols.

Boscolo, Claudia. 1997. 'L'immaginario della navigazione nel medioevo: il volgarizzamento veneto della *Navigatio sancti Brendani*'. Unpublished dissertation, University of Trento.

Bourgeault, Cynthia. 1983. 'The Monastic Archetype in the *Navigatio* of St. Brendan', *Monastic Studies*, 14, 109-22.

Boyer, Regis. 1989. 'The Vinland Sagas and Brendan's *Navigatio*', in *Atlantic Visions*, eds J. de Courcy Ireland and D.C. Sheey. Dún Laoghaire: Boole Press, pp. 37-44.

Bray, Dorothy A. 1995. 'Allegory in the *Navigatio sancti Brendani*', *Viator*, 26, 1-10. Reprinted in Wooding 2000a, pp. 175-86.

Bril, Jacques. 1991. *La Traversée mythique ou le fils accompli*. Paris: Payot.

Brunel, Geneviève. 1976. '*Vida de sant Frances*, versions en langue d'oc et en catalan de la *Legenda aurea*: essai de classement des manuscrits', *Revue d'Histoire des Textes*, 6, 219-65.

Burgess, Glyn S. 1993. 'Repetition and Ambivalence in the *Anglo-Norman Voyage of St Brendan*', in *Anglo-Norman Anniversary Essays*, ed. I. Short. London: Anglo-Norman Text Society, pp. 61-74.

Burgess 1995a. 'Les Fonctions des quatre éléments dans le *Voyage de saint Brendan* par Benedeit', *Cahiers de Civilisation Médiévale*, 38, 3-22.

Burgess 1995b. '*Savoir* and *faire* in the *Anglo-Norman Voyage of St Brendan*', *French Studies*, 49, 257-74.

Burgess 1988. 'La Souffrance et le repos dans *Le Voyage de saint Brendan* par Benedeit', in *Miscellanea Mediaevalia: Mélanges offerts à Philippe Ménard*. 2 vols, Paris: Champion, I, pp. 267-77.

Burgess, Clara Strijbosch, and Giovanni Orlandi, eds. *The Brendan Legend: Texts and Contexts. Proceedings of the Conference held in Gargnano, Italy, 6-9 October 2002*, forthcoming.

Burrell, Margaret. 1997. 'Narrative Structures in *Le Voyage de St Brendan*', *Parergon*, 17, 3-9.

Burrell 1998. 'St Brendan in Occitania: A Study in Confusion and Conflation', *AUMLA*, 90, 21-38.

Carey, John. 1982-83. 'The Location of the Otherworld in Irish Tradition', *Éigse*, 19, 36-43.

Carney, James. 1963. Review of Selmer's edition, *Medium Aevum*, 32, 37-44.

Carp, Teresa. 1984. 'The Three Late-Coming Monks: Tradition and Invention in the *Navigatio sancti Brendani*', *Medievalia et Humanistica*, new series, 12, 127-42.

Carville, Geraldine. 1997. *Birr the Monastic City: St. Brendan of the Water Cress*. Bray, Co. Wicklow: Kestrel Books.

Caulkins, Janet H. 1974. 'Les Notations numériques et temporelles dans la *Navigation de saint Brendan* de Benedeit', *Le Moyen Age*, 80, 245-60.
Chapman, Paul H. 1973. *The Man who Led Columbus to America*. Atlanta: Judson Press.

Charles-Edwards, T. 1976. 'The Social Background to Irish *peregrinatio*', *Celtica*, 11, 43-59. Reprinted in Wooding 2000a, pp. 94-108.

Curran, M. 1984. *The Antiphonary of Bangor*. Blackrock, Co. Dublin: Irish Academic Press.

Daly, Dominick. 1904-05. 'The Legend of St. Brendan', *Celtic Review*, 1, 135-47.

de Paor, Liam. 1997. *Ireland and Early Europe: Essays and Occasional Writings on Art and Culture*. Blackrock, Co. Dublin: Four Courts Press (pp. 105-12).

Dumville, David. 1976. '*Echtrae* and *Immram*: Some Problems of Definition', *Ériu*, 27, 73-94.

Dumville 1988. 'Two Approaches to the Dating of *Nauigatio sancti Brendani*', *Studi Medievali*, 3rd series, 29, 87-102. Reprinted in Wooding 2000a, pp. 120-32.

Dunn, Joseph. 1921. 'The Brendan Problem', *Catholic Historical Review*, 6, 395-477.

Esposito, Mario. 1938. 'Sur la *Navigatio sancti Brendani* et sur ses versions italiennes', *Romania*, 64, 328-46.

Esposito 1960. 'An Apocryphal *Book of Enoch and Elias* as a Possible Source of the *Navigatio sancti Brendani*', *Celtica*, 5, 192-206. Reprinted in *Latin Learning in Mediaeval Ireland*, ed. M. Lapidge. London: Variorum Reprints, 1988, item XIII, and in Wooding 2000a, pp. 27-41.

Esposito 1961. 'L'Édition de la *Navigatio sancti Brendani*', *Scriptorium*, 15, 286-92.

Faarlund, Jan Terje. 1994. 'Old and Middle Scandinavian', in *The Germanic Languages*, ed. by E. König and J. van der Auwera. London: Routledge.

Fingerhut, Eugene R. 1984. *Who First Discovered America? A Critique of Pre-Columbian Voyages*. Claremont, California: Regina Books.

Flint, Valerie I.J. 1992. *The Imaginative Landscape of Christopher Columbus*. Princeton: Princeton University Press.

Forbes, Alexander Penrose. 1872. *Kalendars of Scottish Saints, with Personal Notices of those of Alba, Laudonia, and Strathclyde, an Attempt to Fix the Districts of their Several Missions and the Churches where they were Chiefly had in Remembrance*. Edinburgh: Edmonston and Douglas.

Gerritsen, Willem P., Doris Edel, and Mieke de Kreek. 1986. *De Wereld van Sint Brandaan*. Utrecht: HES.

Görlach, Manfred. 1972. *The South English Legendary, Gilte Legende and Golden Legend*. Braunschweig: Technische Universität Carolo-Wilhelmina zu Braunschweig, Institut für Anglistik und Amerikanistik.

Grignani, Maria Antonietta. 1980. '*Navigatio sancti Brendani*: glossario per la tradizione veneta dei volgarizzamenti', *Studi di Lessicografia Italiana*, 2, 101-38.

Halvorsen, E.F. 1957. '*Brandanussaga*', in *Kulturhistorisk Leksikon for Nordisk Middelalder*. 2 vols, Copenhagen: Rosenkilde and Bagger, II, cols 200-201.

Hamer, Andrew. 1994. 'Moralised Translation in *Strengleikar*', in *Samtíðarsögur: The Contemporary Sagas. Proceedings of the Ninth International Saga Conference*. 2 vols, Ankureyri: n.p., I, pp. 301-315.

Harvey, A., and J. Power. 1997. 'Hiberno-Latin *scaltae*', *Ériu*, 48, 277-79.

Hemming, T.D. 1989. 'Language and Style in the *Voyage of Saint Brendan* by Benedeit', in *Littera et sensus: Essays on Form and Meaning in Medieval French Literature Presented to John Fox*, ed. D.A. Trotter. Exeter: University of Exeter Press, pp. 1-11.

Herbert, Máire. 1999. 'Literary Sea-Voyages and Early Munster Hagiography', in *Celtic Connections: Proceedings of the Tenth International Congress of Celtic Studies, I, Language, Literature, History, Culture*, eds R. Black, W. Gillies and R. O Maolalaigh. East Linton: Tuckwell Press, pp. 182-89.

Herren, M. 1974. *Hisperica Famina*. Toronto: Pontifical Institute of Medieval Studies.

Hughes, Kathleen. 1959. 'On an Irish Litany of Pilgrim Saints Compiled *c*. 800', *Analecta Bollandiana*, 77, 305-31.

Hughes 1960. 'The Changing Theory and Practice of Irish Pilgrimage', *The Journal of Ecclesiastical History*, 11, 143-51.

Illingworth, R.N. 1986. 'The Structure of the Anglo-Norman *Voyage of St Brendan* by Benedeit', *Medium Aevum*, 55, 217-29.

Indrebø, Gustav. 1966. *Gamal Norsk Homiliebok*. Oslo: Universitetsforlaget.

Jacobsen, Peter-Christian. 2000. 'Die *Navigatio sancti Brendani*', in *Beschreibung der Welt: zur Poetik der Reise- und Länderberichte*, eds X. von Ertzdorff and R. Schultz. Amsterdam, pp. 63-93.

Jones, Robin F. 1980a. 'The Mechanics of Meaning in the Anglo-Norman *Voyage of Saint Brendan*', *Romanic Review*, 71, 105-13.

Jones 1980b. 'The Precocity of Anglo-Norman and the *Voyage of Saint Brendan*', in *The Nature of Medieval Narrative*, eds M. Grunmann-Gaudet and R.F. Jones. Lexington, Kentucky: French Forum (French Forum Monographs, 22), pp. 145-58.

Kenney, James F. 1920. 'The Legend of St. Brendan', *Proceedings and Transactions of the Royal Society of Canada*, 3rd series, 14, 51-67.

Kenney 1929. *The Sources for the Early History of Ireland*. Vol. I, *Ecclesiastical: An Introduction and Guide*. New York: Columbia University Press, 1929, 2nd ed., revised by L. Bieler, New York: Octogon, 1966. Reprint Dublin: Irish University Press; New York: Columbia University Press, 1968. Reprint Blackrock, Co. Dublin: Four Courts Press, 1978, 1993.

Kervran, Louis. 1977. *Brandan: le grand navigateur celte du VIe siècle*. Paris: Laffont.

Lane, F.C. 1966. *Venice and History*. Baltimore: Johns Hopkins University Press.

Lapidge, Michael. 1993. 'Israel the Grammarian in Anglo-Saxon England', in idem, *Anglo-Latin Literature 900-1066*. London and Rio Grande: Hambledon Press, pp. 87-104.

Larmat, Jean. 1976. 'Le Réel et l'imaginaire dans la *Navigation de saint Brandan*', in *Voyage, quête, pèlerinage dans la littérature et la civilisation médiévales*. Aix-en-Provence: Publications du CUERMA, pp. 169-82.

Larmat 1985. 'L'Eau dans la *Navigation de saint Brandan* de Benedeit', in *L'Eau au Moyen Age*. Aix-en-Provence: Publications du CUERMA, pp. 235-46.

Lavery, Simon. 1984. 'The Source of the St Brendan Story in the *South English Legendary*', *Leeds Studies in English*, 15, 21-32.

Lecoq, Danielle. 1992. 'Saint Brandan, Christophe Colomb, et le paradis terrestre', *Revue de la Bibliothèque Nationale*, 25, 14-21.

Legge, M. Dominica. 1967. 'Les Origines de l'anglo-normand littéraire', *Revue de Linguistique Romane*, 31, 45-54.

Lehane, Brendan. 1968. *The Quest of Three Abbots: Pioneers of Ireland's Golden Age*. London: John Murray, 1968. Reprinted under the title *Early Celtic Christianity*, London: Constable, 1995.

Little, George A. 1945. *Brendan the Navigator: An Interpretation*. Dublin: Gill.

Mac Cana, Proinsias. 1980. *The Learned Tales of Medieval Ireland*. Dublin: Dublin Institute for Advanced Studies.

Mac Cana 1989. 'The Voyage of St Brendan: Literary and Historical Origins', in *Atlantic Visions*, eds J. de Courcy Ireland and D.C. Sheehy, Dun Laoghaire: Boole Press, pp. 3-16.

McCone, K. 2000. *Echtrae Chonnlai and the Beginnings of Vernacular Narrative Writing in Ireland*. Maynooth: Department of Old Irish.

Mac Mathúna, Séamus. 1994a. 'Contributions to a Study of the Voyages of St Brendan and St Malo', in *Irlande et Bretagne: vingt siècles d'histoire, actes du colloque de Rennes (29-31 mars 1993)*, eds C. Laurent and H. Davis. Rennes: Terre de Brume, pp. 40-55. Reprinted in Wooding 2000aa, pp. 157-74.

Mac Mathúna 1994b. 'The Structure and Transmission of Early Irish Voyage Literature', in *Text und Zeittiefe*, ed. H.L.C. Tristram. Tübingen: Gunter Narr, pp. 313-57.

Mac Mathúna 1996. 'Motif and Episodic Clustering in Early Irish Voyage Literature', in *(Re)Oralisierung*, ed. H.L.C. Tristram. Tübingen: Gunter Narr, pp. 247-62.

McNamara, Martin. 1975. *The Apocrypha of the Irish Church*. Dublin: Dublin Institute for Advanced Studies.

Manfredi, Valerio. 1996. *Le isole fortunate: topografia di un mito*. Rome: L'erma di Bretschneider.

Marsden. John. 1995. *Sea-Road of the Saints*. Edinburgh: Floris.

Massó i Torrents, Jaume. 1902. 'Manuscrits catalans de Vich', *Revista da Bibliografia Catalana*, 2, 229-53.

Morison, Samuel E. 1971-74. *The European Discovery of America: The Northern Voyages*. 2 vols, New York: Oxford University Press.

Nascimento, Aires A. 1992. '*Navigatio Brendani*: aventura e circularidade', in *A imagem do mundo na idade média: actas do colóquio internacional*. Lisbon: Ministério da Educação, pp. 215-23.

Ó Caoimh, Tomás. 1989. 'St. Brendan Sources: St. Brendan and Early Irish Hagiography', in *Atlantic Visions*, eds J. de Courcy Ireland and D.C. Sheehy, Dun Laoghaire: Boole Press, pp. 17-24.

Ó Corráin, Donncha. 1969-70. 'Studies in West Munster History', *Journal of the Kerry Archaeological and Historical Society*, 1 (1969), 46-55, 2 (1969), 27-37, 3 (1970), 19-22.

O'Hanlon, John. 1975-80. *Lives of the Irish Saints with Special Festivals, and the Commemorations of Holy Persons, Compiled from Calendars, Martyrologies, and Various Sources Relating to the Ancient Church History of Ireland*. 10 vols, Dublin: James Duffy; London: Burns, Oates and Co.; New York: The Catholic Publishing Society (vol. 5, pp. 389-472).

O'Loughlin, Thomas. 1999. 'Distant Islands: The Topography of Holiness in the *Navigatio sancti* Brendani', in *The Medieval Mystic Tradition*, ed. M. Glasscoe. Woodbridge: Boydell and Brewer, pp. 1-20.

O'Loughlin 2000. *Celtic Theology*. London: Cassells.

O'Meara, John J. 1978. 'In the Wake of the Saint', *Times Literary Supplement*, 14 July 1978. Reprinted in Wooding 2000a, pp. 109-112.

Ó Néill, Joseph. 1907. 'The Rule of Ailbe of Emly', *Ériu*, 3, 92-115.

Orlandi, Giovanni. 1968. *Navigatio sancti Brendani edidit Ioannes Orlandi. I, Introduzione, II, Edizione provvisoria del solo testo latino*. Milano and Varese: Istituto Editoriale Cisalpino (*Testi e documenti per lo studio dell'antichità*, 38).

Oskamp, Hans P.A. 1969-70. '*Mochen, Mochen, a Brénaind*', *Éigse*, 13, 92-98.

Oskamp 1970. *The Voyage of Máel Dúin: A Study in Early Irish Voyage Literature*. Groningen: Wolters-Noordhoff.

Plummer, Charles. 1905. 'Some New Light on the Brendan Legend', *Zeit-schrift für celtische Philologie*, 5, 124-41. Reprinted in Wooding 2000a, pp. 1-14.

Pomel, Fabienne. 2001. *Les Voies de l'au-delà et l'essor de l'allégorie au Moyen Âge*. Paris: Champion.

Raugei, Anna Maria. 1983. 'Un volgarizzamento inedito della *Navigatio sancti Brendani*', in *Studi di lingua e letteratura lombarda offerti a Maurizio Vitale*. 2 vols, Pisa: Giardini, I, pp. 214-39.

Renan, Ernest. 1854. 'La Poésie des races celtiques', *Revue des Deux Mondes*, new series, 5, i, 473-506. Reprinted in *Essais de morale et de critique*. Paris: Michel Lévy, 1859, 4th ed., Paris: Calmann Lévy, 1889.

Ritchie, R.L. Graeme. 1950. 'The Date of the *Voyage of St. Brendan*', *Medium Aevum*, 19, 64-66.

Sanderlin, Sarah. 1975. 'The Date and Provenance of the *Litany of Irish Saints - II*', *Proceedings of the Royal Irish Academy*, 75, Section C, 251-62.

Schirmer, Gustav. 1888. *Zur Brendanus-Legende*. Leipzig: Pöschel & Trepte.

Seip, Didrik A. 1931. *Norsk Språkhistorie til omkring 1370*. Oslo: H. Aschehoug and Co. (W. Nygaard).

Selmer, Carl. 1943. 'The Beginnings of the St. Brendan Legend on the Continent', *The Catholic Historical Review*, 29, 169-76.

Selmer 1950. 'Israel, ein unbekannter Schotte des 10. Jahrhunderts', *Studien und Mitteilungen zur Geschichte des Benediktiner-Ordens und seiner Zweige* 62, supplementary issue, 69-86.

Selmer 1956. 'The Vernacular Translations of the *Navigatio sancti Brendani*: A Bibliographical Study', *Mediaeval Studies*, 18, 145-57.

Severin, Timothy. 1977. 'The Voyage of "Brendan"', *National Geographic*, 152, no. 6 (December 1977), 771-97.

Severin 1978. *The Brendan Voyage*, drawings by Trondur Patursson. London: Hutchinson (Arrow Edition, 1979, Arena Edition, 1983, Abacus, 1996).

Sharpe, Richard. 1991. *Medieval Irish Saints' Lives: An Introduction to Vitae Sanctorum Hiberniae*. Oxford: Clarendon Press.

Simpson, W. Douglas. 1935. *The Celtic Church in Scotland: A Study of its Penetration Lines and Art Relationships*. Aberdeen (*Aberdeen University Studies*, 111).

Skene, William F. 1877. *Celtic Scotland: A History of Ancient Alban*. 2 vols, Edinburgh: David Douglas.

Southern, Richard W. 1953. *The Making of the Middle Ages*. London: Hutchinson.

Stevenson, Jane B. 1998. 'The Monastic Rules of Columbanus', in *Columbanus: Studies on the Latin Writings*, ed. M. Lapidge. Woodbridge, Suffolk: Boydell Press, pp. 203-16.

Stokes, Whitney. 1888. 'The *Voyage of Snegdus and Mac Riagla*', *Revue Celtique*, 9 (1888), 14-25.

Stokes 1888-89. 'The *Voyage of Mael Duin*', *Revue Celtique*, 9 (1888), 447-95, 10 (1889), 50-95, 264.

Strijbosch, Clara. 2000. *The Seafaring Saint: Sources and Analogues of the Twelfth-Century Voyage of Saint Brendan*. Dublin: Four Courts Press. A translation (by Thea Summerfield) of *De bronnen van de Reis van Sint Brandaan*. Hilversum: Verloren, 1995.

Strijbosch 2002. 'Ein Buch ist ein Buch ist ein Buch. Die Kreation der Wahrheit in *Sankt Brandans Reise*', *Zeitschrift für deutsches Altertum und deutsche Literatur*, 131, 277-89.

Tardiola, Giuseppe. 1986. 'I volgarizzamenti italiani della *Navigatio sancti Brendani*', *La Rassegna della Letterature Italiana*, 90, 516-36.

Thacher, John B. 1903-04. *Christopher Columbus, his Life, his Work, his Remains as Revealed by Original Printed and Manuscript Records*. 3 vols, New York: Putnam's; repr. AMS Press: New York, 1967.

Thrall, William F. 1917. 'Virgil's *Aeneid* and the Irish *Imrama*: Zimmer's Theory', *Modern Philology*, 15, 449-74.

Thrall 1923. 'Clerical Sea Pilgrimages and the *imrama*', in *The Manly Anniversary Studies in Language and Literature*. Chicago: University of Chicago Press, pp. 276-83. Reprinted in Wooding 2000a, pp. 15-21.

Tierney, J.J., ed. 1967. *Dicuili Liber de mensura orbis terrae*. Dublin: Dublin Institute for Advanced Studies.

Walberg, Emanuel. 1935-40. 'Sur le nom de l'auteur du *Voyage de saint Brendan*', *Studia Neophilologica*, 12, 46-55.

Westropp, Thomas J. 1912-13. 'Brasil and the Legendary Islands of the North Atlantic, their History and Fable: A Contribution to the "Atlantis" Problem', *Proceedings of the Royal Irish Academy*, 30, section C, 8, 223-60.

Widding, Ole, Hans Bekker-Nielsen and L.K. Shook. 1963. 'The Lives of the Saints in Old Norse Prose: A Handlist', *Mediaeval Studies*, 25, 294-337.

Wooding, Jonathan M. 2000a. *The Otherworld Voyage in Early Irish Literature: An Anthology of Criticism*. Dublin: Four Courts Press.

Wooding 2000b. 'Monastic Voyaging and the *Nauigatio*', in 2000a, pp. 226-45.

Wooding 2003. 'Fasting, Flesh and the Body in the St Brendan Dossier', in *Celtic Hagiography and Saints' Cults*, ed. J. Cartwright. Cardiff: University of Wales Press, pp. 161-76.

Zimmer, Heinrich. 1889. 'Keltische Beiträge: II. Brendans Meerfahrt', *Zeitschrift für deutsches Alterthum und deutsche Litteratur*, 33, 129-220, 257-338.

(iv) The Manuscripts of the Vernacular Versions

For manuscripts of the Latin and Irish versions of the *Vita Brendani / Betha Brénainn* tradition and for those of the *Navigatio sancti Brendani* see Glyn S. Burgess and Clara Strijbosch, *The Legend of St Brendan: A Critical Bibliography* (Dublin: Royal Irish Academy, 2000), 4-20. Where there is more than one extant manuscript, the base manuscript of the edition or translation found in this volume is indicated by an asterisk.

(a) Benedeit's Anglo-Norman Version

* A. London, British Library, Cotton Vespasian B X (I), ff. 1r-11r. 14th century.

B. Paris, Bibliothèque Nationale de France, nouv. acq. fr. 4503, ff. 19v-42r. End of the 12th or beginning of the 13th century.

C. Oxford, Bodleian Library, Rawlinson D 913, f. 85. Late 12th or early 13th century.

D. York, Minster Library and Archives, XVI, K. 12 (I), ff. 23r-36r. Late 12th or early 13th century.

E. Paris, Bibliothèque de l'Arsenal 3516, ff. 96r-100v. Second half of the 13th century.

F. Cologny-Genève, Fondation Martin Bodmer 17. First half of the 13th century.

(b) The Dutch Version

Two Dutch versions (known as the *Reis*) have been preserved.

* C. Stuttgart, Württembergische Landesbibliothek, cod. poet. et phil. 2° 22 (the Comburg manuscript), ff. 179r-192v. Probably between 1380 and 1425.

H. Brussels, Koninklijke Bibliotheek van België / Bibliothèque Royale de Belgique, 15.589-15.623 (the Van Hulthem manuscript), ff. 1r-11r. Between 1399 and 1410.

(c) The German Version

Two versions of the German *Reis* in verse and one version in prose have been preserved.

(i) In verse

M. Berlin, Staatsbibliothek zu Berlin — Preussischer Kulturbesitz, mgo 56, ff. 13v-50v. 14th century.

N. Wolfenbüttel, Herzog-August-Bibliothek, cod. Guelferbytanus 1203 Helmstadiensis, ff. 81r-107v. Second half of the 15th century.

(ii) In prose

b. Berlin, Staatsbibliothek zu Berlin — Preussischer Kulturbesitz, mgq 1113, ff. 87v-106r. Last quarter of the 13th century.

* g. Gotha, Forschungs-Landesbibliothek, Chart. A 13, ff. 54r-63r. Beginning of the 15th century.

h. Heidelberg, Universitätsbibliothek, cod. Pal. germ. 60, ff. 157r-184r. *c*.1460.

l. London, British Library (bound at the end of a copy of the *Legenda aurea* printed at Lübeck in 1507, shelf mark C.107.g.2).

m. Munich, Universitätsbibliothek 2° cod. MS 688, ff. 231r-260r. Third quarter of the 15th century.

For manuscripts of the translations of the *Navigatio sancti Brendani* into Dutch and German see Burgess and Strijbosch 2000, p. 57.

(d) The Venetian and other Italian Versions

Bologna, Biblioteca Universitaria 1513, ff. 39r-62v. Second half of the 14th century (a faithful rendering of the *Navigatio* in the dialect of Bologna).

Dublin, Trinity College 951 (formerly L.5.19), ff. 154r-157v. Beginning of the 14th century (a fragment of the Venetian version).

Florence, Biblioteca Nazionale, Conventi Soppressi, miscell. C2 1550, ff. 1r-42v. First half of the 15th century (one of the two Tuscan versions).

* Milan, Biblioteca Ambrosiana, D. 158 inf., ff. 1r-37r. Beginning of the 15th century (the Venetian version).

Paris, Bibliothèque Nationale de France, italien 1708, ff. 1r-36v. 15th century (a copy, with lacunae, of the Venetian version).

Tours, Bibliothèque Municipale 1008, ff. 214r-227r. End of the 13th or beginning of the 14th century (one of the two Tuscan versions).

(e) The Occitan Version

A. Paris, Bibliothèque Nationale de France, fr. 9759, ff. 210r-213r. 15th century.

(f) The Catalan Version

Es 2. Escorial, Biblioteca San Lorenzo N. III, ff. 223v-226r. Beginning of the 14th century.

* V. Vic / Vich, Biblioteca Episcopal 174, ff. 512v-522r. First half of the 15th century.

(g) The Norse Version

Oslo, Norsk Riksarkiv, fragm. 68. *c.* 1300.

(h) The *South English Legendary* Version

Not all manuscripts of the *South English Legendary* contain a section on St Brendan. Those which do are:

A. Oxford, Bodleian Library, Ashmole 43, ff. 71v-80v. *c.* 1300.

B. Oxford, Bodleian Library, Bodley 779, ff. 1r-10r. 15th century.

C. Cambridge, Corpus Christi College 145, ff. 67v-77r. 14th century.

D. Oxford, Bodleian Library, Laud. misc. 463, ff. 46r-50r. c. 1400.

G. London, Lambeth Palace Library 223, ff. 112v-122v. 14th century.

H. London, British Library, Harley 2277, ff. 41v-51r. *c.* 1300.

J. London, British Library, Cotton Julius D IX, ff. 74v-84v. Early 15th century.

* L. Oxford, Bodleian Library, Laud. misc. 108, ff. 104r-110r. *c.* 1400.

N. London, British Library, Egerton 2891, ff. 77v-86r (lacking a leaf after f. 83). Early 14th century.

O. Oxford, Trinity College 57, ff. 39r-46r. Late 14th century.

P. Cambridge, Magdalene College, Pepys 2344, pp. 273-87. Late 14th century.

Q. London, British Library, Additional 10301, ff. 80r-90v. *c.* 1400.

R. Cambridge, Trinity College 605, ff. 215r-223v. 15th century.

Rm. Ripon, Ripon Minster, fragment 33 (bookbinding strip). c. 1500.

T. Oxford, Bodleian Library, Tanner 17, ff. 99v-107v. c. 1400.
Wa. Aberystwyth, National Library of Wales 5043E, ff. 2v-3r. Early 15th century.

Wm. Wisbech, Wisbech Town Library Museum, No. 21. Late 14th century.

Y. Oxford, Bodleian Library, Additional C. 38, ff. 109v-118r. Early 15th century.

Index I: Index to the Introductions

Index II: Index to the Vernacular Versions